CHARACTER ETHICS
AND THE OLD TESTAMENT

Also from Westminster John Knox Press:

Character Ethics and the New Testament:
Moral Dimensions of Scripture

Edited by Robert L. Brawley

CHARACTER ETHICS AND THE OLD TESTAMENT

Moral Dimensions of Scripture

EDITED BY
M. Daniel Carroll R.
and Jacqueline E. Lapsley

Westminster John Knox Press
LOUISVILLE • LONDON

Scripture quotations from the New Revised Standard Version of the Bible are copyright © 1989 by the Division of Christian Education of the National Council of the Churches of Christ in the U.S.A. and are used by permission.

Scripture translations not from the NRSV are those of the authors.

Chapter 14, "Tamar's Cry: Rereading an Ancient Text in the Midst of an HIV/AIDS Pandemic," by Denise M. Ackermann, was originally published by Cluster Publications in *Grant Me Justice! HIV/AIDS and Gender Readings of the Bible,* edited by Musa W. Dube and Musimbi Kanyoro. It is published herein with the permission of Cluster Publications.

Book design by Sharon Adams
Cover design by Eric Handel, LMNOP

First edition
Published by Westminster John Knox Press
Louisville, Kentucky

This book is printed on acid-free paper that meets the American National Standards Institute Z39.48 standard. ⊗

PRINTED IN THE UNITED STATES OF AMERICA

07 08 09 10 11 12 13 14 15 16 — 10 9 8 7 6 5 4 3 2 1

Library of Congress Cataloging-in-Publication Data is on file at the Library of Congress, Washington, D.C.

ISBN-13: 978-0-664-22936-8
ISBN-10: 0-664-22936-0

Contents

Foreword

Walter Brueggemann

This collection of impressive essays is gathered from the ongoing annual sessions of the Society of Biblical Literature and the American Academy of Religion on "character ethics." "Character ethics" refers to a way of thinking about and interpreting the moral life in terms of a particular vision of and a passion for life that is rooted in the nurture, formation, and socialization of a particular self-conscious community. In this particular instance, it refers to the communities of Judaism and Christianity as they are informed by the biblical text and its derivative traditions. Such a way of understanding ethics is to contend with every ethical approach that appeals to "universal criteria," for the guidance given here is particular to a historical community and to the dynamic of the text. Character ethics, moreover, resists the formulation of codes, rules, or commandments. Here with reference to "the Bible and ethics," it works against a caricature of the Bible—and particularly the Old Testament—as a set of commandments that are too familiarly labeled as "legalism." The dynamic and generativity of character ethics is based on the conviction that a rightly appropriated social vision and a rightly disciplined habit of behavior will together provide sufficient guidelines and adequate resources for every moral issue, all the while assigning the human person great freedom alongside great responsibility as a moral agent who is embedded in a community and disciplined and informed by a particular text.

It is proper that the essays in this volume are divided into two distinct sections reflecting the agenda of the SBL-AAR seminar for the period of several years. Part 1 features a roster of the most important and most influential scholars engaged in the critical study of the Old Testament. In these essays, the leap from critical study to practical ethics is sometimes made and is often to be inferred. Part 2 features ethical reflection by authors who are not regularly a part of the critical guild of biblical study but who are practitioners engaged in real life-or-death ethical issues in specific and often dangerous places in the world. This second section exhibits a way in which the Bible invites and requires imagination in order to make connections between text and concrete moral issues. The two parts of the volume together model a process of thinking and interpreting that holds text and life closely together.

The opening essays by Ted Hiebert, William Brown, and Tom Dozeman review the now well-established shift in Old Testament studies away from the older view of "God's mighty acts in history" to the shape, permits, and requirements of the structure of creation as willed by the creator. While G. Ernest Wright has been a pivotal figure in the older paradigm and his scholarship is now the focus of much criticism, Brown introduces into the discussion an alternative Wright, Frank Lloyd Wright, who attests that space rather than time is the arena of moral activity. A great merit of Brown's essay is an opening toward Job, who will undoubtedly figure more prominently in time to come in discussions of our general topic, for it is Job more than any other biblical character who moves outside the "box" of commandments into a self-assertive moral self-awareness.

The papers on the Torah by Dennis Olson, Samuel Balentine, and Cheryl Anderson seek to veto any notion of Torah-faith and Torah-ethics as a flat, one-dimensional claim of commandments. The essays make clear that the Torah is a field of dynamic restlessness most often marked by critical interaction between the giver of commands and the receivers. Olson exhibits Moses, as rendered in the text, as an agent of acute moral dialogue. Balentine returns to Job and makes clear that Job—in his moral anguish—refuses the silence commanded by the priestly ordering of reality. His interpretation of Job makes unmistakable the fact that the breaking of the silence of ordered control is a moral responsibility, a moral responsibility that is, moreover, sustained and celebrated by the creator who has made both Job and Behemoth. Anderson provides an inventory of several current studies in Old Testament ethics and then breaks beyond them to show the way in which much Old Testament ethics has, with reference to women, the poor, and non-Israelites, dismissed the "other" as an inconvenience that threatens. By appeal to Emmanuel Levinas, Anderson shows the way in which attentiveness to the other requires a critical stance over against much of what passes for biblical ethics.

The sections of this volume on the Prophets and the Exile likely should be considered together, though the essays in each section refuse any easy categorization. The essays by Kathleen O'Connor, Jacqueline Lapsley, and Daniel Smith-Christopher in various ways concern the response of Israel to acute historical loss, indicating that a rich variety of responses are possible and are variously taken to be effective. It is clear that exilic and postexilic moral reflection had the task of reconstituting the community that was completely depleted through the crisis of the sixth century. It is also clear that the conventional stereotype that emerging Judaism simply retreated into legalism is utterly false. These essays show the venturesome experimentation that was undertaken in order to deal honestly with a loss that could not be denied and with a future that could only grow from loss that had been embraced. Daniel Carroll shows the way in which prophetic expectation is necessarily and deeply connected to the practice of worship as a chance for the resymbolization of a community that had had its symbols voided by historical emergency. The essay by J. J. M. Roberts reminds us of the *Realpolitik* of empire that was important in Israel's politics and in Israel's imagination, and warns against any easy romanticizing of a peaceable vision of the future. Roberts's essay makes a powerful counterpoint to the work of Smith-Christopher, whose subject is an empire "other than our own," an invitation to "laugh at the state." David Pleins provides a playful reflection on two recurring topics of ethics—alcohol and sex—and shows how the text works to construct points of reference for a society open to the sensual.

The four essays in the second part of this volume constitute an important corpus of biblical exposition of a very different kind. Here the accent is upon contemporary context. In these essays the move to contemporary context has already been made by the interpreter, a move that in each case seems inevitable, given the urgency of the contextual issue. Luis Rivera-Rodriguez provides a rich and suggestive taxonomy for a "diaspora hermeneutics." I anticipate that his contribution will be a defining one for future work in Old Testament studies. This is a case in which a contemporary practitioner can feed back to critical work an important insight, since current critical work in Old Testament studies is preoccupied with the Diaspora. The urgency of this textual insistence is indicated in his friendly but altogether serious critique of the work of Smith-Christopher, who has moved farther toward a diaspora hermeneutic than any other mainline critical interpreter. That Smith-Christopher has neglected the resources and references that are important to Rivera-Rodriguez adumbrates a more general neglect in the critical discipline, no doubt including the contributors to the first part of the book.

After Rivera-Rodriguez, the three remaining essays of the collection move toward concrete contexts: AIDS in South Africa by Denise Ackermann, migrants and prisoners by Bob Ekblad, and the recurrence of state violence in Guatemala by Rafael Escobar. Ackermann exhibits the power of lament and narrative in relation to the South African epidemic, Ekblad exposits the trickster character of Jacob as a liminal figure in theology and society, and Escobar takes up the wilderness tradition as he considers the process of vulnerability, both in life and in interpretation, in a culture of exploitation and oppression.

The scope and range of the essays in this volume are both broad and deep. In sum, these essays exhibit an ethic of dynamic interactionism that eschews both the autonomy of modern reason and the rule-bound moralism that marks much religion. It is clear that character ethics depends not simply upon the emergence of "mature character," for that by itself would produce autonomous agents. Rather, character ethics is a practice of being (not doing) that is derived from and referred back to the character of God, the God of the script, who practices sovereignty in mutuality, who invites challenge and engagement, and who authorizes and empowers covenant partners to bold and courageous freedom. It is impossible to overaccent the dynamic of this ethic as evidenced in the biblical text, a dynamism that pushes beyond all conventional notions of ethics, especially those commonly associated with conventional religious practice.

In conclusion, four observations occur to me. First, the reference to Emmanuel Levinas by Anderson is likely to be important for the future of this discussion. Levinas is rooted in the "I-Thou" paradigm of Martin Buber, and behind that lies the covenant of Sinai.[1] This entire trajectory of interpretation insists upon the defining force of the "other," the holy other of God, the justice-insisting other of the neighbor, the other that characteristically produces anxiety and seems to authorize defensive violence. Anderson has shown how the biblical text variously assaults or circumscribes the other.[2] But, of course, it is the same biblical text (witnessing to the same biblical God) that has generated the dynamism of the other in the first instant.

Second, in character ethics, social power is important and defining, as indicated in the final essays. Given that reality, biblically grounded ethics characteristically acts with only "the weapons of the weak." As soon as biblical ethics moves toward power and utilizes "the weapons of the strong," it becomes an idolatrous distortion of the source and reference for ethics in God.[3] In current US society, one can readily see the move toward "the weapons of the strong" in religious communities, and one can, with equal readiness, see how that move is marked by idolatrous self-deception.

Third, I am especially impressed with the ways in which Job variously appears in these essays. This is not Job as a Promethean character or Job who ends as a meek suppliant before God. Rather, this is Job who is celebrated by YHWH as an agent of full freedom. Ernst Bloch, in his great essay on freedom and hope, juxtaposed Moses and Job.[4] This is exactly right for character ethics. Such an ethic is rooted in the dialogic accomplishment of Moses, but reaches beyond any settled tradition about Moses to the restless insistences of Job. After Job has done and said everything, he still refuses silence and insists upon justice for himself, for he is the daring other who addresses the sovereign creator God.

Fourth, as indicated in the first set of essays in this volume, current scholarship has turned away from "God's mighty acts in history" and toward the creation and a priestly sense of order. When we listen to "the facts on the ground" from the last four essays, however, it becomes clear that the focus of character ethics can never be generically upon creation but is always "in history" of a concrete kind. Thus, while we cannot return to any naive supernaturalist notion of God's action in history, we should value that era of scholarship, because the human agents who engage the character of God will inescapably enact their ethical character "in history," that is, in the arena of power and violence and ideology. The attestation of this textual-ethical tradition and its contemporary practitioners is that human agents, at the behest of the God of creation, *do indeed act decisively and transformatively in history*. In doing so, they engage the Lord of history, who wills and authorizes their being in history in effective and specific ways.

At the end, current scholarship and current ethical action concern a moral context that requires freedom and courage, exactly the gifts of the creator God who would redeem the historical process. The claim is that through such human agency, this is the God who will make all things new—ending deathly epidemics, maintaining humanness amid state-authorized violence, and doing justice on behalf of "the others" who are little valued among us but finally not to be forgotten or silenced.

Notes

1. See Emmanuel Levinas, *Totality and Infinity: An Essay on Exteriority* (Pittsburgh: Duquesne University Press, 1969).
2. See Regina M. Schwartz, *The Curse of Cain: The Violent Legacy of Monotheism* (Chicago: University of Chicago Press, 1997).
3. This reference is to James C. Scott, *Weapons of the Weak: Everyday Forms of Peasant Resistance* (New Haven, CT: Yale University Press, 1985). See also Scott, *Domination and the Arts of Resistance: Hidden Transcripts* (New Haven, CT: Yale University Press, 1990).
4. See Ernst Bloch, "Exodus in the Concept of Yahweh," in *Atheism in Christianity: The Religion of the Exodus and the Kingdom,* trans. J. T. Swann (New York: Herder & Herder, 1972), esp. 106–22. See also Gustavo Gutierrez, *On Job: God-Talk and the Suffering of the Innocent* (trans. M. J. O'Connell; Maryknoll, NY: Orbis, 1987).

Contributors

Denise M. Ackermann is Extraordinary Professor of Christian Theology at the University of Stellenbosch in the Western Cape, South Africa.

Cheryl B. Anderson is Associate Professor of Old Testament at Garrett-Evangelical Theological Seminary in Evanston, Illinois.

Samuel E. Balentine is Professor of Old Testament at Union Theological Seminary—Presbyterian School of Christian Education in Richmond, Virginia.

William P. Brown is Professor of Old Testament at Columbia Theological Seminary in Decatur, Georgia.

Walter Brueggemann is William Marcellus McPheeters Professor of Old Testament Emeritus at Columbia Theological Seminary in Decatur, Georgia.

M. Daniel Carroll R. (Rodas) is the Earl S. Kalland Chair of Old Testament at Denver Seminary in Denver, Colorado, and is Adjunct Professor of Old Testament at El Seminario Teológico Centroamericano in Guatemala City, Guatemala.

Thomas B. Dozeman is Professor of Hebrew Bible at United Theological Seminary in Dayton, Ohio.

Bob Ekblad is Executive Director of Tierra Nueva and the People's Seminary in Burlington, Washington.

J. Rafael Escobar R. (Rosal) is Coordinator of the Program for Biblical Formation of CEDEPCA (Centro Evangélico de Estudios Patorales en Centroamérica) in Guatemala City, Guatemala.

Theodore Hiebert is Francis A. McGaw Professor of Old Testament at McCormick Theological Seminary in Chicago, Illinois.

Jacqueline E. Lapsley is Associate Professor of Old Testament at Princeton Theological Seminary in Princeton, New Jersey.

Kathleen M. O'Connor is William Marcellus McPheeters Professor of Old Testament at Columbia Theological Seminary in Decatur, Georgia.

Dennis T. Olson is Charles T. Haley Professor of Old Testament Theology at Princeton Theological Seminary in Princeton, New Jersey.

J. David Pleins is Professor of Religious Studies at Santa Clara University in Santa Clara, California.

Luis R. Rivera-Rodriguez is Associate Professor of Theology and Director of the Center for the Study of Latino/a Theology and Ministry at McCormick Theological Seminary in Chicago, Illinois.

J. J. M. Roberts is W. H. Green Professor of Old Testament Literature Emeritus at Princeton Theological Seminary in Princeton, New Jersey.

Daniel L. Smith-Christopher is Professor of Old Testament and Director of Peace Studies at Loyola Marymount University in Los Angeles, California.

Abbreviations

AB	Anchor Bible
Bib	*Biblica*
BibInt	*Biblical Interpretation*
Bijdr	*Bijdragen: Tijdschrift voor filosofie en theologie*
BIS	Biblical Interpretation Series
BRev	*Bible Review*
BZAW	Beihefte zur Zeitschrift für die alttestamentliche Wissenschaft
CANE	*Civilizations of the Ancient Near East.* Edited by J. Sasson. 4 vols. New York, 1995.
CBQ	*Catholic Biblical Quarterly*
CBQMS	Catholic Biblical Quarterly Monograph Series
CC	Continental Commentaries
CHANE	Culture and History of the Ancient Near East
CurBS	*Currents in Research: Biblical Studies*
CurTM	*Currents in Theology and Mission*
EvT	*Evangelische Theologie*
ExAud	*Ex auditu*
FOTL	Forms of the Old Testament Literature
HBT	*Horizons in Biblical Theology*
Hen	*Henoch*
ICC	International Critical Commentary
Int	*Interpretation*
JAAR	*Journal of the American Academy of Religion*
JANES	*Journal of the Ancient Near Eastern Society*
JAOS	*Journal of the American Oriental Society*
JBL	*Journal of Biblical Literature*
JCS	*Journal of Cuneiform Studies*

JHI	*Journal of the History of Ideas*
JNES	*Journal of Near Eastern Studies*
JPS	Jewish Publication Society
JPSTC	JPS Torah Commentary
JQR	*Jewish Quarterly Review*
JSOT	*Journal for the Study of the Old Testament*
JSOTSup	Journal for the Study of the Old Testament: Supplement Series
JSP	*Journal for the Study of the Pseudepigrapha*
JSPSup	Journal for the Study of the Pseudepigrapha: Supplement Series
KJV	King James Version
LXX	Septuagint
NEB	New English Bible
NICOT	New International Commentary on the Old Testament
NIV	New International Version
NJPS	New Jewish Publication Society
NRSV	New Revised Standard Version
OBT	Overtures to Biblical Theology
OTL	Old Testament Library
RevExp	*Review and Expositor*
RSV	Revised Standard Version
SBL	Society of Biblical Literature
SBLDS	Society of Biblical Literature Dissertation Series
SBLMS	Society of Biblical Literature Monograph Series
SHBC	Smyth and Helwys Bible Commentary
TBT	*The Bible Today*
USQR	*Union Seminary Quarterly Review*
VT	*Vetus Testamentum*
VTSup	Supplements to Vetus Testamentum
WBC	Word Biblical Commentary
WW	*Word and World*
ZA	*Zeitschrift für Assyriologie*
ZAW	*Zeitschrift für die alttestamentliche Wissenschaft*

Introduction

Christendom, the apparent seamlessness of Western culture with Christianity, is now widely recognized to be dead. Whether this fact is hailed or lamented depends on one's perspective, but the fact seems irrefutable. Christian communities are now being cast into the disorienting position of having to think more intentionally about who they are and about the role of Scripture in forming their personal and communal identities. For Jewish communities this is not a new problem. Long and often painful practice at minority religious status forms part of the tradition.

Today Christian communities face several challenges of unprecedented scope. The globe suffers the casualties of horrific wars on several continents, is threatened by the nefarious networks of terrorism, and endures the senseless violence of drug trafficking. The growing pluralism of the public square portends that the Christian voice will no longer enjoy the benefits (or perils) of religious privilege. There are also the multiple pressures exerted by the negative effects of economic globalization, such as trade and industry dissymmetry among nations, massive migration to urban centers in the developing nations of the Two-Thirds World, large-scale emigration (both legal and illegal) to the West, widespread poverty, social disintegration, sex slavery, child labor, and eradicable yet somehow intractable diseases. The effects of these contemporary realities can vary widely depending on the context. How globalization, for instance, impacts South Africa may be quite different from its effects in South Carolina, but the necessity of grappling with the phenomena themselves cannot be avoided.

In a world that continues to contract, these increasingly interrelated realities are unavoidable. People of faith cannot afford to ignore any of them. In order to address these ills in a progressively more complex world in which they are becoming a minority voice, communities of faith must learn to discern the distinctiveness of their own confessional and ethical life. A crucial part of that task is discerning the particular role of Scripture in the process. In recent years interest in Old Testament ethics has grown dramatically, and this renewed interest is to some extent a function of the demands exerted on communities of faith by these worldwide changes. Questions of moral identity and formation have become much more urgent, and uncertainties about how best to address them in a variety of interpretive contexts drive persons of faith back to the Scriptures as an important moral resource. The field of Old Testament ethics in present discussions is rich and diverse and certainly does not limit itself to a few prescriptive "thou shalts" and "thou shalt nots" or what it means for the New Testament to fulfill the Law. Many readers of the Old Testament now operate with a broader perspective that seeks to dig deeper into the worlds evoked and imagined by the Old Testament, to ask how the variety of Old Testament texts exert formative power in the modern context.[1]

The essays in this volume, all delivered over several years at the sessions of the Character Ethics and Biblical Interpretation Group at the annual meetings of the Society of Biblical Literature, revolve around questions of Scripture and moral formation. This is the second book to come out of the group.[2] Despite disparate approaches, the papers are united by their conviction that Scripture, as the revelation of a passionate God, has shaped and continues to shape those committed to God's justice and the desire that all might thrive, especially those who lie outside the walls of the more privileged sectors of society. The field of Old Testament ethics is often taken up with principles and normative precepts, but character ethics, as it is variously understood in these essays, is more concerned with other, often more subtle ways in which Scripture molds believers and their communities. Character ethics is not as widely understood to be constitutive of Old Testament ethics as, say, the legal material in the Bible, but its less visible power to impact every dimension of human existence is nonetheless real and must not be underestimated.

The essays in the first part of this volume cover almost the entire breadth of the Old Testament canon in order to maximize the number of glimpses into its promising potential as a resource for ethics. The great variety in perspective, theology, and historical context that lies behind the texts funds different sorts of moral imaginations, and these essays help the reader to explore the contributions that this great diversity can have for moral life. The second part of the volume contains essays that engage the Old Testament in ethical reflection out of different modern contexts. Walter Brueggemann, a scholar who for so many years has championed the ethical reading of the Old Testament and who encouraged this publication, offers a foreword that summarizes many of these essays and underscores some of the significant issues that are raised.

The first part of the book is meant to reveal some of the possibilities within the biblical witness to generate moral worlds, while the second section attests to a range of contemporary contexts that embrace those alternatives and aspire to be formed by them. Both parts of the volume are crucial to ethical engagement with the Scriptures, but the second part of the book reflects the particular concern to bring into ethical discourse those contexts of interpretation on the margins that historically have been neglected in favor of dominant European and North American viewpoints. Communities in other parts of the world, especially those who suffer in hidden ways or are forgotten by the more secure, read the Bible with a unique set of needs and issues in mind, and it is past time for scholarship to acknowledge this basic reality.

The authors come from various ecclesiological traditions, and they represent theological perspectives that span the spectrum from evangelical to more ecumenical persuasions. The textual methodologies employed in reading the Old Testament also vary. Many of the essays engage in interdisciplinary explorations as well, using the tools of literary and philosophical theory, sociology, and the like in order to seek fresh insights into the biblical text. Nevertheless, despite so much diversity, a common desire to transform Christians, the church, and the world by wrestling with the Old Testament energizes and unites all of the essays. Each one seeks to foster the common good through thoughtful reflection on the Old Testament witness.

This sense of responsibility means that some examine critically how the Old Testament has been used for ethics. Cheryl Anderson, for instance, questions appropriations of Scripture that do not adequately grapple with the situations of women, the poor, and the non-Israelite in ancient Israel. She also steadfastly refuses to soft-pedal texts that could pose problems for modern interpreters. J. J. M. Roberts highlights the imperialistic quality of Isaiah's vision of world peace and challenges Western Christians to realize that they (we!) might be far closer to Isaiah's original political context than they are to that of the New Testament writers. What does it mean to read *as Scripture* an imperial vision of peace from a position within a modern empire? On the other hand, the authors of the second part of the volume read with and for the powerless and so at once disturb and broaden horizons. Luis Rivera-Rodriguez attempts to develop a hermeneutics grounded in the diaspora experiences of the biblical world and those of contemporary Latinos in the United States, and Denise Ackermann reads the rape of Tamar in light of the AIDS pandemic in Africa. Bob Ekblad looks at some of the narratives of Genesis from the location of prison inmates and itinerant Mexican farm workers in the Pacific Northwest, even as Rafael Escobar asks the very different question of how Scripture can reorient Christian life in the violent and racially divided world that has been Guatemala for so many years.

What is the role of the Old Testament in shaping the moral vision of those who claim it as their scripture? Our hope is that this collection can contribute to the ongoing and crucial conversation about what it might mean to live faithfully in light of its guidance in a world of so much need.

M. Daniel Carroll R.
Jacqueline E. Lapsley

Notes

1. To name only a few of the many volumes that have been published recently: Bruce C. Birch, *Let Justice Roll Down: The Old Testament, Ethics, and the Christian Life* (Louisville, KY: Westminster/John Knox, 1991); Waldemar Janzen, *Old Testament Ethics: A Paradigmatic Approach* (Louisville, KY: Westminster John Knox, 1994); William P. Brown, *Character in Crisis: A Fresh Approach to the Wisdom Literature of the Old Testament* (Grand Rapids: Eerdmans, 1996); Gordon J. Wenham, *Torah as Story: Reading the Old Testament Ethically* (Edinburgh: T. & T. Clark, 2000); John Barton, *Understanding Old Testament Ethics: Approaches and Explorations* (Louisville, KY: Westminster John Knox, 2003); John Rogerson, *Theory and Practice in Old Testament Ethics* (ed. M. Daniel Carroll R.; London: T. & T. Clark, 2004).
2. The first volume is William P. Brown, ed., *Character and Scripture: Moral Formation, Community, and Biblical Interpretation* (Grand Rapids: Eerdmans, 2002).

PART I
BIBLICAL
INTERPRETATION

Chapter 1

Beyond *Heilsgeschichte*

THEODORE HIEBERT

In James Muilenburg's 1968 presidential address to the Society of Biblical Literature, entitled "Form Criticism and Beyond," he proposed a new paradigm for the literary criticism of the Bible, one that shifted the interpreter's attention from small units to larger literary strategies and compositions.[1] I would also like to make a case for a new paradigm for biblical interpretation, but one that is conceptual and that goes to the heart of biblical religion. This new paradigm places the center of biblical faith not in history but in the broad range of biblical experience, for which the arena of creation plays a foundational and essential role.

The practice of regarding history as the point of orientation for biblical thought has governed biblical interpretation for the last one hundred years, if not longer, and it has made its way into the literature of almost everyone writing about the Bible. This has certainly been the case inside the guild of biblical scholarship, where commentaries on biblical texts and biblical theologies alike have been based on this premise. But it has also been embraced and promoted by ancient Near Eastern and comparative scholars outside the biblical field per se, whose larger perspective, one might have thought, would have provided them a vantage point to question the traditional but artificial split between the historical religion of the Bible and the natural religions of Israel's neighbors. James Barr has observed, "Historians of theology in a future age will look back on the mid-twentieth century and call it the revelation-in-history period. . . . No single principle is more powerful in the handling of the Bible today than the belief that history is the channel of divine revelation."[2]

Within this historical paradigm that has governed biblical studies, the larger realm of creation is relegated to the background and assigned a marginal status. "It performs only an ancillary function," says Gerhard von Rad. "It is but a magnificent foil for the message of salvation."[3] For Ernest Wright, my distinguished predecessor at McCormick, the natural world also played a decidedly peripheral role in biblical thought; he called it "a handmaiden, a servant of history."[4] This view of nature as peripheral to biblical thought has spread beyond the borders of biblical scholarship, and we find it, for example, in the writings of the great comparative scholar Mircea Eliade. He believed that when ancient Israel first discovered the meaning of history, it transcended or left behind the world of nature, with its archetypes and repetitions. In this transcendence, biblical society emerged, as Eliade put it, "from the paradise of animality (i.e., from nature)."[5]

We are now at a point in contemporary culture and scholarship when a reexamination of the data demands that we move beyond this historical paradigm, which I refer to as *Heilsgeschichte*, a term associated most directly, perhaps, with the theology of Gerhard von Rad but that I use here for the twentieth-century habit of placing history at the center of biblical interpretation and thought and pushing nature to the margins. We must make this move beyond history as the center of biblical interpretation for three reasons: (1) The assumptions on which it was based are no longer tenable, (2) the description of biblical religion it presented is partial and incomplete, and (3) the ethical stance it implies is deeply problematic. Let me address these three reasons in order, dealing first with the assumptions behind the traditional approach.

The historical paradigm for interpreting biblical texts and understanding biblical thought rests on four simple claims, which have become so widely accepted and unchallenged that they have assumed the status of assumptions in modern biblical interpretation. They are: (1) that nature and history are distinct categories, (2) that biblical religion is grounded in history rather than nature, (3) that biblical religion in this regard is distinct from other ancient religions that are grounded in nature, and (4) that the Bible's unique historical consciousness is an advance in the evolution of human thought. If we actually examine these assumptions directly, we soon discover their fatal flaw. They are based solidly in the intellectual worldview of modern biblical interpreters themselves rather than in the ancient worldview of the Bible, and they turn out to be embarrassingly inept at dealing with ancient thought itself.

Perhaps the most fateful modern assumption is that history and nature are distinct categories of thought and that the interpreter can meaningfully connect ancient religions with one category or the other. For the biblical scholars of the last century, this assumption appears to depend most directly on the idealistic philosophical tradition as it was articulated by Hegel. As the great idealists before him, Hegel divided the world into two metaphysically distinct orders, the spiritual and the material, and he used this dualistic perspective to explain the history of religion. The oldest religions of the ancient Near East, according to Hegel, could be assigned to the material side of this ledger in that they identified God directly with nature. The religion of ancient Israel, by contrast, could be assigned to the spiritual side, since it separated God from nature and connected God instead with humanity, spiritual individuality, and freedom, that is, with historical existence. In Israelite religion, according to Hegel, "Man is exalted above all else in the whole creation," while "Nature is represented as thus entirely negated, in subjection, transitory."[6]

The obvious problem with this idealistic approach to the religions of antiquity is that its categories of thought are not those of ancient thinkers, biblical or nonbiblical. The idealistic split between spirit and matter was not part of the conceptual framework of ancient writers, nor was the split between nature and history that accompanied it in Hegelian thought. This is illustrated first and foremost, of course, by the fact that ancient languages such as biblical Hebrew have no equivalent terms, distinguishing neither spirit from matter nor history from nature. Gerhard von Rad himself, one of the great architects of *Heilsgeschichte*, recognized toward the end of his career the philosophical problem here. "The Old Testament draws no such distinction between Nature and history," he wrote, "regarding them as one single reality under the control of God." He went on to assert that such notions as nature and history were "merely vast ciphers, so many images projected" onto reality, and he gave interpreters this challenge: "Anyone who wishes to see the world in some measure as Israel saw it must rid his mind of both mythical and philosophical ways of thinking. It is much easier said than done!"[7] This assertion is, in my opinion, one of von Rad's greatest insights.

A second assumption, which has frequently functioned to reinforce this philosophical distinction between history and nature, is that Israel came to this distinction as a result of its desert origins. This assumption is based upon the tripartite theory of social development popular in nineteenth-century anthropology, the school of anthropology contemporary with the philosophical idealism of Hegel. According to this theory, human culture evolved naturally in linear fashion through three stages: from hunting and gathering to herding to cultivation. With this anthropological framework in hand, biblical scholars took the images of sheep and goats and desert sojourns in the Pentateuch and developed a theory of Israel's desert origins, a theory that included ancient Israel within the expected cultural evolution from herders to cultivators.

The crucial element in this theory for our purposes is the assertion that Israel's desert origins led directly to its unique historical consciousness. This view was put into classical form by Albrecht Alt in a series of essays in the 1920s and '30s that linked the distinctive characteristics of Israel's life and thought with Israel's desert beginnings. In his essay "The God of the Fathers," Alt claims that the link between God and nature was broken in Israel's early desert experience: "The seeds of a completely different development from that of local and nature gods were implanted at the very inception of the cult: the god was not tied to a greater or lesser piece of earth, but to human lives, first that of an individual, and then through him to those of a whole group. . . . The gods of this type of religion show a concern for social and historical events."[8] This same link between Israel's origins and the desert was used by H. and H. A. Frankfort in their widely used introduction to ancient Near Eastern thought, *Before Philosophy: The Intellectual Adventure of Ancient Man*, to argue that Israel broke decisively from ancient Near Eastern mythic thought by connecting revelation with history rather than with nature.[9] One can see this confidence in Israel's desert origins everywhere in biblical interpretation, and it is just as energetically defended in popular culture in books like Thomas Cahill's *The Gifts of the Jews: How a Tribe of Desert Nomads Changed the Way Everyone Thinks and Feels*.[10]

The Achilles heel of the assumption of Israel's desert origins is the now clearly obsolete anthropology on which it was based. The history of human culture does not in fact represent a move from nomadic herding to sedentary farming. Rather, herding developed later than farming, as an offshoot of an agricultural economy. Nor do particular cultures inevitably move in this direction. For all of its stories of herds and deserts, the literature and thought of ancient Israel are clearly grounded in an agricultural way of life, as I have tried to show elsewhere in a study of the Yahwist's perspectives on Israel's environment.[11] Thus, these faulty anthropological assumptions, just as the anachronistic philosophical assumptions we have already examined, doom the history-centered approach to biblical interpretation from the outset.

But I want to mention one more assumption behind this historical paradigm before moving on to some constructive suggestions: the unspoken apologetic mission behind most of this serious historical-critical scholarship. The attempt to differentiate biblical religion from those of its neighbors and then to defend this difference as an evolution in the development of human thought lies ultimately in the desire to see one's own religious and philosophical traditions as unique and more enlightened than those of others. For those in the Jewish and Christian religions, the history-nature dichotomy provided a convenient vehicle to accomplish this apologetic mission. It provided biblical scholars a way to find their highest values in their own traditions, to distinguish their traditions from others, and then by implication—and sometimes by explicit rebuke—to discredit the traditions of others.

The goals of this past scholarship were often laudable. Ernest Wright, for example, took up Hegel's view of the historical character of biblical religion to argue, on the one hand, against the tyranny of systematic and propositional approaches to biblical religion and, on the other hand, against the tyranny of oppressive political systems resistant to change.[12] Today the historical consciousness of biblical religion has been embraced by some liberation theologians as the genius behind the exodus and behind biblical protests against oppressive political structures, which are grounded, as they see them, in the status quo of the eternal verities of nature.[13] Though admirable in their own right, these approaches can now from our perspective be seen to be not only biased and inaccurate, on account of their flawed assumptions, but also, in their devaluation of the natural world, deeply problematic in the light of the values and ethics embedded in them.

I have spent more time than I should have, perhaps, taking on the assumptions behind our historical approach to biblical thought, but they have become so deep and widespread that they are often unnoticed and unquestioned, even by those setting out to interpret the Bible with a new appreciation for the natural world within it. I believe we must do more today than find nature texts in the Bible, or add a short paragraph on nature at the end of a history-centered commentary. I believe we need a whole new way of reading the Bible without the old assumptions. We need a new set of lenses, a new paradigm that goes beyond *Heilsgeschichte*. The new paradigm must incorporate the broad range of human experience in biblical thought, and it must, I believe, recognize that within the biblical understanding of experience, the world of creation is foundational, not marginal, ancillary, disregarded, or repudiated.

To begin this move beyond the partial and incomplete picture of biblical religion that the historical paradigm has bequeathed to us, and to show what a new direction in biblical interpretation might look like, let me start at the very beginning with the creation stories in Genesis. These stories, which describe the world of nature and the human place in it, have customarily been identified as a prologue to what follows. Nahum Sarna's comments in the introduction to his Genesis commentary are representative: "The theme of Creation, important as it is, serves merely as an introduction to the book's central motif: God's role in history. The opening chapters are a prologue to the historical drama that begins in chapter 12."[14] Walter Brueggemann, who wisely wishes not to subsume Gen. 1–11 under 12–50 or vice versa, nevertheless refers to Gen. 1–11 as the "Pre-History."[15] Gerhard von Rad, in his comprehensive reconstruction of hexateuchal traditions, thought that the "pre-patriarchal history" in Gen. 1–11 was added last, deriving, as he put it, "from a totally different sphere of culture and religion" than the indigenous Israelite sagas of the patriarchs and Moses that followed.[16] For each of these interpreters, the history-centered paradigm is clear: Creation is, at worst, alien to and, at best, the prologue for the real historical religion of the patriarchs and Moses.

But let us step back and ask whether this is, in fact, how beginnings function in charter narratives such as this, narratives that found and establish the identity of a people. If we look at other such narratives in the Bible, say the Deuteronomistic History, we can see that beginnings function not as prologues to the real story but rather as defining moments, moments that establish the conceptual framework for everything to follow. The Deuteronomistic History, for example, begins with an account of the covenant and its laws established at Mt. Horeb. This beginning provides the definition of who true Israel is and the standard for interpreting Israelite life and thought from this time forward. Or, take the starting points of other charter narratives, say the life of Christ in the Gospels or the writings of Calvin in the Reformed tradition. Such starting points are not prologues, preliminary or alien in any way to what follows, but founding moments in which the essential identity of their heirs is unalterably established and determined.

If we read the beginning of Genesis according to the rules by which charter narratives normally work, rather than through history-centered lenses, the role of creation in biblical thought looks very different. Creation now stands as the beginning of everything that follows, the foundational and defining moment for civilization itself. The world of nature is thus the starting point, the defining condition, the standard according to which human life is understood. The most basic fact about human identity then is not its social and political existence but its membership in the community of life that makes up creation as a whole.

Just how this actually works can be illustrated by taking a closer look at key details of the Priestly creation account in Gen. 1, where central elements of the cult—the focus of Israelite social, political, and religious life for the Priestly author—are grounded in the orders of creation itself. The most obvious example, of course, is the Sabbath. The ultimate motive behind the overall design of the Priest's seven-day creation account, unique among ancient cosmogonies, was to establish this ritual observance as a part of the cosmic patterns of the universe. To be sure, Sabbath observance is grounded in the Law, specifically in the fourth commandment in the Decalogue revealed at Sinai. But this commandment itself is grounded in creation, as its motivational clause recalling God's creation of the world makes clear (Exod. 20:8–11). Furthermore, the Sabbath, which is grounded in cosmic orders, is the sign of the Sinai covenant itself, the third and climactic covenant in the Priestly history. By serving this function, the Sabbath draws this covenant, which establishes the entire Priestly cult, into the orders of the cosmos. If God's rest on the Sabbath is to be interpreted as a sign of his mastery of primordial chaos and establishment of an ordered world, a common motif in ancient Near Eastern cosmogonies, then human observance in imitation of God is also essentially a celebration of the entire cosmos and its orders.

One could show how many other elements of the Priestly cult, just like the Sabbath, have their foundation in the elemental orders of the cosmos as they are established in Gen. 1. This would include the festivals of the liturgical calendar, grounded in the movements of the heavenly bodies; the dietary system of pure and impure animals, grounded in the three cosmic realms and their prototypical animal life; and the tabernacle or temple itself, whose construction in Exod. 25–40 mirrors the formation of the cosmos. Many of these connections between cosmos and cult have been noticed and investigated by others in more detail than we have time to do here. But their larger significance for understanding the foundational place of creation in biblical thought has seldom been appreciated. In each instance, as in the Priestly narrative as a whole, creation provides the foundation and point of orientation for religious experience. One could also show, as I have tried to do in *The Yahwist's Landscape*, how the Yahwist's creation narrative plays a similar role, grounding Israel's agricultural identity in the orders of creation.

The ethical warrant for this paradigm shift in biblical interpretation will, I hope, be clear to some extent by now. While splitting off history from nature and elevating history to a premier position in biblical religion served laudable ethical goals for many interpreters, most recently the goal of liberation and freedom, it was accomplished at great expense—the marginalizing of nature in biblical thought. This is a fine example of the way scholars can be ethically sensitive and fervent in one area while remaining completely blind in another. By marginalizing nature in this way, scholars denied to creation an integrity in its own right and divorced humanity and its well-being from its natural environment, two perspectives that have led to our thoughtlessness about creation. As I have argued here, these particular dualisms and their ethical problems are more those of the Bible's interpreters than those of the Bible's writers, but it will take a major effort to rethink a century of biblical interpretation.

In conclusion, I would simply like to emphasize the magnitude of the challenge in front of us. To shift paradigms, to move nature from the margin to the foundation of Israelite thought, means nothing less than reconstructing the fundamental nature of Israelite religion, which has been understood for the last hundred years at least as being narrowly historical in character. Such a shift will involve a new investigation of all of the ways biblical writers saw their religious culture—its liturgies, its images of human identity, its daily practices, its values—connected to and grounded in the world of creation in which they lived. This is the sort of work Bill Brown has done in *The Ethos of the Cosmos*, in which he analyzes the way Israel's moral values and perspectives are integrally linked to its various cosmogonies.[17]

It will also involve a new investigation of the relationship between creation and the divine in biblical thought, a relationship that is even more sensitive and controversial than the one between creation and humanity, which we have been examining. The core scholarly concept of God's absolute transcendence of nature, so heavily dependent on the Hegelian dualism of Spirit and matter, simply cannot handle the concept of God in the Bible. One need look no further than the *rûaḥ 'ĕlōhîm*, the "breath" or "wind of God," in Gen. 1:2 to realize that the concept of divine transcendence simply doesn't explain the nature of this deity. The divine and the material, the creator and the creation, are inextricably intertwined and inseparable in the *rûaḥ 'ĕlōhîm*. The old language of "transcendence" and "immanence," of "natural revelation" and "special revelation," will no longer work. To shift paradigms will involve not only a new way of thinking about biblical religion but also a new way of talking about it.

Notes

1. James Muilenburg, "Form Criticism and Beyond," *JBL* 88, no. 1 (1969): 1–18.
2. James Barr, "Revelation through History in the Old Testament and in Modern Theology," *Int* 17, no. 2 (1963): 193–94.
3. Gerhard von Rad, "The Theological Problem of the Doctrine of Creation," in *The Problem of the Hexateuch and Other Essays* (trans. E. W. Trueman Dicken; London: SCM, 1966), 138–39.
4. G. Ernest Wright, *God Who Acts: Biblical Theology as Recital* (London: SCM, 1952), 43.

5. Mircea Eliade, *The Myth of the Eternal Return: Or, Cosmos and History* (trans. Willard Trask; Princeton, NJ: Princeton University Press, 1954), 155.

6. G. W. F. Hegel, *Lectures on the Philosophy of Religion* (trans. E. B. Speirs and J. Burdon Sanderson; London: Routledge & Kegan Paul, 1962), 2:189, 199.

7. Gerhard von Rad, "Some Aspects of the Old Testament World View," in *Problem of the Hexateuch*, 154–55.

8. Albrecht Alt, "The God of the Fathers," in *Essays on Old Testament History and Religion* (trans. R. A. Wilson; Garden City, NY: Doubleday, 1968), 54–55.

9. H. and H. A. Frankfort et al., *Before Philosophy: The Intellectual Adventure of Ancient Man* (New York: Penguin, 1989), 237–63.

10. Thomas Cahill, *The Gift of the Jews: How a Tribe of Desert Nomads Changed the Way Everyone Thinks and Feels* (New York: Doubleday, 1998).

11. Theodore Hiebert, *The Yahwist's Landscape: Nature and Religion in Early Israel* (New York: Oxford University Press, 1996).

12. Wright, *God Who Acts*, 15–38.

13. See, for example, J. Severino Croatto, *Exodus: A Hermeneutics of Freedom* (trans. S. Attanasio; Maryknoll, NY: Orbis, 1981), 13, 34–35.

14. Nahum Sarna, *Genesis* (JPSTC; Philadelphia: Jewish Publication Society, 1989), xiv.

15. Walter Brueggemann, *Genesis* (Interpretation; Atlanta: John Knox, 1982), 1, 11.

16. Gerhard von Rad, "The Form-Critical Problem of the Hexateuch," in *Problem of the Hexateuch*, 63–64.

17. William P. Brown, *The Ethos of the Cosmos: The Genesis of Moral Imagination in the Bible* (Grand Rapids: Eerdmans, 1999).

Chapter 2

The Moral Cosmologies of Creation

WILLIAM P. BROWN

Inspired by the landscape of the Midwest, Frank Lloyd Wright helped to define a truly American style of architecture. He incorporated the natural beauty of the open prairie by building homes with low proportions, gently sloping roofs, horizontal lines, and long bands of windows. Minimizing the distinction between inside and outside, Wright believed that all human habitation should be "organic," that is, derived from the earth. The entrance to a home became part of the continuous flow from one naturally beautiful space "outside" into one "inside." The floor plans for his houses were distinctively open, radiating outward from a central fireplace. In the house he built for himself in Oak Park, Illinois, Wright had the following message carved in the fireplace mantel: "Truth is life. Good Friend, around these hearth-stones speak no evil word of any creature." By reshaping the center of human existence in positive relation to nature, Wright conveyed a moral vision of nature's unity and intrinsic value.

Wright's architectural vision provides a fruitful point of departure for highlighting the moral contours of the biblical cosmologies. Wright wanted to establish continuity, both aesthetically and morally, between natural space and "man-made" place by shaping human habitation in accord with nature. His architectural vision is not without premodern precedent. In their various accounts of creation, the ancient cosmologists of Scripture did much the same thing, but conversely. They were not about building homes so much as depicting the universe *as* a home, an *oikos*. In this way, human beings discovered (or forged) their ecological link to the cosmos and came to know their place within the vastness of the created order.

Like Wright's central fireplace, the creation accounts radiate outward from the human hearth with moral visions *for* the world, while at the same time shaping human identity and agency *in* the world. Contrary to certain modern ecologies, these ancient cosmologies ascribe to human beings an important and constructive role within the created order.[1] They provide meaningful contexts for human life and conduct, offering what William Schweiker calls "moral cosmologies," that is, "sets of beliefs and valuations, often tacit in a culture, about how human beings orient themselves rightfully and meaningfully in the texture of the physical cosmos."[2] For the ancients the cosmos inscribes an ethos, the "'cement' of human society" writ cosmically large.[3] As Wright's work gives visual testimony that nature and human nature can be mutually related, so the biblical cosmologies bear literary witness to the seamless whole of created existence, human and nonhuman. Like Wright's architecture, the creation accounts specify two inextricably related aspects of creation for the purpose of shaping moral identity, namely, *place* and *value*. Both are indispensable for establishing an ecology of community. A modest sampling of the various cosmologies of the Bible will provide sufficient demonstration: Gen. 1:1–2:3; 2:4b–3:24; Prov. 8:22–31; Job 38–41; and Ps. 104. Each cosmology will be examined in terms of its moral "texture," which includes how a given cosmology defines the "outside" in terms of what is "inside" with respect to human habitation and agency.

Animate Icons in the Cosmic Temple

The shaping power of creation for human agency is readily evident in Gen. 1:1–2:3. For unlocking the significance of this preeminent creation account, the pattern is key. Governed by a heptadic (seven-day) literary, perhaps liturgical, structure, the Priestly account methodically constructs an ordered, highly differentiated universe in which each life form (genus or species) has its place within a given domain (sea, land, air). The first six days of creation divide themselves into two halves or, more accurately, two *columns* of three days. But the seventh day distinguishes itself as the day of divine repose from all creative activity. When viewed structurally in two columns of correlating days (1 and 4, 2 and 5, 3 and 6), with the seventh day set apart at the end, the Priestly creation resembles the tripartite architecture of the temple with its gradations of holiness culminating with the Holy of Holies, God's inner sanctum (*dĕbîr*).

Simply put, this account of creation has constructed a cosmic "temple in time" for human *and* divine habitation. Temporally, God rests on the Sabbath; spatially, the seventh day corresponds to divine indwelling of the temple's holiest domain.[4]

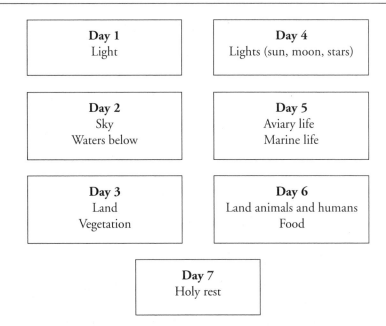

Day 1 Light	Day 4 Lights (sun, moon, stars)
Day 2 Sky Waters below	Day 5 Aviary life Marine life
Day 3 Land Vegetation	Day 6 Land animals and humans Food

Day 7
Holy rest

The temple, thus, sets the defining context of creation and human agency. The specific rubric for human creation is that of "image" and "likeness" of God (1:26). It is the only act of creation throughout the six days that requires the cooperative effort of the divine assembly ("Let us . . . in our image") as well as, possibly, a coordinated effort of the natural elements, particularly earth and water.[5] By virtue of their unique creation, human beings bear a distinctly sacramental quality vis-à-vis the rest of creation. All human beings, regardless of gender, ethnic, and socioeconomic division, have a share in divine power and function. They are "at home" in the cosmic temple as animate icons of the divine realm, the terrestrial counterparts to the "hosts" of YHWH.[6] Akin to the cult statues of various deities that populated the temples of the ancient Near East, human beings embody a self-defining theophanic purpose in the earthly realm, and they do so by mediating God's salutary sovereignty on earth.[7] As bearers of God's image, human beings embody God's creative way in the world, one that enlists and harnesses, rather than subjugates and conquers, the elements of earth and water to realize their life-productive, sustaining potentials.

The command to "subdue" and have "dominion" over the world (1:28), thus, is freighted with qualification: It is a mandate of stewardship, not of exploitation. It is the blessing of gentle, life-giving dominion consonant with the creator's way. For the ancient Israelites, cultivation of the land and animal husbandry were the necessary means to ensure human flourishing in the land. In Gen. 1, such activities are given a dignity that is nothing short of divine; subsistence agriculture is invested with noble, royal purpose.[8] Indeed, the "hero" of the Priestly primordial history is Noah, the first to implement an "endangered species project." In his role as nature preserver, Noah fulfills most fully the command to exercise "dominion" over the earth.

Human identity emerges within a cosmos conceived as a temple-home for *all* living creatures (cf. Ps. 84:2–4 [Eng. 1–3]), one that is established by well-set boundaries. In the language of creation, human agency is cast in terms of blessing, namely, the blessing of procreation (along with the sea creatures and birds [Gen. 1:22]) *and* the blessing of maintaining the cosmic order as established by God, an order whereby demarcated domains are maintained and the flourishing of all life is sustained. Created in God's image, human beings take their vocational cue from God. And since God is described as a sovereign force that orders, coordinates, and enlists, so human beings are to go and do likewise—that is, in *imitatio Dei*. God nowhere wields a weapon or engages in mortal combat in order to create and sustain.[9] The same applies to human beings.

Human activity within the cosmic order, moreover, entails a regular rhythm of work and rest (see Exod. 20:8–11). As the bearers of God's image, human beings are to adopt this divine pattern of activity, exercising a gentle, enabling power that is also held in check, allowing rest for all creatures. And it is in holy *sabbath* rest that the cosmic order is most readily discernible as a *temple* order. Human beings are created in the *imago Dei* insofar as the cosmos is constructed in the *imago templi*. The ordering of creation, thus, has as its implicit goal the praise of the creator from within the cosmic temple.

Cultivating the Garden of Mutual Intimacy

The following creation account, Gen. 2:4b–3:24, replaces the formulaic structure of the Priestly account with messy narrative and focuses more narrowly on the creation of the human family, though not in isolation to the natural environment. Structured around a series of lacks that are subsequently filled, this account takes place within the specific setting of a lush, garden grove (2:9; cf. 1:11–13). The story opens negatively, beginning with the lack of vegetation due to no rain and no tiller (2:4–5). God, consequently, supplies a stream as well as a living, breathing *'ādām*, whom God, as potter, forms from the "dust of the ground," or *'ădāmâ*, and animates by divine breath. As in Gen. 1, origin informs identity and agency: In place of the language of *imago Dei* is that of *imago terrae*. The first human is a "groundling."

The garden is both aesthetically pleasing and materially abundant, a feast to the eyes as well as to the appetite (2:9). It sets the material context for flourishing. But the garden must be tended; it cannot maintain itself. So *'ādām* is placed within it to "serve" (*'ābad*) and to "protect" (*šāmar*) the garden (2:15). Identity, thus, shapes vocation. *'Ādām* is bound to the *'ădāmâ* in service, while the *'ădāmâ* yields utterly to *'ādām* in its productivity. Both are bound to each other in a life of mutual servitude, as it were. More accurately, given their etymological and physical affinity, *'ādām* works in kinship with the *'ădāmâ*. Unlike the creation accounts of Mesopotamia, humans are not created by default to provide labor for the gods, who refuse to perform such labor themselves (e.g., *Atrahasis, Enūma Elish*). Rather, God creates *ʾādām* in order to preserve the formative context that nourishes both him and the rest of creation, the means of self-sufficiency. This "groundling," moreover, is given wide-ranging freedom with only one specific restriction (2:16–17).

But does the garden by itself ensure human flourishing? The garden provides more than sufficient material support for *ʾādām*'s physical welfare. Yet God discovers something amiss about the garden for *ʾādām*'s sake. There remains another lack, one that reaches beyond mere physical need, namely, companionship. *ʾĀdām* lacks a suitable partner, a counterpart (*ʿēzer kĕnegdô*), and the situation is declared by God as "not good" (cf. 1:4, 10, 12, 18, 21, 25, 31), a situation of dire need that, again, requires divine remedy. And so God responds experimentally by creating animals of various species. The animals are brought forth for *ʾādām* to name. He is granted an active role in determining the garden's social topography. Although sharing a level of identity with the animals (they, too, are created "out of the ground"), *ʾādām* does not acknowledge any one of them as a fitting partner. None can provide the kind of companionship that will alleviate his condition of loneliness (2:18). As the search for *ʾādām*'s mutual complement continues, so God fashions another creature, but this time from *ʾādām*'s own material constitution, not from the *ʾādāmâ*'s. Paradoxically, this new creation requires a new lack: A part of *ʾādām* is removed in order to form his complement and, thereby, complete the anthropogony. Without abandoning his original identity, *ʾādām* takes on a new one, namely, his gender as "man" (*ʾîš*). Far from being neutered, *ʾādām* is in fact "gendered" through the act of surgical removal! "Out of man was this one taken" (2:23)—that is, out of *ʾîš* the *ʾiššâ* ("woman") was fashioned. The man's jubilant approbation acknowledges the intimate affinity the woman has with him—not an *indirect* affinity with the man through the medium of the ground but a *direct* affinity of "bone" and "flesh." More than sexual love is celebrated; the kinship of identity is established.[10] The woman and man discover that they are made in the image of each other. *ʾĀdām*, once fashioned in the *imago terrae*, discovers himself to be also created in the *imago feminae*, and the woman in the *imago viri*.

The subsequent story of disobedience and curse, which culminates in the couple's expulsion, highlights all the more the ethos of life within the garden. In the garden there is no fear or shame, even before God. Blame and estrangement have no sway, so also pain that is to be distinctly either the woman's (childbirth) or the man's (exhausting work). The ground is eminently conducive to the man's labors. Life in the garden, thus, is one of fruitful work, delight, and mutual intimacy. The institution of marriage even finds its home *within* the garden, the context of its etiology (2:24; cf. Cant. 4:12–5:1). Life in the garden is harmonious, and it rests upon the delicate balance between freedom and obedience to divine command. But once the balance is upset, a chain reaction of tragic failures commences that leads to expulsion and a life of hardship, pain, and subordination.[11]

But human existence—now turned subsistence—is not left unmitigated. For the author of this tale of human genesis, it is life *within* the garden, not the life of curse, that continues to sustain meaningful existence, however painfully life *outside* the garden falls short. The garden cultivates an ideal, but not an unattainable one. Having planted, as it were, the originating context of the marriage covenant within the garden, this moral cosmology also sets, more broadly, a defining context and ideal for right conduct outside of it, specifically one that fosters partnership within family and community as well as partnership with the soil from which life emerges and is sustained. The garden, thus, sets the context for kinship and, *mutatis mutandi*, for covenantal service to creation. As John Calvin commented about Gen. 2:15 ("serve" and "protect" the garden):

> Moses adds, that the custody of the garden was given in charge to Adam, to show that we possess the things which God has committed to our hands, on the condition, that being content with a frugal and moderate use of them, we should take care of what shall remain. Let him who possesses a field, so partake of its yearly fruits, that he may not suffer the ground to be injured by his negligence; but let him endeavour to hand it down to posterity as he received it, or even better cultivated. . . . Let every one regard himself as the steward of God in all things which he possesses.[12]

Creation as Playhouse: The Delight of Moral Conduct

One of the most aesthetically crafted creation poems in the wisdom literature is found in Prov. 8:22–31, part of wisdom's encomium in chapter 8. The first half of chapter 8 highlights wisdom's unassailable integrity and unsurpassable worth (vv. 6–11), as well as her benefits (vv. 12–16) and preeminent authority (vv. 17–21). Personified as feminine,[13] wisdom seeks to persuade her audience of her legitimacy amid competing voices that populate Prov. 1–9 (e.g., 1:11–14; 7:13–21). The creation poem that follows marks the capstone of her rhetorical agenda (vv. 22–31), bearing testimony to wisdom's genesis within the narrative sweep of God's cosmic work. But more than simply her legitimacy is at stake. Here a distinctly moral cosmology is established, one that both defines wisdom's profile and shapes human agency.

Repeated throughout the poem is wisdom's primordial status. She was birthed prior to earthly creation.[14] Although her preexistent origin is radically distinguished from the origin of the cosmos, wisdom shares a bond with the inhabited world. Indeed, the world, as described by wisdom, sets the context of her place and identity. As Terence Fretheim succinctly notes, "Wisdom needs a world to be truly wisdom."[15] So what kind of world is required for wisdom's flourishing?

As architect and artisan, God carves out the foundations of the earth, anchors the mountains, stabilizes and fills the wellsprings, establishes the heavens, circumscribes the surface of the deep, secures the skies, and sets the boundary between sea and land. In short, God establishes cosmic infrastructures that provide both stability and sustenance. The world is an eminently *safe* place, and limits are assigned so that creation does not collapse upon itself. Everything is made firm and secure. Creation is a home, ready made, but for whom? The poem lacks any reference to the creation of life, human or nonhuman, in the world; only a glancing reference to creaturely life is given in the final verse ("inhabited world" and "human race"). Yet the poem acknowledges something preeminently alive and vibrantly present throughout God's construction of the cosmos. She is wisdom, begotten by God:

> YHWH *created me* in the beginning of his way,
>   the earliest of his works of yore.
> Of old *I was woven*[16] from the beginning,
>   before the earth's inception.
> When the deeps were not, *I was engendered.* . . .
>   In advance of the hills, *I was brought forth.*
>   (8:22–24a, 25b)

> When he established the heavens, *I was there.*
>   (8:27a)

> When he carved out the foundations of the earth,
>   *I was beside him growing up.*[17]
>   (8:29b–30a)

The language of wisdom's creation is not the language of construction and boundary making but that of gestation, birth, and growth. She is a living being, engendered prior to all other creatures. Indeed, she embodies the quintessence of life before and beside God. And what precisely does wisdom do? She plays.

> I have been daily his delight,
>   playing before him every moment,
> playing in his inhabited world,
>   delighting with the offspring of *'ādām.*
>   (8:30a–31)

Wisdom's play serves double duty. Her activity engages both God and creation. She engages God as well as creation in the mutuality of play, holding creator and creation together through the common bond of delight.

Wisdom's place beside God *during* creation informs her role *in* creation. First and foremost, she is in the know regarding the workings of the cosmos. Wisdom is the primary witness of God's creation, and she has not only lived to tell about it, she has "grown up" with creation to sing about it! Indeed, her hymn itself is tangible testimony to her continued delight in creation. She, above all creatures, knows the cosmos as intimately as God does. God has given her birth and let her grow and take delight in her cosmic home. She is no mere instrument of God's creative abilities; she is more than a divine attribute (cf. 3:19). She is fully alive, interdependent with God and the world. Wisdom fully hypostasized is God's full partner in play, and the inhabited world, including that of human beings, is hers to enjoy. The world was made for her sake, for her flourishing and for her delight, and it is her delight that encompasses all the world, sustaining its existence.

As the world was divinely constructed for wisdom's "growth," so the world continues to be conducive for wisdom's flourishing. At the same time, wisdom's delight makes possible the world's ongoing, "daily" life. As an object of appropriation for human beings, wisdom in the cosmos informs humanity's role and place in the world.[18] In this creation poem, wisdom is created in the *imago nati* who grows up. The world is created as wisdom's home inasmuch as the cosmic order was created to be conducive for wisdom's growth and flourishing. Such purpose for creation has its prescriptive counterpart in the narrower world of human intercourse: The social world of humans must be ordered in such a way as to promote growth *in* wisdom. It is incumbent upon human beings to maintain the world in its secure order so that wisdom can thrive in both the mind and heart (see 2:10). Wisdom's growth is nurtured in a life of sheer delight in God and in the order of creation. Her intermediate position between God and the world sets the context for those who aspire to grow in God-given wisdom. That is to say, maturity in wisdom does not discount childlike wonder. Rather, moral formation cultivates it.

Stranger in a Strange Land

Wonder at creation is a central message of YHWH's answer to Job in chapters 38–41. The climax of the book, YHWH's poetic discourse, offers the most panoramic view of creation in all of the Hebrew Bible, but with a particular focus on those corners of creation that lie beyond human apprehension, the fringes of the cosmos. Through probing questions, God gives Job a tour of creation's frontiers, a cosmic field trip of unimaginable proportions. From wastelands to the "recesses of the deep," from the "gates of deep darkness" to the place of the dawn, the extremities of creation come into full view. In addition, Job comes face to face with the animals of the wild: lions and Leviathan, onagers and aurochs. Whereas God brought the animals to ʾādām in the garden in Gen. 2, Job is in effect transported to their remote habitats. Unlike ʾādām, Job is cast far and wide to the very margins of creation, to where the wild things are.

As in Gen. 1, the poetry of creation in Job opens with the establishment of cosmic domains, beginning with the earth's foundations (38:4–7) and proceeding to the containment of the sea (vv. 8–11) and the creation of light (vv. 12–15). The elements of meteorology are depicted, including the rain, which satisfies "the waste and desolate land" apart from human settlement (vv. 25–27). Reference here specifically to creation *beyond* the touch of human encroachment is key, for God enlarges Job's purview to the point of beholding creation at its most "desolate." But it is precisely in the desolation that Job will begin to find creation's dignity, as well as his own.

But Job's tour is not over. Following the description of God's cosmic expanse, Job witnesses a parade of animals, beginning with lions. While dependent upon

God, their provider (e.g., 38:39–41), these denizens of the wild exhibit strength and freedom as they roam the far reaches of the land. The mountain goat kids "go forth and do not return" (39:4); the onager (NRSV, "wild ass") roams freely (v. 5); the auroch (NRSV, "wild ox") resists domestication (vv. 9–12); the ostrich fearlessly flaps its wings (vv. 16–18); the warhorse exults in its strength and "laughs at fear" (v. 22); the raptors, by God's wisdom, soar and thrive, sustaining themselves by their keen sight for prey (vv. 26–30). The two final creatures described in YHWH's second speech to Job assume cosmic proportions: Behemoth and Leviathan, mythically expanded versions of the hippopotamus and crocodile. But these creatures of chaos are invested with entirely positive significance, despite their associations with evil elsewhere in biblical tradition. God admiringly describes them in glorious detail, as if to celebrate their formidable strength. Nothing is said of God's intent to subjugate them; freedom reigns even for these fearsome creatures.

What kind of creation does God paint for Job's instruction? One that is teeming with life, fierce strength, unrequited care, and wild beauty. To be sure, limits are set in place: Earth rests on stable foundations, the sea is contained like a swaddling infant, and the dawn renews the day with some semblance of order (38:4–15). But creation is no static domain, much less a machine set in motion by an indifferent God. Neither is it an object of divine micromanagement.[19] Land, sea, and sky are host to myriad life-forms, all exotic and alien to the human eye,[20] but all affirmed and nurtured by God. The world is God's wild kingdom, and none of its subjects falls under human dominion. Rather, the world pulses with an unrestrained *élan vital*, or, as happily put by Ellen Davis, is shot full of "pizzazz."[21]

What is Job's place, and by extension humanity's, within such a world? On the surface, Job seems bereft of place. No mention is given of humanity's creation, much less of human dominion over creation. This is no anthropocentric world that God so loves. Yet God includes Job:

> Behold Behemoth, which I made with you ['*immāk*];
>   it eats grass like an ox.
>
>   (Job 40:15)

The clue is in the preposition. Behemoth, a creature of strength and fearlessness, is created *with* Job. By association, Job shares some semblance of identity with the denizens of the margins. He is no isolated creation and is clearly not the apex of the created order; rather, he is created in solidarity with a wild and wooly world. When Job earlier *complains* that he is a "brother of jackals and a companion of ostriches" (30:29), ostracized by friends and family, God in effect turns his lament into wonder. As Job is no island, so humanity is no enclave set apart from a potent, thriving world.

God's revelation of Job's place in creation gives shape to Job's vocation. It is not simply, as Fretheim suggests, "to probe the creation more deeply than he already has, but this time with a greater appreciation for the grand design" or "to engage more deeply in his vocation on behalf of God's creatures of great worth and value."[22] Yes, Job's worldview is infinitely expanded, but for what purpose? Simply to awaken his curiosity? Important (and vague) as these vocational purposes are, God's challenge to Job cuts more deeply and bears far greater particularity than most commentators admit. His vocation arises out of a new identity gained from having discerned the world anew. Job is to take back something of the wild, indeed, to embody the wild by recognizing it within himself. He is to see in himself Behemoth's strength and Leviathan's fearlessness when confronting human presumption, but also to find himself among the brood of ravens that needfully "cry out to God" for food (38:41).[23] Job has come to a greater knowledge of the world and, in turn, a deeper knowledge of himself in the world, as one both frail and fearless, as one who sits in dust and ashes (42:6) yet also "surveys all that is lofty" (41:34), incinerating false proverbs into ashes (13:2; cf. 42:19–21). The extremities of the world have exposed the extremities of Job's own life and affirmed them. In the end, Job is vindicated for his unrepentance; he, unlike his friends, spoke of "what is right" (42:8). In sum, Job has come to see himself created in the *imago animalis* and views his role akin to that of God's by caring gratuitously and without restriction for his world. Is it any wonder, then, that Job does something quite unorthodox with his new family? He freely extends an inheritance to his daughters in addition to his sons (42:15), something unexpected in ancient patriarchal practice (cf. Num. 27:1–11). Job has found his way home from the wild; indeed, he has brought something of the wild back home.

More than any other creation discourse in the Hebrew Bible, Job 38–41 turns the familiar, human world inside out. With its intense focus on creation's extremities, the poem focuses resolutely on the "outside" without any familiar template to impose. The world is not a cosmic temple nor a lush, familial garden nor a playhouse for child wisdom. No, the world is viewed from the perspective of the margins, apart from human provenance; it is truly alien, and by extension so is the world "closer to home." Thus, the claim made by Fretheim about Job requires qualification: "With God there are no alien creatures, no outsiders."[24] Yes, no creature resides outside the orbit of God's providential care, but alien creatures remain, utterly strange and fully wild. God's answer to Job does something similar to what Michael Cunningham says about a good novel: "Any good novel helps us understand difference. I can walk down the street in New York, and the people I see might as well be lizard women from other planets. We're so strange to each other."[25]

In Job, creation's "alienness" is fully preserved; indeed, it is lauded, no less, by the creator. The word according to God is made in the *imago peregrini* (cf. Job 19:15). Nevertheless, the aliens that populate the world's fringes are not on the margins. They are "front and center" in God's purview, and now in Job's as well. Amid this alien world a new level of interdependence among *all* creatures is achieved. God's message to Job incorporates what is wild and strange within the orbit of God's care without making it comfortably familiar. The resultant bond forged by God between Job and the creatures of the wild requires Job to affirm, rather than lament, the margins of his own existence, his life *in extremis*, and to move forward in the righteousness in which he has persisted throughout his discourses. That perhaps is what is ultimately meant by God's challenge for Job to "gird his loins" (38:3; 40:6).

The Passion of the Creator and of the Creature

Psalm 104, the most extensive creation psalm in the Bible, could be considered a fitting counterpart to Job 38–41. Indeed, it is tantalizing to imagine Job himself, once restored, having written it in response to his cosmic tour.[26] In any case, Ps. 104 and Job 38–41 form a perfect pairing, for the psalm focuses just as resolutely on the manifold nature of God's creation, Leviathan included, but from the discursive perspective of the human creature rather than that of the creator. Like Gen. 1, creation in the psalm begins with the basic structures of creation but takes a step back; the psalm opens with an acclamation of divinity before proceeding to divine creativity (vv. 1–2). As in Job, the psalm's primary focus is set on animal life: mountain goats, storks, coneys, lions, and finally (as in Job), Leviathan (v. 26b). All are detailed in a tone of rapturous praise given to the creator.

But for all that is comparable between the taxonomies of animal life featured in Job 38–41 and Ps. 104, there is one major difference. Whereas YHWH's response to Job makes scarce mention of botanical life,[27] trees have standing in Ps. 104:

> The trees of YHWH are well saturated;
>> the cedars of Lebanon that he planted.
> There the birds build their nests;
>> the stork has its home in the fir trees.
>> (Ps. 104:16–17; cf. v. 12)

This seemingly minor detail is crucial to understanding the way the psalmist views creation as a whole. Most commentators have marveled over the central theme of provision that pervades the psalm (as also in Job), and appropriately so.[28] God provides springs to give drink "to every wild animal" (v. 11), "waters the mountains" and "the trees" (vv. 13, 16), causes "grass to grow for the cattle" (v. 14), provides bread, wine, and oil for human beings (v. 15), and supplies "prey" for the lions (v. 21) as well as food for all creatures "in due season" (v. 27). The metaphor for such provision is God's "open hand" (v. 28).

But underlying and supporting the various ways God provides is another pervasive cosmological feature, of which the cedar trees offer but just one example. God's first act in creation according to the psalmist is key.[29]

> Who unfurls the heavens as a curtain;
>> who sets the rafters of his chambers upon the waters.
>> (Ps. 104:2b–3a)

God first creates a home, a habitat for divinity, and in turn establishes domiciles for every living creature: streams and trees for the birds (vv. 12, 17), mountains for the wild goats (v. 18a), rocks for the coneys (v. 18b). Even the·waters have their appointed place (vv. 8–9). The lions have their dens, as humans have their homes (vv. 22–23) and Leviathan has the sea (v. 26). The earth is not just habitat for humanity but also habitat for all creatures: "the earth is full of [YHWH's] creatures" (v. 24). Indeed, human beings are scarcely mentioned until v. 23 (cf. vv. 14–15) and only then in consort with the fierce lions, whose only difference from humans is that they take the "night shift" to pursue their living (v. 22). The psalm views creation in thoroughly ecocentric terms; the earth is a place of accommodation for all creatures great and small, people included.

As home is not just a place of refuge but also a source of care and joy, so earth is more than simply a source of sustenance. It is also a place of enjoyment. The earth provides wine "to cheer the human heart, oil to make the face shine" (v. 15a). God *plays* with Leviathan in its abode, the sea, home also for innumerable creatures (vv. 25, 26b). Toward the end of the psalm, the speaker indirectly urges God to "rejoice" (*yiśmaḥ*) in creation (v. 31b), a unique exhortation in the Hebrew Bible. God is to rejoice in creation's abundance, diversity, and capacity to accommodate all creatures.

As for humanity's place and vocation in this cosmic home, the psalmist discerns a fundamental common denominator among all creatures, both alien and familiar, wild and domestic. As rightful occupants of the many rooms of God's cosmic mansion, they are all recipients of God's gracious provision. Humanity constitutes only one class of occupants (there is no "first class"), and this realization ensures a genuine respect for boundaries, like the waters restricted within the boundaries of their appointed place (vv. 8–9). Humanity's work, for example, is consigned to the day, not the night, the temporal domain assigned for the animals of the forest, including the lions, to pursue their living. The wicked, the object of the speaker's scorn at the conclusion of the psalm (v. 35a), have an affinity with the night or darkness (see Job 24:14–17). They act as predators of their own species.

While respect for boundaries, both temporal and spatial, is expressed in the psalm, a degree of freedom is granted to humanity: The ships can ply their trade on the sea, the habitat of Leviathan (no doubt at their own risk). Absent, however, is any hint of human dominion over creation (contra Ps. 8). Human agency is set squarely within the matrix of shared interdependence among all creatures. Vegetation is shared by both cattle and human beings. Deforestation can violate the domiciles of certain creatures. The sense of absolute dependence upon God proscribes both the hoarding of resources and the encroachment of domains by any one species. But the moral power of the psalm extends beyond simply inculcating respect for good boundaries, and it is evoked by the psalm's very tone. The psalmist responds to God's creation, fashioned in wisdom (v. 24b), with awe and praise. It is out of such awe that the psalmist's poetic discourse ("meditation") emerges (v. 34). Psalm 104, as a whole, is an exercise of joy, one that the psalmist encourages even God to join in sharing (v. 31b). As plants are shared, the wine is distributed, and all "are filled with good things" (v. 28), so joy is shared by both creature and creator.

In sum, Ps. 104 brings creation home from the margins, just as Job 38–41 extends creation outward toward the fringes. The exotica of the cosmos are explicitly given homes, their native habitats, whether they be mountain crags, dens, or four-pillared houses. Their fierce freedom is replaced by a domesticity of dependence. In God's cosmic house there are many dwelling places, each fit for each species. Here the world is created in the *imago domi*.

Cultivating Cosmic Values

The contours of the cosmos are distinctively limned in each creation account. Each one in its own way brings the outside in, or, in the case of Job, turns the inside out. Each account unfolds a discrete moral cosmology, whether oriented toward stewardship or play, toward holiness or kinship. Each cosmology extends its own template by which the "blooming, buzzing, confusion" of life (to borrow from William James)[30] is shaped in meaningful ways for human identity and conduct. All the accounts share the conviction that the world is eminently a habitation. Mutual interdependence between human and nonhuman life is a common feature. Each account makes space for human agency, though in varying degrees. In certain cosmologies, human agency is minimized, if not decentered; in other accounts, human freedom and power ("dominion") reign. At the very least, these cosmologies testify to the moral complexity of the world and humanity's place and role within it.

Nevertheless, we cannot leave them as separate, unrelated "world-pictures."[31] Taken together, each account supplements the other, both morally and theologically. The divinely elevated view of humanity in Gen. 1 is tempered in Gen. 2. Humanity, consequently, bears the image of *both* God and ground. The animals are invested with inalienable freedom, as in Job, yet also rendered domestically, as in Ps. 104, along with human beings. Both freedom and dependence characterize not only the human race but all of creation. Regarding creation as a whole, the familiar templates of temple, garden, and home find their limit in Job's outward thrust toward the margins far beyond human habitation. Job reminds us that for every world grasped by human perception, there is always something beyond it, something alien yet sublime. The universe *is* ever expanding!

Perhaps the greatest coherence to be found among these various cosmologies is in the related values they convey for human life and conduct. In the cosmic temple, human beings carry on God's work in the world for the sake of universal life and order. Genesis 1 cultivates a sense of self-awe; human beings, after all, are God's own image. But such awe is not turned inward. Being made in the "image of God" elevates human responsibility for the earth and all its creatures to the highest possible level, in *imitatio Dei*. Humanity is set apart for the responsibility of stewardship for all creatures as much as the Sabbath day is set apart from the rest of creation. Human beings fulfill a distinctly holy service to the world on God's behalf, one that also involves the regular cessation of activity.

Genesis 2–3 ties the holiness of the cosmic temple to the fertile soil of a well-cultivated garden. Animated by divine breath, human beings are formed in kinship with the soil (as *ādām*) and with each other (as woman and man). They are bound together in mutual vocation within the community of creation, both human and nonhuman. According to the garden story, the task of stewardship is best fulfilled in partnership and mutual service. Wisdom in Proverbs adds to human vocation the joyful discipline of learning—"child's play" in the best, most challenging sense. Whereas grasping the "tree of the knowledge of good and bad" out of selfish desire leads to alienation and expulsion from the garden, laying hold of wisdom as God's gift recaptures proper reverence of the creator. The cosmogony in Prov. 8 combines a depiction of an orderly, stable genesis with the lively birthing and growth of wisdom. Wisdom embodies the pursuit of knowledge as an exercise of joy and awe over creation, her playhouse, and so do her "children."

The theme of wonder looks quite different in Job. Gone are the familiar, stable structures of creation. Enter the animals and their inalienable strangeness. This radical awe focuses on the exotica of creation. Once alienated by his own community, Job finds in God's answer a new solidarity with creation as a stranger among strangers. In Job, strangeness is redeemed and freedom reigns, fiercely so. Strangeness captivates rather than threatens; it inspires wonder instead of fear (though, admittedly, only a fine line distinguishes the two). To encounter creation in speechless awe, to see it as if never seen before, and to live accordingly is Job's gift. By living into the wonder of strangeness, one discerns also a solidarity with all creatures great and small, including human beings.

Psalm 104, too, revels in creation's manifold nature but highlights not so much the freedom of its inhabitants as their dependence upon God and each other. Dependence is the tie that binds all creation together. Seizing and exploiting are what the wicked do (see v. 35). Celebrating diversity and dependence in creation, the psalmist sets the stage for creation's praise of God, the provider. And so we have come full circle, back to the "beginning" of Genesis.[32]

Notes

1. A basic statement of this claim can be found in Terence E. Fretheim, *God and World in the Old Testament: A Relational Theology of Creation* (Nashville: Abingdon, 2005), 9.
2. William Schweiker, "Time as Moral Space: Moral Cosmologies, Creation, and Last Judgment," in *The End of the World and the Ends of God* (ed. J. C. Polkinghorne and M. Welker; Harrisburg, PA: Trinity Press International, 2000), 137. Elsewhere, Schweiker talks about "moral ontology," which provides "an account of the meaning of our being in the world and how to orient ourselves in the world" (*Responsibility and Christian Ethics* [Cambridge: Cambridge University Press, 1995], 38).
3. For extensive discussion, see William P. Brown, *The Ethos of the Cosmos* (Grand Rapids: Eerdmans, 2000), 1–26. The quoted phrase is from Paul Lehmann, *Ethics in a Christian Context* (New York: Harper & Row, 1963), 25.
4. For explicit correlation between divine rest and indwelling, see Ps. 132:8, 14.
5. Elsewhere, these primary elements of creation are enlisted by God to participate in the process of creation (Gen. 1:9, 11, 20, 24).

6. See S. Dean McBride Jr., "Divine Protocol: Genesis 1:1–2:3 as Prologue to the Pentateuch," in *God Who Creates: Essays in Honor of W. Sibley Towner* (ed. William P. Brown and S. Dean McBride Jr.; Grand Rapids: Eerdmans, 2000), 16–17. See also a more recent treatment of this theme by J. Richard Middleton, *The Liberating Image: The* Imago Dei *in Genesis 1* (Grand Rapids: Brazos, 2005), who places greater weight on the royal (albeit "democratized") dimensions of the *imago Dei*.

7. From the monotheistic perspective of the Priestly composition, human beings at their very creation replace the gods of the heavenly assembly. See the extensive discussion in W. Randall Garr, *In His Own Image and Likeness: Humanity, Divinity, and Monotheism* (CHANE 15; Leiden: Brill, 2003), 201–40.

8. As often noted, the language of divine image is frequently associated with royal ideology. See, e.g., Garr, *In His Own Image and Likeness*, 144–59, with accompanying bibliography.

9. In contrast, see *Enūma Elish* Tablet IV:30–146.

10. See, e.g., Laban's acknowledgment of Jacob in Gen. 29:14, as well as other instances of the expression in Judg. 9:2 and 2 Sam. 5:1.

11. See Carol A. Newsom's treatment of the dynamics of desire to explain the episode of disobedience in the garden in "Genesis 2–3 and 1 Enoch 6–16: Two Myths of Origin and Their Ethical Implications," in *Shaking Heaven and Earth: Essays in Honor of Walter Brueggemann and Charles B. Cousar* (ed. Christine Roy Yoder et al.; Louisville, KY: Westminster John Knox, 2005), 11–14.

12. John Calvin, *Commentaries on the First Book of Moses Called Genesis* (Grand Rapids: Eerdmans, 1948), 1:125.

13. See Prov. 1:20–33; 4:5–9; 8:1–36; 9:1–6.

14. See vv. 22–25. For detailed examination of the terms of birth, see Brown, *Ethos of the Cosmos*, 272–73, along with accompanying bibliography.

15. Fretheim, *God and World in the Old Testament,* 206.

16. The verb denotes the language of gestation, as in Ps. 139:13.

17. This is frequently translated "master worker" (so NRSV), despite the fact that the Hebrew form is that of a Qal infinitive absolute from the root *ʾmn*. For exegetical details, see Brown, *Ethos of the Cosmos*, 274n14; Michael V. Fox, "*ʾĀmôn* Again," *JBL* 115 (1996): 699–702.

18. Elsewhere in Prov. 1–9, wisdom is cast as an object of understanding, teaching, possession, and even love (e.g., 2:2–4; 3:18; 4:5–8, 11; 5:1).

19. See Fretheim, *God and World*, 235, 239.

20. This is so with the possible exception of the warhorse in 39:19–25, but its strength cannot be entirely tamed.

21. Ellen F. Davis, *Getting Involved with God: Rediscovering the Old Testament* (Cambridge, MA: Cowley, 2001), 139.

22. Fretheim, *God and World*, 243, 242.

23. For greater detail on this point, see Brown, *Ethos of the Cosmos*, 370–75; John Gammie, "Behemoth and Leviathan: On the Didactic and Theological Significance of Job 40:15–41:26," in *Israelite Wisdom: Theological and Literary Essays in Honor of Samuel Terrien* (Missoula, MT: Scholars Press, 1978), 217–31; Kathleen M. O'Connor, "Wild, Raging Creativity: Job in the Whirlwind," in *Earth, Wind, and Fire: Biblical and Theological Perspectives on Creation* (ed. Barbara Ellen Bowe et al.; Collegeville, MN: Liturgical Press, 2004), 52.

24. Fretheim, *God and World*, 282.

25. Quoted in Frappa Stout, "History *and* Imagination," *USA Weekend* (July 15–17, 2005), 11. Not fortuitously, Cunningham's novel *Specimen Days* features extraterrestrial lizard women.

26. This is provided that one can imagine Job ever recovering his voice of praise, absent in the book of Job but so prominent in the psalm.

27. See only Job 40:21–22, which like the psalm details certain flora as the setting for animal life, specifically Behemoth.

28. See Patrick D. Miller, "The Poetry of Creation: Psalm 104," in Brown and McBride, *God Who Creates*, 87–103.

29. God's first act in creation is not, properly speaking, light (v. 2), which is regarded rather as a characteristic feature of divinity. See the parallels in *Enūma Elish* Tablet I: 68 and 138, in which the gods don "mantles of radiance" or effulgent "auras" as markers of their divinity.

30. Quoted in G. D. Kaufman, *God—Mystery—Diversity: Christian Theology in a Pluralistic World* (Minneapolis: Fortress, 1996), 6.

31. The phrase comes from Kaufman.

32. Many thanks to Mark Douglas for having commented on an earlier draft of the paper.

Chapter 3

Creation and Environment in the Character Development of Moses

THOMAS B. DOZEMAN

The opening story of Moses as an adult recounts his killing an Egyptian (Exod. 2:11–15). It is an ambiguous story with regard to motive and character. B. S. Childs writes, "The text does not moralize on Moses' act of violence. Nowhere is there an explicit evaluation that either praises or condemns [him]." In its place, concludes Childs, "a situation is painted with great realism. . . , and the reader is left to ponder on the anomalies of the deed."[1] And interpreters have debated the moral character of Moses and sought to discern the criteria for evaluating his action. Is he a heroic savior who embodies justice, or an immoral murderer who kills in secret?[2] U. Cassuto offers a recent positive reading. Moses looked for aid, according to Cassuto, and when none was evident, he killed the Egyptian, showing "the spirit of a man who pursues justice and is quick to save the oppressed."[3] Not so, concludes W. Propp. Far from a heroic story, Moses' action was impetuous and performed in secret. It is, Propp concludes, "morally wrong."[4]

Two features of the story have been pivotal in the debate over Moses' moral character: the social setting of oppression and a psychological interpretation of the phrase "looking this way and that" to describe Moses before killing the Egyptian. The two motifs are complementary, exploring social context and individual motive in the development of moral character. Yet both motifs also restrict interpretation to an anthropocentric reading of the text. What has received less attention in the history of interpretation is a broader evaluation of setting, one that interrelates individual motive and social setting with a theology of creation, conceived as environment. Does the natural environment of Egypt influence the moral character of Moses in killing the Egyptian? I will argue that it does and that the biblical author accentuates the influence of environment on the character formation of Moses through the motif of adoption in his birth story.

My title, "Creation and Environment in the Character Development of Moses," derives from contemporary humanistic geographers, who describe the interplay between humans and their environment as "place," indicating the reciprocal relationship between nature and human character.[5] It is this dynamic relationship between place and character formation that I wish to explore in the opening stories of Moses. My study will progress through three stages. In the first section I will highlight research on the relationship between creation and justice in ancient Near Eastern royal ideology. The review will anchor the contemporary notion of place in the ancient world. The broad research on creation and justice will provide the background for interpreting the character of Moses in Exod. 1–2. I will conclude with questions about the significance of creation and character formation for contemporary theological and ethical reflection.

Nature and Society in the Worldview of the Ancient Near East

Creation has played a marginal role in biblical theology and ethics during much of the past century. Recent evaluations of biblical theology have documented the way in which the anthropocentric focus of salvation history has pushed creation to the periphery of study.[6] And even when interpreters have focused on the topic of creation, its theological significance has tended to be limited to cosmology and world origin, not social ethics, and certainly not character formation.[7] But creation is reemerging as a more central theme in biblical theology and ethics. A turning point in this process is certainly the work of H. H. Schmid, who, in the early 1970s, argued that creation, not salvation history, is the broad horizon of biblical theology.[8] Schmid advanced three arguments that provide a starting point for my study. His foundational insight is that the primary concern for creation in ancient Near Eastern religion was not with the past origin of the world but with the present structure of the cosmos, particularly the relationship between humans and the natural environment. Two more specific conclusions follow from this. One is that nature and society are interdependent in the worldview of the ancient Near East, meaning that the ordering of the political world and the renewal of nature were bound together. The other conclusion is that creation and law share the same structure, forming an inextricable bond between ethics and creation. Thus, according to Schmid, acts of injustice influence both nature and society in ancient Near Eastern religion. As a result, divine judgment against injustice could come both in the form of a drought and the attack of an enemy.[9]

Schmid illustrates his conclusions with texts from Mesopotamia and Egypt. For our purposes, with an eye on the book of Exodus and its setting in Egypt, the goddess Maat will provide a brief illustration.[10] She is the personification of the world order and nature, while also embracing the concepts of reciprocity, justice, and truth in human society.[11] The gods give the gift of Maat at creation, providing the environment for humans to act in a just manner. The flow of justice from creation to human society is through the cult, led by the king, while human acts of justice also return the gift of Maat to the gods in the same manner, through the king and cultic ritual. The reciprocity between nature and society is illustrated in the iconography of the pharaoh, who is often presented as offering Maat to the gods as an act of worship, an image of social and environmental health, symbolizing the world in balance.[12] Thus, justice in Egyptian religion binds humans, gods, and nature in a reciprocal relationship. E. Horning describes the relationship: "Maat, which came from the gods at creation, returns to them from the hand of the [human]; it symbolizes the partnership of god and [humanity] which is brought to fruition in Egyptian religion." The goal of the relationship, according to Horning, is "to maintain existence and to build a living order."[13] The royal ideology surrounding Pharaoh indicates a focus on society and nature in Egyptian religion, but not exclusively.[14] Maat also shapes individual human character, weighing every human heart at death before the god Osiris.[15]

Schmid argued that the Egyptian view of nature and society also characterizes the worldview of ancient Israel. Law, nature, and religion are all aspects of one comprehensive order of creation. Justice goes out before Yahweh, as Maat before Ra, and it is also the foundation of Yahweh's throne, again recalling Maat.[16] M. Weinfeld reinforces the conclusion of Schmid, affirming that in Israel the divine king establishes justice at the creation of the world, imposing order on the cosmos and making righteousness a foundation of the divine throne (Pss. 33, 89, 93).[17] The result, according to G. M. Landes, is that "to the biblical writers the forces of nature are not morally neutral," prompting his further conclusion that creation and divine liberation are interrelated in biblical literature.[18]

The moral fabric of the cosmos also creates a dynamic and reciprocal relationship between human morality and nature, described by K. Koch as the connection between action and consequence.[19] Human acts of justice strengthen the cosmos; injustice weakens and even pollutes it. The quality of nature, in turn, influences social health and individual moral character. Thus, the moral way (*derek*) chosen by a human evolves into a path or way of life (*derek*).[20] In the process, a reciprocal relationship is formed between actions and their environmental consequences. Within this worldview, justice has its own ecology, requiring the "right atmosphere,"[21] according to Koch, an argument echoed most recently in W. Brown's notion of the "ethos of creation," meaning the habitation that arises from the interplay of human moral actions and environment.[22]

The focus of justice in ancient Israel, as in Egypt, is on the relationship between society and nature, anchored in the royal ideology of the king. The true king must embody the quality of justice in his character, according to Weinfeld, showing compassion.[23] The absence of justice in the king will influence both social stability and the natural order.[24] The prophet Amos attributes environmental pestilence to immoral leadership, while Hosea, too, links ecology and morality in declaring that the land mourns, that all life languishes, and that humans lack insight (Hos. 4:1–3, 6). Yet, as in Egyptian religion, the focus on social justice is not exclusive in ancient Israel. The wisdom tradition, for example, illustrates that the ecology of justice extends beyond the social to include individual morality. We will also see that the ecology of justice is active in the opening stories of Moses on both the social and individual levels.

Creation and Justice in the Introductory Stories of Moses

Recent research has underscored the dynamic interplay of justice and creation in the book of Exodus. Interpretation has focused on the royal ideology surrounding Pharaoh and the influence of his immoral actions on the environment of Egypt. The character traits of Pharaoh, which set in motion the ruin of the land of Egypt, are established in the opening chapters of Exodus. He is a king who perverts wisdom into shrewdness, performing acts of violence and murder in secret to control the Hebrew population. He cautions his advisors to deal shrewdly with the Israelite people (Exod. 1:9–10), and he also directs the midwives in secret to kill male babies (Exod. 1:15–22). The result is both social oppression within Egyptian society and environmental pollution in the land of Egypt.

T. E. Fretheim explores the broader environmental effects of Pharaoh's immoral action, arguing that the plague cycle must be interpreted within the framework of the ancient Near Eastern royal ideology. The symbiotic relationship between ethical and cosmic order means that Pharaoh's oppression of the Israelite people will have environmental implications on the land of Egypt. Indeed, the series of plagues traces the consequences of Pharaoh's immoral acts on nature. They are, writes Fretheim, signs of ecological disaster.[25] The plagues progress through the elements of nature, from water (the sea monster, blood, and frogs) to land (gnats from the earth, flies, cattle) and finally to air (skin boils from ashes thrown into the air, hail, and locusts), before the land of Egypt returns to the primeval state of darkness.[26] Z. Zevit is certainly correct when he concludes that at the end of the plague cycle Egypt is a "land in which creation is undone."[27] In such an environment, where all moral order is lost, even the descent of the deity lacks light, bringing, instead, death at midnight.

The blindness and resistance of Pharaoh to justice, indicated by his "hard heart," places the environmental catastrophe squarely upon the king. The Egyptian officials make the point explicit, stating to Pharaoh, "Do you not yet understand that Egypt is ruined?" (Exod. 10:7). The royal ideology, moreover, is corporate in focus, influencing all humans who live in the land. Egyptians become slave masters, Hebrews act violently against each other, and all suffer from the plagues. Where the writer wishes to separate Israelites from Egyptians, it becomes necessary to designate a distinct location for the Israelite people, in the land of Goshen. The biblical author uses the corporate focus of the royal ide-ology to examine the role of environment in the formation of Moses' character. The early stories of Moses take place in the land of Egypt, not Goshen. Moses' birth, with the motifs of abandonment, rescue, and adoption, anchor him even more firmly in the social environment of Pharaoh and his land. The result, I will argue, is that a theology of creation becomes crucial for interpreting the initial moral actions of Moses. The birth story of Moses establishes the importance of environment in the formation of his character, while his killing of the Egyptian illustrates its destructive effects on the Israelite hero.

The secret birth of Moses and his rescue from the Nile River (Exod. 2:1–10) conform to a common legend in the ancient Near East in which a hero is aban-doned, set adrift in the water, and eventually adopted. B. Lewis has identified no less than seventy-two variations of the story.[28] And as H. Gressmann noted nearly a century ago, the most striking parallel to the story of Moses is the *Legend of Sargon*.[29] Sargon is the infant of a priestess prohibited from conceiving a child. She disobeys, conceives Sargon in secret, and floats the baby on the river in a ves-sel of reeds. Sargon is rescued from the river and adopted by Akki, the water drawer, who raises him as a gardener, before he becomes king of Akkad with the aid of the goddess Ishtar. Most interpreters of the *Legend of Sargon* highlight the theme of identity. The absence of the father's name indicated a problem of legitimacy to Gressmann, particularly the lack of Sargon's royal lineage.[30] Lewis concurs, noting that the motifs of abandonment and adoption emphasize the mysterious origin of Sargon and his humble beginnings, not royal genealogy.[31] Lewis is likely correct, moreover, that the story of Sargon is intended to represent the prototype of the ideal king in Mesopotamian tradition by idealizing the deeds of Sargon, from his initial descent to his eventual rise to power. The tale is, to use a phrase from Childs, a "rags-to-riches" story.[32]

The parallels between the *Legend of Sargon* and Moses' birth story include anonymous parents from the priestly class, an illegal birth, a river ordeal, rescue, adoption, and the protection of women.[33] The similarities suggest that the Israelite historian also wishes to explore the identity of Moses; indeed, the theme of identity is woven throughout the early stories of Moses. The naming of Moses by the daughter of Pharaoh suggests an adoption, while the opening actions of Moses present conflicting perceptions of his identity. Moses identifies himself as a Hebrew but is described as a prince by the Hebrew slave (Exod. 2:14) and then as an Egyptian by the daughters of Jethro (Exod. 2:19) before he marries into the Midianite family of Jethro (Exod. 2:20–21). The theme of identity continues into Moses' commission when he resists the deity with the words, "Who am I that I should go to Pharaoh?" (Exod. 3:11).

The departures from the pattern of the heroic legend provide further focus for interpreting the theme of Moses' identity. Interpreters have underscored two sig-nificant differences in the structure of Moses' story. The first departure is in the reshaping of the birth story itself to maintain the clear ethnic identity of Moses. The expected pattern of the birth legend is the early anonymity of the infant, who remains incognito until becoming an adult and assuming a rule of leadership. But in the case of Moses, his identity is never lost. Pharaoh's daughter recognizes him immediately in the river before adopting him, "This must be one of the Hebrews' children" (Exod. 2:6). And in an additional departure from the pattern, Moses even remains in the care of his Hebrew mother, solidifying his genealogical origin even further (Exod. 2:9).[34] Thus, if the legend is intended to explore identity on the bases of deeds, the biblical author leaves no doubt that the deeds of Moses remain those of a Hebrew, in which case the only variable for evaluating his actions is his environment. G. W. Coates is certainly on target when he concludes that the birth story of Moses is not intended to make Moses an Egyptian but to place him in an Egyptian culture.[35]

The second departure from the heroic legend has more to do with literary context than the reshaping of the birth story itself. The expected pattern of the heroic legend is a rags-to-riches story, in which the hero rises from the threat of death and anonymity to public leadership. The structure of Moses' birth story is inverted. Moses is indeed exalted into the family of Pharaoh but only momentarily, before he returns to the status of a hunted slave when Pharaoh seeks his life (Exod. 2:15). Many interpret the inverted structure against the backdrop of the Israelite slavery and the need for Moses to become a savior of slaves. Propp gives voice to this interpretation: "Whereas the typical hero eventually leaves his lowly environment to assume his rightful glory, Moses flees the Pharaonic court to discover his path first among desert nomads and later among slaves."[36] The social focus of slavery is certainly an important theme in Moses' preparation for leadership. But it does not account for Moses' reversal of fortune.

The pivotal event in the reversal of Moses' fortune is his killing of the Egyptian (Exod. 2:11–14), his first action as an adult, which, as we have seen, is fraught with moral ambiguity precisely because it is a story about the influence of environment on the formation of his character. Moses' killing of the Egyptian probes the influence of Egyptian culture on the hero. It is a story of failed leadership in spite of good intentions. The author introduces Moses with ideal motivations. He enters the scene a savior. He sees the forced labor of his people and their abuse by the Egyptian taskmaster. And he identifies with the Hebrews. Yet he acts in conformity with his environment. The royal ideology of Pharaoh permeates and perhaps even predetermines Moses' action, for he seeks to liberate in secret through violence, recalling the characteristics of Pharaoh that introduced slavery and genocide into the land of Egypt. When the contagion of violence infects two Hebrews the following day, one of them rejects Moses' attempt at mediation, placing him squarely in the world of Pharaoh as a murderer: "Who made you a ruler and judge over us? Do you mean to kill me as you killed the Egyptian?" (Exod. 2:14). The message of the author comes into focus through the accusation: The inclination to liberate becomes murder in an environment already polluted with genocide.

Moses' killing of the Egyptian is a story about creation and character formation. It is morally ambiguous, because it weighs good intentions against environment, underscoring the power of the latter to shape character. Indeed, the influence of environment on the hero, Moses, could not be clearer. He is born a Hebrew baby and declared to be "good" (Exod. 2:2) before being adopted into the family of Pharaoh (Exod. 2:9). He enters the stage as a prince in his first scene as an adult, seeking to liberate through violence, but within verses he exits the stage a fugitive, fleeing for his life from his adopted father. Thus, in the end, Moses' first action as an adult is a negative story of failed leadership. A central point of the tale is that individual motive is insufficient to liberate. The "right atmosphere," to use Koch's phrase, is also necessary in the formation of character. The strong wisdom characteristics in the opening chapters of Exodus, moreover, reinforce the role of creation in the character formation of Moses. The absence of any direct action by the deity aids in exploring the power of environment. As Childs notes, "Everything in the story has a natural cause."[37] If we were to read on in the book of Exodus, we would see that it is only when Moses leaves the pollution of Egypt for the wilderness of Midian that his inclination to liberate takes root (Exod. 2:15–21).

Creation in Biblical Theology and Ethics

I would like to conclude with three reflections on the implications of my reading of Moses for contemporary theology and ethics.

The first conclusion concerns Schmid's thesis regarding the role of creation in biblical theology and ethics. In the past decades we have felt the sting of criticism from writers such as L. White, who argued that the root of our contemporary ecological crisis lies squarely in the anthropocentric focus of Judeo-Christian teleology.[38] Although the charge is in part undeniable, its truth, in my judgment, lies more in the history of interpretation than in the biblical texts. We have only begun to explore Schmid's thesis that creation is, in fact, the broad horizon of biblical theology and ethics rather than the events of salvation history. I am convinced by arguments like Fretheim's that the plague cycle explores the interplay of ethics and creation, and I have sought to demonstrate the same interplay in the character formation of Moses. The environmental contrast between the land of Egypt and the wilderness, moreover, is not limited to Moses but repeats on the national level, when the Israelites also leave Egypt for the wilderness in their pilgrimage for the utopian environment of the promised land. The analogy between hero and nation suggests that the broader story of salvation history is an extended reflection on the power of creation to form a moral society.

I have lingering questions about my reading of the introductory stories of Moses. My final two conclusions probe two areas of ambiguity that I believe require further reflection. To begin with, I am not convinced that the author's presentation of Moses is really about the ethics of character, if by that we mean an analysis of individual virtue, disposition, intention, and so forth. The prominent role of the royal ideology associated with Pharaoh suggests, instead, that the writer is interested in creation and environment in order to probe more the foundations of the ethical life, what we might describe today as metaethics.[39] The

moral ambiguity surrounding the early stories of Moses reinforces this conclusion. His actions are not resolved on the individual level. The contrasting readings of Cassuto and Propp illustrate the point. In view of this, I would suggest
that we must evaluate the moral actions of Moses against the broad canvas of society and environment. If this is correct, then there is a danger in reading the story
of Moses as though it is about individual character formation, when the focus
may be more on the necessary foundations of a good creation and a pure environment as a basis for a just and healthy society.[40]

My second reservation arises from the narrow focus of my reading on the
opening chapters of Exodus. My interpretation has underscored the absence of
God in the opening story of Moses. I would agree with Childs that the wisdom
background of these chapters infuses everything in the story with a natural cause,
thus highlighting the power of environment. But it would be a mistake to read
the opening chapters of Exodus in isolation from the larger thematic development of the book. The book of Exodus is a story about the establishment of
YHWH's cult and the transformation of both creation and human morality,
which occurs when God takes up residency on earth. In view of this, the early
stories of Moses cannot be separated from the establishment of the cult at Sinai,
where the holiness of God purifies both nature and humans, making the formation of both a just society and individual moral character possible.[41] In fact,
Moses' early failure at liberation leads to his initial encounter with God on the
divine mountain (Exod. 3). The focus on the cult in the larger thematic development of the book of Exodus brings us closer to the model of Maat, where the
cult holds nature and society in balance. When the early stories of Moses are read
in the larger context of the book of Exodus, a message of the author for contemporary readers is that metaethics, the foundation of the ethical life, requires worship. It is the encounter with the sacred in worship that creates the dynamic
relationship between creation and the formation of human character.

Notes

1. B. S. Childs, *The Book of Exodus: A Critical, Theological Commentary* (OTL;
   Philadelphia: Westminster, 1974), 44–45.
2. The history of interpretation is summarized in Childs, *Book of Exodus*, 33–42.
3. U. Cassuto, *A Commentary on the Book of Exodus* (Jerusalem: Magnes Press,
   1967), 22.
4. W. Propp, *Exodus 1–18* (AB 2; New York: Doubleday, 1999), 163–66.
5. Yi-Fu Tuan, *Space and Place: The Perspective of Experience* (Minneapolis: University of Minnesota Press, 1977), 6. The literature is extensive and growing. See
   E. Relph, *Place and Placelessness* (London: Pion Limited, 1976); E. Hirsch and
   M. O'Hanlon, ed., *The Anthropology of Landscape: Perspectives on Place and Space*
   (Oxford Studies in Social and Cultural Anthropology; Oxford: Oxford University Press, 1996); E. S. Casey, *The Fate of Place: A Philosophical History* (Berkeley: University of California Press, 1997).
6. See, for example, L. G. Perdue, *The Collapse of History: The Reconstruction of Old
   Testament Theology* (OBT; Minneapolis: Fortress, 1994), and the authors listed
   below in footnotes 7–9.

7. See the excellent summary of creation mythologies from the point of view of world origins in R. J. Clifford, *Creation Accounts in the Ancient Near East and in the Bible* (CBQMS 26; Washington, DC: CBA of America, 1994). R. A. Simkins, *Creator and Creation: Nature in the Worldview of Ancient Israel* (Peabody, MA: Hendrikson, 1994), and T. Hiebert, *The Yahwist's Landscape: Nature and Religion in Early Israel* (New York: Oxford University Press, 1996), each expand the focus of their study of creation to include the topics of culture and value.

8. See H. H. Schmid, *Altorientalische Welt in der alttestamentlichen Theologie* (Zurich: Theologischer Verlag, 1974).

9. H. H. Schmid, "Schöpfung, Gerechtigkeit und Heil: 'Schoepfungstheologie' als Gesamthorizont biblischer Theologie," in Schmid, *Altorientalische Welt in der alttestamentlichen Theologie* (Zurich: Theologischer Verlag, 1974), 10–13. An abridged form of the article is translated as "Creation, Righteousness, and Salvation: 'Creation Theology' as the Broad Horizon of Biblical Theology," in *Creation in the Old Testament* (ed. B. W. Anderson; Issues in Religion and Theology 6; Philadelphia: Fortress, 1984), 102–17.

10. Schmid, "Schöpfung, Gerechtigkeit und Heil," 13; and Schmid, "Jahweglaube und altorientalisches Weltordnungsdenken," in Schmid, *Altorientalische Welt in der alttestamentlichen Theologie*, 42–43.

11. See S. Quirke, *Ancient Egyptian Religion* (London: British Museum, 1992), 34–35 *et passim*.

12. E. Horning, for example, provides illustrations of King Ramesses II offering Maat to Ptah in *Conceptions of God in Ancient Egypt: The One and the Many* (Ithaca, NY: Cornell University Press, 1982), 214–17.

13. Ibid.

14. See H. Frankfort, *Kingship and the Gods: A Study of Ancient Near Eastern Religion as the Integration of Society and Nature* (Oriental Institute Essays; Chicago: University of Chicago Press, 1978).

15. See, for example, the figure of Ankhwahibre's heart weighed against the feather of Maat in T. G. H. James, *Egyptian Painting and Drawing in the British Museum* (Cambridge, MA: Harvard University Press, 1986), 50, fig. 55. For similar iconography, see Quirke, *Ancient Egyptian Religion*, 66.

16. Schmid, "Schöpfung, Gerechtigkeit und Heil," 13; and Schmid, "Jahweglaube und altorientalisches Weltordnungsdenken," 42–43.

17. M. Weinfeld, *Social Justice in Ancient Israel and in the Ancient Near East* (Publications of the Perry Foundation for Biblical Research in the Hebrew University of Jerusalem; Jerusalem: Magnes Press, 1995), 20, 179–214.

18. G. M. Landes, "Creation and Liberation," in Anderson, *Creation in the Old Testament*, 141.

19. K. Koch, "Gibt es ein Vergeltungsdogma im Alten Testament?" *ZTK* 52 (1955): 1–42. An English translation is available as "Is There a Doctrine of Retribution in the Old Testament?" in *Theodicy in the Old Testament* (ed. J. L. Crenshaw; Issues in Religion and Theology 4; Philadelphia: Fortress, 1983), 57–87. Koch broadens his study of the "deed-consequence connection" (*Tat-Ergehen Zuzammenhang*) in his study of the Hebrew motif "way" (*derek*) as both a way chosen and a resulting way of life. See "*derek*," *TDOT* 3.270–93, and *Die Propheten 1–2*, 1:44–46, 2:25–30 (Stuttgart: W. Kohlhammer, 1978). An English translation of the letter is available as *The Prophets*, 2 vols. (Philadelphia: Fortress, 1983). For an evaluation, see P. D. Miller, *Sin and Judgment in the Prophets: A Stylistic and Theological Analysis* (SBLMS 27; Chico, CA: Scholars Press, 1982), 111–36 *et passim*.

20. See Koch, "*derek.*"
21. See Koch, *Prophets*, vol. 1, *The Assyrian Period.* Koch has sought to describe the same dynamic relationship in his research on retribution in wisdom and prophetic literature. God can and does judge human actions externally according to an outside law or norm. But, more often, according to Koch, justice must be envisioned spatially, as a sphere of power that influences the broader environment of human actions. The image of God offered by Koch is not an external judge but a midwife, who "facilitates the completion of something which previous human action has already set in motion" ("Docrtine of Retribution," 63).
22. W. P. Brown, *The Ethos of the Cosmos: The Genesis of Moral Imagination in the Bible* (Grand Rapids: Eerdmans, 1999), 10–33.
23. Weinfeld, *Social Justice in Ancient Israel*, 45–46.
24. See Koch, *Prophets*, 1:56–60.
25. T. E. Fretheim, "The Plagues as Ecological Signs of Historical Disaster," *JBL* 110, no. 3 (1991): 385–96.
26. T. B. Dozeman, *God at War: Power in the Exodus Tradition* (New York: Oxford University Press, 1996), 15–18, 110–17.
27. Z. Zevit, "The Priestly Redaction and Interpretation of the Plague Narrative in Exodus," *JQR* 66, no. 4 (1976): 193–211.
28. B. Lewis, *The Sargon Legend* (ASORDS 4; Cambridge, MA: American Schools of Oriental Research, 1980), 152–95.
29. H. Gressmann, *Mose und seine Zeit: Ein Kommentar zu den Mose-Sagen* (FRLANT 1; Göttingen: Vandenhoeck & Ruprecht, 1913), 8–10.
30. Gressmann suggested a mythological background to the legend, in which the motif of adoption anchored the monarchical authority of Sargon with the gods, underscoring his destiny to be king regardless of his genealogy.
31. Lewis, *Sargon Legend*, 249 *et passim.*
32. Childs, *Book of Exodus*, 9.
33. For a summary of the parallels see, most recently, Propp, *Exodus 1–18*, 155–56.
34. See, among many others, Childs, *Book of Exodus*, 8–14; and Propp, *Exodus 1–18*, 158.
35. G. W. Coates, *Moses: Heroic Man, Man of God* (JSOTSup 57; Sheffield: JSOT Press, 1988), 44.
36. Propp, *Exodus 1–18*, 158.
37. B. S. Childs, "The Birth of Moses," *JBL* 84, no. 2 (1965): 120–21.
38. L. White, "The Historical Roots of Our Ecologic Crisis," *Science* 155 (1967): 1203–7.
39. See W. Frankena, *Ethics* (2nd ed.; Foundations of Philosophy Series; Englewood Cliffs, NJ: Prentice-Hall, 1973), esp. chap. 6.
40. R. Knierim, *The Task of Old Testament Theology: Method and Cases* (Grand Rapids: Eerdmans, 1995), 219–20, explores the contemporary significance of the relationship between cosmic order and history.
41. See J. Z. Smith, *To Take Place: Toward Theory in Ritual* (Chicago: University of Chicago Press, 1987).

Chapter 4

Biblical Laws

Challenging the Principles
of Old Testament Ethics

CHERYL B. ANDERSON

Among all of the distressing images of Hurricane Katrina's effects on New Orleans shown on television in September 2005, one scene was particularly poignant. An African American girl who appeared to be about ten years old was interviewed just outside of the Superdome, where she and thousands of others had been taken in the storm's aftermath. As televised, the young girl said only these words: "I don't want to die here." Although just a child, she was a survivor of two disasters—one natural and the other political—and she could foresee the consequences of putting thousands of people together in that space without electricity and adequate food or water. Places like the Superdome are indeed built to hold thousands of people, but never for more than three hours at a time. This child knew that death was a possible outcome given the neglect, misery, and chaos observable around her.

When this little girl said, "I don't want to die here," she was referring literally to the Superdome, but her words have a broader symbolic meaning. The space that she occupied was not just at the Superdome. She also occupies a space between theory and practice and between policy and application, where the assumptions on which those theories and policies are based are not made explicit and so remain unexamined and uncontested. In this instance, the underlying

37

assumption was that, if warned about an impending storm, all people would want to leave and would have the ability and means to do so. However, that assumption did not prove true for some who were children, poor, or infirm, and the consequences were horrifying. As a person who is young, female, black, and poor, the girl lived in the gap created by policies and practices that ignored her specific circumstances, whether intentionally or unintentionally.

That gap can be found in other contexts, and it is the point of departure for this analysis of biblical laws. My argument is that certain biblical laws ignore the specific circumstances and interests of women, non-Israelites (especially the Canaanites), and the poor, and that consideration of these situations challenges some of the ethical principles commonly drawn from the Old Testament. For example, a woman whose husband accuses her of not being a virgin at the time of their wedding may be stoned to death if proof of her virginity is not offered (Deut. 22:20–21), a slave owner who strikes a male or female slave with a rod is not liable if the slave survives a day or two before dying (Exod. 21:20–21), and those occupying the land now claimed by the Israelites (the Canaanites) are to be annihilated (Deut. 20:17–18). Whatever the underlying policies and rationales might be for these laws in their historical contexts, their foreseeable consequence is the death of particular women, the poor, and Canaanites. In spite of the dramatic separation of time and geography, that little girl in New Orleans seemed to give voice to those who live in these textual gaps when she said, "I don't want to die here." Those for whom death is a possible consequence of these texts probably do not want to die there either. Furthermore, to ignore their circumstances when interpreting these texts means that interpreters become immune to the lethal possibilities created for others. As a result, such consequences for those who live figuratively in a similar space today, like the child in New Orleans, will be ignored as well.

The assertion that biblical laws tend to ignore the possible feelings and circumstances of women, the poor, and the Canaanites can be made from only a cursory survey of some of their provisions. In the case of rape, the husband or father of the woman assaulted is the injured party and not the woman (Deut. 22:23–29).[1] If a slave owner strikes the eye of a male or female slave and destroys it, the owner must let the slave go free to compensate for the eye (Exod. 21:26). However, that person's ability to earn a living has now been severely compromised. From the slave's perspective, a more effective compensation for the lost eye would be to require the slave owner to care for the injured person for the rest of his or her life. Similarly, a problematic law from the perspective of the Canaanites exempts Israelites from permanent servitude but specifies that those from the surrounding nations can be held in permanent servitude and passed on as property to subsequent Israelite generations (Lev. 25:44–46). Considered together, these laws marginalize the perspectives of the nonprivileged, whether that lack of privilege results from being poor, female, or non-Israelite.

Reading these laws today, it seems obvious that they do not provide direct and immutable guidance about how to treat the poor, females, or anyone who is of a different race, ethnicity, or religious affiliation. Whether we recognize it or not, though, the same underlying attitudes shape our own attitudes toward these groups in the contemporary context. The interpretive impact of these laws does not remain locked away in the ancient Near East because Christian scholars use biblical texts in their discussions of Old Testament ethics that encode the same marginalization. As a result, principles of Old Testament ethics are developed and proposed for contemporary contexts that indirectly condone and perpetuate the silencing of marginalized groups.

This essay will examine the ethical principles articulated by Waldemar Janzen, Christopher J. H. Wright, and John Barton. This discussion is not meant to be an exhaustive treatment of how Christians have used or are to use the Old Testament for ethical guidance. Instead, the writings of these three scholars are analyzed to illustrate how biases encoded in biblical texts can be reinscribed in ethical principles and, if they are not actively challenged, brought into our own context. After highlighting the challenges that biblical laws pose to the construction of ethical principles, the final section of the essay will argue that the parameters of ethical inquiry must include a consideration of the very process through which ethical principles themselves are derived. A theoretical understanding for this shift in emphasis away from determining the ethical principle toward following an ethical process will be presented as well.

Waldemar Janzen: The Familial Paradigm

In his book *Old Testament Ethics: A Paradigmatic Approach*, Waldemar Janzen uses "paradigms," biblical models to discern ethical patterns for the church today.[2] His five major paradigms from the Old Testament are familial, priestly, wisdom, royal, and prophetic. But these are interrelated and not separate understandings of "what it means to live rightly before God."[3] In fact, the familial paradigm is the "comprehensive ethic," and the other paradigms are subordinate to it and work together to uphold it.[4] For each paradigm, Janzen identifies relevant biblical stories, and for the familial paradigm those stories are Gen. 13, Judg. 19, and the book of Ruth. Janzen finds that the significant feature in these three stories is that they model primary commitments to family and the Israelite community. In Gen. 13, Abram divides up the land with his relative, Lot, and Janzen approves of Abram's "nonassertive and peaceful disposition [that] makes him willing to yield the choice to Lot, even at the cost of personal disadvantage."[5] In the book of Ruth, Janzen finds the behavior of Ruth and Boaz to be paradigmatic because they act to preserve "a family that might otherwise have become extinct."[6] In Judg. 19, Janzen thinks that the host "holds to the highest ideals of hospitality" because he attempts to protect his guest, the Levite, from the mob and is willing to offer his daughter who "is dearest to him."[7] Janzen does acknowledge initially that "the story is so repulsive and abhorrent to us that we may want to reject it immediately as a text with an ethical message." Yet he goes on to argue that the host and the Levite "outdo each other, as it were, in the greatness of the sacrifice they are ready to offer."[8]

Janzen emphasizes here the importance of commitment and responsibility in communities of faith, but he has done so in a way that continues to marginalize the perspectives and circumstances of women, the poor, and non-Israelites. Abram's gift of land to Lot is considered to be exemplary, but the question of how Abram got the land—or, more specifically, from whom Abram took the land (if Joshua and Judges are followed)—is not raised. In their study of Gen. 12–13, Danna Nolan Fewell and David M. Gunn phrase the appropriate question as follows: "The gift of the land collides with the commission to be a blessing to other families of the earth. How can one be a blessing and yet also supplant?"[9] One can only wonder if the "nonassertive and peaceful disposition" for which Janzen admires Abram is exhibited because Abram is giving away land that belonged to another group (the Canaanites) and not to him in any real sense. At any rate, to praise Abram's actions without even acknowledging that the Canaanites were dispossessed ultimately is to imply that the concerns of Canaanites can be safely ignored.

The story of Ruth does allow a family line to continue, as Janzen contends, but it comes at a cost. Ruth 4:17 refers to those who proclaim that "a son has been born to Naomi." As Amy-Jill Levine states, "Ruth, the ostensible heroine of the story, is left an enigma; her continuing relationship to Naomi, her feelings for her son and husband, and her sense of belonging in Israel are never addressed."[10] By implication, Janzen's use of Ruth's story as a paradigmatic model for Old Testament ethics means that the possible concerns and feelings of women are less important than their appropriate behavior. Furthermore, Janzen considers Ruth's story, where a stranger receives an inheritance, to demonstrate that "Israel's familial paradigm goes beyond the general concern for the preservation of life, of a name, of a family line—though those remain prominent—to a special concern for the disadvantaged, the poor, and the needy."[11] The underlying message, though, is that the disadvantaged must leave their own people, culture, and traditions to improve their lot in life. Phrased differently, the book of Ruth implies that being within the Israelite culture is better than being outside of it. Musa Dube, a biblical scholar from Botswana, counters the notion that Ruth, who abandons her culture, is better off than Orpah, who returns to her culture.[12] In Dube's reflections, Orpah is her country's regent queen and a priestess, and she hopes that Ruth will tell her children about her people, the Moabites—"of their origins, of their kindness, of their hospitality and of their struggles for survival."[13]

Janzen's use of Judg. 19 to illustrate hospitality is troubling. First, he does not condemn the violence against the Levite's concubine as strongly as he might. He does mention that the Levite might have offered himself to the mob. However, he writes that to do so "would have exposed him to homosexual practice," which was ranked elsewhere (Lev. 20:13, for example) as "an abomination" that deserved the death penalty.[14] By structuring his argument in this way, Janzen fails to distinguish between "homosexual practice," as he refers to it, and a violent rape, which is what would have occurred if the Levite had gone out to the mob himself. Furthermore, because the Levite's concubine is indeed raped in the story, the clear implication is that the rape of a female is somehow not as egregious an act as the rape of a male would have been.[15] The concubine's reaction is not given, but it is easy to hear her voice as an echo from a young female in another place: "I don't want to die here."

Second, Janzen only mentions in a footnote, when quoting from Phyllis Trible's *Texts of Terror*, that the hospitality assumed in Judg. 19 only protected males.[16] Janzen then writes in a footnote on the next page that "the modern reader wishes with sadness that this ideal of inclusiveness might have embraced the women in the story equally."[17] Nevertheless, for Janzen to use Judg. 19 as a paradigmatic model, knowing that women were excluded from the hospitality expressed, simply means that their inclusion is not imperative.

It is worth noting that the three biblical stories used by Janzen for his familial paradigm describe an uncle and his nephew (Gen. 13), a mother-in-law and her daughter-in-law (Ruth), and two male members of the same community (Judg. 19)—relationships that are outside of the small nuclear family deemed normative today. Such a difference is not a coincidence. As John Rogerson reports, the family in ancient Israel was "a natural social mechanism that developed initially to meet particular circumstances."[18] In addition, he writes that the biblical family was, among other things, "often polygamous," "the context for rivalry, jealousy, and even fratricide," and "far more advantageous to men than women."[19] He continues: "Anyone who would want to suggest that the Old Testament family as just described should in some sense be a model for the family today could only do so by means of a highly selective and superficial use of the text."[20] Rather than assuming that biblical models apply today, Rogerson calls for new questions to be asked about the effect of family breakups on children, the financial strains that require both parents to work in order to pay the mortgage, and ways to support mothers who also want to have careers, to name a few. He summarizes:

> If the Old Testament says anything to us today, it is that we need to devise theologically driven structures of grace appropriate to our situation that will sustain those aspects of family life which, from a Christian perspective, we deem to be most valuable, and which may be most under threat from the state and powerful interests. This is not something that biblical scholars or theologians can do, without the expertise of lawyers or sociologists.[21]

To answer more justly the questions that our contemporary context raises about responsibilities and commitments in the Christian life, we need to listen to the marginalized voices that have all too often been ignored. In his article "Marriage and Family as Christian Concerns," Stephen Barton proposes that we listen to those whom "we might call the 'outsiders': single people, sexual minorities, the poor, the [physically and sexually] abused, children, and the elderly." For him, the importance of listening to the "outsiders" has been brought to our attention by liberation theology, which is based on "the biblical story where God 'hears' the cry of the slaves in Egypt, and where God-in-Christ responds to the cries for help of the marginalized people of his day." Barton refers to this kind of listening as "an act of love" that "is a quality of attention which contains the seed of transformed relationships, not least in marriages and family life."[22]

Christopher J. H. Wright: What about the Canaanites?

In his book *Old Testament Ethics for the People of God*, a revised version of *Living as the People of God*, Christopher J. H. Wright covers a range of themes and their implications for contemporary society, including ecology, politics, economics, and the legal system. The preface to that earlier book mentions his understanding that "the Old Testament is absorbed with what it means to be the living people of the living God" and his hope that his insights will be used by Christians who work in these and related fields as "a more coherent and effective application of biblical theology and ethics to the particulars of their own environment."[23] Commenting on the addition of an appendix to the 2004 version of his book entitled "What about the Canaanites?" Wright admits in the new preface that he did so

> simply because I get asked that question so often. Invariably, it seems, hearing or reading the phrase, "Old Testament ethics" arouses in people's minds what they regard precisely as the *unethical* dimensions of these texts. This book, however, was never intended as a book about the ethical *problems* of the Old Testament (as we perceive them).[24]

Wright argues in his appendix that there is no contradiction between Israel's election as a "blessing to the nations" and "God's use of them [Israel] to bring such suffering on the Canaanites." As he explains it, God's eschatological purpose is to bless the nations, but "God remains the moral judge of all human action, and it is an equally essential part of the biblical testimony that God acts within history in judgment upon the wicked." In other words, Wright views Israel's actions in Joshua to be an instance of God's use of human agents as "the vehicle of his moral judgment."[25]

He finds further support for his position in texts that attest to the "wickedness of Canaanite society in moral and social terms" (citing specifically Lev. 18:24–25; 20:22–24; Deut. 9:5; 12:29–31) and the fact that "the same YHWH who acted in moral judgment on Israel's enemies would act in precisely the same way on Israel itself."

> So the consistent biblical affirmation that the conquest constituted an act of God's punishment on a wicked society, using Israel as the human agent, must be taken seriously (by those who wish to take the Bible's own testimony seriously) and not be dismissed as self-serving disinfectant for the poison of Israel's own aggression.[26]

By including a discussion about the Canaanites, Wright has not ignored their treatment altogether, but he has clearly made that treatment a marginal issue by addressing it in an appendix, away from the rest of his analysis. The harsh treatment of the Canaanites and other indigenous groups is not just found in the book of Judges; it is also mandated by laws such as Deut. 20:17–18 that require their annihilation. Most importantly, Wright has not considered the possible reactions or perspectives of the Canaanites, undoubtedly none of whom would want to perish under such conditions. Wright can bracket out the ethical questions raised by the Canaanites because he is not one of those against whom the conquest narrative has been invoked.

Robert Allen Warrior, on the other hand, is a Native American who identifies with the Canaanites in the text. In an influential essay, he points out that as the exodus story is usually read, indigenous populations are asked to believe in a "liberationist picture of Yahweh" who has become "Yahweh the conqueror."[27] Just the same, Wright considers the story of Rahab, "set in the midst of the conquest narrative," to demonstrate "the power of 'repentance' and faith and God's willingness to spare his enemies when they choose to identify with God's people."[28] For Warrior, the emphasis on the liberative message of the exodus has meant that, even if the annihilation did not take place, the indigenous people who "put their hope and faith in ideas and gods that were foreign to their culture" were betrayed. "They [the Canaanites] were assimilated into another people's identity and the history of their ancestors came to be regarded as suspect and a danger to the safety of Israel."[29]

Obviously, Wright fails to consider the ways in which the exodus story has been used by European Christians to separate indigenous (nonprivileged) populations from both their cultures and their lands.[30] As Warrior suggests, "We need to be more aware of the way ideas such as those in the Conquest narratives have made their way into Americans' consciousness and ideology." He specifically recalls how Puritan preachers would refer to "Native Americans as Amalekites and Canaanites—in other words, people who, if they would not be converted, were worthy of annihilation."[31] Warrior's words remind us that any notion that God can order the annihilation of a population creates an ethical slippery slope. It becomes far too easy for subsequent groups with adequate force to say, "God has annihilated populations as in Joshua and, since God is on our side, we are acting on God's behalf, which means we can do the same thing in our own time and place."

Wright insists that the annihilation of the Canaanites was prompted by God's interests alone (divine punishment) and not those of the Israelites (land acquisition). However, other scholars who also take the Bible seriously have identified the role of human interest or ideology in the biblical texts. For example, Walter Brueggemann describes the biblical text in general terms as "an act of imaginative remembering" that has been shaped by "real people who live real lives in socioeconomic circumstances where they worried about, yearned for, and protected social advantage and property."[32] Consequently, biblical traditions have been influenced by human interests, and those interests have involved gender, race, class, and ethnic distinctions.

More specifically, Israelite interests are identifiable in the biblical depictions of the Canaanites as sexually deviant. Wright notes that the Canaanites are deemed wicked and worthy of punishment due to their "sexual promiscuity and perversion particularly associated with fertility cults."[33] Yet Robert Oden has written that such accusations do not mean that the Canaanites behaved in such a manner. Instead, he submits that such depictions may have had a role in "defining Israel and Israelite religion as something distinctive."[34] Similarly, Randall Bailey, an African American biblical scholar, points out that to label non-Israelites as sexually deviant is to dehumanize them, and "once this is done, other acts of Israelite oppression or devaluation of these people are readily sanctioned, condoned, and accepted by the reader, both ancient and modern."[35] Furthermore, Bailey argues that the same sexualization of African Americans through negative stereotypes has been used to justify racist oppression in the United States.[36] It would seem that ignoring the human interest or ideology in biblical texts, as Wright does, makes it more likely that the same dehumanizing dynamic can be used to marginalize another group in a different historical period.

Rather than accepting marginalization, Warrior has two suggestions at the end of his essay that are worth noting in the context of this discussion. First, Warrior thinks that "the Canaanites should be at the center of Christian theological reflection and political action" because of the violence and injustice their portrayal has condoned and engendered.[37] Accordingly, the treatment of the Canaanites should not be covered in an appendix to a lengthy treatise. The characterizations of the Canaanites raise fundamental issues about the construction of a national identity and intergroup relationships that are as vital today as they were in ancient Israel, if not more so, and they need to be engaged. Second, Warrior suggests that Christians, whether Native American or not, must learn to participate in a struggle for justice "without making their story the whole story."[38] In other words, Christians need to hear other voices and consider the existence of and need for their different realities.

John Barton: The Basis of Old Testament Ethics

Barton has identified three basic models for ethics in the Old Testament: obedience to God's declared will, natural law, and the imitation of God. Each of these models, however, is problematic when considered from the perspective of women, the poor, and non-Israelites and the biblical laws that affect them. Obedience to God's declared will, according to Barton, reflects the assumption held by "ordinary Israelites as well as those who wrote the biblical books that 'the good' [is] that way of life which God enjoined."[39] Although Barton acknowledges that such obedience is not meant to be blind, difficulties remain. If biblical laws concerning these marginalized groups are considered to express the divine will, then questions about their treatment are discouraged and their marginalization remains unchallenged. For example, there are laws requiring a raped woman to marry her rapist (Deut. 22:28–29) and, as mentioned earlier, a bride's family has to show proof of her virginity if demanded by the groom (Deut. 22:13–21). Challenging such laws in the contemporary context becomes more difficult if they are thought to express the divine will. A more liberative reading becomes possible when the human interest underlying the law is pinpointed, that is, the male interest in ensuring the legitimate paternity of descendants.[40]

Divine guidance is discernable in other parts of the canon, too, but Bruce Birch cautions, "Although it is through Israel that God's word and will are mediated, Israel is not the perfect embodiment of the living out of that divine moral vision." Birch submits that "Israel's unexamined participation in widespread social practices" such as the subordination of women and slavery and "the stories of Israel's sin such as its excesses of nationalism" indicate that "Israel's story is not intended to model normative moral behavior in all of its particulars." As a result, obedience to the divine will must involve a discernment process that distinguishes between divine concern and human interest. As stated by Birch, "Any adequate approach to the Old Testament as moral resource must seek not only to *retrieve* moral perspectives that inform our ethics but in some instances to *reclaim* the biblical text from elements that distort or limit its moral witness."[41]

Another basis for Old Testament ethics, according to Barton, is natural law. However, Barton's use of the term is distinguishable from Western natural law traditions and refers to principles that exist in the biblical text but are not "positive law" as found in law codes.[42] Barton considers natural law and positive law in the Bible to be "two ways by which ethics flows from God: they are not to be opposed as respectively human and divine."[43] Barton sees natural law in two ways: (1) the ethical principles that are inherent to all humankind as alluded to in the oracles against the nations in Amos 1–2 and (2) the ethical concepts that are built into the nature of things, the structure of the world, as evidenced by Isaiah's distress at the state of affairs in Isa. 3.[44]

Nevertheless, the concept of natural law may not be an adequate basis on which to radically change the circumstances of the nonprivileged today. For example, the Decalogue can be thought of as "natural law in practice."[45] Yet the Decalogue condones the subordination of women as well as slavery, and its protections only apply to those within the covenant community, not outsiders. Likewise, Barton finds a commitment to justice ("poetic justice") in the Prophets, as in Isa. 5:8–9, that promises judgment against those who have exploited the poor.[46] It is true that even reducing oppression is beneficial to those who suffer. However, Cyril Rodd has concluded that "what is not found [in the Old Testament] is a belief that the presence of the poor in society is somehow 'wrong,' and that society itself must be changed to remove poverty from its midst."[47] Today, when capitalism has contributed to greater disparities between the rich and the poor around the globe, very fundamental systemic changes may be needed.

Barton's third basis for Old Testament ethics is the imitation of God. For Israelites, it means "to take God's character as the pattern of their character and God's deeds as the model for theirs."[48] This basis is derived from laws such as Deut. 10:17–19 ("The LORD your God is God of gods and Lord of lords . . . who is not partial and takes no bribe . . . and loves the strangers, providing them food and clothing. You shall also love the stranger") and Lev. 19:2 ("You shall be holy, for I the LORD your God am holy").[49] Barton suggests that the moral life here "is envisaged as a cooperative venture between God and humanity. Its commonest image is that of a path, leading to the place where it will converge with the highway trodden by God."[50]

Rodd thinks that such a basis for Old Testament ethics is questionable. He argues that "if the idea of actively *imitating* God and not just living a life which is *similar* in some respects to that of God underlies so much of the Old Testament," it would have been found more often and not just in Deut. 10:17–19 and Lev. 19:2.[51] Furthermore, Rodd contends that "the divine life and the human life run parallel" and the moral actions required of each may differ: "Rather what is required of Israel is to be holy (in its own way) because God is holy (in his), and although human holiness and divine holiness as purity may be thought to coincide, the moral actions which are called out by it need not be."[52] Rodd ends his critique of the imitation of God concept by admonishing those who "read into the Old Testament modern ideas and virtues that are attractive to us" and by underscoring the need to recognize the distance between the world of the Old Testament and our own: "It is a foreign country on which we gaze."[53] Recognizing the historical and cultural differences between the biblical world and our own, as Rodd suggests, might make it easier to determine which norms concerning the treatment of women, the poor, and others are applicable today and which are not. However, Barton's articulation of the basis of Old Testament ethics continues the marginalization of females, the poor, and those who are presumably ethnic outsiders. Moreover, the resultant silencing of those voices is not contested and so appears to be an ethical occurrence. The lack of attention paid to the perspectives of these groups in the biblical texts and Barton's ethical principles must surely be related to the lack of attention paid to the perspectives of these same groups today.

Engaging the Marginalized: The Ethics of Obligation

With only a limited number of examples, the preceding discussion shows how principles of Old Testament ethics have been derived without considering the implications of those principles for women, the poor, and non-Israelites. Judges 9 is read as a model for hospitality, but that hospitality is not extended to women (Janzen). The extermination of the Canaanites in Joshua is justifiable as an act of divine punishment (Wright). A basis for Old Testament ethics is obedience to the divine will, but that approach can merely reproduce the antiquated cultural norms of an ancient context concerning these groups (Barton). The disadvantages imposed in some of the biblical laws upon women, the poor and non-Israelites are reinforced in other parts of the canon and reappear in the principles drawn from them. When biblical scholars consign any discussion of women, the poor, and non-Israelites to a footnote, to an appendix, or ignore them altogether, these groups and their experiences remain marginalized. Over time, that marginalization becomes routine so that their reality and the actual repercussions of decisions and policies on such groups do not have to be considered at all. It should not come as a surprise that the reality of a young, poor, black female in New Orleans in the fall of 2005 had not been considered either.

Clearly, a commitment to engage the circumstances of marginalized groups is needed, whether those groups exist in textual gaps in the Bible or in contemporary society. Frank Yamada, an Asian American biblical scholar, offers a theoretical framework for such a commitment. He outlines a postmodern concept of ethics by relying on the writings of Emmanuel Levinas, among others. Levinas's ideas are particularly helpful for Yamada's project in two ways. First, Levinas not only acknowledges that "the Other" exists, he insists that face-to-face encounters with the Other are the basis of ethics and that ethics is conceived of "within a fundamental relationality with the Other." Second, for Levinas, ethics also involves addressing societal conditions beyond just one's relationship to the Other, thereby "creating the necessity for talking about justice for other human beings and the world."[54]

Yamada recognizes that postmodern ethics does not offer universal or foolproof answers to the moral issues of modern society. But this is probably an advantage, because modernity's attempts to provide such answers may have been its tragic flaw. He continues:

> Postmodern ethicists suggest that life without universals or foundations is not cause for panic but for hope. In the end, ethical decisions are made. The Other beckons us to more authentic ethical relationship. Obligation happens.[55]

A significant difference would be made if biblical interpreters had an obligation to encounter the Other when developing ethical principles from biblical texts. The treatment of women, the poor, and non-Israelites could not be ignored and could no longer be left to the margins. Questions that were previously elided would come to the fore. If a raped woman has to marry her rapist because her marriage prospects are limited, maybe a woman would prefer to be supported financially by inheriting a portion of her father's estate. If force is warranted to discipline a slave, one must wonder if the subordinate conditions under which that slave works should be challenged. If Canaanites are labeled moral deviants, a pattern might be seen in the way negative stereotypes have been used historically to justify exploitation and oppression.

Correspondingly, the ethical principles based on biblical texts that encode the same marginalization would be different. A principle would only be an ethical one if the Other's reality were taken into account. Hospitality, for example, would not be an ethical-biblical paradigm unless it included women, the poor, and the non-Israelites, and biblical texts would be read from that hermeneutical perspective. Ultimately, an obligation to the Other shifts the emphasis in ethics from advancing principles and toward developing a process that ensures the obligation has been met. It means reading the Bible differently and reading our contemporary context differently. Maybe then we could heed the voice of a poor black female child in New Orleans.

Notes

1. See Carolyn Pressler, "Sexual Violence and Deuteronomic Law," in *A Feminist Companion to Exodus and Deuteronomy* (ed. Athalya Brenner; Sheffield: Sheffield Academic Press, 1994), 102–12.
2. Janzen's basic definition of "paradigm" is "something used as a model or example for other cases where a basic principle remains unchanged, though details differ" (Waldemar Janzen, *Old Testament Ethics: A Paradigmatic Approach* [Louisville, KY: Westminster John Knox, 1994], 26). That definition is taken from Christopher J. H. Wright's book *An Eye for an Eye: The Place of the Old Testament Ethics Today* (Downers Grove, IL: InterVarsity, 1983), 43.
3. Janzen, *Old Testament Ethics*, 2.
4. Ibid., 3.
5. Ibid., 10.
6. Ibid., 33.
7. Ibid., 37.
8. Ibid.
9. Danna Nolan Fewell and David M. Gunn, *Gender, Power, and Promise: The Subject of the Bible's First Story* (Nashville: Abingdon, 1993), 41.
10. Amy-Jill Levine, "Ruth," in *Women's Bible Commentary with Apocrypha* (rev. ed.; ed. Carol A. Newsom and Sharon H. Ringe; Louisville, KY: Westminster John Knox, 1998), 90.
11. Janzen, *Old Testament Ethics*, 35.
12. Musa W. Dube, "The Unpublished Letters of Orpah to Ruth," in *A Feminist Companion to Ruth and Esther* (second series; ed. Athalya Brenner; Sheffield: Sheffield Academic Press, 1999), 145–50.
13. Ibid., 150.
14. Janzen, *Old Testament Ethics*, 37.
15. The biblical laws would in fact make that distinction. Homosexual acts are punishable by death, but the rape of the daughter of one's host, if she were not married or betrothed, meant only that the perpetrator had to marry the daughter (Deut. 22:28–29).
16. Janzen, *Old Testament Ethics*, 51n29.
17. Ibid., 52n31.
18. John Rogerson, "The Family and Structures of Grace in the Old Testament," in *Theory and Practice in Old Testament Ethics* (ed. M. Daniel Carroll R.; London: T. & T. Clark, 2004), 132.
19. Ibid.
20. Ibid., 133.
21. Ibid.
22. Stephen C. Barton, "Marriage and Family Life as Christian Concerns," in *New Occasions Teach New Duties: Christian Ethics for Today* (ed. Cyril S. Rodd; Edinburgh: T. & T. Clark, 1995), 168–70.
23. Christopher J. H. Wright, *Old Testament Ethics for the People of God* (Downers Grove, IL: InterVarsity, 2004), 11–12.
24. Ibid., 14–15.
25. Ibid., 473–74.
26. Ibid., 475–76. See also C. S. Cowles et al., *Show Them No Mercy: Four Views on God and Canaanite Genocide* (Grand Rapids: Zondervan, 2003).
27. Robert Allen Warrior, "A Native American Perspective: Canaanites, Cowboys, and Indians," in *Voices from the Margin: Interpreting the Bible in the Third World* (ed. R. S. Sugirtharajah; Maryknoll, NY: Orbis, 1997), 279.
28. Wright, *Old Testament Ethics*, 479.

29. Warrior, "Native American Perspective," 282, 284. It is striking that Wright assumes the annihilation actually took place yet sees the action as unproblematic, whereas Warrior thinks that the story itself, regardless of its historicity, is problematic.
30. Today postcolonial criticism examines the ways in which the Bible has been used to facilitate European imperialism. See, for example, Musa W. Dube, *Postcolonial Feminist Interpretation of the Bible* (St. Louis: Chalice Press, 2000).
31. Warrior, "Native American Perspective," 283.
32. Walter Brueggemann, *An Introduction to the Old Testament: The Canon and Christian Imagination* (Louisville, KY: Westminster John Knox, 2003), 10.
33. Wright, *Old Testament Ethics*, 475.
34. Robert A. Oden Jr., *The Bible without Theology: The Theological Tradition and Alternatives to It* (San Francisco: Harper & Row, 1987), 153.
35. Randall C. Bailey, "They're Nothing but Incestuous Bastards," in *Reading from This Place: Social Location and Biblical Interpretation in the United States* (ed. Fernando Segovia and Mary Ann Tolbert; Minneapolis: Fortress, 1995), 137.
36. Ibid., 124. See also Bailey, "He Didn't Even Tell Us the Worst of It!" *USQR* 59, no. 1 (2005): 15–24.
37. Warrior, "Native American Perspective," 283.
38. Ibid., 284.
39. John Barton, "The Basis of Old Testament Ethics," in Barton, *Understanding Old Testament Ethics: Approaches and Explorations* (Louisville, KY: Westminster John Knox, 2003), 47.
40. See Carolyn Pressler, *The View of Women Found in Deuteronomic Family Laws* (BZAW 216; Berlin: Walter de Gruyter, 1993).
41. Bruce C. Birch, *Let Justice Roll Down: The Old Testament, Ethics, and Christian Life* (Louisville, KY: Westminster John Knox, 1991), 43.
42. Barton, "Basis of Old Testament Ethics," 48.
43. Ibid., 50.
44. Barton, "Natural Law and Poetic Justice in the Old Testament," in Barton, *Understanding Old Testament Ethics*, 34–37.
45. Barton, "Basis of Old Testament Ethics," 52.
46. Barton, "Natural Law and Poetic Justice," 40.
47. Cyril S. Rodd, *Glimpses of a Strange Land: Studies in Old Testament Ethics* (Edinburgh: T. & T. Clark, 2001), 184.
48. Barton, "Basis of Old Testament Ethics," 51.
49. Ibid.
50. Ibid., 53.
51. Rodd, *Glimpses of a Strange Land*, 68.
52. Ibid., 68, 69.
53. Ibid., 76.
54. Frank M. Yamada, "Ethics," in *Handbook of Postmodern Biblical Interpretation* (ed. A. K. M. Adam; St. Louis: Chalice, 2000), 80, 81.
55. Ibid., 84. Yamada's statement here is influenced by John D. Caputo, *Against Ethics: Contributions to a Poetics of Obligation with Constant Reference to Deconstruction* (Bloomington: Indiana University Press, 1993).

Chapter 5

Between Humility and Authority

The Interplay of the Judge-Prophet Laws (Deuteronomy 16:18–17:13) and the Judge-Prophet Narratives of Moses

DENNIS T. OLSON

The sixteenth-century Italian political theorist Niccolò Machiavelli, in his treatises *The Prince* and *The Discourses of Livy*, held up the biblical figure of Moses as an ancient paradigm of a great leader. Machiavelli saw Moses as a ruthless, forceful, violent, and courageous political leader who knew how cynically to manipulate the people's religion in order to maintain and extend his power.[1] For Machiavelli, political self-preservation was the highest good, supplanting all other ethical values and constraints. In making his case, Machiavelli lightly cherry-picked his way through the Moses narratives of the Bible, sometimes distorting biblical texts without closely engaging them. My intention is to revisit the character and virtues of the literary portrait of Moses' leadership by considering in more detail certain clusters of laws and narratives involving the leadership of Moses.

Many studies of Moses' leadership exist, but they tend to focus either on Pentateuchal narratives alone or on Pentateuchal laws alone.[2] In this essay, I seek to bring the two genres into mutual dialogue—the genre of law and the genre of narrative—and explore how they contribute together in the literary characterization of the figure of Moses as a leader of Israel. What is the relationship between what Moses *does* in certain *narratives* involving leadership as compared to what Moses *says* in certain *laws* concerning leadership? Anticipating in part my conclusion, I will argue that a fairly consistent and fruitful dialectic or polarity of competing leadership virtues coexist in these key narratives and laws having to do with Moses and leadership. We will see that a key in holding these seemingly opposed polarities together is a critical theological dimension concerning the leader's relationship to a divine reality that Machiavelli was never able fully to appreciate or embrace.

I will illustrate the leadership of Moses in three literary contexts in the Pentateuch: (1) an important cluster of Deuteronomic laws concerning leadership in Deut. 16–18, (2) two brief narratives concerning the actions of Moses as judge and prophet in Deut. 1 and 34, and (3) a juxtaposed pair of Pentateuchal narratives in Num. 11–12 that involve the leadership of Moses as judge and prophet. This essay is an illustrative probe into a larger project, since numerous other Pentateuchal laws and narratives would need to be considered to gain a full portrait of the character of Moses' words and actions as a leader.

The Deuteronomic Laws of Leadership in Deuteronomy 16:18–18:22

The laws concerning community leaders in Deut. 16:18–18:22 share with the Decalogue's commandment about honoring mother and father in Deut. 5:16 a basic set of values concerning the role and purpose of authority, whether exercised in a smaller family context (so the commandment in Deut. 5:16) or in a larger community or national context (as in Deut. 16:18–18:22).[3] In ancient Israel, parents were primary holders of authority within the family context and thus warranted honor and respect. But parents were not gods, and they were not to be worshiped. Thus, the Deuteronomic laws include strict prohibitions against establishing a cult of dead parents or ancestors (Deut. 18:11; cf. Deut. 14:1; 26:14).[4]

Within the predominantly patriarchal context of ancient Israel, the commandment's inclusion of both father *and* mother as together worthy of honor deserves note. Familial authority is not centered in only one individual. This distribution of authority and power carries over into the leadership laws in Deut. 16–18. These leadership laws outline the decentralization and limitations of authority among multiple offices of judges, kings, priests, and prophets. Deuteronomy's program achieves this distribution of power through the number of different leadership offices as well as the variety of bases of authority by which leaders are legitimated.[5] Thus, kings and Levitical priests serve on the basis of heredity and lines of family descent (17:20; 18:1). Judges serve on the basis of appointment by the community based on their community reputation for fairness (16:18). Prophets derive their authority from claims of divine appointment and prophetic charisma (18:15).[6]

Embedded among these laws concerning the distribution of human power and authority in Deut. 16–18, one also finds a subgroup of laws that strictly centralizes all ultimate authority and loyalty in the one God of Israel. This is but one example of a large number of references in Deuteronomy's laws to the first commandment and its prohibition of any other gods that weave in and out throughout Deuteronomy's statutes and ordinances (12:30, 31; 13:2, 3, 6, 7, 13; 16:21–17:7; 18:20; 19:9; 20:18; 26:16–19). The implication is that one can understand the proper honoring of authorities and leaders only in connection with the laws prohibiting the false worship of other gods. The distribution and fragmentation of human power among several different bases of limited human authority is joined in Deuteronomy by a countervailing tendency to centralize Israel's allegiance in one God who will be worshiped in the one "place that the LORD your God will choose as a dwelling for his name" (12:5, 11, 14, 18, 21, 26; 14:2, 23, 24, 25; 15:20; 16:2, 6, 7, 11, 15, 16; 17:8, 10, 15; 18:6; 26:2, 31:11). Human leaders may be honored, but God alone is worshiped.

The Deuteronomic laws of leadership treat several kinds of leaders: judges, the king, Levitical priests, and prophets. For the purposes of this study on the character of Moses, I will focus only on the laws concerning judges and prophets, since Moses' leadership is explicitly identified in both of these roles within the narrative sections of Deuteronomy itself (Deut. 1:9–18; 34:10–12) as well as within a key pair of narrative texts in Num. 11–12 that we will consider below. The laws concerning judges in Deut. 16:18–17:13 begin by specifying the character of the judges and the criteria for their judgments in arbitrating disputes:

> You shall appoint judges and officials throughout your tribes, in all your towns that the LORD your God is giving you, and they shall render just decisions for the people. You must not distort justice; you must not show partiality; and you must not accept bribes, for a bribe blinds the eyes of the wise and subverts the cause of those who are in the right. Justice [*sedek*], and only justice, you shall pursue, so that you may live and occupy the land that the LORD your God is giving you. (16:18–20)

Concerning this description of the character and function of the judges, the biblical legal scholar Bernard Jackson writes:

> The judges are here told simply to act justly and avoid corruption. They are not asked to follow any particular rules. I am not, of course, suggesting that they are being given an entirely free discretion. The passage has clear wisdom connections, as seen by the proverb used as a motive clause [Deut. 16:19: "You must not accept bribes, for a bribe blinds the eyes of the wise and subverts the cause of those who are in the right"]. That seems to me to be a clue as to the kind of criteria which the judge is expected to apply: a sense of justice is to be tempered by the conventional norms of practical wisdom.[7]

Moreover, Michael Goldberg has argued that the ban on judges accepting bribes is grounded in Deuteronomy in the character of God.[8] According to Deut. 10:17–18, God is one who "is not partial and takes no bribe, who executes justice for the orphan and the widow, and who loves the strangers." Human judicial practice is to be shaped by the character of the divine Judge.

Nestled among these laws for judges are laws for the proper worship of Israel's God and prohibitions against worshiping other gods. The laws include an extended legal case involving an Israelite who "serves other gods" and the judicial requirement of two witnesses to validate the charge (Deut. 16:21–17:7). These laws are immediately followed by instructions to judges "if a judicial decision is too difficult for you." In such cases, the local judge is to "go up to the place that the LORD your God will choose, where you shall consult with the levitical priests [plural] and the judge [singular] who is in office in those days" (Deut. 17:8–19). Judges are human, fallible, limited, and may require assistance in certain difficult cases.

These judicial laws pulse with polarities. Dispersed authority among local judges exists alongside some centralized authority "in the place that the LORD will choose." The appeals court consists of multiple priests and a single judge. A measure of freedom and discretion by judges is balanced by certain guidelines and limitations (seeking justice, practical wisdom, no bribes, worship of God alone, instructions for difficult cases).

We turn next to Deuteronomy's laws concerning prophets in Deut. 18:15–22, which are included in the cluster of leadership laws in Deut. 18:16–18. Moses proclaims, "The LORD your God will raise up for you a prophet like me from among your own people; you shall heed such a prophet" (18:15). The prophet is both "from among your own people" and yet also set apart as one who is raised up by God. The possibility of false prophets is raised: "Any prophet who speaks in the name of other gods, or who presumes to speak in my name a word that I have not commanded the prophet to speak—that prophet shall die" (18:20). But "how can we recognize a word that the LORD has not spoken?" (18:21). The definitive guideline is that a prophetic word or oracle is false if "the thing does not take place or prove true" (18:22). Of course, this guideline is not always self-evident in the immediate circumstance; hearers of prophetic predictions would often simply have to wait and see whether the prophet's words would come true (for example, the prophets Jeremiah and Hananiah, who proclaim contradictory oracles in the Lord's name in Jer. 28:5–9). But what if a prophet predicts something that comes true while speaking in the name of another god? Would such a "successful" prophet be a true prophet like Moses? No, an earlier law in Deut. 13:1–3 makes clear that the first commandment, "You shall have no other gods," overrides any other criterion of true prophecy, even if a prophet's predictive success rate were a hundred percent.

Once again, limits are placed here on the exercise of authority. Prophets who speak in the name of the divine are to be honored but not worshiped. Their words must be tested. The reality is that such tests of truth will at times be ambiguous and may require hearers to wait and see. What counts as fulfillment of a prophetic prediction is itself open to interpretation and dispute. But within this ambiguity, the first commandment, the prohibition of allegiance to other gods, remains a primary guide in discerning the difference between true and false prophets.

Moses as Judge and Prophet in the Narratives of Deuteronomy 1 and 34

Two brief narratives in Deuteronomy itself explicitly characterize Moses as a judge and a prophet in the very beginning (chap. 1) and the very end (chap. 34) of the book of Deuteronomy. In the first narrative that appears in Deut. 1, Moses recalls the time when he distributed his authority as chief leader and judge to other tribal leaders and judges. The story is told earlier in the Pentateuch in two versions in Exod. 18 and Num. 11. Because of the large increase in Israel's population, Moses recalls his collapse under the burden of leadership: "How can I bear the heavy burden of your disputes all by myself?" (Deut. 1:12). The overwhelming leadership demands resulted in his decision to share authority and designate coleaders over groups of thousands, hundreds, fifties, and tens. He instructed the people to "choose for each of your tribes individuals who are wise [ḥăkāmîm], discerning [nᵉbōnîm], and reputable [yᵉduʾîm] to be your leaders" (1:13). The people affirmed Moses' plan as good (1:14). Moses then recalls how he instructed the judges and leaders: "I charged your judges at that time: 'Give the members of your community a fair hearing, and judge rightly between one person and another, whether citizen or resident alien. You must not be partial [literally, "you must not recognize faces" (lōʾ takkîrû pānîm)] in judging; hear out the small and the great alike; you shall not be intimidated by anyone, for the judgment is God's" (1:16–17). Moses retained a role as chief appeals judge: "Any case that is too hard for you, bring to me, and I will hear it" (1:17). The criteria for the selection of judges, the instruction to be impartial, the role of the people in implementing Moses' plan, the recognition that some cases will be too difficult and will require the assistance of a higher judge, and the ultimate accountability to the deity ("for the judgment is God's") all resonate with the laws for judges in Deut. 16:18–17:13.

As we move from the first narrative in Deuteronomy to the last, we encounter the story of Moses' death on the border of the promised land of Canaan. In its present form, Moses' death outside the promised land casts a long shadow over the entire book from beginning to end. The narrative context of Moses' death scene explicitly identifies Moses not only as a judge as in chapter 1 but also as a prophet without peer:

> Never since has there arisen a prophet in Israel like Moses, whom the LORD knew face to face. He was unequaled for all the signs and wonders that the LORD sent him to perform in the land of Egypt, against Pharaoh and all his servants and his entire land, and for all the mighty deeds and all the terrifying displays of power that Moses performed in the sight of all Israel. (34:10–12)

Moses' uniqueness stems from his unparalleled intimacy with God (knowing God "face to face"), on the one hand, and his uniquely powerful "signs and wonders," on the other hand. What is remarkable is that these words ("signs and wonders," "mighty deeds," "terrifying displays of power") are all technical terms applied consistently elsewhere in Deuteronomy to God alone (4:34; 6:22; 7:19; 11:3; 26:8; 29:3). Thus, paradoxically in a narrative that emphasizes his human mortality when he dies as Israel's leader outside the promised land, Moses is also remembered at the same time as a leader with godlike powers.

This paradoxical portrait of Moses as both a strong heroic leader and a fragile and limited human emerges in other ways as well in these last chapters of Deuteronomy. On the one hand, at 120 years old Moses remains exceptionally strong and healthy: "His sight was unimpaired and his vigor had not abated" (34:7). On the other hand, Moses had just three chapters earlier described himself as feeble and weak: "I am now one hundred twenty years old. I am no longer able to get about" (31:2). Another dialectic involves two coexisting but conflicting accounts of why God does not allow Moses to enter the promised land of Canaan, in spite of Moses' urgent requests to do so. Some traditions within Deuteronomy suggest that God forbade Moses to set foot in Canaan because of the *people's sin* (1:37; 3:26; 4:21). Another tradition, also within the present form of Deuteronomy, explains Moses' death outside the promised land as due not to the people's sin but to *Moses' own human failure* in "breaking faith" during the wilderness journey in connection with the rock and water at Meribath-kadesh (32:48–52; cf. Num 20:1–13). One reason portrays Moses as heroic and noble, dying for others; the other reason portrays Moses as flawed and sinful, suffering the consequences of his own failure.

One final tension in this last narrative of Deuteronomy is that Moses is honored but not deified in his burial on Mount Nebo. Moses "was buried in a valley in the land of Moab, opposite Beth-peor, but no one knows his burial place to this day" (34:6). Many interpreters read the passive verb that Moses "was buried" as a divine passive: God is the one who buries Moses, a rare honor in the biblical tradition. But then the story makes a point to emphasize that his burial place is unknown. This latter observation links up with the earlier prohibitions in Deuteronomy that forbid setting up any kind of shrine or cult for a dead human ancestor (18:11; cf. 14:1; 26:14). Leaders, whether of a family or a people, are to be honored but not worshiped. Finally, Moses is designated by the title "servant of the LORD" (34:5), a title that both honors Moses but that also places him under the divine rule of God. Thus, in these Deuteronomic narratives of Moses' leadership as judge and prophet in chapters 1 and 34, we see in Moses the dialectical portrait of a leader who holds together with integrity both a frail humanity and a vigorous and heroic leadership under the ultimate authority of the one God of Israel.

Moses as Judge and Prophet in Numbers 11–12

Numbers 11 and 12 contain two side-by-side narratives in which the leadership of Moses is a central theme.[9] In Num. 11, the wilderness-wandering Israelites complain to Moses about the lack of variety in their boring diet of daily manna. Moses is frustrated by the people's constant complaining and asks God to end his misery as a leader and put him to death (11:14–15). God offers an alternative plan and distributes "some of the spirit that was on [Moses]" onto seventy elders who "prophesied" (*yitnabb'û*) when they received the spirit. Meanwhile, back in the Israelite camp two men, Eldad and Medad, who were not among the seventy elders, also had "the spirit rest upon them," and they too began prophesying

(11:26). Moses' assistant, Joshua, urges Moses to stop this unauthorized prophesying by Eldad and Medad. But Moses seeks to assuage Joshua's anxiety about
unauthorized claims to prophetic inspiration and authority: "Are you jealous for
my sake? Would that all the LORD's people were prophets, and that the LORD
would put his spirit on them!" (Num. 11:29). The characterization of Moses'
leadership here emphasizes his vulnerability, his limits, and his eagerness to share
the burden of leadership not only with elders but also with other "unofficial" or
"unauthorized" claims to prophetic authority.

In Num. 12, the brother and sister to Moses, Aaron and Miriam, function as
his assistant leaders. Whether motivated by sibling rivalry or political envy, they
resist what they perceive to be Moses' exclusivity as the bearer of the divine word
to the community: "Has the LORD only spoken through Moses? Has he not spoken through us also?" (12:2). The narrator's voice then interjects a parenthetical
but literarily authoritative statement: "Now the man Moses was very humble
[ʿānāw mᵉʾōd], more so than anyone else on the face of the earth" (12:3). The
word "humble" [ʿānāw] does not refer so much to a general personality trait of
meekness as it underscores Moses' devotion, obedience, and humility specifically
before God (cf. Zeph. 2:3).[10] God intervenes in the dispute and strongly asserts
the uniqueness and superiority of Moses' prophetic authority:

> Hear my words: When there are prophets among you,
>   I the LORD make myself known to them in visions;
>   I speak to them in dreams.
> Not so with my servant Moses;
>   he is entrusted with all my house.
> With him I speak face to face—clearly, not in riddles;
>   and he beholds the form of the LORD.
>   (Num. 12:6–8)

Moses has unique access, intimacy, and clarity in mediating the divine word. The
legitimacy of other prophetic voices is here affirmed but also subordinated to
Moses' voice. Although superior to any other human voice, Moses himself
remains subject to a higher divine authority, as God identifies Moses as "my servant Moses" (12:7).

In the next scene when Miriam is struck with leprosy, Moses intercedes with
God on behalf of Miriam, who is both his sister and his opponent in the dispute:
"And Moses cried to the LORD, 'O God, please heal her" (12:13). The affirmation of the strong and unique authority of Moses affirmed by this narrative is
joined with a portrait of Moses' leadership that is humble, forgiving, and mag-
nanimous toward an opponent. The people also seem to have some power in this
narrative, as they refuse to set out on the march until Miriam has been brought
in again (12:15).

As with the laws in Deut. 16–18 and the narratives of Deut. 1 and 34, the narratives in Num. 11–12 appear to be carefully crafted in their present form in ways
that hold together seemingly oppositional polarities in the narrative presentation

of Moses' character as a leader: the individual leader versus the empowered community of coleaders, centralized power versus decentralized power, courageous boldness versus humility and devotion. The reader comes to see a subtle interplay of polarities that are managed and negotiated in order to be held together in a fruitful and constructive tension within particular contexts and situations. Specific contexts will require leaning more heavily toward one end of the polarity than another, even while preserving elements of the other end of the polarity.

Conclusion

Perhaps the most distinctive element of this biblical portrait of Moses as leader is the double-edged role which the relationship to God consistently plays in the laws of Deut. 16–18, the narratives of Deut. 1 and 34, and the narratives of Num. 11–12. In each case, leaders like Moses derive, on the one hand, boldness, strength, and authority from their relationship and connection to God. On the other hand, the presence of God prompts leaders like Moses to come face to face with their own human limits, their frailty, their potential to misjudge God's will and purpose, their need for the assistance of others, and their susceptibility to God's judgment and critique as much as God's affirmation and support.

Contrary to Machiavelli's distorted portrait of Moses and his leadership, Moses' success as a leader was not ultimately grounded in expediency, self-interest, or self-preservation. The delicately maintained polarity between claiming bold authority and, at the same time, letting go of that authority is grounded in relationship to a divine reality whose purpose, knowledge, and power far exceed the limitations of human capacities. It is the vitality of this theological conviction of God's presence and activity in the life of the community that underlies the more nuanced and complex portrait of Moses as leader embedded in the details and data of the biblical texts we have examined. The biblical injunction to *honor* human authorities but to *worship* only God provides an important corrective and critique of the Machiavellian depiction of Moses. In the biblical world of these texts, those who exercise authority may be extraordinary and even heroic human beings, but they inevitably will be subject to human limitations, mortality, and a higher divine authority who both empowers and judges those who lead.

Notes

1. See Niccolò Machiavelli, *The Prince* (trans. William Connell; Boston: Bedford/St. Martin's, 2005), chap. 6; and scattered references to Moses in *The Discourses of Livy*, III, 30, in *Machiavelli: The Chief Works and Others* (3 vols.; trans. Allan Gilbert; Durham, NC: Duke University Press, 1965). In one section of *The Discourses of Livy*, Machiavelli discusses the death of thousands of Israelites who rebelled against Moses' leadership in the wilderness: "He who reads the Bible intelligently [which means for Machiavelli without sentimentality or spiritualizing] sees that if Moses was to put his laws and regulations into effect, he was forced to kill countless men who, moved by nothing else than envy, were opposed to his plans" (496). In his study entitled "Machiavelli's Moses and

Renaissance Politics," John Geerken argues that for Machiavelli, religion mirrors politics. Machiavelli believed that the politics as well as the religion of sixteenth-century Italy had become weak and toothless, robbed of virile life and force. Machiavelli sought to restore his brand of virtues to politics: the virtues of strength, self-confidence, glory-seeking forcefulness, physical action, vengeance, courage and ruthless expediency, all dedicated to preserving one's political position and territorial rule. He rejected religiously based characteristics in leaders such as humility, nonviolence, suffering, charity, and patience, except in those instances when pretending to possess them in public displays brought some political advantage or popular support. Such religious virtues, he argued, could be useful to politicians in certain circumstances but not as the core virtues of leadership. (Geerken, "Machiavelli's Moses and Renaissance Politics," *JHI* 60, no. 4 [1999]: 592–95). See also Steven Marx, "Moses and Machiavellianism," *JAAR* 65, no. 3 (1997): 551–71; and Marjorie O'Rourke Boyle, "Machiavelli and the Politics of Grace," *Modern Language Notes* 119 Supplement (2004): S224–S246. For a helpful survey on scholarship on Machiavelli's view of religion, see John Najemy, "Papirius and the Chickens, or Machiavelli on the Necessity of Interpreting Religion," *JHI* 60, no. 4 (1999): 659–81.

2. Studies of the historical, literary, and theological dimensions of the biblical character of Moses are plentiful. Some have focused specifically on the character of Moses' leadership but usually restrict themselves to one genre: biblical narratives or biblical laws. Three notable examples may be mentioned. Aaron Wildavsky, *The Nursing Father: Moses as a Political Leader* (Tuscaloosa: University of Alabama, 1984), reflects on several of the Pentateuchal narratives involving Mosaic leadership and some implications for political leadership. Michael Walzer, *Exodus and Revolution* (New York: Basic Books, 1986), examines how the narratives of Moses' leadership in the exodus have been appropriated by political movements, revolutions, and liberationist struggles in Western history. Norbert Lohfink, "Distribution of the Functions of Power: The Laws in Deuteronomy That Governed Ministries, a Constitution in Terms of Power Distribution, and Catholic Canon Law," in Lohfink, *Great Themes from the Old Testament* (Edinburgh: T. & T. Clark, 1982): 55–76, studies the implications of the Deuteronomic laws on leadership that Moses proclaims in Deut. 16–18. However, no study of which I am aware brings together into dialogue the leadership laws proclaimed by Moses in Deut. 16–18 and key leadership narratives of Moses elsewhere in the Pentateuch.

3. A number of scholars have argued that within the present form of the book of Deuteronomy, the laws concerning Israel's leaders in Deut. 16:18–18:22 function as an interpretative expansion and elaboration of the Decalogue's commandment "Honor your father and your mother" (Deut. 5:16). On the way in which the topics of the laws of Deut. 12–26 generally follow the sequence of the Ten Commandments in Deut. 5, see Stephen Kaufman, "The Structure of the Deuteronomic Law," *Maarav* 1, no. 2 (1979): 105–58; Georg Braulik, "Die Abfolge der Gesetze in Deuteronomium 12–26 und der Decalog," in *Das Deuteronomium, Entstehung, Gestalt und Botschaft*, ed. Norbert Lohfink (Louvain: Leuven University Press, 1985): 252–72. The themes and key words that unify this section of leadership laws in Deut. 16:18–18:22 and also link it to the commandment on honoring parents are noted in Georg Braulik, "Zur Abfolge der Gesetze in Deuteronomium 16,18–21,23. Weitere Beobachtungen," *Bib* 69, no. 1 (1988): 63–82. Thus, for example, the "statutes and ordinances" of Deut. 12–13 explicate the first commandment, "You shall have no other gods" (Deut. 5:7). The next set of laws in Deut. 14:1–21 expand on the second commandment about the wrongful use of the divine name (Deut. 5:11). Deut.

14:22–16:17 explicates the sabbath commandment (Deut. 5:12–15). The leadership laws of Deut. 16:18–18:22 involving community leaders (king, judge, prophet, priest) are an expansion of the commandment regarding parental authority (Deut. 5:16). The question of whether Deuteronomy's leadership laws reflect sociopolitical realities at one or more times in ancient Israel's history is addressed in Udo Rüttersworden, *Von der politischen Gemeinschaft zur Gemeinde: Studien zu Dt. 16,18–18,22* (Frankfurt am Main: Athenaeum, 1987). Rüttersworden detects a movement from an earlier redactional layer of preexilic laws that reflected historical practice in Israel's history to a later exilic layer that changed as Israel moved from a national-political entity (preexile) to a covenant community (postexile). For a fuller discussion and bibliography, see Dennis T. Olson, *Deuteronomy and the Death of Moses: A Theological Reading* (Minneapolis: Fortress, 1994), 62–67, 78–87.

4. The primary thrust of the commandment concerning parents is that authorities (i.e., parental authorities) are to be honored. The primary thrust of the expansive laws of community leaders that explicate the commandment in Deut. 16–18 is that leaders and authorities are to be worthy of the honor they receive. Deuteronomy thus moves beyond what ethicist Paul Lehmann describes as the false opposition between hierarchy and equality to a model of what he calls "reciprocal responsibility" involving both those who hold authority and those who are led. See Lehmann, "The Commandments and the Common Life," *Int* 34, no. 4 (1980): 341–44.

5. The distribution and balancing of human authority envisaged by Deut. 16–18 has been observed in several studies. Norbert Lohfink concludes that in Deuteronomy "an earlier and greater concentration of power in monarchy and priesthood is scaled down and an attempt is made to create a balance of power between four different authorities: the judiciary, the king, the temple priesthood, and free charismatics" (Lohfink, "Distribution of the Functions of Power," 72). Louis Stulman argues that Deuteronomy perceived a grave threat to the community not only from foreigners outside the community but also from leaders within the community itself. Thus, Stulman contends, Deuteronomy is concerned to distribute the base of leadership and power among several competing and varied groups and elements within the community so that exclusive power is not vested in one group or leader alone (Stulman, "Encroachment in Deuteronomy: An Analysis of the Social World of the D Code," *JBL* 109, no. 4 [1990]: 613–32). Cf. Leslie Hoppe, "Deuteronomy and Political Power," *TBT* 26, no. 5 (1988): 261–66; and Moshe Greenberg, "Biblical Attitudes toward Power: Ideal and Reality in the Law and Prophets," in *Religion and Law: Biblical-Judaic and Islamic Perspectives* (ed. Edwin Firmage et al.; Winona Lake, IN: Eisenbrauns, 1990), 101–12.

6. The Deuteronomic conception of the prophet seems to follow a largely charismatic model. However, some prophets from non-Deuteronomic traditions in ancient Israel did have more institutional ties to the central establishments of power such as the royal court. Isaiah of Jerusalem is an example of a Jerusalemite court prophet. See Robert R. Wilson, *Prophecy and Society in Ancient Israel* (Philadelphia: Fortress, 1980), 135–308.

7. Bernard Jackson, "Legalism and Spirituality," in Firmoga et al., *Religion and Law*, 245.

8. Michael Goldberg, "The Story of the Moral: Gifts or Bribes in Deuteronomy," *Int* 38, no. 1 (1984): 15–25. Goldberg has noted that the distinctive Deuteronomic prohibition against judges accepting bribes occurs against a broader context in both the ancient Near East and even Israel's own wisdom literature (Prov.

17:8; 21:14), where the practice of offering bribes to judges and leaders was expected or assumed.

9. For various perspectives on some of the tradition-historical, redactional, and other interpretational issues in Num. 11–12, see Dennis T. Olson, *Numbers* (Interpretation; Louisville, KY: Westminster John Knox, 1996), 61–75. Benjamin Sommer, "Reflecting on Moses: The Redaction of Numbers 11," *JBL* 118, no. 4 (1999): 601–24, argues that two different redactional layers, one pro-Moses and another anti-Moses, have been joined together into the present narrative. David Jobling, *The Sense of Biblical Narrative: Three Structural Analyses in the Old Testament (1 Samuel 13–31, Numbers 11–12, 1 Kings 17–18)* (JSOTSup 7; Sheffield: Sheffield Academic Press, 1978), presents a complex structuralist reading of the two chapters. Thomas Römer, "Nombres 11–12 et la question d'une redaction deutéronomique dans le Pentateuque," in *Deuteronomy and Deuteronomic Literature: Festschrift C. H. N. Brekelman* (ed. M. Vervenne; Louvain: Peeters, 1997), 481–98, surveys recent redactional studies and argues for a later Deuteronomic redaction of Num. 11–12.

10. G. B. Gray, *Numbers* (ICC; Edinburgh: T. & T. Clark, 1903), 123. Zeph. 2:3: "Seek the LORD, all you humble [*'anwê*] of the land, who do his commands; seek righteousness, seek humility [*'ānāwâ*]; perhaps you may be hidden on the day of the LORD's wrath." Cf. George Coats, "Humility and Honor: A Moses Legend in Numbers 12," in Coats, *The Moses Tradition* (JSOTSup 161; Sheffield: Sheffield Academic Press, 1993), 92–94.

Chapter 6

Inside the "Sanctuary of Silence"

The Moral-Ethical Demands of Suffering

SAMUEL E. BALENTINE

How does the Torah's conceptualization of worship shape character and ethics? The primary custodians of the answer to this question are ancient Israel's priests, whose contribution to the final form of the Torah bears witness to the centrality of the sanctuary—and the ritual activity that takes place within it—in shaping Israel's identity. The sheer volume of material in the Pentateuch that deals with the sanctuary is the first indication of its importance in the priestly perspective. Nearly one-third of the book of Exodus is given to detailed instructions for the building of the tabernacle (Exod. 25–31, 35–40), and the entire book of Leviticus—twenty-seven chapters—deals with the rituals performed within its holy precincts (Lev. 1–16), which in turn seed the requirements for ethical behavior in the everyday world outside the sanctuary (Lev. 17–27). In sum, when a band of refugees gather themselves at Sinai to hear God say, "You shall be to me a priestly kingdom and a holy nation" (Exod. 19:6), the priests insist that worship is the principal means by which they become the Israel of God's hopes and expectations.[1]

This priestly preoccupation with worship begs a further question: What goes on in the complex of rituals inside the sanctuary that is so critically important for shaping the character and ethics of the people of God?

Inside the Sanctuary of Silence

In reflecting on this question, I have returned to an observation offered years ago by Y. Kaufmann. Inside the temple, Kaufmann argued, one enters a "sanctuary of silence."[2] Outside the temple, both priests and laity engage in a variety of verbal activities, for example, confession, thanksgiving, praise, and blessing.[3] Inside the sanctuary, however, everyone observes a strict code of silence. The priest executes his duties—lighting the lamps, burning incense, dispersing the sacrificial blood, among other things—and the people bring prescribed offerings, but no word is spoken. Kaufmann attributes this silence to "the priestly desire to fashion a non-pagan cult," that is, one that deliberately breaks away from the magical incantations and mythological allusions that characterized cultic activity in Egypt and Mesopotamia.[4]

Kaufmann's assertion has often been taken as axiomatic, although surprisingly little attention has been devoted to examining his explanation, still less to exploring its theological basis in priestly thinking.[5] Israel Knohl has addressed this need in a number of recent publications by building upon Kaufmann's seminal ideas in two important ways.[6] First, Knohl argues that the silence required inside the sanctuary is an expression of the priests' particular conception of the holiness of God.[7] A holy God is beyond any form and personality, indeed, beyond any notion of morality that invites praise or petition. God's holiness exceeds all human comprehension and thus cannot be reduced to such practical functions. If we cannot say anything about God, then "silence is praise," as the psalmist puts it (Ps. 65:2).[8] If there is a dimension of God's majesty that exceeds every expectation that God acts to meet human need, then prayers of lament and petition lose their significance. "The relationship [with God] that exists in the Temple," Knohl says, "is not one of covenant or dependence. Rather, it is a unilateral pact."[9] Confronted with a holy God, humans become aware of their insignificance and necessarily yield to "feelings of guilt and the need for atonement." In the "ideal cultic system," obedience and contrition are nonnegotiable divine commands. As Knohl puts it, "There is no room for the slightest deviation from the divine command . . . even if it is done out of religious enthusiasm."[10]

A second aspect of Knohl's argument is still more intriguing. The requirement of silence inside the sanctuary reflects not only the priestly theology of God's holiness but also bears witness to a priestly inspired "Copernican revolution" in Israel's understanding of the faith God requires.[11] Within priestly thinking, Knohl argues, we can discern a "dynamic process" of maturation, a shift from the "elementary faith" that characterized the Genesis period to the "exalted faith consciousness" that Moses and Israel exemplify.[12] In the pre-Mosaic period, according to the priestly view in Gen. 1, faith consists in believing that God (Elohim) places human beings at the summit of creation, invests them with responsibility for creation's potential to be "very good," and then tunes the moral order of the world to human behavior. When human beings rightly exercise their God-given stewardship of creation's resources, they may expect God to reward their efforts with abundance and prosperity. Alternatively, when human beings fail to be God's worthy superintendents, not only they but also creation itself pay the price. In sum, the priests recognize that faith *begins* when human beings comprehend that God, "[human]like in his image and his actions," is approachable.[13] But such faith, while foundational and important, is not fully adequate for what God requires.

In the distinctive revelation that comes from God (YHWH) to Moses, the priests discern that faith must ascend to a higher level, for the Tetragrammaton reveals a numinous aspect of divinity that will not be defined by human behavior. A mature awareness of God's centrality requires a recalibration of humanity's place in creation, for God has not created everything in the world to serve the needs of human beings. An increased awareness of the mysterious, intangible, holiness of God requires a recalibration of the world's moral order, for a holy God governs in ways that exceed elementary notions of reward and punishment. In sum, elementary faith, which aspires to a close, personal, and reciprocal relationship with God, is authentic but insufficient and immodest. Inside the sanctuary, one must respond to a fuller revelation from God that requires a higher level of faith. Humility, not self-assertion, silence, not words, convey the worship required by a holy God, who is essentially other and different from human beings.

Knohl's assessment of this dynamic process of faith refinement rests largely on close examination of literary details in two independent priestly sources within the Pentateuch: the Priestly Torah and the Holiness School. Although the details of this argument merit close scrutiny, I have chosen not to engage him at this point. I will focus instead on another aspect of his argument. As if trying to put a human face on this literary analysis, Knohl directs us to the book of Job and thus to a specific example of how one's faith can and should mature according to the priestly discernment.[14] In his words, "The book of Job depicts a dynamic process—the refinement of faith consciousness—generally similar to the shift that occurs in PT [Priestly Torah]."[15] The gist of his argument is that the beginning of the book (Job 1–2) echoes the priestly discernment of the faith consciousness depicted in Gen. 1. At the outset, Job believes there is a direct correlation between his behavior and the behavior of the Creator, who tunes the moral order of the whole world to reward his personal righteousness. However, when Job experiences suffering and loss "for no reason" (Job 2:3), this elementary faith leads him to question God's justice. Not until God (YHWH) invites his contemplation of the mysteries of creation does he come to understand his proper place in the world.[16] According to Knohl, Job ascends to "a higher level of faith" when he responds to this revelation first with silence (40:4–5: "I lay my hand on my mouth. I have spoken once . . . but will proceed no further"), then with contrition ("I knew of you only by report, but now I see you with my own eyes. Therefore I yield, repenting in dust and ashes" [42:5–6 NJPS]).[17] At the end of Job's journey he effectively arrives at the "sanctuary of silence," where priestly rituals of sin and atonement, not words of lament, provide the most authentic theodicy any person ever needs.[18]

Job as a "Test Case" for the Sanctuary of Silence

I find Knohl's discussion of the connections between Job and the Priestly Torah instructive, but I question whether his conclusions do them full justice. A number of clues within the book lead me in a different direction. If we imagine Job as among those addressed by the directives of priests, that is, if Job is the "test case" for their view of worship, is there sufficient evidence in the book that records his story to confirm that he in fact silences his complaints and rises to the higher level of faith—obedience and contrition—that Knohl believes the priests require? I address this question in the nine observations that follow.

1. The Prologue uses four terms to establish Job's extraordinary piety. Two adjectives describe his character, "blameless" (*tām*) and "upright" (*yāšār*), and two verbal expressions describe his ethics, "fearing God" (*yirē 'ĕlōhîm*) and "turning away from evil" (*sār mērā'*). Both Job's character and his ethics are further profiled by the reports in the Prologue and Epilogue that he offers sacrifice. Job 1:5 describes his presentation of "burnt offerings" (*'ōlōt*) on behalf of his children as a preemptive propitiation for any inadvertent sins they may have committed. Job 42:8 reports that he receives the "burnt offering" (*'ōlâ*) presented by the friends, who require his prayer of intercession if God is to forgive their wrongdoings. While neither of these texts envision Job's sacrificial acts as occurring in a formal cultic setting, they invite us nonetheless to see him as one who "plays the part of the perfect priest" within his household.[19] Moreover, instead of locating Job in a specific time and place in the postexilic period, which most agree is the likely historical setting for the book, the narrator retrojects this story into the patriarchal epoch, which invites us to consider how Job's priestly profile relates to the priestly conceptualization of pre-Mosaic worship.[20]

2. Whereas the prose Prologue-Epilogue frames the book as the story of a priest-like Job who extends the rituals of sacrifice to others, the poetic dialogues inside the frame turn the tables. Now it is Job who stands in need of the rituals of comfort that other ministrants may offer him. In short, the priest now requires a priest.[21] The Prologue subtly anticipates this role reversal by reporting that Job has been afflicted with "loathsome sores" (*šᵉḥîn*; 2:7). The same word is used in Lev. 13–14 to identify the skin diseases that make a person unclean and needful of priestly rituals (see 13:18–23). In the midst of two lengthy pericopes detailing the priestly diagnosis of skin diseases (13:1–44) and the requisite purification rituals (14:1–32), two brief verses describe what diseased persons (like Job) should do in the painful interim between affliction and restoration. Until the priest determines that they are "clean," they must live outside the camp, where they tear their clothes, dishevel their hair, cover their mouth, and cry out, "Unclean, unclean!" (13:45–46). The gesture of covering the mouth confirms that they know themselves to have become repugnant to their community. The words "Unclean, unclean!" warn others against coming too close, lest they inadvertently endanger themselves.

3. The Prologue describes affliction as a test of Job's piety, which is to be judged in large part by what does or does not come from his mouth. The *śāṭān* wagers

that Job will curse God. God wagers that the *śāṭān* is wrong. By all accounts, God has placed the better bet. Like the diseased person in Lev. 13, Job responds to affliction with a ritual gesture: He tears his clothes, shaves his head, and falls on the ground. Despite his losses, Job speaks words of blessing and "does not charge God with any wrongdoing" (1:21–22). Despite temptations to speak like foolish persons who question God and scorn the rewards of the righteous, Job remains steadfast. Even as he sits alone on his ash heap of suffering, presumably outside the city, where society consigns the rejected and the destitute, Job does not "sin with his lips" (2:10).[22] When the curtain falls on the Prologue, Job's world is submerged in silence (2:13). Whether this silence is sacred, hence comparable to what the priests require inside the sanctuary, is the question that prepares for the next scene in this drama.

4. When the curtain rises on the next scene, Job opens his mouth (3:1) and moves beyond silence. He speaks seven curses—three against the day of his birth (3:3–5), four against the night of his conception (3:6–9)—that mount a rhetorical assault on the seven days of creation and, by implication, the creator who pronounced the primordial design of the world "very good." To these curses he couples a string of anguished laments, peppered with the question "Why?" (3:11, 12, 20; implied in vv. 16, 23), which press the issues that every subsequent speaker in the book, including God, must address. From Job's perspective, there is much at stake, for he contends that suffering like his calls the whole of the created order into question. If his questions cannot be satisfactorily addressed, then they will continue to rip and tear at the fabric of life until creation itself is undone.

One by one Job's three friends rise to the challenge of providing the answers they believe he needs (Job 4–27). They are not priests, but they are clearly spokespersons for the religious establishment, and much of what they say is consonant with the priestly *tôrôt* concerning sacrifice and repentance.[23] *If* Job confesses that he is a sinful mortal in the presence of a holy God, *then* God will restore him to his rightful place in the world (e.g., 8:5–6; 11:13–15; 22:23–27). Eliphaz speaks for all when he reduces the *torah* that applies to Job to one nonnegotiable mandate: "Agree with God and be at peace; in this way good will come to you" (22:21). Virtually every word of this *torah*, however, only adds to Job's burden. Given the plotline of the canonical story, *if* Job agrees with God, *then* he is innocent and thus cannot atone for a sin he has not committed (1:2, 8; 2:3). *If* religious orthodoxy requires the sacrifice of personal integrity as the price for peace with God, *then* Job must loathe the person God has created him to be, which means per force that he is ever at war with himself and with his creator (e.g., 7:16; 9:20–21, 30–31; 10:1a). Given this conundrum, it is little wonder that Job remains defiant, that he insists his words be preserved for posterity (19:23–24), that the friends, and God, must listen to his words (6:25–26; 7:11–15; 10:1–2; 13:3, 13–17; 16:18; 21:1–5; 23:1–7; 27:1–6; 31:35–37). What do the rituals of the cult offer to one such as Job, whose suffering has been willingly inflicted on him by God? W. Scott Green states the matter bluntly:

> From a cultic or halakhic perspective, there is nothing concrete Job can do to repair his relationship with God. Sacrifice, repentance, and any religious behaviors that develop from them are nugatory under these circumstances. . . . No offering, no change of heart, can appease divine caprice or undo an affliction that happens for no reason.[24]

5. When Job's words are ended (31:40), a fourth friend, Elihu, steps into the story as the "Answerer" Job seeks but has not yet found (Job 32–37). Drawing upon both forensic and cultic metaphors, Elihu seeks to persuade Job that God uses suffering to save his life, principally by turning him away from misplaced pride and toward a public confession of sin (33:15–28). By inviting Job into both the courtroom and the cult, Elihu seems intent on clarifying the distinctions between these two ways of addressing his issues with God. On closer inspection, Elihu seems only to blur the differences. The trial Job seeks is one in which the accused is presumed innocent, until a fair and impartial jury decides that the evidence requires a different verdict (e.g., Job 9–10). When Elihu invites Job into the courtroom, however, he announces before the first word is spoken that Job is in the wrong (33:12). Similarly, when Elihu summons Job to prayer, he declares that the cult provides him only one option. He must speak the words his angelic counselor tells him. He must confess and say, "I sinned, and perverted what was right" (33:27). Prayer, at least as Elihu defines it, is simply another word for legal language that presumes Job's guilt and God's innocence. In short, whether Job presents his case in the courtroom or the cult, the verdict will be the same.

6. The ultimate answer to Job's situation, once he attains the required humility before God, according to Elihu, is to yield to the Lord of creation, whose unfathomable justice (36:5–15) necessarily commands awe and praise (36:22–37:13). Embedded within Elihu's summons to praise is a subtle but telling clue concerning his assessment of where human beings rank among the wonders of God's creation. For all its attention to the intricate details of nature (note, for example, the multiple words for thunder, rain, lightning, and clouds throughout the speech), Elihu's "Ode to Creation" provides almost no place for living creatures, animal or human. To find them in Elihu's world, one must look for the places where they hide (37:7–8).[25] Retreating to their lairs and homes, both animals and humans cower before God, whose awesome display of power seems far more threatening than inviting. Perhaps, given Elihu's reading of creation's grammar, all creatures should be glad to have at least a place to hide. And perhaps in Elihu's world, cowering praise is better than no praise at all. But we may wonder if Job can accept Elihu's invitation into a world of coerced confession and cowered praise. Carol Newsom's questions are mine as well: Can Elihu's world be properly urged upon an innocent sufferer? Is such a world "adequate to the moral demands posed by the presence of Job in his pain"?[26]

7. Elihu's hymn to creation segues to God's dramatic revelation to Job from the whirlwind, which in turn brings us back to the nub of Knohl's observations. In his view, once God invites reflection on the mysteries of creation, Job at last attains the exalted faith the priests aim for. Knohl argues that Job rises to the level

of the modesty required, for now he knows that human beings are not the "crowning glory of Creation. The crown is taken off the human head and placed upon that of a terrible sea monster [Leviathan; 41:25–26]."[27] And he rises to the level of faith consciousness that defines the priestly ideal. Having seen and understood more than before, he bows in silent contrition, for now he knows that the holiness of God comes with one nonnegotiable commandment: obedience. I repeat words from Knohl I have already cited: "There is no room for the slightest deviation from the divine command . . . even if it is done out of religious enthusiasm." Here too, however, other clues in God's revelation to Job invite a different assessment.

8. Unlike Elihu's world, which has almost no place for creatures of any kind, God's world is full of animals, which are described with such attentive detail they seem almost near enough to touch. But what is God's objective? Creation imagery provides the beginning of an answer. God does not bring *the animals to Job* so that he can name them and thus define their existence in relation to himself, as in Gen. 2:19–20. Instead, God brings *Job to the animals,* so that they may teach him something about his own creaturely existence in God's world.[28] The lesson begins with five pairs of animals (38:39–39:30), all but one (the horse) numbered among the wild that frolic in the freedom of being exactly what God has created them to be.[29] When the lesson concludes, God invites Job to say what he has learned (40:1–2). Job responds with the concession "I am small." Placing his hand on his mouth, he retreats in silence. When he agrees to speak no further (40:3–5), Knohl—along with most interpreters—assumes that Job has arrived at the answer God desires. The logic of the revelation, however, suggests otherwise, for with a second speech God pushes past Job's silence with still another request for his response (40:7). Silence, it seems, is not fully adequate.

God now singles out a sixth and final pair of animals, Behemoth (40:15–24) and Leviathan (41:1–34), which require Job's special attention. The structure of this part of the speech suggests that these two animals exemplify the intent of God's work on the sixth day of creation, when God made "wild animals" (*bᵉhēmâ*), along with human beings (Gen. 1:24–27). "Look at Behemoth," God says to Job, "which I made just as I made you" (40:15). Consider Leviathan, God continues, a creature "made without fear" (40:33 [MT 41:25]). What is the lesson for Job? Most commentators argue that God singles out Behemoth and Leviathan, creatures conventionally regarded as wild and hostile to creation, in order to teach Job that God alone has the power to subjugate them. If Job persists in his own creaturely defiance of God, so this argument goes, then he can expect certain defeat. Once again, I believe the text invites a more nuanced reading.

I cite but one of the clues.[30] A critical part of God's discourse on Leviathan is the description of what does and does not come forth from its mouth. What does not come from this creature's mouth are "soft words" (41:3–4 [MT 40:27–28]). In the unlikely event that anyone should ever successfully capture Leviathan and force it into service, even then it would not conform to any "covenantal" (*bᵉrît*) existence that requires it to do or say only what its master permits. Instead, when it opens its mouth (41:18–21 [MT 41:10–13]) what comes out is fire and light, smoke and flames, phenomena typically associated with the strong and compelling appearance of God (e.g., Ps. 18:7–8, 12–15; 29:7–9). Instinctively godlike, Leviathan announces its presence with an awesome fierceness that commands attention and defies coercion. Contrary to the conventional view, when God looks at Leviathan, God sees no cause for opposition. Instead, God celebrates its power, pride, and fierce resistance to domestication, for these virtues exemplify its God-given creaturely royalty (41:33–34 [MT 41:25–26]: "On earth it has no equal. . . . It is king"). If Job's piety is to be judged by what does and does not come forth from his mouth, then the lesson from Leviathan commends strong words, not soft or gentle ones, speech that demands respect, not silence.[31]

9. According to Knohl, Job rises to the level of faith consciousness God requires when he responds to this revelation not only with silent humility (40:3–5) but also with a verbalized confession of sin. Knohl finds this repentance (with a majority of commentators) in Job's last words in the book: "I despise myself, and repent in dust and ashes" (42:6). Most would agree that these words constitute the crux of the book, so perhaps I may be forgiven for not engaging the ongoing debate about the range of legitimate exegetical possibilities that must be considered. Let me simply invite consideration of one issue that all agree is critical. The words "repent *in* dust and ashes" (*niḥamtî 'al*) may be more properly translated, "repent *concerning* dust and ashes." Whereas the conventional translation suggests that Job retreats to the traditional ritual of gesturing forth sorrow for wrongdoing by sitting *in* dust and ashes,[32] the syntax may legitimately be taken to mean that Job "repents" or "changes his mind" *about* dust and ashes. If we pursue this option, then we must be open to the possibility that what finally comes forth from Job's mouth is not a confession of sin but instead a (re)affirmation of his creaturely stature before God. If God does not rebuke Abraham, another mere mortal of dust and ashes who dares to challenge God's justice (Gen. 18:27), then perhaps God will not rebuke Job when he dares to follow Abraham's model of faith.[33]

"Inside the House, an Archaic Rule; Outside, the Facts of Life"?

What then are we to make of the priests' commendation of silence as *the* criterion for the highest expression of faith? On the one hand, Knohl, Kaufmann, and others are on solid ground when they argue that the "outstanding characteristic of this [priestly] sanctuary is the holy silence within it."[34] On the other, there is ample evidence, both within and beyond Priestly texts, that worshipers created in "the image of God" are peculiarly empowered for speech. With mouths opened in the image of the Creator, human beings are birthed into created life with a capacity not only to receive God's words but also to speak their own, words not only of praise and thanksgiving but also of complaint and protest.[35] Indeed, if the "priestly" Job is a reliable script for the words that seek a hearing inside the sanctuary, then we have reason to suspect that the latter was a prominent component of cultic speech, even if the priests provided no place for it within the sanctuary itself.[36] But this only accentuates a larger question, which has been lurking at the edges of my ruminations from the outset. If the priests were well aware of the legitimate role of all forms of human speech to God, why then did they insist that its proper place was *outside* the holy sanctuary, not inside? To return to Knohl's observations, why do the priests insist that silence before God is "the most exalted level of faith"? Let me shape the question more specifically to the concerns of this session. How and why should silence before God be understood as the key to character formation?

I confess that I still falter when trying to formulate a persuasive answer to this question. My dis-ease is not unlike that of the narrator in Saul Bellow's short story "Something to Remember Me By." As a schoolboy brought up in an Orthodox Jewish home, he often felt trapped between high-minded religious commandments and the "grimly ordinary" requirements of life on the Chicago streets: "At home, inside the house, an archaic rule; outside, the facts of life. The facts of life were having their turn. Their first effect was ridicule."[37]

I suspect that we do not need Job's witness to convince us that the grimly ordinary facts of life too often ridicule "high-minded" affirmations of faith. We may, however, take real comfort in thinking that, because of Job's witness, when we limp toward the sanctuary with bruises and wounds exceeding any sin we may have committed, no one will block our entrance by saying, "No protesters allowed beyond this point." By the same token, we likely feel more authentically human, more empowered to meet the moral and ethical demands of life, when we can cry aloud to the heavens—inside the sanctuary—for justice. Given the tragic sense that defines so much of life in this world, "the chiefest sanctity of a temple," as M. de Unamuno says, "is that it is a place to which men go to weep in common. A *miserere* sung in common by a multitude tormented by destiny has as much value as a philosophy," or, I would add, as any theology.[38] Such are the moral demands of innocent suffering on the rituals of worship. The Jobs of this world cannot be fully human in the presence of God if religious authorities require them to stay outside the sanctuary yelling "Unclean, unclean!" Religious authorities who ignore or deny this truth only indict themselves. The charge they can expect to be leveled against them, as A. S. Park has discerned, will place them in the company of Job's friends; when challenged to offer comfort to the "sinned-against," they do not speak "what is right" about God:

> The God of Job is angry at this simplistic sin-repentance formula the church has applied to the victims of sin. . . . It is overdue for us to provide a sensible theology of healing for the victims of sin and tragedy. Our present one-dimensional theology is under God's wrath. Theologians owe burnt offerings to God and our apology to the victims.[39]

But surely Israel's priests knew that their rituals must be meaningful not only to sinners but also to the sinned-against. Even if the sanctuary represents only an idealized "island of silence in a sea of hymn and prayer,"[40] as Knohl puts it, the priests' insistence on silence in the presence of God presses us to do more than simply probe for the weaknesses in their view of worship. Might it be that they have discerned a larger truth than we skeptics have been willing to see? Given the modern tendency to view ourselves as the center of the universe, surely there is virtue in a summons to worship that reorients us, in proper humility and contrition, to a God whose fullness surpasses our needs. Private woes are important—indeed, for those trapped in the clutches of affliction they may be all we can feel, all we can say, all we can believe is real. To be invited—no, according to the priests, to be *commanded*—to silence our words and still our souls is to be reminded that there is a divine dimension to life. In the midst of all that is painfully real and constricting in this world, Israel's priests envision a sanctuary in which the "really real" becomes not only palpable but also freeing.[41] On this point, Barbara Brown Taylor's reflections on God's decentering revelation to Job are instructive. When she looks at the vastness of God's creation through the revelation vouchsafed to Job, two things happen to change her perspective:

> First, my ego undergoes radical shrinkage. Even though I know better, I still work so hard to justify my existence on this earth. I teach classes, I write books, I give to good causes, I work out with weights . . . but what does the night sky care? "You think you're so big, well take a look at *this*!" I am not even a flea on the back of this universe. I know some of those stars by name, but they do not know mine. They look the same when I am happy as they do when I am sad. As beautiful as they are, they ignore me. They remind me of my true size.
>
> The second thing that happens when I look at them is that I feel deeply reassured. Thank God they ignore me. Can you imagine how awful it would be, if you got into a rage one night and knocked nine or ten stars out of the sky with your wrath? Or if you walked into your back yard for a good cry and toppled your favorite shade tree with grief? Some of us dream of being that powerful, but it is a great mercy that such dreams do not come true.[42]

Further, we may take it as truth that silence in the presence of God can be not only freeing but also cleansing. Every speech act is in some sense an interference of thought and a corruption of vision. In her essay "The Aesthetics of Silence," Susan Sontag suggests an analogy that may be useful: "A landscape doesn't demand from the spectator his 'understanding,' his imputations of significance, his anxieties and his sympathies; it demands, rather . . . that he does not add anything to it."[43] Just so, when we stand in the presence of the ineffable God, words are not only inadequate and unnecessary, but they also betray the transcendence of the ordinary we so desperately seek. God does not need our words in order to be fully God, and we, perhaps, only counterfeit the moment of revelation by speaking instead of listening. Silence has the salutary effect of cleansing our world of noise and redeeming us from what Sontag calls the "treachery of words" that encumber, compromise, and often adulterate our proximity to the sacred.[44]

Still, rituals that demand silence in the face of innocent suffering and gross injustice may be guilty of the worst kind of evasion. If the highest level of faith requires that we subtract our voices from this world in order to add to God's heavenly chorus, then can the sanctuary of worship be anything more than a retreat from the ethical mandate not only "to walk humbly" with God but also to "do justice" (Mic. 6:8)? The question is of course one frequently addressed to the priests by Israel's prophets. I believe we can be confident that the priests heard it and responded, though perhaps in ways unexpected. Even within Leviticus, Israel's "book of worship," the priests understand that silence inside the sanctuary (Lev. 1–15) is not the sum total of what is required of the faithful. It is but the first and necessary step toward moral and ethical engagement with the world that lies outside (Lev. 17–27). If one is to "be holy" in creaturely ways that image God's holiness (19:2), then silence is merely the preparation for the action that must follow, not the action itself. Just as narrowing the gauge heightens the compression and increases the velocity, so worship that narrows faith to obedience increases the likelihood that we may go out into the world with a passion for ministry that will not be thwarted. We may be confident that what we do and say outside the sanctuary matters, both to God and to the world. *And* we may take comfort in the truth that our efforts are not all that matters. Relieved of the burden of being God, we are freed to live as God's faithful stewards. In this world, God does not require and we cannot aspire to do more.

I cannot end without acknowledging one further matter that continues to nag at my best efforts to accept the priests' invitation to lay aside all reservations and enter fully into the sanctuary of silence. We may well accept the notion that silent obedience is the better route toward becoming the person God wants us to be. Even so, we cling to the hope that unspoken doubts and worries will not be lost in rituals of silence. In short, we trust that the priest will know our story. Here I take some comfort in a rabbinic clue about the lingering importance of Job for Israel's priests. The Mishnah stipulates a seven-day preparation period for the high priest before administering the rituals for the Day of Atonement, which includes required readings from the books of Daniel, Ezra, Nehemiah, and Job (*Yoma* 1:6). The rabbis do not explain their selection of this lectionary. Daniel, Ezra, and Nehemiah may have been thought appropriate because each contains models of the penitential prayer that the Day of Atonement requires (e.g., Dan. 9; Ezra 9; and Neh. 9). Job may well have been included for the same reason, given the widespread assumption that he too repents in the end. But in the absence of evidence to the contrary, we may wonder if rereading Job's story, the whole of his story and not just selected excerpts, might have sensitized the high priest to the presence of authentically dissonant voices among those he would soon summon to silence.[45]

If so, then I offer one last contemporary reflection on the issue before us. In *Father Melancholy's Daughter*, Gail Godwin describes a scene in which Father Gower, rector of St. Cuthbert's, a small parish in rural Virginia, struggles with the ministry of the sacraments. "The thing about a ritual," he always says, "is that it brings containment and acceptance to people. The sacramental life is a sort of sanity filter against the onslaughts of existence." Father Adrian, his friend and colleague, recognizes the wisdom in this theology and confirms it with a personal anecdote:

> There was a Jesuit studying with me in Zurich, at the Institute. I once asked him, "What if you as a priest stopped believing? What would you do then?" "Make a fist in my pocket," he said, "and go on with the ritual."[46]

I think the Jobs of this world may well take comfort from the thought that the priest who summons them to submit in silence to the rituals of faith does so with a clinched fist. Might that fist be clinched in anger or protest, as if to say, "I don't really want to do this"? I concede that I would like to believe this is so. Might it be clinched as a deep expression of will and determination, maybe even, as Israel's priests might say, of faith? I am not sure, but I suspect there is always something more to be learned from any priest, ancient or contemporary, who resolves, clinched fists and all, to "go on with the ritual."[47]

As language always points to its own transcendence in silence, silence always points to its own transcendence—to a speech beyond silence.[48]

Notes

1. On the theological importance of the Pentateuch's seemingly disproportionate attention to matters relating to worship, see S. E. Balentine, *The Torah's Vision of Worship* (Minneapolis: Fortress, 1999).
2. Y. Kaufmann, *The History of Israelite Religion*, 4 vols. (Tel Aviv: Dvir, 1937–1956; Hebrew), 2:476–77. The first three volumes were abridged and translated by M. Greenberg as *The Religion of Israel* (Chicago: University of Chicago Press, 1960). The fourth volume was translated in its entirety by C. W. Efroymson as *The History of the Religion of Israel: From the Babylonian Captivity to the End of Prophecy* (New York: KTAV, 1977).
3. Priestly and other texts both within and beyond the Pentateuch refer, albeit obliquely and often negatively, to the use of the spoken or sung word alongside the ritual acts of Israel's worship. Within Priestly texts, see Lev. 5:5; 16:21; Num. 5:21–22; 6:22–26. Elsewhere, see, e.g., Deut. 21:1–9; 26:2–10; 1 Sam. 1:3, 10–15; 1 Kgs. 8:5, 12–64; Amos 5:21–23; Isa. 1:13–15; 38:20; 56:7. Special mention should be made of the various psalms ascribed to Levitical families (cf. 1 Chr. 6:16–34; 15:16–24; 16:4–43), especially the Korahites (Pss. 42, 44–49, 84–85, 87–88) and the Asaphites (Pss. 50, 73–83). The conventional assessment is that such examples attest the use of music and psalmody in the temple court-yards, outside the priestly areas. In other words, the "sanctuary of silence" is strictly limited to the priestly rituals of sacrifice at the altar. Cf. J. Milgrom, *Leviticus 1–16* (AB 3A; Garden City, NY: Doubleday, 1991), 60–61.
4. Kaufmann, *History of the Religion of Israel*, 303. On the division of the central temple personnel in Mesopotamia into cult priests, incantation priests, and diviners, see J. Renger, "Untersuchungen zum Priestertum in der altbabylonis-chen Zeit," *ZA* 58 (1966): 112–14. Of particular interest here is the role of the so-called lamentation priest (*kalu*) in voicing the congregational and individual responses to a variety of crises that threaten status quo affirmations of divine justice and punishment. For a convenient summary of the texts and their relevance

for assessing biblical literature, see W. W. Hallo, "Lamentations and Prayers in Sumer and Akkad," *CANE*, 1871–82.

5. Note, e.g., Milgrom's extension of Kaufmann's argument to the priestly polemic against anthropomorphism, which he judges to be an essential plank in the rejection of all forms of idolatry (Milgrom, *Leviticus 1–16*, 58–61; and *Leviticus 17–22* [AB 3B; Garden City, NY: Doubleday, 2000], 1426–28). Idolatry not only seeks to conform God to human thought, it also seduces human beings into believing that they can influence or control God with human speech, on the assumption that the Deity's will is pliable, just like any other human being. The paradigm for the priestly polemic against human speech in the presence of God, Milgrom argues, is Moses, the putative father of the cult, who is typically silent when performing the signs and wonders God commands and whose verbalized prayers are typically private, never public (e.g., Exod. 5:22; 8:8, 25–26; 9:29, 33; 10:18; 32:11–13; 33:7–11), lest it be thought that his words, not divine prerogative, are the reason for God's response.

6. See I. Knohl, *The Sanctuary of Silence: The Priestly Torah and the Holiness School* (Minneapolis: Fortress, 1995), esp. 124–64; "Between Voice and Silence: The Relationship between Prayer and the Temple Cult," *JBL* 115, no. 1 (1996): 17–30; and *The Divine Symphony: The Bible's Many Voices* (Philadelphia: Jewish Publication Society, 2003), 71–85.

7. Knohl, *Divine Symphony*, 73–74; *Sanctuary of Silence*, 148–52.

8. For this translation, which reflects the rendering of *dumiyyâ* in Jewish tradition, see Knohl, *The Sanctuary of Silence*, 149n101.

9. Knohl, *Divine Symphony*, 73. He calls attention to the selective use of the terms *bᵉrît*, "covenant," and *'ēdût*, "commandments, orders," in the Priestly Torah (see *Sanctuary of Silence*, 137–48). The priests typically use the word "covenant," he contends, with reference to the bilateral promises and obligations of God to Noah, Abraham, and their descendants (Gen. 6:18; 9:9–17; 17:2, 4, 9–13, 19, 21; Exod. 2:24). A change takes place with the revelation of the Tetragrammaton (YHWH) to Moses, after which the term *bᵉrît* "disappears" from the Priestly Torah and is replaced by the term *'ēdût*. The "pact" between YHWH and Israel consists solely of the unilateral demands God imposes on Israel, irrespective of any promise or obligation on God's part that invites the notion of "reciprocal utilitarian relations" (*Sanctuary of Silence*, 149n103) between God and human beings.

10. Knohl, *Sanctuary of Silence*, 150–51.

11. Ibid., 146.

12. Ibid., 164; cf. Knohl, *Divine Symphony*, 19–23, 71–74.

13. Knohl, *Sanctuary of Silence*, 146.

14. Ibid., 165–67; Knohl, *Divine Symphony*, 115–22. See also M. Douglas, who notes without discussion that "Leviticus' general reflection on God's justice reaches forward to the Book of Job" (*Leviticus as Literature* [Oxford: Oxford University Press, 1999], 252; cf. 212).

15. Knohl, *The Divine Sanctuary*, 165.

16. A critical component in Knohl's thesis is the distinction between divine revelations from Elohim, El Shaddai, or Eloah, and those from YHWH. The former correlates with Genesis and a first stage in faith consciousness, the latter with the exalted faith of Moses and Israel. The book of Job depicts a dynamic process from the elementary to the mature in a way comparable to the Priestly Torah, with one important difference. According to the priests, an exalted faith consciousness is available only through the complex of rituals inside the sanctuary; it is the legacy of Israel alone. According to the book of Job, an exalted faith consciousness is neither limited to observance of temple rituals nor restricted to

Israel. Job, a non-Israelite, gains access to this revelation through reflection on creation, not through the execution of sacrificial worship, which is mentioned "only at the stage of Job's early faith level" (Job 1:4–5). Knohl, *Sanctuary of Silence*, 165–66; and *Divine Symphony*, 120–22.

17. Knohl, *Divine Symphony*, 118.

18. On cultic rituals, especially the sacrifices for sin prescribed in Lev. 4:1–35, as "the priestly theodicy," see Milgrom, *Leviticus 1–16*, 260–61. His explication of the priestly advocacy of collective responsibility for sin merits citation, for it seems to be a response to the questions one might hear from the Jobs of the world: "[The priests] knew full well that the prophet was justified in protesting 'why does the way of the wicked prosper?' (Jer. 12:1 [cf. Job 21:7, 17–19]), and they provided their answer: the sinner may be unscarred by his evil, but the sanctuary bears the scars, and, with its destruction, he too will meet his doom. . . . That the righteous were engulfed in disaster (i.e., God's retribution) may have been protested by a few biblical voices (e.g., Gen. 18:23; Ezek. 18:1–32), but existential reality and the monotheistic premise make it impossible to conceive God otherwise. . . . The 'good' people who perish with the evildoers are not inno-cent. For allowing the evildoers to flourish, to pollute the sanctuary beyond repair, they share the blame. Indeed, they are the inadvertent sinners who con-tribute to the pollution of the sanctuary. Let a modern—hence, more vivid—example illustrate the point. World War II would have presented no theological quandary for Israel's priests of old. They would have rejected with scorn our con-temporary theologians who have proclaimed that 'God is dead.' Instead of bewailing the silence of God, they would have pointed the accusing finger at the human culprits, the inadvertent sinners, the 'silent majority'—the German peo-ple who voted the Nazis into power and the peoples of the free world who acqui-esced to the annexation of the Saar, Austria, and Sudetenland while barring their own doors to the refugees who managed to escape. A worldwide cataclysm was thus inevitable. Indeed, Israel's priests would have asked: How long under the circumstances could God have been willing to abide in his earthy sanctuary?"

19. N. Habel, *The Book of Job* (OTL; Philadelphia: Westminster, 1985), 88; cf. J. Hartley, *The Book of Job* (NICOT; Grand Rapids: Eerdmans, 1988), 69–70. I believe this assessment holds, despite D. J. A. Clines's important caution: "The story's setting in time and place lies beyond the horizon of priestly law" (*Job 1–20* [WBC 17; Dallas: Word, 1989], 16).

20. However we assess the historical accuracy of this profile, it is instructive to note that Job has often been depicted as a priest in both ancient Near Eastern and Christian iconography. See S. Terrien, who notes that more than forty statues of "Saint Job the Priest" have been preserved in Belgium, Luxembourg, and the Netherlands (*The Iconography of Job through the Centuries: Artists as Biblical Interpreters* [University Park: Pennsylvania State University Press, 1996], 149–58).

21. For a preliminary exploration of these matters, see S. E. Balentine, "Job as Priest to the Priests," *ExAud* 18 (2002): 29–52.

22. The text does not identify Job's location in 2:8. Commentators widely assume that he sits in a place of shame outside the city walls, a judgment that LXX seems to support by translating "ashes" as "the dung heap outside the city."

23. The instructions in Lev. 1–15 consist of ten *tôrôt* or "commandments." Five *tôrôt* deal with sacrifice: burnt offerings (6:2–6), cereal offerings (6:7–16), purifica-tion offerings (6:17–23), reparation offerings (7:1–7), and well-being offerings (7:11–21). Five *tôrôt* concern impurity: animal carcasses (11:1–23, 41–42), childbirth (12:1–8), skin diseases (13:1–59), purification from skin diseases (14:1–57), and genital discharges (15:1–32). See Milgrom, *Leviticus 1–16*, 2.

24. W. Scott Green, "Stretching the Covenant: Job and Judaism," *RevExp* 99, no. 4 (2002): 574.

25. Elihu's last speech contains but three oblique references to living creatures: two to human beings (37:7) and one to animals (37:8). Textual difficulties obscure the meaning in verse 7; about all that is clear is that God uses nature to "seal" or "close up" (*ḥātam*) human beings. The NIV's translation is relatively close to the Hebrew: "He [God] *stops* every man from his labor." Verse 8, likely a parallel statement with respect to animals, provides some clarification. Just as animals seek shelter in their dens when the winter storms arrive, so human beings retreat to the sanctuary of their homes when the weather becomes too severe to carry on with their normal labors.

26. Carol Newsom, *The Book of Job: A Contest of Moral Imaginations* (New York: Oxford University Press, 2003), 232.

27. Knohl, *Divine Symphony*, 118.

28. Cf. William P. Brown, *The Ethos of the Cosmos: The Genesis of Moral Imagination in the Bible* (Grand Rapids: Eerdmans, 1999), 365.

29. Note especially the wild ass, ostrich, and the horse, each of which "laugh" (39:7, 18, 22) in the face of potential danger. The horse is especially instructive, because its fearlessness, described as "might" (39:19; cf. 12:13), "terror" (39:20b; cf. 9:34; 13:21), "majesty" (39:20b; cf. 37:22), and "thunder" (39:25; cf. 40:5) is Godlike.

30. I have explored these matters further in "'What Are Human Beings, That You Make So Much of Them?' Divine Disclosure from the Whirlwind: 'Look at Behemoth,'" in *God in the Fray: A Tribute to Walter Brueggemann* (ed. T. Linafelt and T. K. Beal; Minneapolis: Fortress, 1998), 259–78; and *Job* (SHBC; Macon, GA: Smyth & Helwys, forthcoming).

31. J. G. Gammie also notes that what comes from Leviathan's mouth is a major emphasis in the poem. He suggests that the poet uses this emphasis both to caricature Job's verbal defenses and at the same time to affirm his protests. Gammie, "Behemoth and Leviathan: On the Didactic and Theological Significance of Job 40:15–41:26," in *Israelite Wisdom: Theological and Literary Essays in Honor of Samuel Terrien* (ed. J. G. Gammie et al.; Missoula, MT: Scholars Press, 1978), 223, 225.

32. For references and discussion, see, e.g., S. Olyan, *Biblical Mourning: Ritual and Social Dimensions* (New York: Oxford University Press, 2004), 111–23.

33. The phrase "dust and ashes" (*'āpār wa'ēper*) occurs only three times in the Old Testament: Gen. 18:27; Job 30:19; and Job 42:6. In each case it signifies something about the human condition in relation to God. In Job 30:19, Job laments that God has thrown him into the "mire" (*ḥōmer*; cf. Job 4:19; 10:9; 33:6) of human mortality, where human existence is defined as "dust and ashes." In the context of his suffering, Job understands this to mean that he exemplifies the way afflicted human beings are banished from society (30:1–8), then scorned and terrorized by their peers (30:9–15) and by God (30:16–23). His experience leads him to conclude that as "dust and ashes" he has been consigned to live in a world where he cries out to a cruel God who does not answer (30:20–21). In Gen. 18:27, the phrase "dust and ashes" applies to Abraham. In the context of arguing with God about matters of justice, Abraham acknowledges that he is a mere creature of "dust and ashes" who has entered dangerous territory. Abraham's recognition of his status before God is similar to Job's in 30:19, with one important exception: Abraham persists with his questions, and God answers. Indeed, the Hebrew text of Gen. 18:22—"YHWH remained standing before Abraham"—suggests that God, the "Judge of all the earth" (Gen. 18:25), stands waiting to hear what "dust and ashes" will say on the subject of divine justice.

As E. Ben Zvi has discerned, this picture of Creator and creature locked in dialogue over matters of mutual concern provides a glimpse of how the creaturely pursuit of justice enacts what it means to be made in the image of God: "The text underscores the notion that when the ideal teacher defends the universal order and confronts God with the standards by which God ought to judge the world, *he is in fact fulfilling the role God has chosen for him to fulfill*" (Ben Zvi, "The Dialogue between Abraham and Yhwh in Gen. 18:23–32: A Historical-Critical Analysis," *JSOT* 53 [1992], 39; emphasis added).

34. Knohl, *Divine Symphony*, 71. The argument for a silent sanctuary is surely apt when considering Leviticus, which records no direct response, no specific verbal reply, to God from either Moses or Israel. Moreover, as G. Auld has noted, Leviticus depicts the sanctuary as both a structural and theological sanctuary in the midst of the wilderness, which is a prominent theme in Exodus and Numbers. The "wilderness theme" occurs twelve times in Exodus (*bammidbār*: 3:18; 5:1, 3; 7:16; 8:23, 24; 14:11, 12; 15:22; 16:2, 32; 19:2) and thirty-one times in Numbers (1:1, 19; 3:4, 14; 9:1, 5; 10:12, 31; 12:16; 14:2, 16, 29, 32, 33, 35; 15:2; 16:13; 21:5, 11, 13; 26:64, 65; 27:3, 14; 32:13, 15; 33:8, 11, 13, 15, 36). By contrast, the wilderness is mentioned but twice in Leviticus (7:38; 16:22). Auld, "Leviticus: After Exodus and before Numbers," in *The Book of Leviticus: Composition and Reception* (ed. R. Rendtorff and R. Kugler; Leiden: Brill, 2003), 43. Both before and after Leviticus, that is, in the wilderness, the discourse between God and Israel frequently includes complaint and protest (e.g., in the "murmuring traditions" preserved in Exod. 15–18 and Num. 11–25). Inside the sanctuary, however, the tabernacle is an oasis of obedience; those who might address God differently in other places now respond with reverent silence.

35. Space limitations permit no more than a footnote reference to ancient Near Eastern texts describing the ritual of "washing" (*mis pi*) or "opening" the mouth (*pit mi*) of cultic images for the deity, which appear to have been in existence throughout Mesopotamia from at least the eighth to the first centuries BCE. Although no extant text preserves the complete *mis pi* or *pit mi* ritual, it seems to involve two essential acts. First, the ritual specialist performs a symbolic act by which the deity opens the mouth of the statue, thereby indicating that it is able to breathe, that is, it has been ritually birthed into the world of created life. Then the ritualist adds incantations, which empower the image to speak and to be spoken to by human beings with whom it now shares its existence. For translation and assessment of the extant texts, see C. Walker and M. B. Dick, "The Introduction of the Cult Image in Ancient Mesopotamia: The Mesopotamian *mis pi* Ritual," in *Born in Heaven, Made on Earth: The Making of the Cult Image in the Ancient Near East* (ed. M. B. Dick; Winona Lake, IN: Eisenbrauns, 1999), 55–121.

The existence of such precedent rituals in the ancient Near East begs an important question of the priestly insistence that human beings are created "in the image of God" (Gen. 1:26). Despite the polemic against both cultic images and the anthropomorphism they typically conveyed in so-called pagan cults, could Israel's priests have been completely unaware of the implication that human beings, created in the image of the God, whose mouth is open, not closed, are peculiarly shaped for communication both *from* and *to* God? On this question, see the insightful comments of my colleague Andreas Schüle in his essay "Made in the 'Image of God': The Concept of Divine Images in Gen 1–3," *ZAW* 117, no. 1 (2005): 1–20. Pondering the question, the words of George Steiner may help us to bridge from ancient texts to contemporary discernments: "It is the Hebrew intuition that God is capable of all speech-acts except that of monologue which has generated our arts of reply, of questioning and counter-creation. After the Book of Job . . . there *had* to be, if man was to bear his being, the means of dialogue with God, which are spelt out in our poetics, music, art" (Steiner, *Real Presences* [Chicago: University of Chicago Press, 1989], 225).

36. For all his attention to Job as a model for "exalted faith consciousness," Knohl never quite succeeds in getting him completely inside the sanctuary of silence. Job's role, according to Knohl, remains that of the outsider who speaks truth to truth. As Knohl says, "We can recognize that there is a place for, and significance to, the kind of debate in which the *other* view may also be a reflection of divine truth" (*Divine Symphony*, 146). Moreover, Knohl affirms that the tension between Job's cacophonous words outside the sanctuary and the sublime silence that characterizes the liturgy inside the sanctuary is necessary and should not be blurred. "Inevitably, there was a tension between the silent inner circle and the outer circles, a tension between the Priestly theology concentrated upon the sanctity of God and the popular religion that cared for the satisfaction of everyday human needs. At the same time, the different beliefs gave rise to a single, unified, holy system, where sound and silence found their place in harmony" (Ibid., 74).

37. S. Bellow, "Something to Remember Me By," in *Saul Bellow: Collected Stories* (New York: Viking, 2001), 415, 431.

38. M. de Unamuno, *The Tragic Sense of Life* (New York: Dover, 1954), 17.

39. A. S. Park, "The Bible and Han," in *The Other Side of Sin: Woundedness from the Perspective of the Sinned-Against* (ed. A. S. Park and S. L. Nelson; Albany, NY: SUNY Press, 2001), 51.

40. Knohl, *Divine Symphony*, 73.

41. On the capacity of religion's sacred symbols to distinguish between the "real" (the realities of everyday life) and the "really real" (wider realities that correct and complete), see C. Geertz, "Religion as a Cultural System," in Geertz, *The Interpretation of Cultures: Selected Essays* (New York: Basic Books, 1973), 110–12.

42. B. Brown Taylor, "On Not Being God," *RevExp* 99, no. 4 (2002): 613.

43. S. Sontag, "The Aesthetics of Silence," in Sontag, *Styles of Radical Will* (New York: Farrar, Straus & Giroux, 1966), 16.

44. Ibid., 5, 15.

45. The comment in *Yoma* is frustratingly oblique. Similar references to the reading of Job in connection with Daniel, Ezra, and Nehemiah occur in Tosefta *Kippurim* (4:4) and in relevant discussions of the Talmud to *Yoma* 1:6, but none provide an explanation. I am grateful to Jack Neusner, who graciously responded to my inquiries concerning the rabbinic treatment of Job by pointing out that in reading Job, the rabbis deemed his story kosher, that is, "proper" or "suitable for use according to Jewish law" (see *Dictionary of Judaism in the Biblical Period 450 B.C.E. to 600 C.E.* [J. Neusner, ed. in chief, W. S. Green, ed.; New York: Macmillan, 1996], 374).

46. G. Goodwin, *Father Melancholy's Daughter* (New York: Avon, 1991), 274.

47. With deep gratitude, I acknowledge that the shaping of this last paragraph owes much to the comments of Bill Green, one of my most valued conversation partners, who helped me to think deeply about what the image of the priest's clinched fist might convey.

48. Sontag, "Aesthetics of Silence," 18.

Chapter 7

The Book of Jeremiah

Reconstructing Community after Disaster

KATHLEEN M. O'CONNOR

Approaching the book of Jeremiah through the dual lens of moral character formation and survival of disaster entails the various ethical assumptions about
human character that underlie prophetic works, as Jacqueline Lapsley has shown
in her work on Ezekiel.[1] I am, however, interested in ways the book of Jeremiah
seeks to rebuild the moral character of the community in the aftermath of disaster. I want to know how the book, in the words of Marcia Riggs, "expands capacities of hearts and minds to make meaning in a world destroyed and to take action
suited to that meaning"—that is, how does concern with survival reframe the
character of Jeremiah's community?[2]

The book of Jeremiah is a complex, multilayered response to disaster. No
matter when the book or its parts were composed, the disaster in question I
assume to be the tragic events surrounding and following Babylon's invasions of
Judah (597–537 BCE). Given the superscription dating the words of the prophet
from "the days of King Josiah . . . until the captivity of Jerusalem" (1:1–3), it
becomes clear that the entire book in its final form assumes the disaster has
occurred. The community's survival of this disaster is the book's chief subject.
Every poem, narrative, or sermon relates to it in one way or another, announc-
ing, explaining, or offering hope for living through it.

The term "disaster" refers to a colossal collapse of the world, a vast interruption of life, what Louis Stulman calls "a cosmic crumbling."[3] Daniel Smith-Christopher brings disaster studies to bear upon the book of Ezekiel and says that disaster is "disastrous only when the events exceed the ability of the group to cope, to redefine and reconstruct" their world.[4]

This essay proposes that the book of Jeremiah seeks to reconstruct the community in the aftermath of disaster by

(1) its relentless portrayal of the disaster;

(2) its alteration of the community's self-understanding;

(3) its rhetoric of blame;

(4) its portrayal of Jeremiah as ideal survivor;

(5) its vision of a future community;

(6) its characterization of God;

(7) its literary structure, or lack thereof.

I am not concerned here with sources or compositional processes. I do assume that in its final form the book is a symbolic tapestry, a metaphoric world, a rich stew of meaning emerging from the nation's fall.[5]

The Book of Jeremiah Reconstructs the Community in the Face of Disaster by Portraying the Disaster, Endlessly and Repeatedly

For the first twenty chapters, disaster is a coming event, an onrushing attack by the mythic foe from the north (1:14; 4:6). Following the call narrative of chapter 1, three poetic collections anticipate disaster: poems about the broken family (2:1–4:2), poems about mythic battle (4:3–6:30), and poems about weeping (8:18–9:22).

Family Poems: The Broken Family

The broken family poems (2:1–4:2) portray the story of YHWH's tragic relationships with Israel and Judah in symbolic form. The nation's past, present, and future appear in an implied narrative of two marriages, divorces, invitations from God to return (šûb; 3:12–14), and the acceptance of the invitation, not by unfaithful wives but by the children (3:22–25).[6] The disaster is the fault of the people, figured as wives. Restoration is possible for the children, the next generation, if they "return" (šûb), and, in 3:22–25, they do.

Military Poems: The Destroyed City

After 4:2 the family recedes, while divine discourse on the mythic battle moves to the foreground (4:6–6:30 and less abundantly 8:4–10:27), and terror overtakes blame.[7] YHWH sends "the foe from the north," a superhuman force, against weakling Daughter Zion.[8] Like the family poems, the military poems also present a symbolic interpretation of the nation's collapse.[9] The inequity of power between the foe and the puny female Zion emphasizes the overwhelming nature of the attack, and so does God's description of the coming invasion. The attacker

> will devour your harvest and your bread;
> he will devour your sons and daughters;
> he will devour your sheep and cattle;
> he will devour your vines and your fig trees;
> he will shatter with a sword your fortified cities which you trust.
> (5:17; emending to the singular)

The attack will even crush the cosmos. Light, mountains, hills, birds, and the cities will return to primeval "waste and void" (*tōhû wābōhû*, 4:23–26; cf. Gen. 1:2).[10]

Poems of Weeping

In Chapters 8–10, poems of weeping decenter family and battle (8:18–9:23). With anticipatory grief, the mourning women further mark the totality of the disaster:

> Death has come up into our windows,
>   it has entered our palaces,
> to cut off the children from the streets
>   and young men from the squares.
> . . . .
> Human corpses shall fall
>   like dung upon the open field,
> like sheaves behind the reaper,
>   and no one shall gather them.
> (9:21–22)

The more mixed literary materials of chapters 11–20 stress the disaster's inevitability. The covenant sermon (chap. 11), for example, contains no blessings, only curses, for their accomplishment is a foregone conclusion. YHWH announces, "I am going to bring disaster upon them that they cannot escape" (11:11). Although scholars dispute literary divisions across chapters 11–17, Mark Smith correctly identifies a pattern among the larger units to include: a superscription, a prophetic story to indict the people, and a prophetic lament to illustrate their guilt.[11] Disaster is inescapable.

Chapters 18–20 then accomplish the disaster in symbolic performances. First, the potter destroys the pot (18:1–14), then Jeremiah heralds the nation's destruction by breaking the jar before the elders (19:1–15), and finally the priest imprisons Jeremiah in the stocks of the temple, signaling the captivity of God's word and of the nation (20:1–6). Only now is the mythic foe from the north historicized as Babylon.

Having accomplished the disaster symbolically in chapters 1–20, the book thereafter largely assumes historical destruction has occurred. It now moves to instructions for living in the aftermath, setting out "the way of life and the way of death" (21:8).[12] The book, therefore, is a compilation of materials wherein disaster appears as a coming event and materials wherein disaster is a permanent situation within which the community must struggle.[13]

But why is this book so utterly preoccupied with disaster? In its obsession with disaster, the book provides language, indeed a symbolic world, for the community to see itself. If, according to philosopher and literary critic Elaine Scary and psychologist Judith Herman, physical and emotional pain destroy language, then by repeatedly portraying the disaster, by viewing it from multiple interpretive angles, the book gives the community language to speak of its pain.[14] It makes collective experience conscious and public. It gives survivors the vocabulary and grammar to reenter the tragedy and begin to come to terms with it. It offers the community speech to overcome the isolation and numbness that accompany trauma to create of them a community of sufferers.

Such use of language, as James Boyd White insists about other texts, is a political and moral act, a performance of words that reshapes the ethical character of the community.[15] The book provides it with an essential ingredient of ethical living—a mirror of itself, that is, knowledge of its reality. This knowledge is the only place from which rebuilding of the community can begin.

The Book Shapes the Community's Character in the Face of Disaster by Altering Its Self-Understanding

The community is not what it used to be; the past is over. Everything has been plucked up and torn down—the nation, the kingship, the temple, and the ancient hope for landed security. Judah's habitat is broken, the tent destroyed, cords snapped, and the children gone into exile (10:20). The people have lost a coherent sense of themselves, for the institutions that shape communal identity are broken beyond repair. Kings fail "to execute justice in the morning" (21:12) and prophets speak lying words, "saying, 'Peace, peace,' when there is no peace" (6:14; 8:11). Idolatry has made them like Shiloh (7:4, 12). They all commit adultery, walk in lies, and strengthen the hands of evildoers (23:14). When the community accepts the disaster's magnitude and "the end of [its] nationalist-religious aspirations," it can go forward, but not on the same terms as before.[16]

Grandiosity, pride, and false security have no place in the community (5:12; 7:4, 10; 8:8; 13:9). Past glories will not return, nor can hopes for a renewed nation be sustained. To survive, the community must break from delusions of its safety:

> Do not listen to the words of the prophets who prophesy to you; they are deluding you. They speak visions of their own minds, not from the mouth of the LORD. They keep saying to those who despise the word of the LORD, "It shall be well with you. . . . No calamity shall come upon you" (23:16–17; cf. 28:1–17; 27:9; 29:8; 39:9).

The people's new identity is that they are wounded, tattered stragglers from the nation's collapse who can hope only to gain their lives as "a prize of war": "You who stay in this city shall die by the sword, by famine, and by pestilence; but those who go out and surrender to the Chaldeans who are besieging you shall live and shall have your lives as prize of war" (21:9). The phrase "to gain your life as a prize of war"—in Hebrew, literally, "you will have yourself for booty" (v̊həyṯâ l̊kā napš̊kā l̊šālāl)—occurs four times, creating a thin thread of realism through the latter part of the book (21:9; cf. 38:2; 39:18; 45:5). "Having yourself as booty" means "yourself is all you have for booty." You have survived, you are alive, but nothing is the same.[17] With the exception of chapters 30–33 and a narrow stream of vague future visions, the book promises little more than survival.[18] By radically altering the people's identity from nationalist dreamers to broken survivors, the book reconstitutes the moral character of the nation. Its people must renounce false nationalist hopes and embrace the truth of their present broken reality.

The Book Reconstitutes the Character of the Community by Its Rhetoric of Blame

At face value, the book seems immensely more concerned with blaming humans for the disaster than with offering means to survive it. It accuses, shames, and attacks. Because blame and shame are such strong themes, scholars usually entitle the book's first twenty-five chapters "oracles of accusation and judgment against Judah and Jerusalem" or some variation thereof.[19] The key word here is "against." The prophet speaks against people, priests, prophets, and kings. All citizens are responsible for the disaster, not God. From a plethora of blaming texts, here is but one:

> How can I pardon you?
>   Your children have forsaken me,
>   and have sworn by those who are no gods.
> When I fed them to the full,
>   they committed adultery
>   and trooped to the houses of prostitutes.
> They were well-fed lusty stallions,
>   each neighing for his neighbor's wife.
>   (5:7–8)

Jeremiah judges the community to be sinful, and from the least to the greatest (6:13), they caused the nation's fall.

This hermeneutics of blame is a theodicy, and it also tries to evoke human repentance, but against intuition, Jeremiah's blaming and shaming are also coping mechanisms in the midst of disaster. They help the community survive by urging upon it an ethic of responsibility. As Smith-Christopher argues, "Shame is a mark of honesty . . . an admission that allows transformation. . . . It offers hope that the new way will not repeat the acknowledged mistakes of the old way."[20]

Survivors of disaster and trauma often evaluate their situations in self-blaming speech. Blame gives meaning to otherwise incomprehensible predicaments. Smith-Christopher points to Cambodians who interpret the enormous destruction under the Pol Pot regime to have been the result of the nation's "bad karma."

This interpretation excuses the Buddha from blame for the catastrophe and enables the people to hold on to their tradition. Survivors are not victims in an arbitrary and chaotic universe but actors who brought disaster upon themselves.[21] Because they caused it, they can also change their ways and control their future. Alice Miller says something similar about survivors of child abuse.[22]

When survivors blame themselves, their larger worldview stays intact and God (or the parent) remains reliable, even if also harsh and destructive. According to this analysis, the more theologically appalling imagery of Jeremiah, such as God's attacks upon Daughter Zion in the mythic battle (4:5–6:30) and God's rape of Jerusalem due to the nation's sin (17:20–27) help the community explain the collapse of their world and offer them a sense of agency for the future. They may be broken survivors, but they are not passive victims.

As an interpretation of historical causality, this discourse of blame is frightfully inadequate. As discourse for reconstitution of the community, however, Jeremiah's blaming gives meaningful structure to chaotic and vacuous experiences. It makes the best of the community's suffering by understanding the disaster as the application of God's refining fire (6:27–30; 9:7; 13:27; 33:8). It encourages communal responsibility and insists on the survivors' capacity to be moral agents. The contours of this moral agency find expression, at least in part, in the figure of the prophet Jeremiah.

The Book of Jeremiah Reconstitutes the Community through Its Portrayal of Jeremiah as "Ideal Survivor"

Of all the prophets in the Old Testament, we have the most putative "biographical information" about Jeremiah. Scholarly preoccupation with historical questions about his life has yielded a thin broth of historical meaning and has, until recently, left the prophet's "persona" underinterpreted.[23] But as Pauline Viviano and Corrine Patton also claim, the text conveys ideology, point of view, and meaning, not only through prophetic oracles but also through characterization.[24]

Jeremiah is a rich symbol, a figure straddling two opposing symbolic directions.[25] At one level, his suffering is unique to his role as a prophet. The "confessions" (11:18–12:6; 15:10–21; 17:14–18; 18:18–23; 20:7–18)[26] portray him as the victim of his family and people, of the priest Pashur (20:1–6), of other prophets (chaps. 27–28), and of unnamed enemies who oppose him because he speaks against them (11:19; 15:15; 17:15, 18; 18:18–23; 20:7–8). He is their adversary, allied with God against them. About this there is no interpretive dispute.

But at another level, Jeremiah symbolizes the plight of the people and embodies virtues they need for survival. He stands over against his community, as Fretheim insists, *and* he symbolizes the fate of the nation.[27] Even as prophet—courageous, persistent, and at odds with his people—Jeremiah is not a heroic figure of epic proportions. He is an anguished survivor, a kind of antihero, wounded, isolated, and broken like the community in the grip of disaster.

His celibacy, for example, echoes the end of domestic life in the land (16:1–4) when there will be no more giving and taking in marriage, no voice of gladness, no voice of bride or bridegroom (16:9). His solitary state is emblematic of the devastation of domestic life caused by invasion. His repeated captivities (20:1–6; 26:1–24; 37:11–21; 38:1–6), escapes from death (26:24; 36:19; 37:21; 38:7–13; 39:11–14), attacks upon him (11:18–19, 21–23; 20:1–6; 26:1–24), and his exile to Egypt (chaps. 42–44) parallel the people's historical sufferings. His experience of God's abandonment (20:14–18) evokes the situation of a community destroyed (8:14).

Jeremiah's own survival is of great symbolic import for the community. Interpreters frequently puzzle over the absence of information about the end of his life or about his death. But Jeremiah *must* survive and endure in the book, for so must the people, even up to seventy years in Babylon (29:10). By the end, all Jeremiah and Baruch (45:5) have gained are their lives for booty (chaps. 42–44). Jeremiah is the ideal survivor who, even as he opposes his people and is opposed by them, exhibits the loyalty to God they must practice to reconstitute themselves as covenant people. In this way, his life offers language of social definition.[28]

Loyalty   Jeremiah is absolutely loyal to YHWH. His loyalty is in counterpoint to the behavior of the community, which he accuses of abandoning YHWH to follow after other gods, a theme that spills across chapters 1–20 (see, for example, 2:1–4:2).[29] Jeremiah's loyalty is evident at every turn, most particularly in the first-person laments called the "confessions" (11:18–12:6; 15:10–21; 17:14–18; 18:18–23; 20:7–14). Despite attacks on his life (11:18, 21–23; 12:6; 20:10), isolation from others (15:17), abandonment by his community, and, above all, by God (12:1; 15:18; 20:7), Jeremiah stays engaged with God. The confessions are about that engagement. They show the community how to rage and struggle with God in the midst of devastation. Jeremiah is the one fully obedient to God's word even as he resists it, wrestles with it, and is "burned" by it (20:9).

The book portrays him as a mystic, a contemplative who knows God, communes with God, argues with God. He is seduced and raped, yet he remains loyal (see 11:18–12:6). He speaks in brutal truth to God and thereby offers survivors permission to do the same. They too can pray for vengeance/justice, for God's word to come to fruition, for hope amidst despair. Jeremiah clings to God in his suffering. So must they.

Resistance   Resistance to the governing powers of his own nation expresses his allegiance to God. That loyalty undermines and overrides any loyalty to rulers—monarchical (chaps. 37–38), prophetic (chaps. 27–28), or priestly. By counseling cooperation with conqueror Babylon, he urges survivors to do the same, most notably in his letter to the Babylonian exiles (chap. 29).

Spirit of Communal Cooperation   Jeremiah benefits from cooperation with others inside and outside the community. Ahikam, son of Shaphan, mysteriously rescues him after his trial (26:24). Officials of King Jehoiakim counsel Baruch and Jeremiah to hide for their lives when Jeremiah's scroll is read to the king

(36:11–19). Ebed-melech, the Ethiopian slave of the king, rescues Jeremiah from the cistern (36:7–13). Jeremiah survives only because others help him.

Implicit in these accounts is a call for a spirit of openness in the community, of a willingness to seek survival in cooperation with others, insiders and outsiders. Exilic survivors must similarly seek cooperation from others, for Babylon's shalom is their shalom (29:7). Because Babylon is God's agent (25:8–14), cooperation with the enemy also expresses loyalty to YHWH. Absolute loyalty to God remains central to survival (29:13–14).[30]

The Book of Jeremiah Addresses the Moral Formation of the Community by Its Vision of a Future Community

The lyrical chapters of the "little book of consolation" address survivors for whom disaster has become a permanent reality, and they also offer grounds for reconstituting the character of the community. Obviously, the projection of a future for this community aids survival by claiming divine intention to restore and rebuild. It creates hope by suggesting the community can move on and begin again in a city rebuilt, a land replanted and with social relations restored. Jeremiah's life again symbolizes the community's survival when he redeems his cousin's field in the midst of invasion and imprisonment (32:6–15).[31] The restored community will be different from the old.

Although these chapters exalt the exiles at the expense of the people of the land, the new world will be built on social arrangements of justice and reversal. Wounded survivors will lead the procession home: the blind and the lame, those with child, those in labor. With weeping they will come—the vulnerable, the scattered, the defeated. There will be a new song, a new radiance, a new abundance of grain and wine for young, old, for women and men—all will be filled, including the priests (31:7–16).

The community will not only survive; it will flourish. Farmers and those who wander with flocks will live together, the weary will be satisfied, and God will replenish the faint (31:24–25). Each generation will have moral responsibility; each generation will die for its own sins and not for the sins of ancestors (31:29–30). Under a new covenant, the community will live in absolute loyalty to God, for God will write the divine law on their hearts, "for they shall all know me, from the least of them to the greatest" (31:34). And both Israel and Judah will return to Zion.

The Book Reconstitutes the Community by Its Characterization of God

God, not Jeremiah, is the book's principle character, the agent of everything else I have described—blamer, accuser, sender of the foe from the north, commander of the army, appointer of Babylon, and restorer of fortunes.[32] God is a highly emotional figure, lamenting and weeping, brokenhearted about the community's infidelity and reluctant to punish. If nothing else, the book defends God to help the community maintain continuity with its past and to keep God engaged in the present disaster.

The disaster afflicts God, who participates in the community's loss. God also is wounded, weeps, and laments. And God is principle authority and instrument in the community's reconstitution, demanding repentance and loyalty. A new relationship between the community and God is the ground upon which the future will be built. God causes the disaster, is the community's companion in the affects of the disaster, and is therefore the one who can lead them out. "I will put my law within them, and I will write it on their hearts; and I will be their God, and they shall be my people" (31:33).

The Book's Structure or Lack Thereof Forms the Moral Character of the Community

The book of Jeremiah is a notorious literary conundrum.[33] Prose contradicts poetry, sermons appear without preparation, stories and superscriptions exhibit no chronological order, destruction and hope intrude upon each other, and, most notably, in the Masoretic text, the book has multiple endings: chapter 45, chapter 51, chapter 52. This makes what Brueggemann calls "an ending that does not end."[34]

There are many scholarly assessments of these data, but I propose the book's confused arrangement implicitly "performs" the collapse of the world. It enacts the fracture of linear time and the rupture of continuous, narrative meaning. Or put differently, the book faces the audience with the disaster not simply by its content but also by its jumble of genres and its blurring, swirling, conflicting "polyphony" of voices.[35]

The interrupting structural features yield a sacred text wherein readers share the predicaments of the text's content.[36] Its parataxis—the ways it sets complex materials side by side without connecting clues—creates confusion, "smatterings from and of a broken world."[37] The book repeatedly forces readers to try to make sense of events that cannot be harmonized, and so reproduces the difficulties of the world itself. It requires readers to find their own way through competing symbolic formulations, and it places responsibility upon them to make sense of it all.[38]

Such a literary strategy—if that is what it is and not merely editorial chaos—honors readers as agents capable of making meaning in a world destroyed. As such, the book is an ethical speech-act in search of dialogue. Its mosaic of broken pieces invites the formation of a new text, a new community, a new world in the aftermath of disaster.[39]

Notes

1. Jacqueline E. Lapsley, *Can These Bones Live? The Problem of the Moral Self in the Book of Ezekiel,* BZAW 301 (Berlin: Walter de Gruyter, 2000).
2. Marcia Riggs, "The Character Education Imperative: The Whole Community's Responsibility," paper presented at International Denominational Center at a conference on "Teaching and Learning beyond Boundaries," March 2, 2002.
3. Louis Stulman, *Order amid Chaos: Jeremiah as Symbolic Tapestry* (Biblical Seminar 57; Sheffield: Sheffield Academic Press, 1998), 57.
4. Daniel Smith-Christopher, *A Biblical Theology of Exile* (OBT; Minneapolis: Fortress, 2001), 79.

5. A turn to the symbolic in the interpretation of Jeremiah can be found in Stulman, *Order amid Chaos*; A. R. Pete Diamond, "Deceiving Hope: The Ironies of Metaphorical Beauty and Ideological Terror in Jeremiah," a paper presented to the Episcopal Association of Biblical Scholars; and Diamond, "Metaphor in the Book of Jeremiah," paper presented at the annual SBL 2001 International Meeting in Rome, July 2001; in essays in A. R. Pete Diamond, Kathleen M. O'Connor, and Louis Stulman, eds., *Troubling Jeremiah* (JSOTSup 260; Sheffield: Sheffield Academic Press, 1999); and John Hill, *Friend or Foe? The Figure of Babylon in the Book of Jeremiah MT* (Biblical Interpretation Series 40; Leiden: Brill, 1999).

6. For extended study of this text, see A. R. Pete Diamond and Kathleen M. O'Connor, "Unfaithful Passions: Coding Women Coding Men in Jeremiah 2–3 (4:2)," *BibInt* 4, no. 3 (1996): 283–310 (reprinted in Diamond et al., *Troubling Jeremiah*, 123–45).

7. See Louis Stulman, "Insiders and Outsiders in the Book of Jeremiah: Shifts in Symbolic Arrangement," *JSOT* 66 (1995): 65–85. Leo G. Perdue (*The Collapse of History: Reconstructing Old Testament Theology* [OBT; Minneapolis: Fortress, 1994], 141–46) has recognized the cohesiveness of these battle poems in their blending of creation traditions with the mythic battle of the foe from the north. He places all the poetry in 4:5–6:30 under the rubric of mythic battle and includes much of the poetry in 8:4–10:27 as well.

8. The people (5:8, 19), Jeremiah (4:10, 19, 23–26a; 5:4–5, 10–11; 6:26), the enemies (6:4–5) and female Jerusalem/Zion (4:20b, 31) speak about the invasions.

9. Interest in historical origins of individual poems and the generic grouping of the poetry in chaps. 2–25 as "accusations against Judah and Jerusalem" has in the past obscured the predominance of battle language in these chapters. Robert P. Carroll, *Jeremiah* (OTL; Philadelphia: Westminster, 1986), is a notable exception.

10. Although it seems to change the subject, the prose temple sermon serves as a parenthetical comment on the disaster in which insiders, not the foe from the north, threaten Jerusalem's destruction. See Louis Stulman, "The Prose Sermons as Hermeneutical Guide to Jeremiah 1–25: The Deconstruction of Judah's Symbolic World," in Diamond et al., *Troubling Jeremiah*, 51–53; also see Stulman, "Insiders and Outsiders," 65–85. Much of the material in this paragraph is from Kathleen M. O'Connor, "The Tears of God and Divine Character in Jeremiah 2–9," in *God in the Fray: A Tribute to Walter Brueggemann*, ed. T. Linafelt and T. K. Beal (Minneapolis: Fortress, 1998), 172–85.

11. Mark S. Smith, *The Laments of Jeremiah and Their Contexts* (SBLMS 42; Atlanta: Scholars Press, 1990), 34–39.

12. Kathleen M. O'Connor, *The Confessions of Jeremiah: Their Interpretation and Role in Chapters 1–25* (SBLDS 94; Atlanta: Scholars Press, 1988), 143–46.

13. This insight is from J. Severino Croatto, who graciously read an earlier version of this essay. This analysis differs slightly from Louis Stulman's division of the book at the end of chap. 25, a division into two scrolls (*Order amid Chaos*, 23, 72).

14. See Elaine Scary, *The Body in Pain* (New York: Oxford University Press, 1985); and Judith Lewis Herman, *Trauma and Recovery* (New York: Basic Books, 1992).

15. See James Boyd White, *When Words Lose Their Meaning: Constitutions and Reconstitutions of Language, Character, and Community* (Chicago: University of Chicago Press, 1984).

16. Diamond, "Deceiving Hope," 13.

17. See Martin Kessler, "Jeremiah 26–45 Reconsidered," *JNES* 27, no. 2 (1968): 81–88. Survival is the promise to the Rechabites (35:1–19). Because they are obedient to the ways of the ancestor Jonadab, not drinking wine but living in tents, that is, deliberately electing to live as wanderers—unsettled peoples perhaps like those displaced by the disaster—they are promised that they "shall not lack a descendant for all time." (35:19). They will simply survive. Of course, the condition necessary to bring about survival is obedience, in contrast to chap. 34, where the people disobey Zedekiah's order to release the slaves but then take them back into bondage so that the towns of Judah will not survive (34:22). On the relationships between chaps. 34 and 35, see Gerald Keown, Pamela Scalize, and Thomas G. Smothers, *Jeremiah 26–52* (WBC 27; Dallas: Word, 1995), 193–94.

18. See Kessler, "Jeremiah Chapters 26–45 Reconsidered."

19. See, e.g., Carroll, *Jeremiah*, 86; and E. W. Nicholson, *Jeremiah 1–25* (Cambridge Bible Commentary; Cambridge: Cambridge University Press, 1973), 14.

20. Smith-Christopher, *Biblical Theology of Exile*, 122.

21. Ibid., 79–80. Here Smith-Christopher cites the work of Marjorie Muecke.

22. See Alice Miller, *The Drama of the Gifted Child: The Search for the True Self* (New York: Basic Books, 1981).

23. Classic historical renderings include John Bright, *Jeremiah: A New Translation with Introduction and Commentary* (AB 21; Garden City, NY: Doubleday, 1965); and W. L. Holladay, *Jeremiah 1 (chapters 1–25)* and *Jeremiah 2 (chapters 26–52)* (Hermeneia; Minneapolis: Fortress, 1986, 1989, respectively). For more symbolic interpretations of the prophet, see Walter Brueggemann, *A Commentary on Jeremiah: Exile and Homecoming* (Grand Rapids: Eerdmans, 1998), 11–12; Timothy Polk, *The Prophetic Persona: Jeremiah and the Language of the Self* (JSOTSup 32; Sheffield: Sheffield Academic Press, 1984); Hill, *Friend or Foe?*; Stulman, *Order amid Chaos*; and J. G. McConville, *Judgment and Promise: An Interpretation of the Book of Jeremiah* (Winona Lake, IN: Eisenbrauns, 1993), 61–78.

24. Pauline Viviano, "Characterizing Jeremiah," *WW* 22, no. 4 (2002): 361–68; Corrine Patton, "Layers of Meaning: Priesthood in Jeremiah MT," unpublished paper, 2003.

25. Hill (*Friend or Foe?* 40–54) sees Jeremiah as a metaphor of divine grief. See Polk, *Prophetic Persona*, who sees Jeremiah as an ambiguous, symbolic literary figure.

26. Interpreters dispute the breakdown of these laments into five or six, but all agree that these texts belong in the confessions.

27. Terence E. Fretheim, "Caught in the Middle: Jeremiah's Vocational Crisis," *WW* 22, no. 4 (Fall 2002): 351–60; See Heinz Kremers, "Ledensgemeinschaft mit Gott im Alten Testamentum," *EvT* 13 (1953): 122–40. Kremers, with unfortunate christological intentions, is right about the importance of Jeremiah's suffering, though for wrong reasons.

28. White, *When Words Lose Their Meaning*, 72.

29. See Diamond and O'Connor, "Unfaithful Passions," 130, for a more detailed study of this theme of human abandonment of God.

30. I need to do more study to determine if repentance appears enough in connection with the prophet to determine if he is a full embodiment of the virtue of repentance, but God does call him to repent, as God also calls the community to repentance repeatedly (4:1–4; 23:22). Commentators often wonder why God requires Jeremiah to repent, since Jeremiah is innocent when set against the idolatry of his people. "If you turn back, I will take you back," invites God in Jeremiah's second confession (15:9).

31. Diamond finds Jeremiah's land purchase "to be so eccentric a command that even Jeremiah is left incredulous" (Diamond, "Deceiving Hope," 11).

32. See Terence E. Fretheim, "The Character of God in Jeremiah," in *Character and Scripture: Moral Formation, Community, and Biblical Interpretation*, ed. W. P. Brown (Grand Rapids: Eerdmans, 2002), 211–30. Jack Miles, *God: A Biography* (New York: Alfred A. Knopf, 1995), does not treat Jeremiah's characterization of God directly.

33. It appears "to have been constructed in a long and complicated growth process" (William McKane, *Jeremiah* [ICC; Edinburgh: T. & T. Clark], 1:xlviii).

34. Walter Brueggemann, "An Ending That Does Not End: The Book of Jeremiah," in *Post-Modern Interpretations of the Bible: A Reader* (ed. A. K. M. Adam; St. Louis: Chalice, 2001), 117–28.

35. See Mark Biddle, *Polyphony and Symphony in Prophetic Literature: Rereading Jeremiah 7–20* (Studies in Old Testament Interpretation 2; Macon, GA: Mercer University Press, 1996). Brueggemann calls this book "unreadable" because "it reads the abyss" ("Meditation upon the Abyss: The Book of Jeremiah," *WW* 22, no. 4 [2002]: 340–50).

36. White, *When Words Lose Their Meaning*, 54.

37. Ibid., 52. White is referring in this quotation to the *Iliad*.

38. Ibid., 106.

39. Another version of this paper was presented at the Catholic Biblical Association Annual Meeting, San Francisco, 2003. My thinking has been immensely aided by conversations with colleagues Marcia Riggs, Mark Douglas, Walter Brueggemann, and J. Severino Croatto.

Chapter 8

A Feeling for God

Emotions and Moral Formation
in Ezekiel 24:15–27

JACQUELINE E. LAPSLEY

Emotions and the Moral Life

It requires only a brief acquaintance with the book of Ezekiel to realize that the anthropology implicit in the book is rather pessimistic. Ezekiel does not have much good—anything good, really—to say about the people who appear in the book, and it does not require much extrapolation to expand the scope of his pessimistic view to include humanity in general. Broadly speaking, the first half of the book excoriates human beings (specifically the Israelites) for their transgressions that have brought about the total catastrophe, while the second half of the book envisions a new harmonious existence, but one that is fairly denuded of people, as though their very presence might unleash chaos. It is difficult to get a handle on the question of moral formation in the book when the prophet's overall view of humanity is so grim. Yet I think that one entrée into this issue is through a consideration of the way emotions function in the moral formation of the people. The book betrays a deep ambivalence about the ethical import of emotions. On the one hand, the character of the prophet is depicted as highly emotional, while on the other hand, the people's emotions are portrayed as malforming their moral decision making, as leading them away from a God-centered life.

What do emotions have to do with the moral life anyway? Much of the philosophical and theological tradition has not been interested in this question, at least not in any positive way, but recent trends in science and philosophy have begun to suggest that the emotional life is intimately tied to the moral life. In the field of neuroscience, Antonio Damasio has argued that the health of the part of our brains that controls emotional response directly affects whether we make good rational decisions—that, in short, far from being opposed to one another, emotion constitutes part of rationality.[1] Damasio demonstrates that persons who lack emotions due to damage to the area of the brain where emotions "reside" are perfectly capable of intelligent, so-called rational thought, but are utterly incapable of making any kind of moral decision or evaluation—they lack any sense of engagement between themselves and the world. On the philosophical side, Martha Nussbaum argues that emotions are necessary in the moral life because they constitute judgments of value; they are "value-laden ways of understanding the world."[2] From their respective disciplines, Nussbaum and Damasio advance the idea that emotions provide human beings "with a sense of how the world relates to [their] own set[s] of goals and projects. Without that sense, decision making and action are derailed."[3]

If emotions are so important in the moral life, as Nussbaum and Damasio, among others, assert, then it seems worthwhile to consider how emotions relate to the moral life in a prophetic book with so much apparent ambivalence about the emotional life—the prophet himself is highly emotional, but the people are subject to emotions, especially desire, that draw them away from God (this is most clearly evident in Ezek. 16 and 23). To come at this question in a manageable way, I want to focus on one specific emotion, love (or, more narrowly, desire), in forming the moral character of the people in Ezekiel. Many texts in the book clamor for attention with respect to this question (e.g., chaps. 16 and 23), so I want to further narrow my topic to the role that desire plays in one short text, Ezek. 24:15–27, where, as a sign to the people, the prophet is denied the possibility of mourning the death of his wife.

The Prophet's Grief Suppressed

This passage deserves attention because it brings the first twenty-four chapters of the book to a close and with it the torrent of judgments against Israel that began in chapter 2. This sign-act involving the death of Ezekiel's wife, and its interpretation, are in some way the last word of judgment against Israel before the oracles against the nations and the words of hope that mark the second half of the book. Most commentators on this passage understand Ezekiel to be prohibited from engaging in the customary mourning rituals following the sudden death of his wife, an act of suppression that serves as a sign in the second half of the passage that the Israelites too will be prohibited from ritually expressing their grief over the loss of the temple and the loss of their children.[4] Ezekiel does not act without precedent in denying the people appropriate lamentation of the dead. In

Jer. 16:5–9, the prophet, and subsequently the people, are prohibited from mourning the dead in the usual way, since YHWH has withdrawn "wholeness" (*šᵉlômî*) from the people.[5] As with other motifs common to both books, Ezekiel takes this notion and, in the words of chef Emeril Legasse, "kicks it up a notch." The language used to describe the deprivation of mourning rituals is much more graphic and intense in Ezekiel than in Jeremiah, and with an apparently different aim.

The text does not disclose the reason for the suppression of mourning rituals, and so we commentators rush to fill the void. It is the result of the people's emotional rigidity, indifference, or moral callousness, some have suggested,[6] while others, such as Blenkinsopp, have more sensibly suggested that the people refrain from mourning "since the customary rites of mourning will be totally inadequate, faced with such an unparalleled disaster."[7] Still, this is not wholly satisfying. In this essay I argue that the reason the mourning rituals are suppressed is intimately connected with Ezekiel's wrestling with, and proposed solution to, the problem of human nature and what he views as its inherent defectiveness. Connected to this argument, I propose that Ezekiel understands the people's love and desire to be once again misdirected—for within the book Ezekiel never depicts the people's desire as appropriately directed—but that he here leaves open the possibility that their love might one day find its true object, namely, YHWH. In order to tease out both the reason for the suppression of the mourning rituals and the moral function of desire in the passage, two aspects of the passage require particular scrutiny. First, the way in which the text presents Ezekiel's feelings for his wife and, in parallel fashion, the people's feelings for the temple in Jerusalem require attention. Second, we will need to attend carefully to what kinds of emotional expression are permitted and what kinds are proscribed.

In verse 16 Ezekiel's wife is described as "the delight [*maḥmad*] of [his] eyes," and in verses 21 and 25 the temple is similarly "the delight [*maḥmad*] of [the people's] eyes." The temple is further described as the "passion of [the people's] life" (*maḥmal napšᵉkem*), as Block felicitously translates (v. 21).[8] Further on in YHWH's announcement that the temple will be "taken," it is described as the people's "stronghold," "their joyous glory," and as "the longing of their life" (*maśśā' napšām*) (v. 25).[9] A classic critique of the pervasive temple theology is evident here. The people idolatrously placed their confidence in this "stronghold," and now YHWH will be the one to destroy that confidence along with the temple.[10] Of particular interest, however, is the intensity of the language describing the people's love for the temple. The analogy is straightforward enough: As the prophet's wife is an object of his love and desire, so the temple is an object of love and desire for the people.[11] Yet the language describing the people's feelings for the temple suggests an intensity of feeling that is not present in the description of Ezekiel's feelings for his wife. The people's passion for the temple is extreme; as the presence of the *hapax maḥmal* and the variations on the phrase "passion of their life" suggest, the people's feelings for the temple press the boundaries of what is expressible in language.[12]

Mourning versus Groaning

If these are indeed the passionate feelings of Ezekiel for his wife and even more so of the people for the temple, then their anguish at the loss of wife and temple respectively must be equally intense. Yet YHWH wills that such intensity of feeling not be permitted traditional expression: Ezekiel is charged not to mourn (*sāpad*) or weep (*bākâ*), nor to allow his tears to come (v. 16). The people are similarly admonished in verse 23. The first verb (*sāpad*) commonly denotes ritual mourning of the dead, with its customary attendant actions.[13] *Bākâ* is a more general term for weeping, expressing human grief in the Hebrew Bible over a hundred times. As with mourning and weeping in this verse, tears are associated with the expression of human emotion—these are the usual and often ritualized means for people to express their grief—yet these are the very actions that are denied them in this passage.

This may seem a bit tautological. Of course mourning and weeping are human activities—what else would they be? But establishing these behaviors as particularly human is important for seeing the contrast to what follows. In verse 17 the prophet is commanded to "groan softly; observe no mourning for the dead" (*hē'ānēq dōm mētîm 'ēbel lō' ta⁽ʿ⁾śeh*). The translation and meaning of this verse are contested, with the primary issue surrounding what to do with the odd form *dōm*, here translated "softly."[14] Of more immediate interest here is the first word, "groan" (*hē'ānēq*). The type of groaning this verb envisions is the primal groaning of the wounded (Jer. 51:52; Ezek. 26:15, both in qal), or the equally primal groaning of those who react viscerally to the abominations in the temple in Ezek. 9:4 (*niphal*, as in our verse). The primal nature of this type of noise contrasts with the now prohibited but structured "mourning" (*sāpad*) from the previous verse. This is made quite explicit in the subsequent clause: "Observe no mourning [*mētîm 'ēbel lō' ta⁽ʿ⁾śeh*] for the dead." "Mourning" (*'ēbel*) here includes "all of the conventional mourning customs performed over the whole extended period of mourning."[15] Inarticulate "groaning" is permissible, then, but formal mourning is not. A quiet, primal moan is allowed, but nothing that might provide a structure within which the prophet and people might make sense of their overwhelming experience of loss.[16] Making sense of their experience is specifically disallowed.

Loss of Meaning and Dehumanization

Ezekiel is to put on his turban and his sandals and to leave the lower part of his face uncovered, all actions contrary to the customary behaviors associated with mourning: exposing the head to dust and ashes, removing sandals, and veiling the lower part of the face.[17] Again, those actions that might provide a framework within which the prophet could assign meaning to his wife's death are prohibited. Human beings are meaning makers, but it is specifically this human desire for meaning that is excluded here. The denial of what is particularly human is further apparent in a textual conundrum at the end of this same verse: "nor shall you eat the bread of human beings [*'ᵃnāšîm*]" (v. 17). Unable to make much sense of "bread of human beings," translators and commentators often opt to emend the text to "bread of mourners."[18] But the text is not so difficult that recourse should be so readily made to emendation. It may well be, as Friebel suggests, that "bread of human beings" means "customary, ordinary," that is, food customarily brought to a mourner by friends and relatives.[19] This too is part of the ritual of grief, so its prohibition fits with the prior rejection of other mourning rituals. But the phrase speaks at another level as well: The prophet is refused human ways of grieving, being permitted only animal-like groans, and is now denied specifically *human* food. The occurrence of "bread of human beings" twice in the passage (cf. v. 22) intensifies the emerging contrast between the permissible but inarticulate and animalistic groans, and the proscribed but human-specific behaviors.

The accrual of prohibitions against specifically human activities, however, suggests something beyond the simple withdrawal of human structures for interpreting experience. It goes further to evoke a process by which the prophet is dehumanized, stripped of those features that make him human. So the "bread of human beings" is not simply a circumlocution for "ordinary," much less a textual blunder, but a precise articulation of what is being denied the prophet, that is, what it means to be human in the context of loss. The prophet must confront loss without those structures of meaning that human beings need in order to interpret their complex experience. Instead, YHWH requires him to have the complex experience but withdraws the means of interpreting it. He feels the loss of what he loved but is incapable of anything but inarticulate groaning.

And so it will be for the people when YHWH pollutes the object of their desire, the temple. The language becomes even more vivid here. Like the prophet confronting the death of his wife, the people, faced with the loss of their beloved temple, "will not mourn or weep" (v. 23). But new elements appear here that were absent earlier. Not only will there be no customary mourning ritual, but the people shall "rot" (*nᵉmaqqōtem*) in their iniquities. This verb is elsewhere used to describe the decaying and festering of organic substances.[20] Earlier in Ezekiel the verb occurs in the context of famine: Lacking bread and water, the people "will be decimated, each and his neighbor, and they will rot in their iniquity" (4:17). The lack of bread here recalls the denial of bread in our passage; the "rotting" is a form of wasting away from lack of sustenance. This image of decaying flesh aptly captures Ezekiel's view of the people's predicament, as attested in the quote assigned to the people in 33:10 that sums up their situation: "Our transgressions and our sins are upon us, and in them we are rotting [*nᵉmaqqîm*]; how can we live?" The image of organic decay evoked by this verb in 24:23 contributes to the sense that the people are undergoing a process of dehumanization; they are literally decaying.

The second half of the verse intensifies this effect. As they decay, the people will also "groan [*nᵉhamtem*] to one another." The English translation disguises a significant difference between this type of groaning and the groaning in verse 17.

With the earlier verb (*hē'ănēq*), the sound was animal-like in its inarticulacy, but the attested subjects of the verb were human. By contrast, the verb in verse 23 nowhere appears in the Hebrew Bible with human beings as its subject, with one exception. In the majority of occurrences, lions are the ones groaning/growling, and in one case it is the groaning/roaring of the sea.[21] This choice of verbs, similar to the one in verse 17, is crucially different, however. Now the people will be rotting away and groaning explicitly *as animals groan*.

We are now in a position to summarize the movement of the passage. First, the distinctively human means of coping with loss are proscribed, with only inarticulate moans, albeit those usually associated with human beings, permitted. Then the people are described in terms of physical decay, with the only sound emanating from them the raw, unmediated, uncontrolled groans of an animal. The progressive dehumanization of the people, and of the prophet as a sign to the people, has now reached its completion.[22]

Making Room for God

What is the point of prohibiting mourning rituals? Why this diminishment of the human to what is less than human? For punishment alone, or for some larger purpose? Ezekiel continually reiterates that all of God's actions have one goal: "so that the people may know that YHWH is Lord." But how does the stripping away of human categories of meaning here serve this end? How does the resulting emotional chaos help the people know that YHWH is Lord? For Ezekiel the people's love/desire for the temple, intense as it is, is misdirected. They loved the temple, but they failed to love the one whom the temple represents. The only cure for this, in Ezekiel's view, is radical. It is a process by which the people are stripped of what makes them human and are reduced to an animal-like state.

Strong emotions attendant on the death of a loved one require ritual acts of mourning in order to rein in the potential chaos of uncontrolled emotions, to set "boundaries on the unbounded," as Gary Anderson has observed.[23] Yet Ezekiel skewers the Israelites' tendency to make order out of chaos for its naive self-sufficiency; it leaves no room for the activity of God. The critique here of the human propensity for order is reminiscent of the divine speech in Job, in which Job's desire for structures of value and meaning is contrasted with the chaos represented by Leviathan. Carol Newsom observes the conflict between the "blessed rage for order" characteristic of human beings and "that which resists rational organization into structures of meaning and human purpose." In Job, she suggests, "the face of Leviathan exposes the hubris and the self-deception of the human rage for order."[24] The situation in Ezekiel offers some suggestive parallels: Instead of Leviathan, here the stripping away of orders of value and meaning to the point where people resemble animals embodies the unstructurable, unorderable elements of the cosmos that do not yield to symbolic organization. For Ezekiel, their human-generated categories are closing the people off, shielding them from knowing the presence and activity of God. Eliminating these meaning-making forms leaves the people with the chaos of their raw emotion and so prepares them to receive the activity of God, to "know that YHWH is Lord." The Israelites' tendency is to resolve their grief over the temple too easily and only by means of their own ritualized mourning, a mourning in which God is not an active player. Their reduction to an animalistic state allows them to feel their loss with all its attendant pain and without analgesic. The irresolvability of their grief leaves open a space for the radical action of God, space that was previously closed off in the well-ordered culture of ritualized mourning.

This is a very hard ethic. The necessity of being denuded of precisely that which makes us human cannot, should not, be integral to anyone's theology. Having examined this austere logic, should we not reject its claims? Possibly, but not without first considering what insights it might reveal. Ezekiel relativizes all human categories of meaning; they are inadequate and insufficient to deal with reality, and they deny the radical action of God. For Ezekiel, only through a progressive dehumanization can the people be prepared for new life. Nothing of the old nature can be retained. Later in the book (chap. 37), the re-creation of humanity can only be initiated after the people are declared dead; they are brought to new life with nothing of the old life remaining except their bones. The people must be crushed so low that they no longer seek piecemeal solutions for their desperate situation, such as setting their hearts on the temple or mourning its loss in the usual, customary ways. The symbolic ordering of experience (religion, culture) must be violently disturbed before the people can perceive the divine action that ultimately seeks to restore them to their full humanity (in Ezekiel divine salvific action is unilateral; humanity can only receive it).[25] Yet for all its austerity it does not seem far from the mark in terms of the way radical change sometimes happens. The oppressed will only rise up when their oppression becomes unbearable. Slight improvements in policy may have the effect of delaying much-needed, but more radical, change. Similarly, Ezekiel's concern that precisely observed mourning rituals serve to comfort the bereaved at the expense of a genuine sense of the radically contingent and dependent nature of the human condition is one that might be expressed in our own time.[26]

Conclusion

We seem to have wandered far from the question of desire in moral formation, but let me see if I can make the necessary links back to that larger question. Readers of Ezekiel have long remarked that, in contrast to many other biblical traditions, the relationship between God and humanity is never characterized by love. Honor plays a significant role in that relationship but not love. Despite the emotional character of the prophet himself, the divine-human relationship is emotionally bare. But if desire is absent from the divine-human relationship in the book, it appears, albeit in misshapen form, in other contexts. Human love and desire are evoked, but they never have an explicitly acceptable object (with the possible exception of Ezekiel's feeling for his wife, 24:16). Desire is always misdirected, as when it finds its target in the illicit "lovers" of chapters 16 and 23. Even desire for the temple, as we have seen, misses the mark.[27] From this it appears that Ezekiel holds to a purely negative view of the relation between love, desire, and the moral life: These emotions will always lead you astray. Desire, at least in practice, is always idolatrous desire. The process of moral formation involves eradicating these elements of human nature in order to direct the self toward God.[28] Once again, the prophet offers us a severe portrait of the human condition insofar as the extensive barriers to a faithful relationship to God appear to reside within the human condition itself.[29]

Everything happens so that the people "will know that YHWH is Lord." How can this take place given the prophet's dire estimation of the human situation? Can human emotion be redirected away from these inappropriate objects toward God? Or do human feelings have no role to play in the restored creation and humanity (chaps. 36–48)? Ezekiel does not explicitly work out a positive role for emotion in the new creation, but a few points are worth observing by way of conclusion. Ezekiel's grand culminating vision of redemption is of a temple (chaps. 40–48), and while there are not very many people in or around the temple—Ezekiel is too skittish about human nature to include them—nonetheless the temple once again mediates God's presence to human beings. The success of this vision must implicitly rely on the human love for the temple so fleetingly and scathingly evoked in chapter 24. Presumably this new sanctuary will successfully direct the people's love toward God, although Ezekiel characteristically never uses the language of love or desire. We perceive only a few linguistic hints: The water that flows from the new temple will be "healing" (*tĕrûpâ*, 47:8–12), and God's covenant will be one of "wholeness" (*šālôm*, 37:26). These images hint at a reversal of the process of dehumanization carried out in chapter 24 and gesture toward a restored humanity, complete with desire and love, now finally directed as it should be, toward God.

Notes

1. See especially Antonio R. Damasio, *Descartes' Error: Emotion, Reason, and the Human Brain* (New York: Avon, 1994); and Damasio, *The Feeling of What Happens: Body and Emotion in the Making of Consciousness* (San Diego: Harcourt, 1999).
2. Martha C. Nussbaum, *Upheavals of Thought: The Intelligence of Emotions* (Cambridge: Cambridge University Press, 2001), 88.
3. Ibid., 117.
4. Margaret Odell does not see the suppression of emotion at the core of the passage but perceives Ezekiel's symbolic act as constituting a symbolic transfer of power from Jerusalem to the exiles (Odell, "Genre and Persona in Ezekiel 24:15–24," in *The Book of Ezekiel: Theological and Anthropological Perspectives* [ed. M. S. Odell and J. T. Strong; Atlanta: Society of Biblical Literature, 2000], 195–219).
5. In the Jeremiah text, it seems that the prohibition on mourning functions both as punishment and as a sign of the enormity of the catastrophe. The reason for the denial of ritual in Ezekiel is more obscure and is one of the questions being

pursued in this essay. See Walther Zimmerli, *Ezekiel 1: A Commentary on the Book of Ezekiel, Chapters 1–24* (Hermeneia; trans. R. E. Clements; Minneapolis: Fortress, 1979), 506; and G. A. te Stroete, "Ezekiel 24:15–27: The Meaning of a Symbolic Act," *Bijdr* 38 (1977): 163.

6. See Daniel I. Block, *The Book of Ezekiel* (NICOT; Grand Rapids: Eerdmans, 1997), 1:794, for references to these views. See also te Stroete, "Ezekiel 24:15–27," 164–66.

7. Joseph Blenkinsopp, *Ezekiel* (Interpretation; Louisville, KY: Westminster John Knox, 1990), 105. Block, following te Stroete ("Ezekiel 24:15–27," 174) suggests (a bit oddly, given the text) that the exiles will not mourn because they will recognize in the destruction of the temple and city the "dawn of a new age." The news of the collapse of the city would thus "in effect be welcome news" (*Book of Ezekiel*, 1:794). For a list of other views, see Kelvin G. Friebel, *Jeremiah's and Ezekiel's Sign-Acts: Rhetorical Nonverbal Communication* (JSOTSup 283; Sheffield: Sheffield Academic Press, 1999), 340–45.

8. The NRSV opts for "your heart's desire," and NJPS has a variant of this.

9. The NJPS translates "longing of their hearts"; NRSV: "their heart's affection."

10. Block, *Book of Ezekiel*, 1:797.

11. Julie Galambush discusses the metaphorization of the temple as Yahweh's wife in *Jerusalem in the Book of Ezekiel: The City as Yahweh's Wife* (SBLDS 130; Atlanta: Scholars Press, 1992). On Ezek. 24:15–27, see pp. 140–41.

12. The root suggests an element of tenderness in the people's love for the temple.

13. Zimmerli, *Ezekiel 1*, 506.

14. For a thorough discussion of the issues and an argument for deriving *dōm* from *d-m-m* II, see Baruch A. Levine, "Sound, Silence, and the Phenomenology of Mourning in Biblical Israel," *JANES* 22 (1993): 89–106. For another thorough, but opposing, discussion, see Friebel, *Jeremiah's and Ezekiel's Sign-Acts*, 332–36.

15. Friebel, *Jeremiah's and Ezekiel's Sign-Acts*, 330n563. Friebel observes that some of the ritualized laments are paralinguistic, but unlike the groans permitted to Ezekiel here, they function within a context of meaning afforded by the ritual.

16. "Here, a more subtle distinction is suggested between sounds like groans and moaning, which are virtually involuntary, and the more formal and intentional acts that comprised mourning in ancient Israel, such as words of eulogy and those traditional formulas uttered while weeping (Jer. 22:18; 34:5), prescribed radical changes in attire, and the donning of a mask to cover the lower part of one's face" (Levine, "Silence, Sound, and the Phenomenology of Mourning," 100).

17. For extended discussion and biblical references to these practices, see Friebel, *Jeremiah's and Ezekiel's Sign-Acts*, 329–32. For a dissenting view, see Odell, "Genre and Persona," 195–217.

18. The NRSV makes this emendation based on the Vulgate and Targum, a dubious text-critical judgment. Since the same expression appears again in v. 22, even a supposed parallel with Hos. 9:4, "bread of mourners" (*'ônîm*), does not provide enough evidence to favor the emendation.

19. Friebel, *Jeremiah's and Ezekiel's Sign-Acts*, 331n577.

20. Cf. Ps. 38:6 (subject: wounds) and Isa. 34:4 (subject: the host of heaven). A similar usage to the one in question occurs in Lev. 26:39 (the people will "rot" in their iniquity).

21. Prov. 19:12; 20:2; 28:15; Isa 5:29; 5:30 (sea). Prov. 5:11 has the only human subject: "At the end of your life you will groan [*nāhamtā*], when your flesh and body are consumed." This, too, fits the context of physical decay evident in Ezek. 24.

22. The allegory of the corroded pot in the first part of chap. 24 in many ways parallels the sign-act of the second half of the chapter: Everything found in the pot

is eliminated, even its rust, yet the "corruption" remains in the pot. The allegory suggests that the pot, that is, Israel, can never be made clean, even after YHWH has "emptied" Israel of everything. The dynamic in our passage is similar: The people are "emptied" of their human responses to grief; they are reduced to a subhuman existence. The two processes of diminishment parallel each other. On the corroded pot, see Jacqueline E. Lapsley, *Can These Bones Live? The Problem of the Moral Self in the Book of Ezekiel* (BZAW 301; Berlin: Walter de Gruyter, 2000), 97–103.

23. Gary A. Anderson, *A Time to Mourn, A Time to Dance: The Expression of Grief and Joy in Israelite Religion* (University Park: Pennsylvania State University Press, 1991), 96.

24. Carol A. Newsom, *The Book of Job: A Contest of Moral Imaginations* (Oxford: Oxford University Press, 2003), 252–53.

25. For more on this, see Lapsley, *Can These Bones Live?* esp. 159–84.

26. I am thinking here of personal grief, but also corporate grief. The multitude of emotions emergent after 9/11 quickly found expression in ritualized displays (e.g., flag flying), but this often served to obscure deeper issues raised by the disaster.

27. Furthermore, the people are punished through their desire—that is, they loved the temple, and now they will experience the destruction of what they loved, so that its idolatrous nature can be exposed. Block explains: "Yahweh is determined to deliver a final blow to official and popular theology. So long as the temple stood in Jerusalem, the Judeans, including the exiles, continued to be hopeful. As a symbol of the divine patron's presence in the city, the temple guaranteed the nation's future. Ironically, the more the military crisis around Jerusalem intensified, the more desperately its inhabitants clung to what they considered to be the unconditional promises of God. Ezekiel hereby declares that Yahweh himself would put an end to such vain notions" (Block, *Book of Ezekiel*, 1:792).

28. Block rightly perceives Ezekiel's ultimate goal in the whole incident of the death of Ezekiel's wife: "In and through his inexplicable tragedy he is called on to point his compatriots away from the temple, the object of their affections, to God himself" (Block, *Book of Ezekiel*, 1:794).

29. John F. Kutsko, "Ezekiel's Anthropology and Its Ethical Implications," in Odell and Strong, *Book of Ezekiel*, 119–41, argues that the priestly notion of the *imago Dei* operates in Ezekiel's anthropology. It would be interesting, albeit outside the scope of this essay, to consider Kutsko's claim in relation to my own reading of Ezekiel's anthropology.

Chapter 9

"He Has Told You What Is Good"

Moral Formation in Micah

M. DANIEL CARROLL R.

Things that we experience often can be the driving force for how we read the Bible and where we go within its pages. In my case, living for fifteen years in Guatemala (1981–1996) during the time of the war there between the government and the coalition of guerrilla forces, with bloody conflicts also to the south in El Salvador and Nicaragua, generated a keen interest in the ethics of the prophets. Those years helped me to resonate in very palpable ways with the social, political, and military critiques of the Minor Prophets, as well as appreciate the powerful attraction of their hope for a day beyond the death and dying. But my time there also underscored for me that extensive structural change, which was (and still remains) urgent and necessary to be able to move away from the excesses of oppressive regimes and unjust economies, was not enough. The formal end of hostilities that came with the signing of the peace accords and the subsequent stumbling steps toward some semblance of democracy did not bring a significant change in the *moral climate* of our countries: corruption flourishes, suffering by the poor continues, and new forms of violence have appeared. What is missing is a different kind of sociocultural and ethical environment with a deep commitment to justice and peace. This deficiency has sparked my interest in the virtues and the importance of character.

103

Until the last few years, however, scholarly interest in prophetic ethics has usually concentrated its efforts in other directions. For example, research has tried to identify the possible theological traditions that informed the prophets' ethical discourse or to clarify the setting and specific target of their words with the aid of various social sciences. It has been the historical narratives and the Wisdom literature that have generated most of the study of the virtues in the Hebrew Bible. Happily, attention to issues of character in the prophets recently has begun to surface as well, both in broader treatises on Old Testament ethics as well as in several publications that deal more specifically with prophetic ethics.[1]

This essay will look at one particular Minor Prophet, the book of Micah. This is my first foray into Micah (most of my work has been in Amos), but its powerful moral message has drawn me inexorably into its pages. The discussion that follows is limited to 3:1–4:5 and 6:1–8 and uses the final form of the text.[2] My goal is to attempt to utilize insights from virtue ethics in order to reflect upon the moral messages of these two passages in new ways.

The Perversion of the "Good" (3:1–4:5)

A fundamental element of any virtue or character ethics is its articulation of the "good." The good is that supreme end (or *telos*) which should define and orient all existence at both individual and communal levels. It is in achieving this good that a person and a people best fulfill the purpose of what it means to be a human being. This good is community specific in that each community establishes for itself what the good is for its members and (ideally) tries to mold them in accordance with it. Its traditions explain the nature of human society and the meaning and purpose of life—all of which, in turn, point to the desirability and advantages of the good. This foundational and transcendent good to which all other finite goals (and goods) ultimately should point is not limited to some quantifiable material gain or emotional satisfaction. It is inseparable from the virtues—that is, those dispositions of character, habits of life, and emotional responses that one must possess to embody the good.[3] Lastly, this good should be modeled by exemplars, persons who best embody a commitment to the good and the requisite virtues.

At first glance, it might seem somewhat anachronistic to appeal to a technical philosophical term such as the "good" to analyze a prophetic text. The term, however, is an ancient one; it was a topic of Greek moral philosophy.[4] More importantly (and irrespective of its provenance), it can serve as a helpful heuristic conceptual tool to probe how the prophetic literature envisions the ethical ideal, which the people of God should flesh out in their day-to-day existence. The Hebrew term *ṭôb*, "good," does appear in several passages in the book of Micah,[5] and several components of this philosophical notion of the good actually do emerge in the two texts under consideration.

First, the term is used in the first oracle of 3:1–4:5—that is, in 3:1–4, which denounces the leadership of the nation.[6] Micah 3:2a describes these leaders as "haters of good and lovers of evil." The "good" here is not defined explicitly in any systematic fashion, but its general intent is made clearer through a constellation of images and ideas throughout this section of the book. To begin with, we can appreciate what the good is by recognizing what it is not. This line contrasts the good with "evil,"[7] which then is pictured in a strikingly graphic—and shocking—manner as dismembering and cannibalizing the people (3:2b–3).[8] This evil, then, is in no way a disinterested or dispassionate treatment of those without power or prestige; rather, it is deliberate and destructive cruelty. This conscious involvement in evil is repeated (although again without concrete particulars) in the last clause of the oracle: "They have practiced evil deeds" (3:4b).[9] YHWH refuses to respond to the prayers of this kind of people.

This feature of violence against the less fortunate runs like a thread through the next two oracles of chapter three (3:5–8, 9–12) as well. On the one hand, the prophets "sanctify war" (Heb. *qidd^ešû milḥāmâ*; "declare war" NRSV) against those who do not give them remuneration for their message of (ironically) peace (3:5b).[10] On the other hand, the leaders of verse 2 surface again in 3:9–10 as those who have built the capital "with blood"—another vivid expression that can be interpreted as describing how some prosper, personally and institutionally, at the expense of others.[11] McKane describes them thus: "The possession of power, access to wealth, the thirst for prestige and self-advertisement, has changed them into monsters emptied of moral sense."[12] To begin with, then, the implication is that the good is unlike this merciless evil that runs roughshod over the powerless.

Second, the "good" in 3:2 is juxtaposed to "justice" (Heb. *mišpāṭ*; 3:1b). In the Hebrew Bible *mišpāṭ* can refer to the judicial process, to the laws and decisions of that process, as well as to the virtue of justice; context determines its particular sense in any given passage. In philosophical ethics, the essence of justice is often defined as *suum cuique*, "to each his due."[13] From this perspective, the virtue of justice would be that consistent endeavor to grant to each person what is rightfully theirs; eventually this should find tangible expression in equitable socioeconomic, legal, and political relationships. While this virtue at one level could be evaluated by external criteria, such as fulfilling the laws of the land, the passion for equity is not reducible simply to legality. One can be just in a strictly legal sense without having a just character.

In the case of this section in Micah, the leaders fail on the counts of legality and character (and both are in view). They do not "know" justice (3:1b), and their abhorrence of it is demonstrated in the manipulation of the judicial process, where verdicts are bought and sold for bribes (3:9–11; cf. 7:3). There is little pretense of legality here, and any vestige of the virtue of justice is absent. The repetition of "rulers" and "chiefs," along with the verb "hate" in verse 9b (Heb. *t'b*), connects it back to verses 1 and 2 and gives the vagueness of that description of evil some specificity. In the prophet's mind, the good must include justice within the legal system and as a virtue.

Alisdair MacIntyre has stressed that societies often witness conflict between competing understandings of justice. Although his narrative of the history of moral thought expresses his belief that contemporary Western societies have arrived at a state of moral incoherence, his words are apropos to the situation described in the Micah text:

> So theories of justice and practical rationality confront us as aspects of tradi- , tions, allegiance to which requires the living out of some more or less system-atically embodied form of human life, each with its own specific modes of social relationship, each with its own canons of interpretation and explanation in respect of the behavior of others, each with its own evaluative practices.[14]

The prophet is battling the different understanding of the nature and practice of justice of the leaders of Judah. They loathe the justice of God, and "all that is straight they pervert" (3:9b). Their justice is controlled, self-serving, and oppres-sive, but one can suppose that, if confronted, they would defend their system with some sort of appeal to historical precedent, the privileges of their social sta-tion, or the like. In an earlier passage, they are surprised and protest the reversal of that twisted process; they now are the victims of "poetic justice" (both legally and rhetorically, 2:4). Clearly, in their minds "justice" has not been served! In chapter 3 they do not see why YHWH might not defend them. Surely, Jerusalem, the city that they have built and control, is safe in his hands (3:11c; cf. 3:4)!

Third, the good is inseparable from the inner person. It is something one either loves or hates (3:2a). The good, in other words, is not an abstract moral principle.[15] In this section of Micah, those who despise it are motivated by greed. The fulfillment of political, social, and sacral tasks is commercialized (note the variety of leadership spheres mentioned in 3:11), and everything and everybody has a price (3:5, 11). As a consequence, life is cheap; human beings are dispens-able commodities to be consumed to further other ends (3:2b–3, 5b, 10).

In sharp contrast to this attitude and the actions of the nation's leaders stands the prophet in 3:8.[16] The good ideally should be embodied in the life of exem-plars, and the prophet is presented as such in this verse. Micah has "power," but this comes from YHWH and not from his social position. He does not only sup-port or defend justice; he is *filled* with justice. It is part of who he is, and his "might" is committed to this end. How different this is from all of those he has singled out, those (especially the other prophets and the priests) who should have reflected the standards of the God of Israel but who abuse justice and dedicate themselves to violently taking advantage of others![17] Moreover, unlike those prophets, who sell their words and who thus will be disgraced by profound dark-ness and the silence of God (3:5–7; cf. 2:6–11), he is filled with the very spirit of YHWH.[18] Here and elsewhere the book suggests a conflict between Micah and other prophets (2:6–11; 7:6, 10).[19] In other words, this is no empty boasting by a demagogue; rather, these are the words of someone who has had the courage (a concomitant virtue of justice) to denounce the injustice and the unjust. His demand for justice is more than posturing; it is Micah's mission.

If we return to the idea that virtues have an affective component, we can appre-ciate the rhetoric of this section in a new light. Gilman explains how certain "empathetic emotions" comprise an important dimension of the virtue of justice.[20] He lists the sense of responsibility, the centrality of memory, indignant anger, and gratitude. Here we focus on anger. An anger appropriate to justice is moral outrage. This sentiment could be driving the powerful descriptions of the violence of the nation's leaders. The word pictures of cannibalism and the shedding of blood could be more than stylistic techniques designed to try to shock the listener/reader; they very well might reflect the deep indignation that the prophet feels toward the perpetrators of injustice and his profound commitment to defend its victims.[21]

But anger can also be accompanied by hope—more specifically, the hope for redemption and the definitive reversal of the wrong.[22] This kind of hope fits well into how this section develops. The contrast in *character* in 3:1–12 is followed by a contrast in *context* in the opening oracle of the following chapter (4:1–5). The juxtaposition of this oracle with 3:9–12, therefore, is fitting. The future will be the inverse of the present.[23] The devastated "height" of 3:12 will be established as "the head of the mountains" (4:1). Unlike what the country was now experiencing, where Jerusalem is distinguished by legal compromise and stands condemned, in "the last days" Zion will be a center for justice (not only for Judah, but for the nations as well). Other peoples will join the pilgrimage to the temple in order to learn the basis and meaning of a different kind of existence illuminated by the *tôrâ* of God (4:1–2). In addition, instead of the ongoing internal violence of the leaders and the imminent violence of YHWH's judgment, that future time will be marked by the absence of armed conflict (here again, not only for Judah but for all nations), because of the supreme and final jurisdiction of YHWH.[24] The weapons of war will be transformed into agricultural tools, and the constant fear of military aggression will be replaced by the experience of abundance and security (4:3–4). The mouth of YHWH makes this promise sure (4:4b).

What might be the moral impact of this oracle? How might it add to this reflection on the good? To begin with, like Micah the exemplar, the contrast presented in this vision is an indictment of the leadership—of who they are (enemies of the good) and of what Jerusalem has become under them (a place where the good is violated). But this vision does more than highlight evil in a new way; it also functions as a call to live a life in the present that is dedicated to the good (4:5). It has been suggested that verse 5 was penned by someone who was skeptical of the utopia of 4:1–4 and wanted to bring Judah back to an awareness of everyday tasks.[25] My reading argues just the opposite. However other peoples might live ("walk"), this verse says, those who trust in the promise will live differently: "we will walk in the name of YHWH our God forever and ever"—that is, they would live in accordance with the instruction and judgments of God, both now and into that future era.

For those who suffer in the present, these alternative images of reality can empower them to endure and to reorient their perceptions of the cruelties and the apparent inevitableness of actual social existence. Reality is reimagined, and this hope for a new kind of moral world is nurtured (4:4a).[26] This picture of agricultural tranquility and of property that has not been violated ("under *his own*"), and the absence of fear—and thus of war—envisions something very different from the present. That more idyllic time will not be a false prosperity for a few (built on the backs of the many) that will disintegrate once its unfair foundation is exposed (cf. 1 Kgs. 5:5 [Eng. 4:25]; 12:4), nor will it come in the form of a taunt or manipulative promise (cf. 2 Kgs. 18:31; Isa. 36:16). This comes as a sure word from the mouth of God (4:4b).

Finally, in addition to the clarification of the good by its opposite, its connection with justice and the role of virtues for its embodiment, one final element merits mention: the cult. The temple and ritual are part of the background of the message of chapter 3 in the indictment of religious functionaries, such as the prophets (3:5–6, 11; who perhaps are connected with the sanctuary), the priests (3:11) and others (3:7), and the announcement of the destruction of Zion in 3:12. One wonders, too, if the "blood" of 3:10 might be an ironic reference to the blood of the sacrifices in the temple, even as it is an indictment of the cruelty of the leaders.[27] Whereas Zion should be the center of proper sacrifices of animals, it has devolved into the sacrifice of the powerless. The second phrase of 3:10 ("and Jerusalem with iniquity") could be rhetorically designed to bring the reader/ listener up short, much in the same way that Amos would say, "Go to Bethel . . . and sin[!]; go to Gilgal and . . . sin yet more[!]" (Amos 4:4). The cult is more prominent, of course, in the vision of 4:1–5, where the temple is mentioned twice ("the house of YHWH," v. 1; "the house of the God of Jacob," v. 2).[28]

It is possible to explore the importance of the sanctuary and ritual for our ethical focus in at least three ways. To begin with, cultural anthropology has demonstrated the centrality of religion for reflecting and nurturing a worldview and its corresponding sociopolitical system. Balentine, for example, appeals to the work of anthropologists like Geertz and the Old Testament studies of Brueggemann and Gorman to establish his theoretical context for analyzing the worship prescribed in the Torah.[29] These studies recognize that worship can serve as rituals of maintenance of the status quo and thus as religious instruments of social control. The liturgies, periodic festivals, multiple ceremonies, and religious personnel all can legitimate a social reality. This can be a positive or negative function, depending on what that social construct is really like. Ideally, the cult should call the people of God to reflect the moral design of creation and remind them of the ethical demands of the covenant that must govern all the spheres of life.[30]

In addition, the cult can provide and nurture a vision of the present different from that of other dominant destructive worldviews, which either might be imposed on the people of God from the outside by another nation or perpetuated by a certain sector (or sectors) within the community. The latter is what Micah denounces here. He witnesses a cult that renders to those in power what they desire to hear. The prophetic word and priestly sacrifices and pronouncements respond to bribes; those guilty of oppression are not condemned, and the nation is not warned. The cult predicted in 4:1–4, however, will sustain another kind of reality. In other words, the prophetic hope is both moral and cultic. It must be so, since these two dimensions of Israel's social life are inseparable. To read 4:5 in this light would suggest that "to walk in the name of the LORD" perhaps could be related to that pilgrimage to Zion to learn the ways of God.

Virtue ethics can add yet another element to this brief consideration of the cult. From this perspective, worship can be considered to be a "practice." A practice is a "coherent and complex form of socially established cooperative activity" that can help the various (internal and external) goods of the individual and of the community be achieved.[31] Since these goods are inseparable from the virtues, it is an activity through which the virtues should be evoked, modeled, and extended for both the individual and the community. That is, one can neither understand nor possess the virtues apart from practices, and practices cannot serve the realization of the good without the virtues. Several other points are pertinent. First, in light of the connections to the virtues and the good, these practices are interrelated and interdependent within the social fabric of any society. Second, practices can be assessed by their impact on character and the life of the community. Last, because practices are organized social activities, they also are sustained by corresponding social institutions.

It is not difficult to see how the cult fits into this theoretical framework. It is a communal activity that should provide the opportunity for encouraging the embodiment of the virtues—such as mercy and justice—for sustaining the common good of all the people of God. The temple precinct and personnel, of course, would be the institutional context for the practice of worship. In the prophet's mind, the cult had compromised the integrity of the worship of YHWH. The 'goods internal to the practice' of worship had been subverted through the greed of the religious functionaries, and those attitudes and actions that could promote the good (especially the welfare of the marginalized) beyond the walls of the sanctuary had been opposed to the gain of a certain part of the population.[32] This point underscores the relationship between practices: In this case, the negative impact of the practice of worship on other fundamental practices, such as those connected to the rural families of ancient Judah (farming, parenting, household activities) and the administration of justice at the town gates. For example, think for a moment on the effect of debt and unjust economic practices on family life in the countryside, where the vast majority lived: changing or forfeiting crops to pay back loans, debt slavery of family members (particularly children) with the resulting emotional loss and the pragmatic redistribution of daily tasks, or even the taking away of property inherited across generations.

The very institution that should have been the beacon of virtue had become its graveyard. Again, an observation by MacIntyre is a fitting comment for what is found in the text, even though it is directed at another time and place:

> Practices are often distorted by their modes of institutionalization, when irrelevant considerations relating to money, power and status are allowed to invade the practice. The relationships of those within the practice to each other or to those in the wider community may be informed not by that of justice which assigns to each what is her or his due, in virtue of her or his

contribution and place in the practice and in the community, but by externally based judgments deriving from unrecognized prejudice.[33]

What occurs in the practice of worship at the sanctuary is a wicked distortion, which profoundly impacts the broader social fabric. One day, Micah says, all of this will be replaced by a renewed Zion.

These insights from cultural anthropology and virtue ethics call into question some traditional scholarship that has bifurcated the prophets and their message of social justice from the cult. The classic proposal of an "ethical monotheism" for the eighth-century prophets would appear to misunderstand the relevance—and power—of ritual and ceremony for the socioethical construction of reality, especially in religious cultures. An appreciation of the importance of the cult for social self-understanding and social structures can help explain the vehemence with which the prophetics denounced the worship of their day.

In sum, the ethical perspective that focuses on character and the virtues can illuminate some of the dimensions of the demanding messages of the prophets. The concept of the "good" underscores the importance of analyzing the moral ideal(s) that the community should have sought to embody, the dispositions and structures that this required, and the role of key social practices (such as worship) in the realization (or frustration) of the good. We now turn to Micah 6:1–8, to see how these insights might be further developed.

What God Requires: The "Good" and the Liturgy (6:1–6)

Form-critical scholars have debated what might be the genre or combination of genres of these verses.[34] The opening lines announce that YHWH is contending (*rîb*) with his people (vv. 1–2). The passage then recounts stellar events in the nation's historical tradition (vv. 3–5) and concludes with what some have labeled an entrance liturgy (vv. 6–7; cf. Ps. 15, 24) and a wisdom-type saying (v. 8; cf. Qoh. 6:12). These three pericopes are interconnected in several ways. The entire section deals with what YHWH demands of his people. There is also shared vocabulary, in particular "his/my people" (vv. 2, 5) and the interrogative "what" (vv. 3, 5, 6, 8). The passage, then, interweaves genres, but this creative and unified conglomeration can have great rhetorical effect, as it draws in the reader/listener through the call to account, the posing of questions, and the move to a climax of a lesson for life.

Several connections also exist between these verses and 3:1–4:5. For example, there are lexical and conceptual links: the command to "hear" (*šimᶜû-nāʾ*) reappears (6:1; cf. 3:1, 9), as do the notion of walking in the ways of God (6:8; cf. 4:2, 5), the cult (6:6–7; cf. 3:11–4:5), the pursuit of justice (6:8; although in 4:2–3 this is a future hope that is extended to all nations), and the importance of the good (6:8; cf. 3:2). So, although the literary strategy is different, there is some continuity with the concerns of the earlier section. We will again use character ethics in this brief consideration of 6:1–8 by looking at three items: the function of narrative (vv. 4–5), the notion of the good (v. 8), and the cult as a practice (vv. 6–8).

First we turn to the recital of YHWH's deeds on behalf of his people in 6:4–5. The events that are mentioned here (from the exodus through to the entrance into the land) serve to counter the implied complaint by Israel in verse 3 of divine neglect ("My people, what have I done to you? And [in] what have I wearied you?"). From the point of view of character ethics, narratives have particular moral relevance.[35] The narratives of a community play an important part in establishing its identity. They explain where the community has come from and what it has come through, and they can direct that community as to how it should live to extend that narrative into the future. To change these foundational narratives, or deny them, suppress them, use them in other ways, or simply forget them would alter that community's identity. The purpose of this retelling of the history of the people is that they might "know the righteous acts of YHWH" (da'at ṣidqôt yhwh, 6:5c). For them to remember their story would be to see the folly of their attitudes; to contemplate the past could make them consider how they might act redemptively toward one another in the present and thus emulate within the community what God had done for them in their history. To not take hold of these narratives is to become something other than they were called to be.

In other words, narratives not only can ground identity; they also clarify accountability. Narratives present the roles and mutual obligations that are consistent with the tradition. They offer examples of appropriate as well as negative behavior and attitudes (note in these verses the mention of various individuals) and thereby function as a historical framework for evaluating community life in the present. These sorts of narratives, though, are more than theoretical reference points; they are to be embodied in the practices of the community. This takes us to the second point.

Narratives have a beginning, a middle, and an end. Throughout the book the prophet announces what the end, the future, will bring: restoration beyond the judgment. We saw this in 3:1–4:5. Micah 6:4–5 provides the beginning, as it were, to that story line; the present state of affairs would be the middle. Narratives do lay out this sort of ordered sequence, but ultimately this is designed to direct the community to reflect upon the *telos* of their existence, the good. They portray the nature and meaning of that good and so help its embodiment. It may not be a surprise, then, that we hear that "he has *told* you what is good" (6:8a). What YHWH has "told" them could be a reference to the requirements of the Torah and/or the messages of other prophets (cf. 3:8b), but in context might it not also include the traditions of his dealings with them—those righteous acts of 6:4–5—that are cited just a few verses earlier?[36] If so, then once more the people are called to return to their narratives and learn about a life that would please God.

The verse declares that the good is something that the people already should know.[37] Therefore, they are beyond excuse. It is what YHWH continually seeks[38] from each one that would worship him at the sanctuary.[39] In addition to what they have been told previously about the good, here it is defined specifically by three phrases loaded with ethical implications: to do justice, to love *ḥesed*, and to have a life characterized ("to walk") by an attitude of humility.[40] This is a wonderful combination of social-moral demands. It includes definite actions on behalf of others, as well as inner dispositions before God and the community. Once again, as in 3:1–4:5, the prophet points to the ideal of important virtues for community life.[41]

Finally, as YHWH is about to begin the recounting of his "righteous acts," he challenges his people to answer him, to explain their attitude (6:3). The series of questions in verses 6–7 functions literarily as their response to him.[42] With God just having voiced his displeasure, these questions follow quite naturally: First, how can I "approach" YHWH after this estrangement? Second, how might I "bow down" before him to demonstrate obeisance and loyalty, and what is it that I might give to "please" him? It often is taken for granted that these questions reflect the voice of one (whether truly or hypothetically) who sincerely recognizes his or her sin (*piš'î, ḥaṭṭ'at napšî*, v. 7b) and anxiously desires reconciliation with YHWH. From this perspective, the worshiper poses these questions in order to receive a priestly orientation and then suggests a series of offerings in order of increasing extravagance, climaxing with the desperate proposal to present the firstborn as a sacrifice.

To put these verses against the religious backdrop of the rest of the book, however, renders a different reading. Our earlier passage, 3:1–4:5, underscored the celebration of an unacceptable kind of cult that did not comprehend (or that had rejected) the requirements of the virtues that worship was to inculcate. Prophetic condemnation of the cult appears elsewhere in the book too (e.g., 1:5–7; 2:6–8, 11; 5:10–14). Consequently, it makes more sense to interpret these questions as yet another instance of the people's misconceptions of the nature of worship and another example of mouthing words that are self-condemning (cf. 2:4, 6, 11; 3:11; 7:10).[43] Even as the nation's leaders (including its religious leaders) could be bought off, might not YHWH himself be bought off with the delicacy of year-old calves and offerings of huge proportions (cf. 1 Kgs. 8:5, 62–66)? The answer to the rhetorical questions, therefore, would not be "no"—which is the answer of the modern reader, who already knows the proper response—but rather a resounding "yes!" A person who believes that God can be pacified and his anger assuaged with gifts would say "yes" to every question, each one raising the stakes even higher to the most costly sacrifice of all. YHWH would be very pleased![44]

If this is correct, then what follows in verse 8 is not a wise word of priestly guidance. Rather, it comes as a stinging rebuke. It serves as a transition to the denunciations and announcement of judgment in the next passage (6:9–16) and thereby is consistent with the other prophetic-divine words in the book. What is the implication of this reprimand? Does the sharp contrast that 6:8 makes with the previous two verses argue that morality is the acceptable alternative to the cult?[45] To hold that view returns us to the "ethical monotheism" that was demonstrated to be inadequate in 3:1–4:4. If the cult is interpreted within the framework of character ethics as a practice, then 6:8 is not to be set over against the cult but instead is designed to reemphasize precisely what the cult is designed to do: promote the good and nurture the virtues. The cult is where the people are to be taught justice, mercy, and humility and learn about the God who seeks such qualities from the nation. But the present worship at the cult has misconceived God and, unavoidably then, has misconstrued what it is that he requires of them in their daily life together and before him. The dialogue on the cult in 6:6–7, therefore, like the narratives alluded to in 6:3–5, points to the good.

Conclusion

The goal of this essay has been to demonstrate how the perspective of character or virtue ethics can provide helpful insights into the ethical message of the book of Micah. The discussion has revolved around the concept of the good—how it is defined and how it is to be related to the cult. My reading of 3:1–4:4 and 6:1–8 has tried to show that a variety of literary genres and rhetorical strategies are used to communicate what is that good which YHWH wants embodied among his people. The good requires certain virtues that are to be lived out (especially in deeds of justice) within the community; these virtues are central to the practice of worship, which in turn is to solidify and extend the good.

This is but an initial analysis of just two sections of this prophetic text. Some scholars question some aspects of the picture of God that is presented here and elsewhere in the book, specifically as it relates to the nature of divine judgment.[46] This necessary and difficult sort of reflection moves into the complex topics of the nature of biblical language about God in the prophetic literature and how it might be conceived within a character ethics approach, issues that lie beyond the purview of this essay.[47]

Nevertheless, many of the words of the prophet Micah continue to endure as important ethical markers for those who try to do justice, to love ḥesed, and to walk humbly before YHWH. They can sensitize us to the plight of the oppressed and help us unmask liturgies that work against the good. Even those who are critical of particular passages can still sound an appreciative word for the prophet's contribution to ethical reflection.[48]

Notes

1. Such broader works include Bruce C. Birch, *Let Justice Roll Down: The Old Testament, Ethics, and Christian Life* (Louisville, KY: Westminster/John Knox, 1991), 240–79; and Waldemar Janzen, *Old Testament Ethics: A Paradigmatic Approach* (Louisville, KY: Westminster John Knox, 1994), 154–78. On prophetic ethics specifically, see, e.g., Jacqueline E. Lapsley, *"Can These Bones Live?" The Problem of the Moral Self in the Book of Ezekiel* (BZAW 301; Berlin: Walter de Gruyter, 2000); M. Daniel Carroll R., "Seeking the Virtues among the Prophets: The Book of Amos as a Test Case," *ExAud* 17 (2001): 77–96.
2. For a recent survey of views regarding the authenticity and history of composition of the book, see Jan A. Wagenar, *Judgment and Salvation: The Composition and Redaction of Micah 2–5* (VTSup 85; Leiden: Brill, 2001), 3–45 (Wagenar

opts for a redactional history approach). For the purposes of this essay, I appeal to Mignon Jacobs's notion of the "cohesiveness" of the text, which is based on its "conceptuality." She argues that the book holds together in various degrees through common themes and vocabulary and that these links can be exploited to appreciate an overarching message (Mignon R. Jacobs, *The Conceptual Coherence of the Book of Micah* [JSOTSup 322; Sheffield: Sheffield Academic Press, 2001]). Others, of course, will argue for authenticity on historical grounds. Another recent synchronic reading is David Gerald Hagstrom, *The Coherence of the Book of Micah: A Literary Analysis* (SBLDS 89; Atlanta: Scholars Press, 1988). Note the comments by Francis I. Andersen and David Noel Freedman in *Micah* (AB 24E; Garden City, NY: Doubleday, 2000), 16–29. Contrast this with J. David Pleins, who attempts to isolate the ethical messages of the A, B, and C layers of Micah (*The Social Visions of the Hebrew Bible: A Theological Introduction* [Louisville, KY: Westminster John Knox, 2001], 381–90). I hold in abeyance matters of social and historical background (which would be related to the Assyrian crises of the eighth century, especially the siege of Jerusalem by Sennacherib in 701 BCE). My references to the "prophet Micah" are to the persona in the text. Mine is an initial attempt to begin to understand the ethical message of the book; it is suggestive, and in no way exhaustive. Cf. M. Daniel Carroll R., *Contexts for Amos: Prophetic Poetics in Latin American Perspective* (JSOTSup 132; Sheffield: Sheffield Academic Press, 1992), 149–56; Carol J. Dempsey, "Micah 2–3: Literary Artistry, Ethical Message, and Some Considerations about the Image of YHWH and Micah," *JSOT* 85 (1999): 117–28.

3. Treatises on virtue ethics do not always treat the emotions in any detail. Note, however, James E. Gilman, *Fidelity of the Heart: An Ethic of Christian Virtue* (Oxford: Oxford University Press, 2001).

4. Note, e.g., Aristotle, *The Ethics of Aristotle: The Nicomachean Ethics* (rev. ed.; trans. J. A. K. Thomson; London: Penguin, 1976). Different communities define the good in different ways. For Aristotle, it was "happiness" (63–90). Cf. Alisdair MacIntyre, *After Virtue: A Study in Moral Theory* (2nd ed., Notre Dame, IN: University of Notre Dame Press, 1985).

5. See 1:12, 3:2, 6:8, and 7:4; the verbal root (Heb. *yāṭab*) is used in 2:7 and 7:3. The noun (e.g., Isa. 5:20; 7:15–16; Amos 5:14–15; Hos. 8:3) and verb are not uncommon in the eighth-century prophets. I am not suggesting that the Hebrew term is equivalent to the Greek one, but it is interesting that both cultures/languages have a similar broad ethical term to express important ethical demands.

6. Scholars debate the identity of the leaders and whether in context "heads" and "rulers" are parallel terms or refer to two different groups. Other issues include whether these are government officials, local elders, or judges; whether they include the person of the king; and whether the term "rulers" (Heb. *qʿṣînîm*) here refers to military commanders (cf. Josh. 10:24; Judg. 11:6, 11). In light of the Jerusalem context and the parallel in 3:9, it seems best to consider the "rulers" to be public authorities who make policies and in some way influence the judicial system. For an extended discussion, see William McKane, *The Book of Micah: Introduction and Commentary* (Edinburgh: T. & T. Clark, 1998), 98–102. Those who understand the *qʿṣînîm* to be a reference to military leaders relate these oracles to the siege of Jerusalem (e.g., Charles S. Shaw, *The Speeches of Micah: A Rhetorical-Historical Analysis* [JSOTSup 145; Sheffield: Sheffield Academic Press, 1993], 109–11; Marvin A. Sweeney, *The Twelve Prophets* [Berit Olam; Collegeville, MN: Michael Glazier, 2000], 2: 369).

7. Heb. *rāʿ* (*qʿrê*); also in 1:12; 2:1; 7:3; *rāʿâ* appears in 2:3; 3:11 (in 3:2 as *kʿtîb*).

8. Pedro Jaramillo Rivas calls this pericope "una de las denuncias más crudas de la literatura profética" in *La injusticia y la opresión en el lenguaje figurado de los*

profetas (Institución San Jerónimo 26; Navarra: Verbo Divino, 1992), 250. His exposition appears on pp. 235–51.

9. The term "deeds" (*maʿălālîm*) in some cases can describe actions that are inherently evil (e.g., Gen. 44:15; Exod. 23:24; Isa. 59:6; Hag. 2:14). The choice of imagery here could imply that they were done by violent means (i.e., a degree of a literalness to the metaphor). The evil is described in 2:1–2 as seizing the property (and, thereby, the livelihood) of others. The verbs *gzl* (3:2b; 2:2a) and *pšt* (3:3a; 2:8b) also serve to connect this pericope with chap. 2.

10. These prophets are described as "the ones biting with their teeth." This echoes vv. 2b–3 and connects the ethical character of these spokespersons of God with the leaders of the first oracle.

11. It is more appropriate to link the meaning of "who build Zion with blood" with the earlier metaphorical depictions of the violence of oppression than to seek a literal referent (cf. e.g., Andersen and Freedman, *Micah*, 383; Jaramillo Rivas, *La injusticia y la oppression*, 256–64). Andersen and Freedman posit an allusion to human sacrifice and connect the phrase to 6:7 (*Micah*, 382–83). In addition, the participle in v. 10 ("build") is singular, although most versions render it as a plural. Is the singular a collective, or is it a reference to a specific individual, like the king? Some also specify the historical background of these words (e.g., many connect it with Hezekiah's building of defenses before the siege of Sennacherib). Lastly, some turn to passages like this one to suggest that for the prophet there was a fundamental opposition between the countryside (the place of origin of the prophet Micah) and urban culture (e.g., Pleins, *Social Visions of the Hebrew Bible*, 389–90), but the prophetic critique does not seem to be overly determined by this. Also note n. 27 below.

12. McKane, *Book of Micah*, 112.

13. Note the discussion in Aristotle, *Ethics*, 171–202. Cf. André Comte-Sponville, *A Small Treatise on the Great Virtues: The Uses of Philosophy in Everyday Life* (trans. C. Temerson; New York: Henry Holt, 2001), 60–85. Justice can be catalogued as *procedural* (the rules to be followed in legal disputes) and *substantive*. Some differentiate between *reciprocal* (between individuals), *distributive* (by which society acts in a proper manner to individuals), and *legal* (that to which all ideally adhere).

14. Alisdair MacIntyre, *Whose Justice? Whose Rationality?* (Notre Dame, IN: University of Notre Dame Press, 1988), 391.

15. In his discussion on Micah, José Luis Sicre lists passages from Proverbs that describe what YHWH detests—things that have to do with the legal process and improper business practices. See Sicre, *"Con los pobres de la tierra": La injusticia social en los profetas de Israel* (Madrid: Cristiandad, 1984), 288–89.

16. The contrast is highlighted syntactically by the use of the strong adversative *ʾûlām* and the personal pronoun. This verse appears in the oracle against other prophets (3:5–8), but lexical and conceptual connections clearly link it to 3:1–4 and 9–12 as well.

17. Ironically (and in my mind contrary to the thrust of the book), George V. Pixley argues that Micah called on peasants to stage an armed revolt against the cities and their governors ("Micah—A Revolutionary," in *The Bible and the Politics of Exegesis: Essays in Honor of Norman K. Gottwald on His Sixty-Fifth Birthday* [ed. D. Jobling et al.; Cleveland: Pilgrim, 1991], 53–60).

18. The awkward syntax of the phrase need not be an argument for its deletion (see *BHS*) but rather could be a literary emphasis on the spirit of YHWH as the source of the prophet's character and actions. Note McKane's striking turn of phrase: "The seers and diviners will be discomfited and demoralized (v. 7), the elaborate sham of their pose destroyed by the relentlessness of truth. This

exposure will produce signs of mourning, a mourning that the coziness of a well-rehearsed fraud has given place to a comfortless reality" (McKane, *Book of Micah*, 107). In the ancient Near East prophets often went through training and were remunerated; here the issue is the sense of a betrayal of YHWH's true message to his people by these prophets, not, I believe, the reception of payment per se (cf. Andersen and Freedman, *Micah*, 364–67).

19. Some have argued that 2:12–13 also comes from the mouth of false prophets. For a survey of views, see McKane, *Micah*, 92–94.

20. Gilman, *Virtue of the Heart*, 102–31.

21. Several passages express the emotions of the prophet vis-à-vis what he sees and experiences (e.g., 1:8; 7:1–7, 8–10). It is impossible to know how accurate these descriptions are, but they clearly are a reflection of a deeply felt point of view.

22. Gilman, *Virtue of the Heart*, 115–17.

23. At the level of sources, this pericope could very well be an insertion, not least because of its relationship to Isa. 2:2–4. At the literary (and, some might say, redactional) and ideational levels, however, the connections with chap. 3 are explicit and very intentional. Marvin A. Sweeney offers a helpful discussion of this passage's literary connections with the surrounding material in "Micah's Debate with Isaiah," *JSOT* 93 (2001): 111–24, although I am not convinced by his historical reconstruction.

24. We learn from other passages that this vision of peace centered at Jerusalem probably involved the return of dominion under a Davidic king, characterized by the end of hostilities both within and beyond the borders of Judah (4:8, 13; 5:1–8 [Eng. 5:2–9]; 7:11–17). See J. J. M. Roberts, "Zion in the Theology of the Davidic-Solomonic Empire," in *Studies in the Period of David and Solomon and Other Essays* (ed. T. Ishida; Winona Lake, IN: Eisenbrauns, 1982), 83–108. James L. Mays comments that this is not a vision of "a world subject in humiliation to a triumphant Israel. The nations bring their crises to YHWH. . . . They are not dominated and incorporated in a power structure, but helped and led to a new policy that makes for life" (Mays, *Micah* [OTL; Philadelphia: Westminster, 1976], 98–99). This is the very kind of perspective that some now question.

25. McKane, *Book of Micah*, 126.

26. Note, e.g., Walter Brueggemann, *Theology of the Old Testament: Testimony, Dispute, Advocacy* (Minneapolis: Fortress, 1997), 625–49. This has long been his argument in other publications as well. See also his "Vine and Fig Tree: A Case Study in Imagination and Criticism," *CBQ* 43 (1981): 188–204.

27. Sweeney, *Twelve Prophets*, 2:374. This possible double meaning of blood is similar to the indictment of Isa. 1:11, 15–18, where the cult and social ethics also are intertwined. Andersen and Freedman speculate that the singular participle ("he who builds") could refer to a specific individual, King Ahaz, and the "bloods" to the possible sacrifice of his sons (2 Kgs. 16:3; cf. 1 Kgs. 16:34) (Anderson and Freedman, *Micah*, 382–83).

28. Some even suggest that 4:1–4 is some sort of cultic oracle.

29. Samuel E. Balentine, *The Torah's Vision of Worship* (OBT; Minneapolis: Fortress, 1999); Frank H. Gorman Jr., *The Ideology of Ritual: Space, Time, and Status in Priestly Theology* (JSOTSup 91; Sheffield: JSOT Press, 1990). Cf. Walter Brueggemann, *Israel's Praises: Doxology against Idolatry and Ideology* (Philadelphia: Fortress, 1989); M. Daniel Carroll R., "Reexamining Popular Religion: Issues of Definition and Sources: Insights from Interpretive Anthropology," in *Rethinking Contexts, Rereading Texts: Contributions from the Social Sciences to Biblical Interpretation* (ed. Carroll R.; JSOTSup 299; Sheffield: Sheffield Academic Press, 2000), 146–67 (154–57).

30. In addition to Gorman and Balentine, see William P. Brown, *The Ethos of the Cosmos: The Genesis of Moral Imagination in the Bible* (Grand Rapids: Eerdmans, 1999).

31. Note, e.g., James Wm. McClendon Jr., *Systematic Theology*, vol. 1, *Ethics* (Nashville: Abingdon, 1986), 159–86; Jonathan R. Wilson, *Gospel Virtues: Practicing Faith, Hope, and Love in Uncertain Times* (Downers Grove, IL: Inter-Varsity, 1998), 119–39. Both appeal to MacIntyre, *After Virtue*, 181–203 (the phrase quoted here is taken from his oft-cited definition on p. 187); cf. MacIntyre, "A Partial Response to My Critics," in *After MacIntyre: Critical Perspectives on the Work of Alisdair MacIntyre* (ed. J. Horton and S. Mendus; Notre Dame, IN: University of Notre Dame Press, 1994), 283–304 (284–90).

32. These might include, e.g., training in the skills of the worshipers for properly fulfilling the ceremonial requirements, the attitudes that were designed to be fostered in worship (such as reverence, humility, compassion), and ethical actions toward others (giving to the periodic tithes for the poor, including resident aliens, widows, and orphans in the celebrations, etc.) in the worship itself and beyond.

33. MacIntyre, "Partial Response to My Critics," 289.

34. For recent surveys and discussion, see Ehud Ben Zvi, *Micah* (FOTL 21B; Grand Rapids: Eerdmans, 2000), 143–44, 149–52; and Andersen and Freedman, *Micah*, 507–11. In the past this passage often was taken as an example of a "covenant lawsuit." The very existence of such a genre, whatever its possible origin, is now being questioned. See, e.g., Dwight R. Daniels, "Is There a 'Prophetic Lawsuit' Genre?" *ZAW* 99, no. 3 (1987): 339–60.

35. See MacIntyre, *After Virtue*, 204–25. His *Whose Justice? Which Rationality?* develops further the notion of the impact of the narratives and histories of traditions on ethics, in particular in regard to justice. Cf. Gilman, *Fidelity of the Heart*, 27–30, 107–12.

36. Hans Walter Wolff also observes this in his *Micah: A Commentary* (CC; trans. G. Stansell; Minneapolis: Augsburg, 1990), 179–80.

37. In terms of the syntax of this verse, I follow the option that makes the entire verse a declaration of what YHWH requires (NJPS). Other options include: (a) the recital of moral responsibilities (v. 8b) are a response to the question in v. 8a ("What does YHWH require of you?"; NEB, NIV, NRSV); (b) the question continuing from v. 8a through to the end of the verse (KJV, RSV).

38. Qal participle (*dôrēš*). Many translations have "require" (e.g., NRSV, NJPS).

39. Scholars debate the referent of *ʾādām* here. I follow Wolff, *Micah*, 179–80. Other options include humanity in general, humanity as well as the nation, and the king as the one most responsible to establish these qualities.

40. This is the only place in the Hebrew Bible that one finds the combination "to love *ḥesed*."

41. The following passage, 6:9–16, serves as a contrast and details how some abuse others. As in the case of 3:1–4, the good can again be understood by what it is not.

42. These questions are put in the mouth of an individual ("I"). Perhaps this person stands as the representative of the entire nation. In vv. 3–5 the nation is addressed in the second-person masculine singular.

43. It is interesting to compare the referents for "my people" in chaps. 3 and 6. In 3:3, 5 (cf. 2:4, 8, 9; 6:16) the term appears to apply to the victims of oppression within the nation, whereas in 6:2, 3, 5 (cf. 1:9) it refers to the nation as a whole. There is a sense, then, that the entire nation has an incorrect view of God and the cult. If this also is true among the oppressed, then the tragedy is that they believe and perpetuate the lie that legitimizes the very system that abuses them.

44. This confusion about the cult might also explain the unconventional use of cultic vocabulary (i.e., *qādam*, *kāsap*). Cf. Delbert R. Hillers, *Micah: A Commentary on the Book of the Prophet Micah* (Hermeneia; Minneapolis: Fortress, 1988), 78; Wolff, *Micah*, 177–78. The suggestion of human sacrifice, too, could demonstrate how erroneous is the offer to YHWH. This was a prohibited practice. Scholars debate the historical origins of this sacrifice and its existence among YHWH worshipers and practice. For a recent discussion, note, e.g., Mark S. Smith, *The Early History of God: Yahweh and the Other Deities in Ancient Israel* (2nd ed.; Biblical Resource Series; Grand Rapids: Eerdmans, 2002), 171–81. For the most extensive treatment among the commentaries, see Andersen and Freedman, *Micah*, 532–39.

45. Andersen and Freedman relate 6:8 to 1 Sam. 15:22 and, therefore, take the term *ṭôb* in a comparative sense to avoid the sharp dichotomy with 6:6–7 (*Micah*, 528).

46. See Carol J. Dempsey, *The Prophets: A Liberation-Critical Reading* (Minneapolis: Fortress, 2000), 23–33; Dempsey, *Hope amid the Ruins: The Ethics of Israel's Prophets* (St. Louis: Chalice, 2000), 56–58; Erin Runions, "Called to Do Justice? A Bhabhian Reading of Micah 5 and 6:1–8," in *Postmodern Interpretations of the Bible: A Reader* (ed. A. K. M. Adam; St. Louis: Chalice, 2001), 153–64. Cf. Andrew Davies, *Double Standards in Isaiah: Re-evaluating Prophetic Ethics and Divine Justice* (BIS 46; Leiden: E. J. Brill, 2000).

47. See the thoughtful essay by Terence E. Freitheim, "The Character of God in Jeremiah," in *Character and Scripture: Moral Formation, Community, and Biblical Interpretation* (ed. W. P. Brown; Grand Rapids: Eerdmans, 2002), 211–30.

48. See e.g., Dempsey, *Prophets*, 32–33; Dempsey, *Hope amid the Ruins*, 72–73, 115–17.

Chapter 10

The End of War in the Zion Tradition

The Imperialistic Background of an Old Testament Vision of Worldwide Peace

J. J. M. ROBERTS

In days to come the Mountain of the house of YHWH will be established
   as the tallest of the mountains,
   and it will be exalted above the hills;
And all the nations shall look to it with joy,[1]
   and the many peoples will go and say:
"Come and let us go up to the Mount of YHWH,
   to the house of the God of Jacob;
That he may teach us of his ways,
   and that we may walk in his paths."
For from Zion shall go forth instruction,
   and the word of YHWH from Jerusalem.
Thus he shall judge between the nations,
   and arbitrate for the many peoples.
And they shall beat their swords into plowshares,
   and their spears into pruning hooks.
Nation shall not lift sword against nation,
   and they shall no longer learn war.
O House of Jacob, come that we may walk in the light of YHWH,
   for you have forsaken your people, O House of Jacob.

(Isa. 2:2–6a)

This oracle, found in slightly variant form in Mic. 4:1–5, is one of the classic texts often cited as providing a biblical vision for world peace. It is also often cited prescriptively. The prophet's indicative prediction that the nations will one day beat their swords into plowshares and their spears into pruning hooks, that nation will not take up sword against nation, and that they will cease to learn war, is often taken as an imperative injunction for how God's people ought to act now. Perhaps the most sophisticated presentation of this approach is that of H. W. Wolff: "The community of Yahweh even now should (Isa. 2:5) and will (Mic. 4:5) obey his instructions and his word; even now it is to make its swords into plowshares and not learn war anymore."[2] Despite the sophistication of Wolff's argument, however, his interpretation is in my opinion unconvincing, because it pays insufficient attention to both the conceptual and historical setting of this oracle.

The opening imagery of the oracle, in which the mountain on which YHWH resides is elevated above all the other mountains of the world, is a traditional way of stressing the supremacy of YHWH and his royal residency over any divine or political rival. Such imagery is attested as early as Ps. 68, where Mount Hermon is rebuked for looking with envy on the mountain YHWH chose as his dwelling: "O divine mountain, Mount Bashan, O many peaked mountain, Mount Bashan, why do you look with envy, O many peaked mountain, at the mountain God desired for his dwelling? Indeed, YHWH will dwell [there] forever" (Ps. 68:15–16 [Heb. 16–17]). The same text speaks of the kings of the earth bringing tribute to YHWH in Jerusalem (vv. 29–31 [Heb. 30–32]). Such imagery is also found in Ps. 48:1–2 [Heb. 2–3]: "Great is YHWH and greatly to be praised in the city of our God. His holy mountain, beautiful in elevation, is the joy of the whole earth. Mount Zion, the heights of Zaphon, is the city of the great king." The expression "great king" (*melek rāb*) implies that YHWH is suzerain over the other nations, who are conceived of as YHWH's vassals. The same concept is found in many other psalms that celebrate YHWH as the imperial ruler who has the legitimate power to govern and judge the other nations (Pss. 2, 47, 82, 95, 96, 98, 99). But the imperial exaltation of YHWH is at the same time the imperial exaltation of Zion/Jerusalem, YHWH's imperial residency.

In the oracle in Isa. 2 and Mic. 4, the nations recognize the supremacy of YHWH and go up to Jerusalem for instruction, because YHWH's rulings are issued from there. The nature of those rulings is suggested by the lines "he shall judge between the nations, and arbitrate for the many peoples, and they shall beat their swords into plowshares," and so forth. To understand these lines it is important to enter the conceptual world of ancient imperialism, and I know of no better access than a celebrated case from the late Hittite empire.[3] Ammistamru II of Ugarit and Sausgamuwa of Amurru were kings of neighboring states, and both were vassals of the Hittite suzerain, Tudhaliya IV. Diplomatic marriages were common in that time, and to cement the good relations between Ugarit and Amurru, Ammistamru married the sister of Sausgamuwa. But diplomatic marriages are often unhappy, and this one was a disaster. The sister of Sausgamuwa committed a great sin against her husband Ammistamru, probably adultery, but before she could be apprehended and punished for her crime, she fled to the protection of her brother in Amurru. There was apparently no question about the woman's guilt, so Sausgamuwa tried to soothe the rage of Ammistamru with diplomatic concessions, but Ammistamru would not be soothed; he demanded his wife back so that he could put her to death. When Sausgamuwa refused to extradite his sister to certain death, Ammistamru plotted to take her by force, and when the Amorite king discovered this plot, he threatened military action against Ugarit. At this stage in the conflict, when his two vassals were threatening to go to war against one another, the Hittite suzerain ended the conflict by imposing binding arbitration on the two kings, enforced by the explicit threat of Hittite military intervention should either party reject the imperial judgment. The edict issued from the Hittite provincial capital at Carchemish ruled that Sausgamuwa must return his sister to Ammistamru for execution, but for this privilege and to save the honor of the Amorite royal family, Ammistamru must pay Sausgamuwa an indemnity of over ten talents of gold. Thus, the wrongdoer was punished, ongoing blood revenge was prevented, and war between the two vassals was averted. To return to our oracle in the light of this conceptual analogy, the reason the nations can discard their weapons of war is that they are all vassals of YHWH, and as his vassals they are not permitted to go to war against one another to settle their disputes; instead, their disputes will be settled by YHWH's binding arbitration issued from the imperial capital in Jerusalem.

The destruction of the weapons of war in our oracle seems to be related to a similar motif found in several psalms celebrating the imperial God's protective presence in Jerusalem. In Ps. 46, after describing tumult among the nations as a potential threat to the security of God's city that is ended with the utterance of God's voice (v. 6 [Heb. 7]), verse 9 [Heb. 10] characterizes God as "the one who causes wars to cease to the end of the earth, who shatters the bow and cuts the spear in pieces, who burns the wagons with fire," and verse 11 concludes with God's self-assertion, "Desist and know that I am God. I will be exalted among the nations. I will be exalted in the earth." Psalm 76:2–3 [Heb. 3–4], after identifying YHWH's abode as Salem/Zion, continues with the statement, "There he shattered the fiery shafts of the bow, shield, and sword, and war." The psalm concludes with all those around God bringing tribute to this awesome God "who curbs the spirit of princes, and is awesome to the kings of the earth" (76:11–12 [Heb. 12–13]). One should also compare Ps. 48:4–7 (Heb. 5–8) and Ps. 2. Psalm 2 is particularly interesting, because it characterizes the rebellion of the nations as a rebellion against YHWH and his anointed (Ps. 2:2). As God says in his rebuke to the rebels, "I have set my king on Zion, my holy mountain" (v. 6). In other words, the submission of the nations to YHWH's imperial rule on Mount Zion is at the same time a submission to God's Davidic regent, to whom God has given the ends of the earth as a possession (v. 8).

This last point raises a question with regard to the oracle in Isa. 2 and Mic. 4. How did these prophets visualize the manner in which God's instructions would be issued from Mount Zion? Neither version of the oracle is explicit on this matter; the human agency of God's arbitration is not mentioned. One could argue that such silence with regard to human agency excludes human agency, that the prophet envisioned a future in which God in person, using no human agents, would deal directly with the nations.[4] But the silence of the text certainly does not require that interpretation, nor does it seem very probable. It is not unusual for biblical texts to focus on God's actions to the exclusion of God's human agents, even when the activities of those human agents are clearly implied in the cultural context.

Before illustrating this point from Isaiah, let me emphasize the importance of this observation, because the failure to recognize it is the fundamental weakness in Millard C. Lind's attempt to make the theology of warfare in ancient Israel more amenable to his pacifist stance in his *Yahweh Is a Warrior*.[5] Lind argues that the old victory hymn in Exod. 15 portrays YHWH as fighting alone, without Israel's help, in the fundamental victory over the Egyptians that led to Israel's deliverance. Moreover, this paradigmatic event and the way it was celebrated in this old hymn forever shaped Israel's ideal understanding of war. It was ideally an event of pure miracle, God's action of deliverance without any participation of human agency, and any deviation from this ideal in Israel's later history is a move away from true Yahwism. Unfortunately, the hymn in Exod. 15 will not bear the weight Lind puts on it. It is after all a hymn, and hymns tend to concentrate on God's mighty acts, not on those of his human community. The Babylonian hymn celebrating Marduk's victory over Elam totally ignores the Babylonian king's role in that victory and attributes the whole victory to the deity, though we know from other contemporary inscriptions of a different genre that the Babylonian king and his army were very much involved in the fighting that led to this victory.[6] One simply cannot reconstruct the mundane realities of a human event from a hymn. Since the prose accounts in Exod. 14 are much later and probably dependent on the hymn in Exod. 15, our sources do not allow us to say with any certainty whether a human battle between the Egyptians and Israel took place on this occasion or not.

In any case, the Israelite writers of Exodus did not read the hymn as discouraging human participation in YHWH's wars. Only two chapters later, in Exod. 17:8–15, one finds the account of the war with Amalek, where Moses commands Joshua to choose troops and engage the enemy while Moses sits on a hilltop and holds aloft his magic staff. Lind gives curiously little attention to this passage, where human participation in YHWH's war is clearly commanded. Moreover, God promises to punish Amalek in the future for its actions on this occasion, and it is to fulfill that promise that the prophet Samuel commands Saul to lead the Israelite army in a campaign to annihilate Amalek in 1 Sam. 15:1–3. Contrary to what Lind suggests, it is not Israel's paganizing kings that are primarily guilty of introducing and promoting human participation in the violence of war. It is Samuel, not Saul, who hacks Agag to pieces before the Lord, and as 1 Kgs. 20:35–43 indicates, the Yahwistic prophets remained the most rabid upholders of the merciless exercise of *herem* well into the late ninth or early eighth century.

But to return to Isaiah, the prophet complains that rebellious Judah does not seek God's counsel or inquire of his mouth (Isa. 30:1–2), that Judah does not look to the Holy One of Israel or inquire of YHWH (Isa. 31:1). Neither of these passages mentions any human agent of YHWH, but on a very concrete, human level, what both passages mean is that the royal officials are making policy decisions without first getting their decisions approved by obtaining positive oracles from the prophets, the human agents of the *dᵉbar Yahweh*.[7] Does that suggest then that the *tôrâ* and *dᵉbar Yahweh* issued from Jerusalem in Isa. 2:3 implies priests or prophets as the human agents for communicating God's decisions? Perhaps, but once any human agency is allowed, the question of a royal figure must be raised.

The two oracles in Isaiah about a future Davidic king share with Isa. 2 a vision of peace. In Isa. 9:5–6, this ruler is named "the prince of peace," and under his rule there "will be no end to peace," as he establishes his rule in "justice and righteousness." In Isa. 11:3–4, this ruler will judge and arbitrate (the same two verbs used in Isa. 2:4) in righteousness and equity, and the result will be an idyllic, peaceable kingdom, for the knowledge of YHWH will fill the earth (11:5–9). The final verse of this text, Isa. 11:10, is worth quoting in full: "In that day the root of Jesse, which remains standing, will be like a flag for the peoples, to him the nations will go to inquire, and his resting place will be glorious." This text, though different, offers some remarkable parallels to the vision in Isa. 2:2–5. Rather than the divine mountain being exalted to catch the attention of the nations, it is the king from the root of Jesse who stands out like a flag, and it is to him that the nations go to inquire. The word translated "inquire" here is *dāraš*, and it probably should be understood in its technical sense of seeking a decision from God. In other words, this Davidic king is the human agent for rendering God's verdicts to the nations seeking arbitration. Moreover, while the emphasis in Isa. 11:10 is on the king rather than his royal city, his residency is not ignored, "and his resting place [*mᵉnûḥātô*] will be glorious." The term "resting place" is a traditional designation for God's abode in Zion, as can be seen from Ps. 132:14.

In short, one could at least hazard the suggestion that Isaiah's vision of world peace adjudicated from a renewed Jerusalem presupposes an idealized Davidic king and his court, as well as priests and prophets, as the human agents of YHWH's imperial rule over the nations. One could make a similar argument for the text in Micah as well, since it is followed by passages that speak of YHWH ruling as king over his people in Mount Zion (Mic. 4:7), that promise that the former dominion will return to Jerusalem (Mic. 4:8), and that speak of God's new human king from Bethlehem who will be great to the ends of the earth (Mic. 5:1–3). In my view, this complex of texts in both Isaiah and Micah arose out of late eighth-century BCE hopes and expectations for the renewal of the idealized Davidic empire. But even if many of these texts are much later, as some scholars argue, the conceptual world behind the texts is still that of an imperial state centered in Jerusalem. The peace of which Isa. 2 and Mic. 4 speak is as much an imperial peace as the *Pax Romana* of the first few centuries of the common era.

This is evident even from a cursory survey of the clearly exilic and postexilic prophecies concerning the Davidic king and Jerusalem. The promise of a new

Davidide or Davidic line is found in Jeremiah (23:1–6; 33:14–26)[8] and Ezekiel (34:23–24; 37:24–28) in the early exilic period, and while Second Isaiah seems to drop this expectation, referring the Davidic promises to the people as a whole (Isa. 55:3), the hope for a new Davidide reemerges with new energy in the early postexilic period with Haggai (2:20–23) and Zechariah (4:6–14; 6:9–14). They appear to pin this hope on their contemporary Zerubbabel, the Davidic governor of Judea whom they persuaded to rebuild the temple in Jerusalem. Their messianic expectations for Zerubbabel were disappointed, but this disappointment did not dampen the expectation for a renewal of the Davidic line. It continued in the later Zechariah tradition (Zech. 12:7–8; 13:1) and remained a vibrant hope into New Testament times. The imperialistic background to the Old Testament vision of world peace is even clearer, however, if one looks at the late texts that glorify the restored Jerusalem.

One strand of expectations elaborates Isaiah's notion of God's strange work (Isa. 28:21), in which God first besieges Jerusalem to purge it of evil, and then, when God's purging judgment has accomplished its purpose, God suddenly steps in to rescue Jerusalem from the foreign nations gathered against it (Isa. 29:1–8; 31:4–5; cf. 10:5–15). One finds this strand well represented in Ezekiel's vision for the future of Israel after the fall of Jerusalem in 587. In Ezek. 36–37 the prophet promises the return of Israel to its land—a veritable resurrection of the nation from its Babylonian grave—the reunification of the north and the south under a single Davidic ruler, and a reestablishment of God's dwelling place among them. Then in Ezek. 38–39 God summons the nations of the north against the land of Israel, but when Israel's enemies reach the mountains of Israel, God slaughters them and Israel despoils its enemies, collecting such a mass of their broken and abandoned weapons that the wood from these weapons will suffice for all of Israel's firewood for seven years. Then Ezekiel's vision of the renewed Jerusalem and the new temple complex follows in chapters 40–48. This strand is also found in Zechariah. It is touched on in Zech. 12:1–9, where the nations that besiege Jerusalem will be destroyed by God with the active participation of the clans of Judah, the inhabitants of Jerusalem, and the house of David. It is elaborated in even greater detail in Zech. 14. As in Isa. 29:1–8, God will summon the nations to do battle against Jerusalem, and they will capture the city, looting and raping and taking half the city into exile, but at the very moment of the nations' victory, YHWH will intervene and turn the tide. The Mount of Olives will be split in two, living waters will flow out of Jerusalem, Jerusalem will be exalted as the only high mountain in the vicinity, and the city and its surviving inhabitants will dwell in security. All the nations who fought against Jerusalem will be hit with a plague that instantly rots their flesh, and God's people will plunder the wealth of the nations in great abundance. Those who survive of the nations who came up against Jerusalem will make a yearly pilgrimage to Jerusalem to worship the real king, YHWH of Hosts, and to celebrate the feast of booths. Any nation that does not make the pilgrimage to Jerusalem to worship YHWH of Hosts as king, thereby refusing to acknowledge YHWH's imperial suzerainty, will receive no rain. If Egypt fails to make the pilgrimage, it will be hit with the plagues that will afflict all the nations that do not make the pilgrimage. Apparently it is not just the withholding of rain that will afflict the rebellious nations but the rotting plague mentioned earlier.

The same tradition seems to lie behind Joel's vision of God's summoning of the nations to the valley of Jehoshapat for judgment (Joel 3 [Heb. 4]). God calls the nations to the land of Israel, to the valley of Jehoshapat, for war. In a striking reversal of the oracles of Isaiah and Micah, God commands the nations, "Beat your ploughshares into swords and your pruning hooks into spears," and rather than the nations learning war no more, God urges the least warlike to become a warrior: "Let the weakling say, 'I am a warrior'" (Joel 3:10 [Heb. 4:10]). But, as in Ezekiel and Zechariah, God intervenes, roaring from Zion and thundering from Jerusalem, where YHWH is a refuge for his people (Joel 3:16 [Heb. 4:16]), and the enemies of Israel will be destroyed. Jerusalem, however, will be established in security and well-being for Judah and the inhabitants of Jerusalem, since it will be the dwelling place of YHWH, and as in Ezek. 47 and Zech. 14:8, a stream will come forth from the house of YHWH to water the Wadi Shittim. It is not entirely clear in Joel 3:13 (Heb. 4:13) who is being addressed with the command "Put in the sickle, for the harvest is ripe. Go in, tread, for the wine press is full. The wine vats overflow, for their wickedness is great." It can hardly be the nations, since it is their wickedness that is addressed in the chapter (3:1–8 [Heb. 4:1–8]), but it could be either God's heavenly armies or Israel itself, or perhaps both. That God's people are included in the address and thus commanded to participate in God's judgment on the nations is suggested by the parallel in Mic. 4:11–13. There again the nations are gathered against Jerusalem, though contrary to the nations' expectations, God has gathered them as sheaves to the threshing floor. Then God commands, "Arise and thresh, O daughter Zion, for I will make your horn iron and your hoofs bronze; and you shall beat in pieces many peoples, and shall devote their gain to YHWH, their wealth to the lord of the whole earth."

Second and Third Isaiah place far less emphasis on Israel's participation in the divine judgment on the enemy nations, but they do stress YHWH's imperial rule over the nations, the nations' pilgrimage to Jerusalem bearing their tribute, and the enrichment of Israel from the wealth of the nations. According to Isa. 49:22–23, God will summon the nations to bring back Zion's children, and when they do, the kings and queens of the nations will bow down to Zion with their faces to the ground and lick the dust of Zion's feet—a clear indication of the imperial status of YHWH's renewed Zion. Isaiah 60–61 speaks extensively and in detail of foreigners bringing their wealth to Zion and serving Zion's inhabitants, but one quotation will suffice for our purposes: "For the nation and kingdom that will not serve you [Zion] shall perish; those nations shall be utterly laid waste" (Isa. 60:12). It is in this context of the imperial glorification of Zion that one should read Third Isaiah's portrait of the renewed Jerusalem (Isa. 65:18), in which the prophet takes the old peaceable kingdom motif from First Isaiah (Isa. 11:6–9) and reemploys it in a description of the new imperial Zion: "The wolf and the lamb shall feed together, the lion shall eat straw like the ox; but the serpent—its food shall be dust! They shall not hurt or destroy on all my holy mountain, says YHWH" (Isa. 65:25).

Having established that the conceptual background to the prophets' glorification of the renewed Jerusalem is that of an imperial state with the divine king, YHWH, residing in and ruling from Zion, let us return to the oracles in Isa. 2 and Mic. 4. It is necessary to analyze the argument that Wolff draws from them. Wolff argues that the content of YHWH's instruction can be abstracted from the consequences of that instruction. Since God's instructions result in the nations giving up their weapons of war, the contents of that instruction can be summarized by simply rephrasing these consequences as divine commands: "Beat your swords into plowshares and your spears into pruning hooks." The logic is flawed, however. While a suzerain might demand that his vassals not go to war with one another, what made that possible was the suzerain's just adjudication of the disputes that provoked the threat of war in the first place. It is these just and sagacious rulings on the concrete sources of conflict between the quarreling vassals that must be seen as the content of the *tôrâ* and *dᵉbar Yahweh* that is issued from Jerusalem. In our texts, disarmament is merely the result of the settlement of the disputes between the nations, not the settlement itself. Moreover, the conceptual imagery presupposes that the suzerain can use force to impose a binding settlement. This is explicitly said of the ideal Davidic ruler in Isa. 11:4, whose righteous judgment of the poor and fair arbitration for the meek of the earth involves smiting the violent with the rod of his mouth and killing the guilty with the breath of his lips.

But the oracle in both Isaiah and Micah envisions a future reality, not the present, and yet the different endings of the oracles suggest that this vision of the future has implications for behavior in the present. Micah ends with the statement "Though all the nations walk each in the name of its god, we will walk in the name of YHWH our God forever and ever" (4:5). In effect, though the nations do not yet come to Zion to learn YHWH's ways, even now Israel will live according to God's guidance. Contrary to Wolff's logic, this does not imply that Israel was committing itself to unilateral disarmament or that the prophet was calling it to such a stance. Indeed, other oracles in the following context call upon Zion to rise up and thresh, to crush the many peoples into small pieces and dedicate their plundered wealth to YHWH, the lord of all the earth (Mic. 4:13), or promise that in the future the remnant of Israel would be like a lion in a herd of sheep, and its hand would be exalted against its enemies, all of whom would be cut off (Mic. 5:7–8). Only if one reads Mic. 4:1–5 in splendid isolation from the rest of the literary composition of which it is a part can one justify a pacifist reading of this text. The call of the text is for Israel to live according to God's demands for righteousness and justice, but there is no indication that in ancient Israel such demands ever excluded the just use of violence.

The ending in Isaiah is different and suggests a particular historical setting: "O house of Jacob, come let us walk in the light of YHWH. For you have for-

saken your people, O house of Jacob." As I have argued at great length in an earlier article, the two occurrences of "house of Jacob" in Isa. 2:5–6 refer to the
northern kingdom and are to be read as vocatives.[9] At the time of the Syro-
Ephraimitic War, the house of Jacob had forsaken its own people, the Judean
inhabitants of the southern kingdom, by joining in a coalition with the Arameans
and Philistines to attack Jerusalem, which had been the imperial capital of both
Israel and Judah and the abode of YHWH, their national deity before the split
into two separate states. In the light of the vision of Jerusalem's and YHWH's
return to imperial splendor, Isaiah is urging the northern kingdom to abandon
its foreign alliances and join Judah in walking in the light of YHWH's teachings
that emanate from Zion. Thus, the appeal is both religious and political. The call
is not to disarmament—though misplaced trust in military strength, wealth, and
foreign allies is certainly condemned in the following verses—but a call to solidarity with Israel's Judean coreligionists and their common commitment to the
righteous requirements of YHWH, the God of Jacob as well as David.

If the argument of this essay is sound, these texts from Isaiah and Micah provided ancient Israel and still provide us with a glorious vision of the future when,
under the imperial rule of the one true God, all the nations of the world will be
at peace. But they did not and do not provide a prescriptive vision for how that
future divine rule and the concomitant peace will be realized. Their vision of the
future was offered as an encouragement to God's people, even in the uncertain
present in which they and we still live, to walk in obedience to God's ways, for one
day God's triumph will be evident to all. But neither text offers the promise that
such obedience will be the catalyst to bring about this triumphant rule and inau-
gurate this idyllic future. Nor do these texts, read in their cultural contexts, suggest that God's ways demanded of either Israel or Judah unilateral disarmament,
the absolute renunciation of lethal force in any defense of their national existence.

Of course, one may dismiss the original cultural and historical contexts of these
passages as irrelevant, insisting that they must be read through the lens of the New
Testament's allegedly more pacifistic stance, as some prominent Christian ethicists
maintain. Before following them in what amounts to a quasi-Marcionite reduction of the Christian canon to a selectively read New Testament, however, one
might do well to reflect on a possible reason for the larger canon. The New Testament writings all stem from a period in which the faith community exercised no
control over its own political existence either at a national or imperial level. The
early Christians were not responsible for governing the state, and even had they
desired, they were unable to project political power to benefit anyone. Many of
the Old Testament writings, by contrast, come from periods when members of the
faith community did have both the responsibility and the power to govern their
nation, and in many cases, even other nations subject to them. For modern Christians in Europe and North America, our political and cultural context, in that
regard, is far closer to the Israelites of the Old Testament than to the Christians
of the New Testament. One should think twice, therefore, before dismissing the
witness of that part of the canon that actually addresses believers who, like us—as

different as our context may in many ways be—nonetheless have the power and responsibility to govern according to God's will.[10]

Notes

1. For this translation of the expression *nhr 'l*, see the similar use of the expression in Jer. 31:12, another passage that describes a pilgrimage of people, this time clearly remnants of the northern kingdom, to Mount Zion.
2. Hans W. Wolff, "Swords into Plowshares: Misuse of a Word of Prophecy?" *CurTM* 12, no. 3 (1985): 143.
3. The textual sources for this case are found in Jean Nougayrol, *Textes Accadiens des archives sud* (Le palais royal d'Ugarit IV; ed. Claude F.-A. Schaeffer; Paris: Imprimerie Nationale, 1956), 129–48, text nos. 17.116; RS 16.270; 18.06 + 17.365; 17.459; 17.372A + 360A; 17.228; 17.450A; 17.318 + 349A; 17.82.
4. So Delbert R. Hillers, *Micah: A Commentary on the Book of the Prophet Micah* (Hermeneia; Philadelphia: Fortress, 1984), 51.
5. Millard C. Lind, *Yahweh Is a Warrior: The Theology of Warfare in Ancient Israel* (Scottdale, PA: Herald, 1980).
6. See J. J. M. Roberts, "Nebuchadnezzar I's Elamite Crisis," in *The Bible and the Ancient Near East: Collected Essays* (ed. Roberts; Winona Lake, IN: Eisenbrauns, 2002), 83–92, esp. 90.
7. See J. J. M. Roberts, "Blindfolding the Prophet: Political Resistance to First Isaiah's Oracles in the Light of Ancient Near Eastern Attitudes toward Oracles," in *Oracles et Prophéties dans l'Antiquité, Actes du Colloque de Strasbourg 15–17 juin 1995* (ed. Jean-Georges Heintz; Université des Sciences Humaines de Strasbourg, Travaux du Centre de Recherche sur le Proche-Orient et la Grèce Antiques 15; Strasbourg: De Boccard, 1997), 135–46.
8. The omission of Jer. 33:14–26 in the LXX raises questions about the authorship and precise date of this passage, though it is clearly an elaboration of the earlier promise in Jer. 23:1–6. Whoever the author, the passage seems to antedate Zech. 1–6, which seems to presuppose such a promise to both the priestly and royal lines.
9. J. J. M. Roberts, "Isaiah 2 and the Prophet's Message to the North," *JQR* 75, no. 3 (1985): 290–308.
10. A version of this paper appeared with the same title in *HBT* 26, no. 1 (2004): 2–22.

Chapter 11

The Quiet Words of the Wise

Biblical Developments toward Nonviolence as a Diaspora Ethic

DANIEL L. SMITH-CHRISTOPHER

Diaspora Literature: The Exemplary Hebrew in Diaspora

Recent work on the significance of biographical stories in the Persian period and later has almost always focused on at least some aspects of the ethical norms apparently advocated by these tales. Certainly the stories of Daniel, Esther, Joseph, and Tobit have received increased attention in recent years. I want to direct particular attention to Daniel and Tobit as examples of this genre.

In 1973, W. Lee Humphreys published his influential article in which he referred to the court stories of Daniel, and the very similar stories such as Esther, as stories that advocated a "life-style for the Diaspora." John J. Collins, S. Nidith and R. Doran, and A. Meinhold have each elaborated on the notion of a diaspora novella, or "court tale," and the genre of court tale has recently been explored at great length by Lawrence M. Wills.[1] The work on the court tale, for obvious reasons, has tended to focus on Daniel as the main example of this genre. In his early article, Humphreys suggested that the function of the court tale was to show that "one could, as a Jew, overcome adversity and find a life both rewarding and creative within the pagan setting and as a part of this foreign world; one need not cut himself off from that world or seek or hope for its destruction."[2]

In some of my work on the book of Daniel, I have had frequent occasion to note how Humphrey's work seems to have inaugurated a line of interpretation of the court stories in Daniel, namely, that these tales advocate a largely *positive* assessment of the foreign kings and thus a hopeful attitude toward the possibilities of life in the Diaspora. Collins, for one, disputes the late assignment of the Daniel stories to a Maccabean date largely on the basis of these positive views of the foreign kings, which he considers incompatible with Jewish contempt for Antiochus Epiphanes IV, and further states that "we might assume that these stories reflect the aspirations and concerns of upper-class Jews in the eastern Diaspora."[3] Wills further comments, with regard to these tales, that collectively they represent

> a popular genre, but it probably does not extend to the lower classes. It reflects the orientation of the administrative and entrepreneurial class. The scribal ideals inherent in the stories might restrict this circle somewhat to the extended court circles, for example, to the local administrative courts that might correspond to the training offered by Ben Sira's school. In Daniel 1–6, however, a distinction must be maintained between the various source layers and the redaction, the latter reflecting a more intensely pious outlook.[4]

The popularity of associating Wisdom literature with the court tales has led to a further extension of this thesis that the court tales have a scribal context. Calling these tales "didactic stories," Philip Davies emphasizes this scribal context and suggests that they actually had a *practical* importance for those who may have found themselves in situations similar to the setting of the tales themselves. These tales, states Davies, are "essentially a product of the scribal class, those professionally educated administrators who, virtually alone possessing the gift of literacy, served the governing class."[5] Davies, who has otherwise expressed some helpful reservations about the political and sociological assumptions about the setting of Daniel, nevertheless writes of his agreement with similar views expressed in Collins's work on Daniel:

> I agree with Collins that we should not automatically take the court-tales as representing the life-style of the authors. But it is hard to imagine them rejecting such an ambition; had they, one might have expected some hint of disapproval of Daniel's lifestyle. . . . [Yet] the court remains the center of interest of the entire work.[6]

These working hypotheses—(1) the association of wisdom themes with these tales (from the work of von Rad especially), (2) the alleged upper-class roots of Wisdom literature, and (3) the practical interest in these tales as training for the managerial classes have together resulted in an interesting attempt to play down aspects of these tales that do not fit the emerging professional profile. Take, for example, the uncomfortable fact that civil disobedience is a central theme in these tales.

So, for example, when it comes to Daniel, there are clear attempts to play down Daniel's defiance of Darius's order in the sixth chapter of Daniel. Andre

LaCocque states that "Daniel. . . simply perseveres in the exercise of his faith in the living God. Daniel's resistance lies in his constancy and faithfulness. There is no bravado or provocation on his part."[7] Norman Porteus argues that "it was not a question of flaunting his religion and so gratuitously courting trouble. Rather was it that a man like Daniel was not prepared to lower his flag when trouble threatened."[8] John Goldingay writes that the book of Daniel "portrays a world in which alien Judeans work with the government rather than against it. Its implicit sociology is consensual rather than conflictual. Its stance corresponds to the Davidic rather than the Mosaic trajectory."[9] It is thus not hard to cite examples, like the suggeston of Louis Hartman and Alexander DiLella, of the conclusion that "the fact that Daniel and his companions are said in chs. 1–5 to have achieved high position in the Babylonian court may perhaps suggest that life for the Israelites in exile was not all hardship and distress."[10]

While I cite this illustrious list of Daniel scholars as exemplars of biblical analysis, nonetheless I continue to disagree with this line of interpretation of the nature of the court tales, as well as the alleged ethical conservatism of Wisdom literature and the resulting assessment of the conditions of the Diaspora. Instead, I find myself much more in agreement with Dana Fewell:

> In every story in Daniel 1–6, the sage is called upon to hold to values that somehow oppose the existent political authority. The story of deception in ch. 1 lays the ground work for the remaining stories. In [the] first story, the young Judeans, by refusing to eat the food from the king's table, affirm that, although they are willing to serve the king, the source of their wisdom and the subject of their ultimate fidelity is their god, not their king. In this story and the ones that follow, the sages show that they are ready to oppose political power for higher values—whether this challenge entails speaking the truth about an unpleasant dream or vision (chs. 4, 5) or disobeying the command to pay ultimate allegiance to some king who thinks his sovereignty to be supreme (chs. 1, 3, 6).[11]

My own attempts to argue the stories of Daniel as exemplifying forthrightly *oppositional ethics* in the face of Babylonian, Persian, or Hellenistic authority has not met with wide acceptance; nevertheless, I will here press the argument a bit further, particularly experimenting with implications of the possible wisdom connections to these didactic tales and citing Tobit studies as a further case worth considering.[12]

Daniel and the Connection with Wisdom

As Collins points out, although scholars had anticipated von Rad's famous argument in his classic work *Wisdom in Israel*, it was von Rad's strong statement that apocalypticism was actually derived from Wisdom literature that defined the lines of a debate in Old Testament scholarship with regard to Daniel and Wisdom.[13] James Crenshaw does not give this view much credence, claiming that its "widening of the net threatens to distort the meaning of wisdom beyond repair."[14]

Murphy does not even discuss the matter.[15] While there have been some continued attempts to read a common movement or mindset behind both the development of wisdom and the Diaspora tales,[16] I want to suggest an approach to this
issue from the perspective of an exilic challenge during the Diaspora—a challenge
directed toward the readers of the tales of these Diaspora advisors to foreign rulers.

As I tried to argue in my book that attempts to outline a "theology of exile,"
one helpful entry to this issue is provided by reviewing Susan Niditch's ideas about
"trickster tales."[17] Niditch's important work in comparing folklore motifs of "tricksters and underdogs" with certain biblical stories of clever heroes points to the
importance of reading these biblical stories with an understanding of the nearly
universal figure of the trickster. Often admired precisely for their underhanded or
deceptive ingenuity, stories of the trickster (in all their variety across many cultures), writes Niditch, "[are] a subtype of the underdog. A fascinating and universal folk hero, the trickster brings about change in a situation via trickery."[18]
Niditch contrasts the talents and values appropriate to tricksters and wise men in
relation to biblical figures, such as Joseph the wise over against Jacob the clever:

> Joseph, an innocent youth with mantic talents, matures into a court wise
> man, winning a position of power in the establishment that he maintains
> until his death. Jacob, an antiestablishment trickster, matures into a more
> institutionalized figure who declines into senescence much as did his own
> father. Appropriate to roles of wise man and trickster are *alternative views* of
> authority and alternative settings.[19]

I wonder, however, whether the ethics of the trickster, with its definite lack of
respect for "establishment ethics," is really so different from the ethics of wisdom,
especially late developments within Israelite wisdom? Certainly part of the reason why these are seen as different kinds of ethical traditions is the almost uni-
versally presumed notion that wisdom comes from the elite classes of Israel and
has its roots in the privileged scribal class of the monarchy, even if much of the
material was edited during the exilic/Diaspora period. Thus, it is also almost uni-
versally assumed that wisdom ethics are "establishment ethics" par excellence.
This has led to an interesting disagreement about the social context of Wisdom
literature in the Persian period.

Wisdom and Privilege? Questioning Wisdom
as "Establishment Ethics"

The presumed association of wisdom and economic privilege has rarely been the
subject of much debate, but such a discussion may be overdue. Consider, on the
one hand, C. L. Seow's commentary on Ecclesiastes, which has been widely
quoted, particularly his suggestion that during the Persian period there were
many "entrepreneurial opportunities" for Judeans.[20] Christine Yoder, for example, finishes her interesting summary of Persian period Palestine by suggesting
that it

was not a distant, isolated corner of the Persian Empire. Rather, communication, people, and goods flowed in and out freely. Letters and documents traded hands. Travelers journeyed from place to place. Migrant workers set up shop and then moved on. Foreign merchants settled in the cities and gathered at the marketplaces to sell their wares. And imperial troops passed through or were stationed at regional outposts.[21]

But can one make too much of evidence from Persian sources, such as the Persepolis Tablets, that certainly suggests imperial priorities and troop movements? Another example may give pause. It has often been assumed that the Murashu business documents reveal a healthy economy within which Jews would have found some economic opportunities for success in the Diaspora. But Matthew Stolper suggests that the texts establish a clear orientation toward maximizing the advantages of the central regime. Joseph Bryant's reading of Persian economics tends to support a more limited view of economic opportunities:

> The Persian Great Kings were the very embodiment of unrestrained autocracy. As self-proclaimed earthly representatives of the creator god Ahura-Mazda, their every whim had the force of sanctioned command, and summary executions of subordinates who displeased were not uncommon. . . . There was the great pomp and circumstance that exalted the majesty of the royal person and symbolically projected his immense wealth and power: the banquets that fed thousands at a time; the imposing works of monumental architecture, suitably graced by the stern visage or imperious proclamations of the supreme ruler.[22]

Surely this more negative economic setting is the reality that is reflected in Ezra's prayer about the "rich yield" of the lands of Palestine going "to the kings whom you have set over us because of our sins" (Neh. 9:37), a passage that certainly does not sound like Yehud was a land of opportunity in the Persian period. Perhaps the economics of Wisdom literature were not of the nature of market-driven advantages for a rising entrepreneurial class but of the nature of an economics of an occupied people attempting to insulate its communities from the reach of imperial control.

Obedience and Disobedience in the Diaspora: Some Thoughts on Tobit

In his important commentary on Tobit, Joseph Fitzmyer echoes much of the work on Daniel with his observations that passages such as 4:3–19 and 14:3–11 provide wisdom-influenced "instructions about how Jewish people should live uprightly even in a diaspora context."[23] Benedikt Otzen agrees, noting that the author of Tobit "sees, of course, the problem of the Diaspora behind the theme of the exile."[24] So the notion of righteousness in exile is a central concern of the fictional tale.[25]

But consider the *kind* of righteousness that Tobit is praised for! While it is true that he obeys the traditional laws of the Hebrews and even goes to Jerusalem when the northern kingdom tries to establish its own cult against that of the house of David, his "righteousness" also leads to conflict. He resists assimilation into the Assyrian imperial culture ("but I kept myself from eating the food of the Gentiles," 1:10–11) and secretly buries murdered Israelites in the dangerous days of Sennacherib (1:16–20). The story of his blindness begins with yet another case of a murdered Israelite (2:3). Amy-Jill Levine notes that Tobit's "frequent contact with corpses shows the chaos of the Diaspora."[26]

Secrecy, civil disobedience, constantly facing the threats and dangers of Diaspora life, giving alms to the poor—is this really a story about "getting ahead" in the bureaucracy of the Assyrian Empire? Tobit portrays the stratagems of survival when one is a minority in a hostile dominant culture. Thus, the "wisdom" taught by Tobit is arguably not entirely an establishment ethic but a survival ethic—to use the vernacular, "street smarts" that amount to "watching your back." There is little to suggest that Tobit finds any good in the Assyrian system—only the means to survive, while taking care lest one is caught living a subcultural ethic. (Tobit's willingness to take risks to properly bury fellow Israelites was a virtuous aspect of his character.) The parallels to the constant threats in Dan. 1–6 seem obvious, and even Esther is not without its ethics of challenging the Persian system, which are well represented by Mordecai's warnings.

It is furthermore interesting to note Fitzmyer's observations (citing other writers as well) about the thematic connections between Tobit and the patriarchal and matriarchal traditions of Genesis. He notes the similarity of concerns with burial (a frequent theme in Genesis, of course) as well as the parallels with sending sons on journeys and the importance of marriage to the "right" person and into the right people (again, an obvious minority concern).[27] Once again we see potential connections between Jacob's trickster ethic, Abraham's "necessary lies," and Joseph's subterfuge. Is this also a wisdom theme?

Reading Wisdom in Occupied Palestine

If one reads the book of Proverbs from the same social perspective as the subaltern ethics of Tobit and Daniel or the trickster tales of Jacob, some interesting alternatives suggest themselves. Mark Brett, for example, is well aware of the potential for this, as intimated in his reading of Genesis as ultimately a Persian period document that frequently polemicizes against authority figures. Of Jacob's famously questionable integrity, Brett writes:

> Folkloric texts often contain the theme of trickery, and, as many scholars have suggested, this theme appeals to an "underdog" audience which has no other means of combating the dominant culture. Thus, we should not expect the representation of God in folkloric texts to cohere with the God who upholds ethical standards in some of the other Genesis traditions.[28]

This approach reminds me of James Scott's analysis of the "hidden transcripts" of the subordinated in their opposition to power, particularly when he points out that certain behaviors are seen as part and parcel of survival:

> A . . . vital aspect of the hidden transcript that has not been sufficiently emphasized is that it does not contain only speech acts but a whole range of practices. Thus, for many peasants activities such as poaching, pilfering, clandestine tax evasion, and intentionally shabby work for landlords are part and parcel of the hidden transcript. For dominant elites, hidden-transcript practices might include clandestine luxury and privilege, surreptitious use of hired thugs, bribery, and tampering with land titles.[29]

Similarly, Luigi Lombardi-Satriani writes that "folk culture . . . marks the outer limit of the hegemonic culture, whose ideological tricks it reveals, contesting at times only with its own presence, the universality, which is only superficial, of the official culture's concepts of the world and of life."[30]

In my work on exilic theology, I have had a number of occasions to cite significant illustrations of precisely these "subaltern" or "subcultural" ethics in some of the recent work about the creation of "refugee cultures" in modern relief work. John Knudsen, for example, writes of the significance of carefully crafted stories told to the relief workers in refugee camps. These camps, writes Knudsen, provide little opportunity for building trust. The refugee quickly learns which kinds of stories will result in early departure and which stories will result in arrest.[31] Eftihia Voutira and Barbara Harrell-Bond are a bit more forthright:

> As one refugee summed it up, "To be a refugee means to learn to lie." Although this situation of mistrust may be taken as characteristic of the different ways in which the "us" and "them" relate, the actual situation is far more complicated as regards the relevant interests of the two groups that are at stake.[32]

What would happen if we attempted to read Wisdom literature as a genre that is related to the genre of biblical trickster *and* Diaspora tales and thus also a product of the social circumstances of exilic subordination? Can we speak of proverbial wisdom as consisting of "subcultural ethics"? I contend that some of the problems of wisdom ethics become more intelligible under such a reading strategy.

Wisdom as Diaspora Ethics

In his classic commentary on Proverbs for the International Critical Commentaries series, written in 1899, Crawford H. Toy first argued that the opening advice of Proverbs may well refer to "organized banditry"[33] in the Hellenistic urban context, and thus the "sinners" who try to "entice" the young man are actually fellow Jews calling on him to join in social banditry:

> My child, if sinners entice you,
>   do not consent.
> If they say, "Come with us, let us lie in wait for blood;
>   let us wantonly ambush the innocent;
> like Sheol let us swallow them alive
>   and whole, like those who go down to the Pit.

> We shall find all kinds of costly things;
>   we shall fill our houses with booty.
> Throw in your lot among us;
>   we will all have one purse"—
> my child, do not walk in their way,
>   keep your foot from their paths.
>   (Prov. 1:10–15)

Toy argued that "the organized robbery here referred to suggests city life of the later time, the periods when, under Persian and Greek rule, Jerusalem and Alexandria sheltered a miscellaneous population, and a distinct criminal class became more prominent."[34] Toy related this to other biblical texts that sounded to him like allusions to urban violence, such as Hos. 4:2; 6:8–9; and 7:1; as well as Ps. 10:8. While not frequently taken up in contemporary commentaries, Toy's suggestion deserves a second look and can be quite suggestive of a different context in which to read Wisdom literature and also to relate Wisdom literature back again to the tales of Daniel and Tobit. To state it another way, do Proverbs and Ecclesiastes contain the wisdom of the minority group that particularly focuses on lessons in how to survive? Such lessons, whether explicitly called "lessons" or not, are familiar to every member of a minority group who has sat around the dinner table listening to parents tell them how to "get ahead by not making trouble." Here is also the connection with the tales of Tobit and Daniel. Not entirely unlike Jacob, Daniel and the characters in Tobit lived, and indeed "got ahead," but "watched their back" as members of a minority people in a diaspora situation. That we have previously not read Daniel or Proverbs in this light is due not in small measure to the context from which we *have* read this material—usually not as subordinates in an imperial regime, much less like minorities in a dominant culture.

Nonviolence: Strategy of Minority Survival?

In my work on a theology of exile, I have advanced the notion that part of this ethic of survival actually gives rise to a certain kind of nonviolence; it is an ethic of survival that rejects violence as suicidal, even while it accepts the possibilities of martyrdom. What I found interesting is that there appear to be suggestive parallels between the largely nonviolent examples of Daniel and Tobit on the one hand, and the questioning of violence in wisdom ethics on the other.

Nili Shupak's work on Egyptian wisdom literature opens the discussion by suggesting some interesting parallels with biblical wisdom values. Shupak notes that a certain "quietism" is typical of the Egyptian ideal:

> The ideals of quietness and self-control hold pride of place in the *weltanshauung* of the Egyptian sage and of his Hebrew counterpart. Words in praise of restraint—evinced principally in silence and in the avoidance of dispute and quarrel—are a consistent theme in Egyptian and Biblical wisdom.[35]

This ideal can be further enumerated, as Shupak suggests:

> The "silent man" is he who is thoughtful in manner and modest in conduct; he eschews strife and garrulousness; he is kind and gives of his possessions to others; he is honest and obedient towards his superiors. The "silent man" is the devoted pious man, and his lips and heart are one.[36]

While Shupak argues that the exact equivalent is not present in biblical literature, she recognizes that one who is "slow to anger" is certainly present in Proverbial wisdom.[37]

> One of the most important virtues in Biblical wisdom, as in the Egyptian wisdom, is moderation and restraint. The ideal man is tolerant, cool-tempered, balanced in his conduct, sparing of speech, keeps secrets and eschews quarrels. . . . "Silence" as part of the proper behaviour of the believer who submits to the god, expressed in later Egyptian literature beginning with the New Kingdom Period (esp. in hymns of personal piety) is present in the Bible only in non-wisdom books.[38]

This contrast between the Egyptian "silent man" and Hebrew ideals of restraint, however, can be exaggerated, especially when one reads Prov. 17:27–28:

> One who spares words is knowledgeable;
>> one who is cool in spirit has understanding.
> Even fools who keep silent are considered wise;
>> when they close their lips, they are deemed intelligent.

Furthermore, there is an interesting change in the wisdom literature that we have available to us from Egyptian sources, particularly noting that the latter text was written by Egyptians under foreign domination. Consider a series of ethical maxims of restraint over a period of time from the Sixth Dynasty (in any case, pre-2000 BCE) work, *The Wisdom of Ptahhotep*, to the Persian period with *The Instruction of Ankhsheshonq*. *The Instruction of Ankhsheshonq* is written on the premise that it is the collected sayings of an Egyptian priest in prison (for participating in a palace revolt?)[39] and is written to a general populace of Egypt, not an elite.[40] First, from the older writing of Ptahhotep:

> Don't be proud of your knowledge,
> Consult the ignorant and the wise;
> The limits of art are not reached,
> No artists' skills are perfect. . . .
> . . . .
> If you meet a disputant in action;
> a powerful man, superior to you,
> Fold your arms, bend your back,
> To flout him will not make him agree with you.
> Make little of the evil speech
> By not opposing him while he's in action;
> He will be called an ignoramus,

Your self-control will match his pile (of words).
If you meet a disputant in action,
Who is your equal, on your level,
You will make your worth exceed his by silence,
While he is speaking evilly,
There will be much talk by the hearers,
Your name will be good in the mind of the magistrates.
If you meet a disputant in action,
A poor man, not your equal,
Do not attack him because he is weak,
Let him alone, he will confute himself.
Do not answer him to relieve your heart,
Wretched he is who injures a poor man.[41]

. . . .

This kind of advice—which clearly presumes that you have superiors in addition to those below you—can be read either as advice for succeeding in the civil service or as advice that calls for a very self-serving idea about staying clear of trouble. *Ptahhotep* has most often been read in the former manner, as an ethics for civil service. But consider the growth of what some have called "cynicism," or perhaps greater self-interest, that is typical of *Ankhsheshonq*. After an introduction that enumerates all people to be served, the later advice with regard to superiors is interesting. There are the expected calls to respect station in life:

> 7:13 Do not insult your superior.

> 7:15 Do not neglect to serve your master.

> 7:16 Do not neglect to serve him who can serve you.

But there is also a clear level of advice that admonishes self-interest and local loyalties:

> 8:11 Do not go to court against your superior when you do not have protection against him.

> 9:13 Do not be a neighbor to your master.

> 10:7 You may trip over your foot in the house of a great man; you should not trip over your tongue.

> 16:6 Do not deliver a servant into the hand of his master.

> 16:19 Do not conceal yourself from a stranger who comes from the outside.

> 18:10 He who battles together with the people of his town will rejoice with them.

> 22:18 If you come to say something to your master count on your fingers till ten.

23:10 A slip of the tongue in the royal palace is a slip of the helm at sea.

25:11 Learn how to sit in the presence of Pharaoh.[42]

In his survey of Egyptian wisdom literature as a prologue to the study of Proverbs, William McKane evaluates *The Instruction of Ankhsheshonq* in rather negative terms: "The earthiness of Ankhsheshonq is unmistakable. It harks back to the soil and addresses itself to those who engage in the back-breaking tasks of cultivation and are resigned to the unpredictability of agriculture."[43] Contrasting this work with the rather high-mindedness of older wisdom works, such as Ptahhotep, McKane states, "It does not give advice to a clientele of high calibre, who have expectations of eminence and power. It has to do with less distinguished individuals who have adjusted themselves to life at lower levels and whose claims to self-fulfillment are modest."[44] He does not make note of the introduction of a certain cynicism that is reminiscent of Ecclesiastes, however:

26:5 There is imprisonment for giving life.

26:6 There is release for killing.

26:7 There is he who saves and does not profit.

I propose that it is not "earthiness" that is evident in these teachings; rather, it is the growing awareness of "watching your back" that seems to have disturbed McKane. But it is precisely this change that is interesting, given the political occupation of Egypt in the Persian period. I am, of course, not an Egyptologist, and I do not know if I could ultimately sustain my observed differences between the older text and the more recent *Ankhsheshonq*, but I think there is a similar shift in self-interested loyalties in biblical Wisdom literature as life under empire settles into the realities of Diaspora existence.

Ecclesiastes: Dark Humor in Occupied Palestine?

It is often noted that Ecclesiastes exhibits far less confidence in the established ways of the world than most Wisdom literature. It is precisely in the somewhat cynical observation that "things do not always work out the way they are supposed to" that introduces an interesting level of self-interest. It could be argued that these admonitions seem to call into question the "myths" of general social well-being, and perhaps an admonition to be wary of what I am calling, after Scott, the "official transcript." It is perhaps in this context that we should read the "subcultural observations" of Eccl. 9:11–12:

> Again I saw that under the sun the race is not to the swift, nor the battle to the strong, nor bread to the wise, nor riches to the intelligent, nor favor to the skillful; but time and chance happen to them all. For no one can anticipate the time of disaster. Like fish taken in a cruel net, and like birds caught

in a snare, so mortals are snared at a time of calamity, when it suddenly falls upon them.

What then is this sage's advice to minority existence in Persian or Ptolemaic imperial Palestine?

> I have also seen this example of wisdom under the sun, and it seemed great to me. There was a little city with few people in it. A great king came against it and besieged it, building great siegeworks against it. Now there was found in it a poor wise man, and he by his wisdom delivered the city. Yet no one remembered that poor man. So I said, "Wisdom is better than might; yet the poor man's wisdom is despised, and his words are not heeded."

> > The quiet words of the wise are more to be heeded
> > than the shouting of a ruler among fools.
> > Wisdom is better than weapons of war,
> > but one bungler destroys much good.
> > (Eccl. 9:13–18)

This call to seek counsel instead of brute strength is not necessarily a principled nonviolence in the sense of a universal ethical wisdom; rather, it appeals to a profound sense of diasporic practicality: Why die for this state? Why pretend that the present political reality exists according to some deserved status or dominant virtue beyond brute strength? This cool attitude can perhaps help us to understand other sober assessments of Ecclesiastes:

> > The wise have eyes in their head,
> > but fools walk in darkness.
> > Yet I perceived that the same fate befalls all of them.
> > (2:14)

> So I saw that there is nothing better than that all should enjoy their work, for that is their lot; who can bring them to see what will be after them? (3:22)

> With many dreams come vanities and a multitude of words; but fear God.
> If you see in a province the oppression of the poor and the violation of justice and right, do not be amazed at the matter; for the high official is watched by a higher, and there are yet higher ones over them. But all things considered, this is an advantage for a land: a king for a plowed field. (5:7–9)

Ecclesiastes is dated by Crenshaw to 250–225 BCE.[45] While Ecclesiastes is clearly more critical than Proverbs, do we already have signs of self-interested, rather than official, ethics for "getting ahead" and attaining advantage even in terms of being subservient? In short, Ecclesiastes reads far more subversively if the famous "cynicism" is directed not toward a Jewish state or even toward traditional Jewish values of social existence, but rather toward the *Gentile* state. Do some of the proverbs already show signs of this ironic teaching about "watching your back" and learning cleverness as strength—in other words, the survival tactics of the tricksters?

I suggest that Ecclesiastes sounds like the musings of a Jacob-like trickster! Ecclesiastes is upsetting for the same reason trickster ethics are offensive to dominant cultures. They represent a lack of trust and faith in "the system," a cynical disbelief that the political realities under which they are living are either inevitable or good. In such a case, one cannot trust the system to have your best interests at heart—you must fend for yourself! With regard to Ecclesiastes, then, I tend to agree with the sentiment expressed recently by Elsa Tamez:

> Qoheleth's day was not the time for liberation, as was the case in the past when Israel was formed as a people. The Jews would soon come into struggle with the Seleucids. But Qoheleth does not announce, much less promote, the Maccabean revolt. For him, the time of revolution is not propitious. His advice takes another route: resist wisely in the face of absurdity. This is the most important message of his discourse: how to survive with dignity in a dehumanizing and annihilating reality.[46]

Rereading Proverbs from Below

In contemporary refugee studies, it has been noted that among the realities of the dispossessed and the forcibly resettled, there is a certain temptation to break ranks, to perpetuate rivalries in the competition for resources that only eventually come to the foreigners. As Patrick Matlou observes:

> The deprivation and uncertainty that refugees often suffer sometimes lead them into conflict with each other over scarce rewards. In this regard, exile often serves as an arena for the continuation of conflicts begun at home and leads to the intensification of discriminatory practices that were already in place.[47]

Similarly, Voutira and Harrell-Bond note:

> Despite the apparent commonality of their experience vis-à-vis their country of origin, one seldom finds a sense of political solidarity among refugee populations. More often than not, refugee populations are highly factionalized in relation to their different strategies for resolving the causes that led to their flight.[48]

In this light, consider the advice of Prov. 3:28–30:

> Do not say to your neighbor, "Go, and come again,
>   tomorrow I will give it"—when you have it with you.
> Do not plan harm against your neighbor
>   who lives trustingly beside you.
> Do not quarrel with anyone without cause,
>   when no harm has been done to you.

Does Proverbs council against "breaking ranks" with your fellow minority-group member? Along similar lines, it has often been noted that some pieces of advice in Wisdom literature seem contrary to the spirit, if not also the letter, of the Mosaic legislative texts. For example, loans are not prohibited in Deuteronomic law, including loans to foreigners. The difference is only in the matter of interest charged, according to Deut. 23:19–20:

> You shall not charge interest on loans to another Israelite, interest on money, interest on provisions, interest on anything that is lent. On loans to a foreigner you may charge interest, but on loans to another Israelite you may not charge interest, so that the LORD your God may bless you in all your undertakings in the land that you are about to enter and possess.

Is the difference in attitude noted in Proverbs simply a sage disagreement with Mosaic law, or has the social circumstance changed so dramatically that circumspection is now valued more highly than the proverbial generosity of Deuteronomic law? Proverbs 11:15 famously counsels against loans to strangers, though stopping short of contradicting the law: "To guarantee loans for a stranger brings trouble, but there is safety in refusing to do so." It is not difficult to argue that the Proverbial spirit differs significantly from a sentiment such as that in Deut. 15:11: "Since there will never cease to be some in need on the earth, I therefore command you, 'Open your hand to the poor and needy neighbor in your land.'" Is it an error to suspect that a certain self-interest among exiles or occupied peoples is at work here?

Again, despite the spirit of Exod. 22:26, a spirit even further elaborated in Deut. 24:12, 17, where garments must not be kept overnight, Prov. 20:16 seems to be written in the opposite spirit, surely representing some attitudes that are concerned more with the safety of the loan and not the comfort of the person: "Take the garment of one who has given surety for a stranger; seize the pledge given as surety for foreigners."[49] While we may argue that different social classes are being addressed here, wouldn't another way of accounting for this difference be that circumstances have changed? Or, to argue in a somewhat different way, Otzen has noted the number of scholars of Tobit who have made reference to the theme of almsgiving in Tobit as a significant motif. This is often interpreted as a kind of mutual aid among exiles. As Otzen suggests, "The developed practice of almsgiving is a necessity to preserve a Jewish society in the Diaspora."[50] Is it possible, then, that some of the more conservative economic values expressed in Prov. 20:16 are values toward non-Hebrews, which contrast with the "in-house" almsgiving? Such an ethical norm is only problematic for those who are not a part of a marginalized group and thus not used to the significant values of "taking care of one's own—because no one else will!"

Such a presumed wisdom in situations of marginality would further illuminate why Proverbs is speaking to those outside of the circumstances of political power and influence. The following series of images in Prov. 30, often noted for their "zoological observations," are in fact united by one interesting element— they advise *unsupervised responsibility*:

Four things on earth are small,
   yet they are exceedingly wise:
the ants are a people without strength,
   yet they provide their food in the summer;
the badgers are a people without power,
   yet they make their homes in the rocks;
the locusts have no king,
   yet all of them march in rank;
the lizard can be grasped in the hand,
   yet it is found in kings' palaces.
                              (30:24–28)

Finally, it is hard not to believe that the following pieces of advice seem to fit with the circumstances of Hebrew folklore in the Daniel stories:

The dread anger of a king is like the growling of a lion;
   anyone who provokes him to anger forfeits life itself.
                              (20:2)

Do not desire the ruler's delicacies,
   for they are deceptive food.
                              (23:3)

Take away the wicked from the presence of the king,
   and his throne will be established in righteousness.
Do not put yourself forward in the king's presence
   or stand in the place of the great;
for it is better to be told, "Come up here,"
   than to be put lower in the presence of a noble.
                              (25:5–7)

As I have argued, the Daniel tales can be read to illustrate some of the exact same self-guarding wisdom advocated in the book of Proverbs. While I am not arguing for a strong relationship between the two, I am simply noting that when one reads Proverbs under the context of a potential threat, or as an exile or occupied and colonized citizen of imperial Persian or Ptolemaic Palestine, the possibility becomes even stronger. Let us now return to the argument that Daniel (and, I would argue, Tobit) exhibits a Proverbial ideal of clever (e.g., trickster) wisdom.

The Wisdom Warrior: Diasporic Cleverness over Imperial Brute Strength

As I have argued, Daniel and Tobit exemplify a diasporic ethics of wise, clever, and largely nonviolent survival—the ethic of a minority. The Persian period of the Hebrew people (597–333 BCE) began a process of unprecedented contact with peoples and ideas of the ancient Near East that was accelerated dramatically with the conquests of Alexander the Great. The great studies of Judaism in the

Hellenistic period emphasize the enormity, not to mention the complexity, of this exposure to varieties of ideas and cultures and its impact in the later development of Judaism and early Christianity.[51] However, did the very facts of imperial existence, with its concomitant realities of coexistence by different religions, attitudes, peoples, and cultures under an overarching military and administrative presence bring about the need to rethink previous attitudes? Did cleverness come to replace older military and "civic" virtues of the monarchical period?

John Collins first proposed that the book of Daniel represented a "pacifistic" religious document from a group known as the "wise ones."[52] His reading of Dan. 11:34 (as a critique of the violent resistance as "little help"), however, has been challenged by Gordon Zerbe.[53] Zerbe argues that, based on a review of extensive apocalyptic literature, there is very little evidence to support the idea that there are "pacifistic strains" in apocalyptic writing, and thus it seems difficult for Zerbe to accept Collins's view with regard to the authors of Dan. 7–12. However, as I have here argued, the apocalyptic literary tradition is not the only religious and ethical tradition that the book of Daniel builds upon. Daniel does represent an alternative to the violent Hebrew ethics of nationalist preservation, but this does not arise from the apocalyptic tradition but rather from the wisdom tradition of clever, strategic, and personal "quietism." Wisdom, Daniel, and Tobit are examples of what we might call the "Wisdom Warrior."

The Wisdom Warrior: An Ideal Type in Wisdom Literature

Wisdom literature famously employs a number of images in teaching about wisdom, preeminently Lady Wisdom/Sophia, but also the fool, the wicked, the father, the mother, and the young. Among the less prominent images used are those borrowed from warfare. Social conflict, therefore, is obviously an aspect of life from which wisdom is most certainly not removed as an operant series of principles to be attended to. Therefore, in Proverbs and Ecclesiastes there emerges an image of what I will call the "Wisdom Warrior." I have intentionally avoided "Wise Warrior," because that is precisely part of my point. We are not dealing simply with a warrior who has added wisdom to his arsenal. Rather, we are intended to contrast the *Wisdom* Warrior with *standard* warriors! The Wisdom Warrior is different. He is calm and self-restrained, as Prov. 17:27 advises: "One who spares words is knowledgeable; one who is cool in spirit has understanding."

Of course, many scholars have compared this image to the cool-headed ideal of Egyptian wisdom, and the connection seems possible. The Wisdom Warrior seeks to end conflict before it begins, as Prov. 17:9 enjoins: "One who forgives an affront fosters friendship, but one who dwells on disputes will alienate a friend." Note also 17:14: "The beginning of strife is like letting out water, so stop before the quarrel breaks out" (cf. 25:8–10, which advises that one settle matters out of court, which sounds like Matt. 25).

The Wisdom Warrior will not return evil for evil but seeks the welfare even of his enemies. Proverbs 17:13 suggests that "evil will not depart from the house of one who returns evil for good," and 24:29 repeats the thought more directly by demanding that the wise one must not say, "I will do to others as they have done to me; I will pay them back for what they have done."

Particularly when contrasted with militant Hellenistic virtues of the gallant hero-warrior, the Wisdom Warrior appears ineffectual. However, even in his apparent weakness, the Wisdom Warrior is nevertheless protected by God (Prov. 2:7: "He stores up sound wisdom for the upright; he is a shield to those who walk blamelessly"; 16:7: "When the ways of people please the LORD, he causes even their enemies to be at peace with them"; 18:10–11: "The name of the LORD is a strong tower; the righteous run into it and are safe. The wealth of the rich is their strong city; in their imagination it is like a high wall").

It is particularly interesting how often wisdom is contrasted with the fortifications of a town, such as in Prov. 16:32: "One who is slow to anger is better than the mighty, and one whose temper is controlled than one who captures a city."[54] The key here is the contrast between the ways of the strong warrior (who is successful, after all, in this proverb) and the self-control, the restraint, and indeed peacefulness, of the wise. This is particularly evident in 21:22: "One wise person went up against a city of warriors and brought down the stronghold in which they trusted." On reflection, it seems clear that we are not intended to imagine a Samson-like conquest of an entire city by brute strength, since it is precisely apparent strength that is being contrasted with wisdom. (Perhaps we are to think of the power of wisdom, as noted in 25:15: "With patience a ruler may be persuaded, and a soft tongue can break bones."). Compare this with 25:28: "Like a city breached, without walls, is one who lacks self-control," which also, in a similar fashion, contrasts apparent strength with the strength of wisdom.

This theme of the "one wise person" against military strength is reflected elsewhere in Wisdom literature. In his commentary, McKane suggests that this tradition of the single wise person refers to military strategists, whose counsel can turn defeat into victory through their superior tactics. Similarly, Michael Fox suggests, "Ingenuity provides power. It enables one to devise clever stratagems capable even of delivering a city from siege (9:13–15). Hence it is more powerful than a warrior's might (9:16) and weapons of war (9:18)." Fox presumes that ingenuity at warfare is the central point here. Much more consistent, however, would be wisdom in *avoiding* conflict.[55] This can be further advanced on the basis of the famous passage in Eccl. 9:13–18a. How can these images of the single person against warriors make any sense? Some commentaries have pointed to the divine war tradition to explain this, citing, for example, Josh. 23:10 ("One of you puts flight to a thousand"). Certainly we have the comparison of one versus many. But we do not have wisdom contrasted with military strength in this older tradition; indeed, in the Joshua passage, greater strength is the issue.

A more helpful comparison is with the tradition of the "wise women" in 2 Samuel. Claudia Camp and Jacob Hoftijzer have made important contributions to our understanding of the two famous cases of "wise women" who intervene in military circumstances.[56] Camp's study is intended to establish women in positions of family and tribal leadership by recognizing their importance as advisors and local leaders. Although her study does not go in the same direction as this one, she has made many observations relevant to my argument. First, it is clear that the wise woman of Abel practices a form of proverbial wisdom in her dealings with Joab, and exercises considerable diplomatic skills. Camp then compares this with a number of other occasions for "discussions at the city wall" in narrative literature. But Camp, although alluding to the possibility, does not go so far as to say that, for the wise woman of Abel does not have a military role, but rather a peacemaking role! The wise woman of Abel is wise, especially when compared to Wisdom literature dealing with city walls, precisely because she avoids warfare. Her Solomonic decision is hardly Gandhian (she cuts off the head of the fugitive who has threatened the city), but commentators have missed the connection between her single act and the single act of the wise against warriors in Wisdom literature. Indeed, except for the gender of the terms, the Ecclesiastes passage is a striking parallel to the story of the woman of Abel. This is not necessarily to suggest that there is an actual connection between the story and the Ecclesiastes passage, but rather that both illustrate the ideal of practical peacefulness against military solutions—negotiation rather than indignation.

In Sam. 20 and 25, women again act as peacemakers in situations that clearly bode ill for military violence. This raises interesting questions about the interpretation of Prov. 24:5–6:

> Wise warriors are mightier than strong ones,
>   and those who have knowledge than those who have strength;
> for by wise guidance you can wage your war,
>   and in abundance of counselors there is victory.

The abundance of counselors is contrasted with an abundance of soldiers. We may well be in the realm of divine war theology, where the number of soldiers is irrelevant when faith is the controlling issue (this would be supported by a proverb, such as 21:31: "The horse is made ready for the day of battle, but the victory belongs to the LORD"). But in Wisdom literature, we may also be dealing with a decidedly nonmilitary ideal of wisdom, which would also be consistent with the tendency in Proverbs to contrast wisdom with military strength. It is not that the wise are pacifists, but there is a clear preference in Wisdom literature for settling matters peaceably rather than with force.

That Daniel embodies precisely this ethic of the Wisdom Warrior is clear from an examination of only some features of Prov. 1–6. While I cannot go into detail about the stories of Daniel here, I wish to simply point out that these tales, like Tobit, arise from cross-cultural encounter. This encounter, as all cross-cultural encounters, was both fascinating and threatening—that is to say, it was exotic, and at the same time it was dangerous. The setting is in the most sumptuous circumstances imaginable for Jews in late Persian and/or Ptolemaic or Seleucid Hellenistic cultures: the very court of the Babylonian or Persian emperors. In virtually all the Diaspora stories, the exotic enticements include political influence and wealth. But the encounter is also dangerous. There are always threats of death—threats often spectacular in their calculated frightfulness, like burning in overheated furnaces or mauling by starved wild animals. Thus, we find the ambiguities of minority existence illustrated in the folklore of the Diaspora, and the ethics these tales espouse are particularly rational as minority ethics in a hostile, dominant majority culture.

"And Daniel Laughed"—Diasporic Nonviolence: Laughing at the State

I have suggested that there is a direct connection between the clever wisdom advised by Proverbs—a wisdom contrasted with brute strength—and the stratagems of Tobit, Daniel, Esther, Jacob, and many others. This becomes particularly clear in the level of satire and irony in the Bel and the Dragon stories in the Septuagint tradition of the book of Daniel, where Daniel actually laughs at the naive gullibility of the emperor for believing that an idol actually eats (Daniel's laughter forms an inclusio of the solution to the "mystery" of the eating idol: Bel 7, 19).

Where is the nonviolent witness of the Hebrew Bible? If we look for a "Hebrew Gandhi," we will not find such a person. Principled nonviolence as a tactic of *national politics* is not a diasporic virtue and thus is arguably not the Hebraic form of nonviolence. The nonviolence of the Hebrew diasporic ethic is based on the radical irrelevance of the empires within which the Hebrew people lived. In other words, for the Wisdom Warrior, the nonviolence of the Hebrew Diaspora is based on the wise awareness that the empire, despite all its attempts to convince itself otherwise, is not of ultimate significance. It is not worth losing sleep over (it is the emperor's sleep that is disturbed in Dan. 2); much less is it a reason for killing others. It is the clever and wise insight of the Diaspora community that their life as the people of God is far more important than the success or failure of the empire, which is, after all, merely a statue whose dust will be blown with the wind (Dan. 2:35). Indeed, one may well serve the emperor, only as long as it does not conflict with the *real* world.

In conclusion, I would argue that Diaspora ethics are first and foremost subcultural ethics that are not couched in the language of, or heavily invested in, issues of social order and social betterment as values. These kinds of "responsible" ethical discussions are the privileges of a dominant elite. Attempts to read Wisdom literature from the perspective of virtue theology, especially if read in the elitist context of an Aristotle, seriously run the risk of missing the subversive character of ethics in the context of marginalization.

Trying to construct an ethics of civil responsibility from Diaspora sources is like one who is fond of patriotic anthems listening for the first time to Billie Holiday sing the blues. Diaspora ethics may be guided by a prior concern for self-preservation and survival. But it is possible, of course, for these same subcultural ethical traditions to provide the raw materials of a radical critique of the center from the perspective of the margins—thus challenging the very notions both of "civil" and "responsibility."[57]

Notes

1. W. Humphreys, "A Life-Style for Diaspora: A Study of the Tales of Esther and Daniel," *JBL* 92, no. 2 (1973): 211–23; John J. Collins, "The Court Tales in Daniel and the Development of Apocalyptic," *JBL* 94, no. 2 (1975): 218–34; S. Nidith and R. Doran, "The Success Story of the Wise Courtier," *JBL* 96, no. 2 (1977): 179–93; A. Meinhold, "Die Gattung der Josephsgeschichte und des Estherbuches: Diasporanovelle I, II," *ZAW* 87, no. 3 (1975): 306–24; 88, no. 1 (1976): 79–93; Lawrence M. Wills, *The Jew in the Court of the Foreign King* (Minneapolis: Fortress, 1990).
2. Humphreys, "Life-Style for Diaspora," 222.
3. John J. Collins, *Daniel* (FOTL; Grand Rapids: Eerdmans, 1984), 35–36.
4. Wills, *Jew in the Court of the Foreign King*, 197.
5. Philip R. Davies, "Didactic Stories," in *Justification and Variegated Nomism*, vol. 1, *The Complexities of Second Temple Judaism* (ed. D. A. Carson, Peter T. O'Brien, and Mark A. Siefrid; Grand Rapids: Baker Academic, 2001), 101.
6. Philip R. Davies, "Reading Daniel Sociologically," in *The Book of Daniel in the Light of New Findings* (ed. A. S. van der Woude; Louvain: Leuven University Press, 1993), 355.
7. Andre LaCocque, *The Book of Daniel* (Atlanta: John Knox, 1979), 113.
8. Norman W. Porteus, *Daniel: A Commentary* (OTL; Philadelphia: Westminster, 1965), 90.
9. John Goldingay, "Story, Vision, Interpretation: Literary Approaches to Daniel," in van der Woude, *Book of Daniel in the Light of New Findings*, 306.
10. Louis Hartman and Alexander A. DiLella, *The Book of Daniel* (AB 23; Garden City, NY: Doubleday, 1978), 34.
11. Dana Fewell, *Circle of Sovereignty: A Story of Stories in Daniel 1–6* (Bible and Literature 20; JSOTSup 72; Sheffield: Almond, 1988), 154–55.
12. Although it is similar to my approach about the laughter of Daniel at the end of this essay, I want to here acknowledge that Kathleen M. O'Connor's work on Esther is an important exception to the general tendency to see in the Diaspora literature an establishment ethic. Her reading of Esther as humorous exaggeration in the face of Persian dominance is, in my view, right on the mark. See her essay "Humor, Turnabouts, and Survival in the Book of Esther," in *Are We Amused? Humour about Women in the Biblical Worlds* (ed. Athalya Brenner; JSOTSup 383; London: T. & T. Clark, 2003), 52–64.
13. John J. Collins, "Wisdom, Apocalypticism, and Generic Compatibility," in *In Search of Wisdom: Essays in Memory of John G. Gammie* (ed. L. G. Perdue et al.; Louisville, KY: Westminster/John Knox, 1993), 166n9.
14. James L. Crenshaw, *Old Testament Wisdom: An Introduction* (Atlanta: John Knox, 1998), 41.
15. See R. E. Murphy, *The Tree of Life: An Exploration of Biblical Wisdom Literature* (Grand Rapids: Eerdmans, 1990).
16. A helpful survey of the literature is provided by B. A. Mastin, "Wisdom and Daniel," in *Wisdom in Ancient Israel: Essays in Honour of J. A. Emerton* (ed. J. Day, R. P. Gordon, and H. G. M. Williamson; Cambridge: Cambridge University Press, 1995), 161–69.
17. Daniel L. Smith-Christopher, *A Biblical Theology of Exile* (OBT; Minneapolis: Fortress, 2002).
18. Susan Niditch, *Underdogs and Tricksters: A Prelude to Biblical Folklore* (San Francisco: Harper & Row, 1987), xi.
19. Ibid., 124; my emphasis.

20. C. L. Seow, *Ecclesiastes: A New Translation with Introduction and Commentary* (AB 18C; Garden City, NY: Doubleday, 1997); see esp. 21–36. Seow cites Matthew Stolper to buttress his argument that the Preacher could have been a well-off entrepreneur who had taken advantage of some of these "opportunities." However, too much can be made of this. Stolper, however, can be read to say that the Persian economy did not have great opportunities for advancement. It seems Seow and I have read different parts of Stolper's famous work on the Murashu Archives! See Stolper, *Entrepreneurs and Empire: The Murashu Archive, the Murashu Firm, and Persian Rule in Babylonia* (Istanbul: Nederlands Historisch-Archaeologisch Instituut, 1985), esp. 154.

    Seow's somewhat more sanguine reading of the Persian period economy has influenced later commentaries and summaries, such as Richard Clifford, *The Wisdom Literature* (Nashville: Abingdon, 1998), 100–101; and Robert Brown, *Ecclesiastes* (Interpretation; Louisville, KY: Westminster John Knox, 2000), 7–9. Contrast this with Leo Perdue's observation that in Yehud, "times were hard during Persian rule" (Perdue, "Wisdom Theology and Social History in Proverbs 1–9," in *Wisdom, You Are My Sister: Studies in Honor of Roland E. Murphy on the Occasion of His Eightieth Birthday* [ed. Michael L. Barré; Washington, DC: Catholic Biblical Association of America, 1997], 78–101). It seems that Seow wants to locate Ecclesiastes in a monied social setting and so must establish that it was possible to be a wealthy Hebrew in the Persian period.

21. Christine Roy Yoder, *Wisdom as a Woman of Substance: A Socioeconomic Reading of Proverbs 1–9 and 31:10–31* (Berlin: Walter de Gruyter, 2001), 48.

22. Joseph Bryant, *Moral Codes and Social Structure in Ancient Greece: A Sociology of Greek Ethics from Homer to the Epicureans and Stoics* (Albany, NY: SUNY Press, 1966). This view is echoed in Peter Green, *From Alexander to Actium: The Historic Evolution of the Hellenistic Age* (Berkeley: University of California Press, 1990).

23. Joseph A. Fitzmyer, *Tobit* (Commentaries on Early Jewish Literature; Berlin: Walter de Gruyter, Berlin, 2003), 34.

24. Benedikt Otzen, *Tobit and Judith* (Guides to Apocrypha and Pseudepigrapha; London: Sheffield Academic Press, 2002), 43.

25. The increased interest in Tobit is noted, for example, in Richard A. Spencer's helpful summary article, "The Book of Tobit in Recent Research," *CurBS* 7 (1999): 147–80. See also Alexander A. DiLella, "The Book of Tobit and the Book of Judges: An Intertextual Analysis," *Hen* 22, nos. 2–3 (2000): 197–206; Carey Moore, "Scholarly Issues in the Book of Tobit before Qumran and After: An Assessment," *JSP* 5 (1989): 65–81; Otzen, *Tobit and Judith*; and specific issue studies such as Will Soll, "The Book of Tobit as a Window on the Hellenistic Jewish Family," in *Passion, Vitality, and Foment: The Dynamics of Second Temple Judaism* (ed. L. M. Luker; Harrisburg, PA: Trinity Press International, 2001), 242–74.

26. Amy-Jill Levine, "Tobit: Teaching Jews How to Live in the Diaspora," *BRev* 8, no. 4 (1992): 44.

27. Fitzmyer, *Tobit*, 35.

28. Mark G. Brett, *Genesis: Procreation and the Politics of Identity* (London: Routledge, 2000), 92.

29. James C. Scott, *Domination and the Arts of Resistance: Hidden Transcripts* (New Haven, CT: Yale University Press, 1990), 14.

30. Luigi Lombardi-Satriani, "Folklore as Culture of Contestation," *Journal of Folklore Institute* 11 (1974): 119.

31. John C. Knudsen, "When Trust Is on Trial: Negotiating Refugee Narratives," in *Mistrusting Refugees* (ed. E. V. Daniel and J. C. Knudsen; Berkeley: University of California Press, 1995), 18.

32. Eftihia Voutira and Barbara E. Harrell-Bond, "In Search of the Locus of Trust: The Social World of the Refugee Camp," in Daniel and Knudsen, *Mistrusting Refugees*, 216.

33. Crawford H. Toy, *A Critical and Exegetical Commentary on the Book of Proverbs* (ICC; Edinburgh: T. & T. Clark, 1970), 14–16.

34. Ibid., 14.

35. Nili Shupak, *Where Can Wisdom Be Found? The Sage's Language in the Bible and in Ancient Egyptian Literature* (Fribourg: Vandenhoeck & Ruprecht, 1993), 150.

36. Ibid., 165.

37. Ibid., 170.

38. Ibid., 182.

39. Crenshaw, *Old Testament Wisdom*, 215.

40. "The aura of the court, which could be detected in the older instructions, is absent; Ankhsheshonq is writing for ordinary people, not for officials." Roland Murphy, *The Tree of Life: An Exploration of Biblical Wisdom Literature* (Grand Rapids: Eerdmans, 1990), 167.

41. *Ancient Egyptian Literature: A Book of Readings*, trans. Miriam Lichtheim (Los Angeles: University of California Press, 1980), vol. 1: *The Old Kingdom*, 64–65.

42. *Ancient Egyptian Literature*, vol. 3: *Demotic Literature*, 159–84.

43. William McKane, *Proverbs: A Commentary* (OTL; Philadelphia: Westminster, 1970), 118.

44. Ibid., 122.

45. Crenshaw, *Old Testament Wisdom,* 132.

46. Elsa Tamez, "Ecclesiastes: A Reading from the Periphery," *Int* 55, no. 3 (2001): 256.

47. Patrick Matlou, "Upsetting the Cart: Forced Migration and Gender Issues, the African Experience," in *Engendering Forced Migration: Theory and Practice* (ed. D. Indra; Oxford: Berghahn Books, 1999), 136.

48. Eftihia Voutira and Barbara E. Harrell-Bond, "In Search of the Locus of Trust," 218.

49. McKane suggests that it should be read as concern to secure debts: "If you are to have dealings with a person who is a bad risk and is liable for dubious debts, secure yourself immediately!" (McKane, *Proverbs*, 543). Either way, this spirit is clearly not the same as that of Deuteronomy.

50. Otzen, *Tobit and Judith*, 43.

51. See E. Bickermann, *From Ezra to the Last of the Maccabees: Foundations of Post-Biblical Judaism* (New York: Schocken, 1962); M. Hengel, *Judaism and Hellenism: Studies in Their Encounter in Palestine during the Early Hellenistic Period* (Philadelphia: Fortress, 1974); and V. Tcherikover, *Hellenistic Civilization and the Jews* (Philadelphia: Jewish Publication Society of America, 1959).

52. See John J. Collins, *The Apocalyptic Visions of the Book of Daniel* (HSM 16; Missoula, MT: Scholars Press, 1977).

53. See Gordon Zerbe, "'Pacifism' and 'Passive Resistance' in Apocalyptic Writings: A Critical Evaluation," in *The Pseudepigrapha and Early Biblical Interpretation* (ed. J. H. Charlesworth and C. A. Evans; JSPSup 14; Sheffield: Sheffield Academic Press, 1993), 65–95.

54. Toy, *Critical and Exegetical Commentary on the Book of Proverbs*, 333. Toy compares this with the Greek virtue of *sophroyne*, but notably, Helen North's impressively sweeping survey of this virtue in Greek literature includes no examples of this virtue as a contrast to warfare or the spirit of the warrior. See Helen North,

Sophrosyne: Self-Knowledge and Self-Restraint in Greek Literature (Ithaca, NY: Cornell University Press, 1966).

55. Michael V. Fox, "Wisdom in Qoheleth," in Perdue et al., *In Search of Wisdom*, 117–18.

56. See Claudia Camp, "The Wise Women of 2 Samuel: A Role Model for Women in Early Israel?" *CBQ* 43, no. 1 (1981): 14–29, and Jacob Hoftijzer, "David and the Tekoite Woman (2 Sam 14:1–24)," in *VT* 20, no. 4 (1970): 419–44.

57. For example, I would argue that the important role of such originally "marginal" theologies such as Anabaptism is to be found precisely in this ability to offer a critique of, and alternative orientation to, the predominant Reformed tradition in the American theological enterprise.

Chapter 12

Wine, Women, and Song (of Songs)

Gender Politics and Identity Construction in Postexilic Israel

J. DAVID PLEINS

Watch out! If you use sociological and materialist methods to dissect great works of literature, literary critic Harold Bloom will call you one of the "resenters." Apparently those who use sociological, materialist, and postmodern methods are cultural ingrates who, to quote Bloom, "resent literature, or are ashamed of it, or are just not all that fond of reading it."[1] Thus, I knew I was in trouble when I wanted to include the Song of Songs in my book-length study of the social ethics of ancient Israel.[2] Although I understood that the Song of Songs was not a tract for social justice or feminist liberation, I also felt that blandly labeling the Song of Songs "great literature" in no further need of analysis would leave an unforgivable lacuna in my book. There and in this presentation, rather than privilege literary analysis over sociocultural questions à la Bloom, I propose a close inspection of wine, women, and song in the Hebrew Bible, with a primary focus on two striking texts, the Song of Songs and the story of Noah's drunkenness. The triangulation of wine, women, and song, or, more broadly, drink, gender, and imagination in these texts functions to demarcate male identity and social dominance in ancient Israel, an identity rooted in traditional patriarchal authority and male gender structures.

Wine-Induced Wantonness

While Ps. 104 assures us that "wine . . . cheers the hearts of men," elsewhere Scripture tells us that decadence, depravity, and divine judgment are more often wine's by-products. In biblical narrative, scenes of wine-induced wantonness include the tale of Noah's drunkenness (Gen. 9), Lot's daughters' dalliances with their father (Gen. 19), Rebekah's deception of Isaac (Gen. 27), the rape of the Levite's concubine (Judg. 19), Nabal's foolishness (1 Sam. 26), the murder of Amnon (2 Sam. 13), Ahasuerus's exploitation of Vashti (Esth. 1), and Haman's imputed intent to ravish Esther (Esth. 7), and drinking serves as the proximate cause of the loss of Job's children (Job 1). On occasion, wine typifies the opulence of foreign powers, calling forth acts of moral courage in figures like Esther and Daniel who seek to evade the taint of royal folly. Such narratives, in other words, reinforce suspicion that wine serves up a hefty dose of decadence, depravity, and divine wrath.

Periodic calls for abstinence crop up here and there in Scripture. In Leviticus, abstention for Aaron and sons is enjoined as a permanent marker of the line that separates the sacred from the profane at the tent of meeting (Lev. 10:8–10). Likewise, abstinence is integral to the Nazirite vow (Num. 6), a fact that takes narrative form in Samson's birth story when his mother is exhorted by the angel not to drink wine or intoxicants (Judg. 13). Impurity due to wine drinking stands behind Eli's denunciation of Hannah, even as she dedicates her future son to God in a Nazirite-styled vow (1 Sam. 1). Daniel's abstinence is a late version of values encoded in the Nazirite vow and the Rechabite ideal (Dan. 1, 10). For Jeremiah, the abstinence of the Rechabites elevates the virtue of moral fortitude in an otherwise unsavory age (Jer. 35). In Amos, the image of a drunken Nazirite signifies a society turned upside down (Amos 2:12). While Lady Wisdom in Proverbs may have the wine of wisdom on tap, warnings against actually consuming wine litter the text (Prov. 9:2, 5; 20:1; 21:17; 23:20, 31; 31:4). Marriage to virgins and abstention from wine are the order of the day in Ezekiel's future temple (Ezek. 44:21).

In the prophetic writings, wine is linked to harsh divine judgment, either as a sign of the decadent lifestyle of the elite or as a symbol of the drunken madness that attends God's fury against the unjust deeds of the affluent (Isa. 5:11–12, 22; Jer. 13:12; 23:9; 25:15; Hos. 4:11; 7:5; Joel 1:5; 4:5; Amos 2:8; 6:6; Mic. 2:11; 6:15; Zech. 9:15). The elite's decadence is perhaps best captured by their motto "Eat and drink, for tomorrow we die!" (Isa. 22:13). When judgment takes place, the lack of wine is a sign of the land's disgrace at God's hands (Isa. 16:10). Where there is no wine, there can be no song or celebration (Isa. 24:9). The image of the vine's failure, in other words, signifies the demise of the land under the weight of God's judgment (Amos 5:11; Zeph. 1:13; cf. Deut. 28:39).

It is true that the Hebrew Bible crafts visions of the nation's renewal in terms of the revitalized cultivation of the vine. This is a factor in a few late prophetic texts (Amos 9:14; Zech. 10:7). Presumably these late texts reflect the Deuteronomic vision of renewal. Deuteronomy encourages the consumption of tithes of grain, wine, and oil, calling for the purchase of wine and foodstuffs for feasting before God (Deut. 14:22–26). Despite this statement in Deuteronomy and related Deuteronomic additions to the prophetic writings, on the whole wine carries largely negative connotations in Scripture. One curious passage in Deuteronomy deserves comment. This seemingly later addition suggests that the forty years of wandering in the wilderness without wine was so that the people "might know that I the LORD am your God," using words that sound like a priestly updating of Deuteronomy to reflect a very different vision of wine production and the land (Deut. 29:5).

The Social World of Wine, Women, and the Song of Songs

We come then to the Song of Songs. On the surface, the casual reader may have the impression that wine and sex stand in a positive relationship in this text. Here, after all, lust is celebrated heartily and, apart from pomegranates, wine is the sexual stimulant of choice in these poems. We seem to be in a different world of sensuality in the Song of Songs, far from the abstemious realm of so much of sacred Scripture. The decadence that deserves divine condemnation is far from view. The delirium of judgment is set aside. The injustices of the drunken elite are overlooked. Is all as it seems in this collection? Have profane *eros* and gender egalitarianism triumphed over sexual depravity, the prophetic condemnation of the elite, and the male regulation of female sexuality? Is the Song of Songs the Israelite equivalent of the erotic Egyptian Papyrus 55001, offering a pornographic excursion of ancient Israel's erogenous zones?[3] Or does so much superficial sensuality mask a much more conservative social order in which the text is very much at home?

From earliest times there were those whose attitude was that of Origen's, namely, that in the study of Scripture, "this book of the Song of Songs should be reserved for study till the last."[4] In this, these interpreters tacitly acknowledge that a materialist reading, that is, a reading that takes seriously the character of the book as human love poetry, more naturally suggests itself as one encounters this "scandalous" inclusion in the canon of Scripture.

From the sociohistorical standpoint, Egyptian love poetry bears striking similarities to the Song of Songs, perhaps offering alternative keys for unlocking a less theologically antagonistic and more culturally sensitive reading of the text.[5] The various poems of Papyrus Chester Beatty I offer us the same balance of voices (male-female), the same rich body language and nature-linked descriptions, the same motifs of longing and quest, the same sickness and pining over love, the same sorts of euphemisms about locks and doors, and the same "brother" and "sister" language that we find throughout the Song of Songs.[6]

Likewise, the collections found in Papyrus Harris 500 and the Cairo vases 1266 and 25218 afford comparable phrases about the unity of the lovers, the concern over what to tell "mother," the search for the beloved, the snare of love, and the verbiage about "brother" and "sister" that mark the Song of Songs.[7] While some of these themes may simply be a product of the universal character of love poetry, still their assemblage and concentration are too close to the Song of Songs not to suggest that the Song extends the cultural legacy of the court poetry of ancient Egypt. To be sure, the text of the Song of Songs, with its preponderance of Aramaisms, Persian loan words, and late Hebrew vocabulary, qualifies such attempts at connection, but the Egyptian imperial contacts in Canaan are long lived, suggesting that precursors to the Song of Songs were likely part of the royal life and elite imagination of ancient Israel and Judah (cf. Cant. 1:1–5, 12; 3:7–11; 7:5 [Heb. 7:6]; 8:11–12).[8]

The urban character of the texts is also more simply reflected in the shift of locales from Jerusalem and city to the countryside (Cant. 1:5; 3:2, 5, 10; 5:7–8, 16; 6:4), and in the plethora of royal allusions and military images (1:12; 3:7–8; 4:4; 6:10, 12; 7:4–5 [Heb. 7:5–6]; 8:10). Most importantly, however, the urban character of this literature is betrayed by its idealization of the garden motif (Cant. 1:6; 2:15; 4:12–15, 16; 5:1; 6:11; 7:12 [Heb. 7:13]; 8:11–12). Such a tradition of agricultural idealization is no doubt shared with the Mesopotamian texts regarding the goddess Ishtar's relationship to the shepherd Dumuzi (Tammuz), a poetry that undergirded the *hieros gamos* rituals of the royal court in the very ancient period of the region's history and that carry on in later settings apart from the Ishtar-Dumuzi theme.[9] While not wanting to turn the Song of Songs into such a set of sacred marriage texts, we cannot help but notice that these motifs are integral to the movement of the collection in a way not found in the Egyptian materials (Cant. 1:1, 4–5, 8; 3:7, 9, 11; 7:5 [Heb. 7:6]; 8:11–12).[10]

As an urban work, the Song of Songs imposes on lived reality a grid for what is imaginable, from an androcentric perspective, in terms of celebratable sensual relations, doing so under the literary guise of idealized types and forms. Jack Sasson's distinction is worth noting in this regard:

> I would argue that love poetry ordinarily ignores *gender* differences, focusing instead on *sexual* equality and that, written mostly by males, erotic poetry indulges a male fantasy, wherein females are made to seek out lovers with the determination that is supposed to be stereotypical of the male.[11]

In other words, the egalitarianism of the lovers is only apparent and is not inconsistent with the distribution of social power and roles accorded women elsewhere in the biblical text.[12] Indeed, this poetry would normally reinforce a conservative social structure, as do the *wasf* poems in Syria often linked to the Song of Songs.[13] Athalya Brenner's study of the gendering of food and drink in the Song of Songs lends weight to these considerations, even if she sees in the text a social transformation that I do not discover there. In general, Brenner discerns that it is the female figure in the Song of Songs who "flows with the produce of the Promised Land, with the milk and honey and wine and pomegranates."[14] The male figure, as agent, cultivates and feeds off this female object. She is the locus of productivity; he is the beneficiary. As Brenner states, "The male lover eats and drinks his female lover."[15] Even more succinctly Brenner writes, "She is the wine, he drinks it."[16] Like so much of the Bible, the Song of Songs uses the image of the dominant male to imagine for women what it is to be women. It is true that Scripture is often transfixed by female sexual boldness, as A. Bloch and C. Bloch have observed in their commentary and translation of the Song of Songs.[17] Yet cases like Delilah, Bathsheba, Tamar, or even Ruth hardly suggest that in ancient Israelite culture unchecked female passion was seen as a good or that women felt free to carve out their own sexual turf inside the canon of Scripture or in that social world.

Seen in the light of the foregoing, the Song of Songs is very much a part of the world of wine presented to us elsewhere in Scripture. In terms of its stark sexuality, the Song of Songs reinforces the idea that unbridled sensuality can be a source of decadence and discord in society. Brenner downplays the violence associated with sensuality, yet the Song of Songs is frank about such violence, as the watchmen beat the woman who roams the town outside of her proper bounds (Cant. 5:7). But stories of decadence and depravity reinforce those boundary lines throughout Scripture. While the Song of Songs may seem to be indulgent to an extreme, one can also argue that, like Mardi Gras, one moment's excess can actually serve to reinforce a fairly conservative social structure.

That the Bible is obsessed with regulating female sexual activity may simply reflect the social reality that such activity was indeed under scrutiny. One hardly imagines that the world of the ancient Israelite was some sort of brothel, the Song of Songs notwithstanding.

Noah's Drunkenness

In this part of the essay, I want to set the seemingly positive sensuality of the Song of Songs beside the much more sinister sexuality implied in the story of Noah's drunkenness. Among the Bible's portraits of heroes, none closes more oddly than the tale of Noah. Presented initially as the most righteous figure of his generation, Noah is selected by God to save the human race from its corruption. Only he and his immediate family are spared as the rest of the world is swept away in a horrific flood. As the cataclysm rages, God turns the tide at the very moment when "God remembered Noah." We are led to think of Noah as a noble hero. We hardly expect the story's denouement, which presents Noah in a drunken stupor, the apparent victim of a sexual outrage at the hands of his son Ham (whose own son, Canaan, is cursed by the decrepit patriarch).

The peculiarity of the story has exercised the imaginations of interpreters over the centuries.[18] From the sordid stories of the rabbis, to the racist justifications of slavery by proslavery advocates in the American South in the nineteenth century, to the queer-bashing of fundamentalists, the drunkenness tale keeps turning up like a bad penny. Perhaps one is less surprised when this happens in fundamentalist circles, but conflicting (and conflicted) interpretations also show up in more established, scholarly quarters. The drunkenness passage has been susceptible to five sorts of interpretations.

Sexual Sleuthing and the Potency of Alcohol

A clever, if ultimately dissatisfying, reading is given to us by H. Hirsch Cohen in *The Drunkenness of Noah*. Cohen wonders "why a man worthy enough to be saved from the waters of the flood should be portrayed later as lying naked in a drunken stupor?"[19] Why, indeed? To find the answer, Cohen engages in a bit of what he calls "philological sleuthing."[20] Taking his lead from erotic paintings and sexually suggestive poetry from the ancient Mediterranean, Cohen observes that ancient cultures frequently linked wine, fire, and the male genitalia. Alcohol, he argues, was understood to contain those fiery procreative juices that were needed, especially by older people, to ensure successful sexual intercourse. Wine was for the ancients what Viagra has become for us.

Quaffing his viticultural Viagra, Noah was hard at work trying to follow God's command, "Be fruitful and multiply! Swarm throughout the world! Increase in it!" (Gen. 9:7). At age 600, Noah needed whatever help he could get to carry out those orders. In Cohen's words, "Noah's determination to maintain his procreative ability at full strength resulted in drinking himself into a state of helpless intoxication."[21] By placing the powers of alcohol in their proper procreative perspective, Noah reclaims his image as an obedient servant of God.

Sadly, however, the morally upright Noah became the undeserving victim of Ham's wiles. Here too, Cohen thinks interpreters have failed to grasp the import of the story. To look is to acquire. Ham looked and in the process gained Noah's procreative powers. Noah had artificially boosted his sexual powers with alcohol and was engaged in the very act of sexual intercourse at the moment Ham barged in and slipped out with the sexual goods. Upon waking, Noah recognized that something had gone terribly wrong—presumably having sensed, like Superman in the presence of kryptonite, that his vital energies had dissipated.[22] Strangely, though, he curses Ham's son Canaan and not the perpetrator himself. Apparently, Ham's successful appropriation of Noah's procreative powers explains why Noah could not curse Ham. Having lost his potency, Noah could not retrieve it from Ham. Before it was too late, however, Noah cursed Ham's descendant Canaan to thwart any attempt to pass that potency on to his son.[23]

Cohen's clever commentary makes sense out of aspects of the story that have confounded generations of Bible readers. The seemingly free sensuality of the Song of Songs finds tempered criticism in such a text. If Cohen is right, the very drink that can revive the libido is also the drink that drives even the greatest of patriarchs mad. If the Song of Songs is an endorsement of wine, the story of Noah's drunkenness is a cautionary tale.

One cannot but feel, however, that Cohen uses so many keys in so many farflung locks in an effort to open up the story that the essential meaning of the text has slipped through his fingers. Cohen is hardly the first or the last interpreter who has been eager to fill in the blanks in a text that resists easy explication.

Noah, Racism, and African American Enslavement: The "Curse of Ham"

The worst offenders have given the passage a racist tinge. Afrikaners in South Africa made use of the Ham story to justify apartheid and resist democratic elections in that country,[24] but the most notorious use of this passage was in the efforts of slaveholders and preachers in the antebellum, southern United States to justify the enslavement of African Americans.

In tract after tract and book after book, proslavery writers in nineteenth-century America invoked this very passage to defend the view that slavery was a legitimate product of the "curse of Ham." Ham was seen to be the ancestor of the Africans, and the curse of Noah was thought to have come to fruition in the institution of slavery. T. Stringfellow wrote in his *Scriptural and Statistical Views in Favor of Slavery*, "God decreed this institution before it existed" and has "connected its *existence* with Prophetic tokens of special favor, to those who should be slave owners or masters."[25]

That it was Noah who was drunk in the first place was beside the point for southern writers. What mattered, as Stephen Haynes argues, was that Ham acted with dishonor against his father.[26] The image of Noah as a planter who deserved respect resonated well with the social world of the nineteenth-century South. Southern writers papered over the profligate behavior of the patriarch Noah, ignoring those story elements that inconvenienced their argument. What mattered was that Ham had the audacity to dishonor his father.

White Southerners saw themselves as the heirs of Noah's son Japheth, carrying out God's eternal plan by enslaving African Americans, the descendants of Ham, in a land once dominated by the Indians, the descendants of Noah's son Shem.[27] This fantasy was deeply internalized. One writer of the period portrayed an heir of Japheth instructing a descendant of Ham about this grand white destiny, while Ham's heir humbly submitted to God's design for Japheth's descendants.[28] The myth not only came to encode white superiority but imagined black acceptance of white domination as the black contribution in God's enduring plan for America.

If myths can go wrong, this one certainly did so in the American South. Obviously the story originally had nothing to do with black slavery, but that did not stop white Christians from filling in the blanks. While this use of the text went beyond the surface meaning of the story, we can nonetheless wonder if, in fact, the text contains its own codes of domination that came to be invoked in the later American context. Such a reading does not take us as far afield from the Song of Songs as one might at first think. The Genesis story would seem to encode particular lines of familial respect and authority that also skulk about in the Song of Songs, though the latter does this in terms of the mother figure (Cant. 1:6; 3:4; 3:11; 6:9; 8:1–2).

Ham's Handiwork and Homosexuality

Then, of course, there is the homosexual interpretation of the Noah story. Randall Bailey argues that the "ambiguity" of the story leads the reader to resolve that something sexual has transpired, so unlike the slavery interpretation we are safely back on Song of Song's sensual turf, though this time with a same-sex sexuality in view.[29] Given the text's failure to specify Ham's transgression, many speculate that what happened between Ham and Noah in the tent that day was some sort of homosexual act. Fundamentalist writer Gordon Lindsay, for example, assumes that Ham's sin was homosexuality. That assumption is supported, Lindsay claims, in Gen. 10:15–19, where we learn that Ham's son Canaan carried on the family tradition and settled in the land named after him—a land in which the immoral Sodom and Gomorrah continued Ham's and Canaan's wicked legacy.[30] The homosexual interpretation is "obvious" to most fundamentalists.

The problem with this interpretation, of course, is that the text is rather vague at the very point where the deed occurs. Noah is drunk, and Ham does something inappropriate that warrants the curse of a drunken hero. What did Ham do? Whatever Ham did, Shem and Japheth were able quickly to remedy the situation. Perhaps we are to see in the story no more than what it says, namely, that Ham exposed (or even simply observed) Noah's private parts and that the other sons covered their father up. This would certainly qualify as a repellent event in the ancient Israelite value system, but it is hardly the dire homosexual misdeed that fundamentalist interpreters see in the text. Who is the real biblical literalist here?

Fundamentalists are not alone in this regard. The homosexual interpretation has taken up residence among biblical scholars. Regina Schwartz, hardly a fundamentalist, is confident that the Ham story is a statement against homosexuality, or rather, "homosexual incest, father-son incest, to be precise."[31] By showing the disaster that results from Ham's deed, Schwartz argues that the text reinforces "the general biblical hysteria about homosexuality."[32]

Schwartz's analysis begs many questions. Is incest now to be equated with homosexuality? Marti Nissinen, in his comprehensive study *Homoeroticism in the Biblical World*, insists on making the distinction, arguing that the Ham story concerns Ham's rape of Noah as an act of incest and power, not a homosexual deed.[33] We may also ask whether there truly is a general hysteria about homosexuality in the Hebrew Bible. After all, the topic is mentioned very infrequently (Lev. 18:22; 20:13; Deut. 23:17). Can we be so precise about texts that are so fraught with literary and cultural ambiguities? At this point, fundamentalists usually bring in the story of the destruction of Sodom and Gomorrah (Gen. 19). Yet no one would use the gang rape in Judg. 19, where the concubine is brutalized and murdered, to condemn heteroeroticism, so why call on the Sodom text to support a blanket condemnation of homosexuality? That Ham or the men of Sodom were "gay" hardly seems to be the point of the text.

While this line of interpretation is actually more problematic than many seem to think, I suggest that if the antihomosexual thrust of the Noah story can be sustained, then we are seeing in this text a kind of limit to sexual conduct that reinforces the norm of heterosexuality found in the Song of Songs. However, I suspect that the Song of Songs stands at the other end of the continuum. Its free-spirited sexuality is no more a cultural norm than the homosexuality inferred from the

Noah tale. The vast middle ground and actual social practice would seem to be filled in by the rest of the Hebrew Bible, where a more self-restrained sexuality is cultivated.

Lecherous Libido?

Perhaps the text has something more outrageous in mind. Peter Gomes, author of *The Good Book: Reading the Bible with Mind and Heart,* points to rabbinic suggestions "that Ham had engaged in immoral sexual conduct on the Ark."[34] Some rabbis believed that while the other people aboard the ark remained celibate, Ham joined the dog and the raven as the only beings to have sexual relations while on board; presumably Ham found an animal or two to satisfy his lusts.[35] Others taught that, after the flood, Ham "castrated Noah so that there could be no more heirs from his father's loins."[36] One rabbinic tradition holds that Canaan gazed first, and in so doing became an accomplice to Ham's misdeeds.[37] In another, Canaan castrates Noah after binding a thread around his circumcised penis.[38] In this tradition, Ham merely looks on as Canaan does the dirty work but then goes outside to joke with his brothers about the incident, thereby dishonoring his father and neglecting his duties as a son. If any of these horrifying possibilities is implied by the story, the extreme harshness of Noah's response becomes more intelligible. Ham would represent uncontrolled libido at its worst.

This approach is fascinating, but it seems to go far beyond the text. We get a tour of the sexual proclivities and anxieties of the later interpretive tradition, but hardly any additional insight into the meaning of the original text. This line of interpretation finds its counterpart in some of the more imaginative readings of the Song of Songs, where every line is made to contain layers upon layers of sexual innuendo. Titillating to be sure, but hardly demonstrable to an independent observer.

All in the Family: The Incest Question

There is yet one last angle for approaching the drunkenness story in its own theological and literary terms. Some interpreters focus on the phrase "father's nakedness." Insight is provided here by Lev. 18:7–8: "Do not uncover your father's nakedness, that is, the nakedness of your mother. She is your mother. You shall not uncover her nakedness. Do not uncover the nakedness of your father's wife. She is the nakedness of your father." Leviticus 20:11a concurs: "When a man lies with his father's wife, he uncovers the nakedness of his father."

These passages suggest that a reference to the uncovering of a father's nakedness is really a reference to an act of sexual impropriety with one's own mother or stepmother (see also Deut. 22:30 [Heb 23:1]; 27:20; Ezek. 22:10). As F. W. Bassett explains, "The idiom is used to describe not homosexual but heterosexual intercourse, even when it speaks of a man seeing another man's nakedness. 'To see a man's nakedness' means to have sexual relations with his wife."[39]

Robert Gagnon, who seems to want to find modern homosexual analogues in every nook and cranny of the Bible as he searches for ammunition to condemn modern homosexual practice, acknowledges in this case that "father's nakedness" refers to *maternal* incest. Yet even here he inexplicably insists on reading the Ham passage as "incestuous, homosexual rape."[40]

If Bassett's interpretation is to be preferred to that of Gagnon—and I think it should be—then the "father's nakedness" refers to Ham's violation of his own mother. If this interpretation is more authentic to the linguistic nuances of the text than Gagnon's reading, the tragic irony is that a text that is designed to horrify us about *heterosexual* misconduct has come to be used as a sledgehammer against gays and African Americans.

However, as tantalizing as the incest interpretation is, we cannot be entirely certain that the incest categories of Leviticus ought to govern our reading of Genesis. The similarity in language may be coincidental, and we may be guilty of reading more into the story than was intended. After all, the final form of the text, as Bassett acknowledges, turns on Ham's merely gazing at the nakedness of his father. In this, we return to Cohen's suspicion that there is power in gazing, though without the excessive trappings of Cohen's analysis. The story of Noah's drunkenness prompts us to ask what sort of "nakedness" the Song of Songs finds acceptable. Tellingly, the word "nakedness" does not appear in the Song of Songs. One might also find it curious to consider that despite reveling in the body, many passages in the Song of Songs actually focus on seeing the lover's face and peering behind the veil (Cant. 1:10; 1:15; 2:9, 14; 4:1–3; 5:10–13, 16; 6:5–7; 6:13 [Heb. 7:1]; 7:4–5 [Heb. 7:5–6]; 7:10). Gazing at one's lover is in its own right a key factor for the Song of Songs. On the other hand, the story of Noah's drunkenness and the rest of the tradition sees fit to patrol the border regions where gazing is forbidden.

Ancient Israel's Sociological Currency

The Song of Songs and the story of Noah's drunkenness would appear to be two sides of the same sociological coin. This coin trades not in drunkenness or sexual excess per se but in rather conservative social sexual patterns and practices. The stock in trade of Scripture is a society in which gender lines are clearly marked and in which female sexual activity is regulated to perpetuate the male's social status. The Hebrew Bible as a whole seals this social destiny for both partners. Men shall enjoy wine, women, and song in a land of divine plenty. Women will embody that plenty in fruitful heterosexual relationships dominated by males. This ideology may be a social fantasy, but we do a disservice to the texts if we turn them into documents more congenial to the modern, liberated mind.

One lesson here is a negative one but is no less important for its negativity. Mythographer William Doty warns of the "danger of getting stuck in fundamentalisms that leave us trapped in dysfunctional mythostories."[41] In ancient times, the biblical text may have authorized the Israelite subjugation and enslavement of the Canaanites. In our own day we must beware of the easy assumptions that permit those in control to use the text to authorize repression in God's name.

Rather than fall prey to first impressions when reading texts, we must ask what social configurations are hidden by biblical texts that turn women into free sexual spirits and patriarchs into drunkards. Such texts demarcate fault lines between those on the inside who do not drink (or who know when to drink) and those on the outside who are drunkards, those on the inside who have good sex and those on the outside who presumably do not, those on the inside who tell the right stories and sing the right songs and those on the outside who bear the curses. We find that an idealized male and national identity is bound up with factors such as drink, social power, the delineation of sex lines, and the need to control libidinal impulses that are thought to be as much violent as they are procreative.

Another lesson gained is that we must affirm, against Bloom, that the Bible's legacy is not enhanced by treating the book as "great literature." However wonderful the Song of Songs is as ancient poetry or however carefully constructed the Noah tale is as narrative, we will only make progress on matters of historical interpretation when we struggle with the sort of world the Bible wishes to construct, while not overlooking the need to fashion a postbiblical world free of its counterproductive social constraints. We can for this very reason affirm with Bloom that there is value in letting the text retain its own cultural stubbornness and blinders. Perhaps this justifies juxtaposing these two rather disparate texts.

Our study of these diverging texts may leave us with more of a postmodern muddle than a clear postexilic sociohistorical view of wine, women, and song in the Hebrew Bible. However, reading behind and around the text reveals the underlying social strategy of the tradition. Each text seeks in its own way to create the same set of social conditions and sexual norms, reinforcing particular attitudes about consumption, gender, and the sacred. The free spirit of the Song of Songs is not quite so free in a world where fear of the father's nakedness and the glare of a mother's stern eyes delimits an entire culture's expression of its subterranean sensual sensibilities.

Notes

1. Harold Bloom, *The Western Canon: The Books and School of the Ages* (New York: Harcourt, Brace & Co., 1994), 521.
2. J. David Pleins, *Social Visions of the Hebrew Bible: A Theological Introduction* (Louisville, KY: Westminster John Knox, 2001).
3. See J. Omlin, *Der Papyrus 55001 und seine satirisch-erotischen Zeichnungen und Inschriften* (Turin: Fratelli Pozzo, 1973).
4. Marvin H. Pope, *Song of Songs: A New Translation with Introduction and Commentary* (AB 7C; Garden City, NY: Doubleday, 1977), 117.
5. See Michael V. Fox, *The Song of Songs and the Ancient Egyptian Love Songs* (Madison: University of Wisconsin Press, 1985); Miriam Lichtheim, *Ancient Egyptian Literature*, vol. 2, *The New Kingdom* (Berkeley: University of California Press, 1976), 181–93.
6. Lichtheim, *New Kingdom*, 182–89.
7. Ibid., 190–93; see also Marcia Falk, *Love Lyrics from the Bible: A Translation and Literary Study of the Song of Songs* (Bible and Literature Series, 4; Sheffield: Almond, 1982).

8. Ariel A. Bloch and Chana Bloch, *The Song of Songs: A New Translation with Introduction and Commentary* (Berkeley: University of California Press, 1998), 23–25.

9. See Samuel Noah Kramer, *The Sacred Marriage Rite: Aspects of Faith, Myth, and Ritual in Ancient Sumer* (Bloomington: Indiana University Press, 1969).

10. See J. S. Cooper, "Sacred Marriage and Popular Cult in Early Mesopotamia," in *Official Cult and Popular Religion in the Ancient Near East* (ed. E. Matsushima; Heidelberg: Universitätsverlag C. Winter, 1993), 81–96; Fox, *Song of Songs*, 239–43; E. Matsushima, "Les Rituels du Mariage Divin dans les Documents Accadiens," *Acta Sumerologica* 10 (1988): 95–128; D. Reisman, "Iddin-Dagan's Sacred Marriage Hymn," *JCS* 25 (1973): 185–202.

11. Jack M. Sasson, "A Major Contribution to Song of Songs Scholarship," *JAOS* 107 (1987): 735.

12. Contrast Dianne Bergant, "'My Beloved Is Mine and I Am His' (Song 2:16): The Song of Songs and Honor and Shame," *Semeia* 68 (1996): 23–40.

13. Pope, *Song of Songs*, 56–57.

14. Athalya Brenner, "The Food of Love: Gendered Food and Food Imagery in the Song of Songs," *Semeia* 86 (1999): 109.

15. Ibid., 108–9.

16. Ibid., 108.

17. Bloch and Bloch, *Song of Songs*, 13.

18. See J. David Pleins, *When the Great Abyss Opened: Classic and Contemporary Readings of Noah's Flood* (New York: Oxford University Press, 2003).

19. H. Hirsch Cohen, *The Drunkenness of Noah* (Tuscaloosa: University of Alabama Press, 1974), vii.

20. Ibid., x.

21. Ibid., 8.

22. Ibid., 21–22.

23. Ibid., chap. 2.

24. See H. F. Stander, "The Church Fathers on (the Cursing of) Ham," *Acta Patristica et Byzantina* 5 (1994): 113–25.

25. T. Stringfellow, *Scriptural and Statistical Views in Favor of Slavery* (Richmond, VA: J. W. Randolph, 1856), 9.

26. Stephen Haynes, *Noah's Curse: The Biblical Justification of American Slavery* (New York: Oxford University Press, 2002), 65–104.

27. Thomas V. Peterson, *Ham and Japheth: The Mythic World of Whites in the Antebellum South* (Metuchen, NJ: American Theological Library Association, 1978), 5.

28. Ibid., 94.

29. Randall C. Bailey, "They're Nothing but Incestuous Bastards: The Polemical Use of Sex and Sexuality in Hebrew Canon Narratives," in *Readings from This Place*, vol. 1, *Social Location and Biblical Interpretation in the United States* (ed. F. F. Segovia and M. A. Tolbert; Minneapolis: Fortress, 1994), 134.

30. D. G. Lindsay, *The Genesis Flood: Continents in Collision* (Dallas: Christ for the Nations, 1992), 227.

31. Regina Schwartz, *The Curse of Cain: The Violent Legacy of Monotheism* (Chicago: University of Chicago Press, 1997), 107.

32. Ibid., 111.

33. Marti Nissinen, *Homoeroticism in the Biblical World: A Historical Perspective* (Minneapolis: Fortress, 1998), 52–53.

34. Peter Gomes, *The Good Book: Reading the Bible with Mind and Heart* (New York: William Morrow, 1996), 49.

35. Talmud *b. Sanhedrin* 108b; *Rabbah Gen.* 36:7.

36. Gomes, *Good Book*, 49; cf. Talmud *b. Sanhedrin* 70a.

37. *Rabbah Gen.* 36:7.

38. *Pirke de Rabbi Eliezer* (London, 1916; trans. G. Friedlander; New York: Hermon Press, 1970), 170.

39. F. W. Bassett, "Noah's Nakedness and the Curse of Canaan: A Case of Incest?" *VT* 21, no. 2 (1971): 235.

40. Robert A. J. Gagnon, *The Bible and Homosexual Practice: Texts and Hermeneutics* (Nashville: Abindgon, 2001), 64.

41. William G. Doty, *Mythography: The Study of Myths and Rituals* (2nd ed.; Tuscaloosa: University of Alabama Press, 2000), 46.

PART II
THE BIBLE
IN MODERN CONTEXTS

Chapter 13

Toward a Diaspora Hermeneutics

LUIS R. RIVERA-RODRIGUEZ

In the introduction to his edited volume *Interpreting beyond Borders*, Fernando Segovia anticipated that "in the years ahead diasporic criticism will become increasingly popular and increasingly sophisticated."[1] In a more recent publication, R. S. Sugirtharajah considers that "diasporic biblical interpretation is still in its infancy."[2] This essay is a contribution to emerging models of diaspora hermeneutics in biblical and theological studies.

This reflection comes from a male Protestant and Puerto Rican theologian who made the option to live and work in the USA. I have established a long-term residency in this country of which I am a citizen by birth but a social and cultural first-generation "immigrant" by experience.[3] This reflection grows out of three main processes in my life: (1) the quest to understand my personal journey and transformation of identity as a diasporan; (2) my practices of preaching in Latino churches, teaching Latino religious leaders, and my learning from other Latino/a theologians; and (3) my professional agenda of contributing to the hermeneutical practices of teachers, preachers, theologians, and biblical scholars who are members of different diaspora communities and take that location as a point of reference for the theological interpretation of sacred texts.[4]

My proposal presents a way of practicing diaspora hermeneutics that builds on the insights that Fernando Segovia[5] has developed but looks to complement his model by engaging in dialogue with disciplines in the social sciences that study the social and historical phenomenon of diaspora communities.[6] My claim is that if the experience of diaspora is going to be recognized as a social location, then we need to get acquainted with empirical studies that theorize and describe the experiences of diaspora people, communities, and congregations. A dialogue with these disciplines allows us to develop a critical and empirical understanding of diaspora communities as social formations and locations in their variety, complexity, conflicts, identities, politics, and dynamics.

I am interested, like Segovia, in developing a diaspora hermeneutics of "flesh and blood" diasporic people. By this expression I mean specifically two kinds of people in diaspora communities. A diasporic person is anyone who left his or her native country and culture and settled down in another country. This person (1) claims membership in the country of origin, (2) maintains a feeling of loyalty to the homeland, (3) reproduces cultural practices and identities related to the sending country, and (4) engages in some kind of transnational exchanges across borders. They are what I call "first-order" diasporans because they have the experience of translocality, that is, they have gone through the processes of exiting, traveling, entering, and settling in countries other than their native lands. This applies to both first- and 1.5-generation immigrants.[7] This is my experience, and this is the voice that I want to highlight.[8]

Diasporans are also children of first-order diasporans who are born in host lands but claim some form of membership in and develop a sense of emotional attachment to the homelands of their parents. This sense of belonging to the homeland of their parents might come from a combination of factors: (1) education in the family, (2) claims of homelands over their diasporas, (3) the political status as foreigners that host countries impose on the children of immigrants, and (4) the option to construct personal identity as a diasporan that children of immigrants practice at times for personal and/or political reasons. "Second-order" diasporans develop some type of transnational concerns and practices in different degrees, and construct their ethnic and social identities as a variation of any of the diasporic mentalities that I will identify below. I call them "second-order" diasporans because they do not go through the concrete experience of being born in and leaving a native country.

My project of theological diaspora hermeneutics privileges the experience and reading strategies of first-order diasporans.[9] This essay is an attempt to articulate a method for diaspora hermeneutics done from the perspective of what I have defined as first-order or first-generation diasporans. It contains the first part of a twofold project in which I am trying to answer this question: What does it mean to interpret biblical texts "diasporically," and how do we go about doing it?[10]

Toward a Diaspora Hermeneutics (of Diasporic People)

Definition and Description of the Model

Diaspora hermeneutics is the practice and study of the process of interpreting texts and readers from the social situation of diaspora communities and the social locations and interests of diasporic people. More concretely, to read a text diasporically means to interpret its meanings and functions: (1) in terms of the practices and power relations, the social locations and identities, the interests and ideologies, and the traditions and worldviews of diaspora communities and diasporic people; and (2) for the sake of promoting a political, ethical, and religious vision and lifestyle of communal, personal, and congregational life in diaspora. Diaspora hermeneutics pays particular attention to the ways in which first-order diasporans interpret texts in their quest to produce meaning, reproduce their social locations and identities, and determine ways to act politically and religiously as members of diaspora communities and congregations.[11]

My model for a diaspora hermeneutics contains two parts. In the first part, I develop a grid with four components or "lenses" with insights from the social sciences: (1) an interpretation of six dynamics in diaspora communities, (2) a typology of diaspora politics, (3) a typology of diasporic identities of first-generation migrants, and (4) an inventory of socioreligious functions in diasporic congregations. The second part of my model consists of three reading strategies in which these lenses are used. I identify these reading tasks as follows: reading *through* diaspora, reading *from* diaspora, and reading *for* diaspora. Before explaining in detail this model, I will offer my working definitions of diaspora groups and communities.

Defining Diaspora

One of the outcomes of migratory processes is the formation and development of diaspora groups and communities in receiving countries.[12] *Diaspora groups* are conglomerates of individuals and families who leave their home countries, for different reasons and under different circumstances, and come to live and work in foreign countries. These people live in proximate residential locations in countries of destination and interact with one another through simple or complex group networks. These groups may not survive as diaspora communities in foreign countries. They can move or be deported to other countries. Under certain circumstances, they can be disbanded, assimilated, or destroyed in the countries of arrival. On the other hand, diaspora groups can develop into diaspora communities.

Diaspora communities are stable and organized conglomerates of immigrant families and groups, and their descendants, who have established a long-term residency in a host country and who carry out their social action and cultural existence through their own networks and within the power networks of three fundamental social fields: the diaspora community itself, the host land, and the homeland. What marks the transition from transient diaspora groups to communities is a combination of the following factors: (1) the growth and concentration of coethnic migrant populations in particular geographical areas; (2) an increasing incorporation into the social, political, and economic structures of the receiving country, along with the development of an economic infrastructure in the diaspora community itself; (3) a stability of immigrants' residential patterns; (4) the development of networks and organizations run by immigrants; and (5) the emergence of cadres of economic, civic, and political leadership within the community, mostly members of the first generation.[13]

Based on this partial description of diaspora communities, I would like to propose a kind of grid that informs my proposal of diaspora hermeneutics. Diaspora hermeneutics interprets texts and readers out of some theoretical perspective of the profile and characteristics of the formation, dynamics, and behavior of diaspora communities. I engage in diaspora hermeneutics by examining texts and readers in light of these four sets of "lenses."

A Grid for Diaspora Hermeneutics

Six Dynamics in Diaspora Communities

Diaspora groups and communities are constituted and characterized by the dynamics of six sets of practices that I call translocality, communality, transnationality, interculturality, marginality, and diaspolitics. *Translocality* involves the complex and diverse processes by which people leave their native countries, travel to their destination countries, and establish permanent residency there. *Communality* is the development of a stable, organized, and established immigrant community with organizations and leadership that work out simultaneously strategies of economic, political, and cultural autonomy and incorporation in the country of destination. *Transnationality* refers to the multiple forms of engagement in economic, political, and cultural exchanges across geographical, political, and cultural borders through formal and informal networks that connect diaspora communities with their homelands and/or coethnic diasporas around the world.

Interculturality is the range of practices associated with three processes of cultural production that takes place at the intersection of the three social worlds in which diasporas exist, struggle, and survive: the homeland, the host land, and the diaspora community. First, there is the practice of affirming and nurturing ethnocultural identities and traditions through which they claim loyalty and membership to their homelands (affirming the vernacular). Secondly, there are the processes of negotiating economic, political, and cultural incorporation and adaptation that diverse sectors in diaspora communities practice differently. Finally, there is the production of cultural hybridity, that is, the many patterns of selecting, incorporating, and mixing aspects of cultural practices, beliefs, values, and traditions present in the three constitutive social fields.

Marginality has to do with the process by which diaspora communities experience and affirm, on the one hand, relative levels of cultural and political self-differentiation and distantiation from majority groups and other minority groups in countries of destination. On the other hand, it has to do with relative levels of cultural and political subordination and domination imposed by majority and other minority groups in host countries.[14]

Diaspolitics is a term I have coined to refer to the political practices and ideologies present in diaspora communities and its sectors. Diaspora communities are conflictive and contested social formations in which there is a diversity of political ideologies and projects sponsored by different elites and grassroots groups. Diaspora politics can be distinguished according to the three social fields that intersect in diaspora communities: the immigrant community, the host country, and the homeland. An analysis of diaspolitics should always consider the connection of the political options and programs advanced by diaspora groups in reference to the different power structures of social hierarchy and control (class, gender, sexual orientation, race, ethnicity, nationality, generations, etc.).

Gabriel Sheffer has published an important book on diaspora politics. His typology of political strategies in diaspora communities in their host countries is an important theoretical suggestion for diaspora hermeneutics.[15] He discusses seven of such strategies.

The *assimilationist* strategy consists in adopting the ethnic identity and political and social goals of the majority sectors in the host society. This happens through a process of voluntary or forced incorporation into the economic, political, social, and cultural structures, dynamics, and traditions of the receiving society. It also involves processes of decreasing identification and interaction with the countries and cultures of origin. The *integrationist* strategy seeks to achieve a higher degree of social, economic, and political participation and recognition as members in the host country, without the consequences of assimilation. It promotes a sense of primary loyalty and belonging to the new society but keeps a subordinated sense of connection to the ancestral cultural and ethnic heritage. An example of this is the mindset of hyphenated identities in minority groups in multicultural societies.

The *communalist* and *corporatist* strategies pursue the goals of keeping a strong allegiance and exchange with the homeland, preserving an ethnonational identity related to the country and culture of origin, and participating actively and with a "relative degree of absorption" in the economic, political, and cultural life of the host country as an immigrant group and a political minority. The difference between these two has to do with the organizational practice of achieving these goals. The communalist strategy relies on the creation and work of "diaspora organizations and trans-state networks to connect the diaspora to its homeland and to other dispersed segments of the same nation."[16] The corporatist strategy employs the option of constituting formal organizations that the legal and political system of host countries allow and recognize for diaspora communities to represent and advocate for their interests. The *autonomist* strategy aims at seeking a degree of self-standing political space for resident aliens by negotiating "special political and cultural rights and freedoms" for the members of diaspora communities in receiving countries.[17]

The last two strategies are the options of diaspora communities whose "historical homelands have been taken over by other ethnic groups and host countries." The *irredentist* strategy seeks to separate a region in the homeland, now under the control of the host country, "in order to establish a national state within the boundaries of the diaspora's historical homeland." The *separatist* strategy intends "to establish an independent state in a diaspora's former historical homeland and facilitate the return of all or most segments of its ethnic nation."[18]

The recognition of different and competing political projects and their moral voices in diaspora communites should help us consider their impact in the production of religious texts and their interpretation by readers in diaspora communities and congregations.

Diasporic Identities

All human groups engage in the practice of ethnogenesis, that is, the social and symbolic process by which groups construct their socioethnic identity. The process of ethnic construction includes a dual process of self and other-definition within internal and by external groups. The ways groups define self- and other-identities will depend on the dynamics of competition, cooperation, or conflict that might exist between the groups involved in relationships.[19] I would like to suggest that this multilayered and complex process of ethnogenesis manifests in four main expressions of diaspora mentalities, particularly among first-generation immigrants.[20] I speak of the exilic, sojourner, resident alien, and diasporic identities.[21]

Exilic Identity

Some immigrants are forced to leave their countries against their will. This is the experience of people who are deported as prisoners, slaves, and indentured workers. This is also the case in the expulsion of native populations due to state persecution or extermination as in the cases of political, religious, or ethnic refugees. Finally, this is the experience of uprooted and displaced national people affected by deep economic and environmental crises.

For many of these migrants the experience of leaving the homeland and resettling in a host land is articulated in negative terms. They perceive themselves as expatriates away from the homeland and as strangers in foreign lands. Their geographical translation makes them feel uprooted or displaced, resulting in a sense of being homeless in the new country.

Diasporans with an exilic mindset maintain a very strong orientation and allegiance to their country of origin, and little or no attachment and loyalty to the new society. They also have a heightened perception of distance and differentiation from the new sociocultural environment. The majority of exilic diasporans have a strong desire for a prompt return.

Sojourner Identity

Other immigrants decide to leave their countries under pressure but not compulsion. There are people who leave because they think the integrity or quality of their lives is limited in their homelands. We may say that they are pushed but not forced to leave. This is the experience of some religious and ideological dissidents; landless people and unemployed or underemployed workers; some people displaced by war, economic, or environmental crises; and professional workers seeking to maintain or improve the standards of living for themselves and those they leave behind.

There are others who leave their countries driven by a sense of opportunity and even adventure. This is the case of those who sojourn as colonizers, explorers, pilgrims, merchants, missionaries, entrepreneurs, military and diplomatic personnel, professionals, workers, students, and scholars.

Many of these people exhibit a "sojourner mentality." Some may have a sense of duress and loss in leaving their countries, or of opportunity and potential gain, accompanied by a sense of having made a voluntary decision. They have moved away from home on a temporary basis. They develop a sense of differentiation and distantiation from the social and cultural environment in the receiving country. If they are well received and count with appropriate skills, education, and the language, as well as access to resources, then they can adapt more easily to the new situation without the psychological trauma of those who are forced to leave. The expectation of return is not imminent but is surely part of their future plans. With time, however, many exilic and sojourner diasporans find themselves staying longer than anticipated or making the decision to stay for good in receiving countries. When this happens there is a shift toward the resident alien and diasporic identities.[22]

Resident Alien Identity

Resident aliens have postponed indefinitely, but not completely, their home return. Though home is still the country of origin, there is a sense in which the country of destination has become a temporary or secondary home. The new country and its culture are not experienced as completely alien, though the native culture is still the primary point of reference for their identity. Resident aliens can exhibit different levels of knowledge, identification, management, and enjoyment of elements of the new sociocultural environment. Likewise, different levels of biculturalism are present in these sectors.

Diasporic Identity

Immigrants with a diasporic identity can be characterized by the following factors: (1) a decision to make permanent residency in the country of destination; (2) a dual sense of home, that is, a sense of belonging and loyalty to both homeland and host land, sometimes with priority given to the host land; (3) a higher degree of biculturalism with a deeper consciousness of living and struggling "in between and betwixt" the two sociocultural worlds; and (4) a clear decision not to return to the homeland.[23]

The recognition of the diversity of mindsets among first-generation migrants and the plurality of identities among generations in diaspora communities should help us consider their impact in the production of religious texts and their interpretation by readers in diaspora communities and congregations.[24]

Functions of Diaspora Religions

Sociologists of religion have started to study immigrant congregations and diasporic religions. Their research reveals that diaspora religious communities engage in several basic primary socioreligious functions. Diasporic congregations meet religious needs and foster religious identity in continuity with religious traditions and organizations of their country of origin. They forge ethnic communities and identities by preserving, reproducing, or even challenging imported patterns of cultural distinctiveness, including the practice of hierarchical systems. Diaspora communities of faith adapt the religious-ethnic identity to the new sociocultural environment, and they market their religion to coethnics, second and future generations, and outsiders. They provide informal and formal networks of social services and advocacy, and engage in transnational practices through religious and nonreligious networks that operate across national borders. They also generate compliance with or defiance of the structures and strategies of dominant groups to incorporate immigrant and minority groups into the political, economic, social, cultural, gender, and racial-ethnic stratification systems.[25]

These findings help diaspora hermeneutics to understand critically the socioreligious dynamics that can be present in diasporic religious groups and that inform the production of religious texts and the interpretations in diaspora communities and congregations. Again, the recognition of these socioreligious functions in diasporic congregations should help us theorize how they impact the production of diasporic religious texts and their interpretation by diasporic readers, as well as the consequence of this in our own readings as diasporic and nondiasporic readers.

In interpreting texts and readers, diaspora hermeneutics employs theories and methods of analysis from a diversity of disciplines that study the experiences and dynamics of diaspora people and communities and their religiosity. In principle, diaspora hermeneutics can work with more than the "four lenses" I have used. For example, diaspora hermeneutics can integrate insights from immigration studies; diaspora studies; cultural studies; postcolonial studies; minority, race, and ethnicity studies; feminist studies; sociological and anthropological research on diaspora religions; social stratification studies (gender, race, class, ethnicity); intercultural studies; border studies; and all sorts of literary and hermeneutical theories. My approach is just a model and an example of the contribution of social sciences that study empirically and comparatively the historical, social, and global phenomenon of diaspora.

Reading Strategies of Diaspora Hermeneutics (of Diasporic People)

The second part of my diaspora hermeneutics model consists of three sets of reading practices that are done simultaneously.[26] First, we look at the *inscription* of diaspora in the production of texts and the interpretations of readers who are primarily first-order diasporans. By "inscription of diaspora" I mean the representation of diaspora as a social situation and location that texts and readers work with. This is what I call reading *through* diaspora.

The second task of diaspora hermeneutics has to do with the *description* of the diaspora situation as part of the human condition. We examine critically the ways in which texts and readers develop a picture of the "diasporic self and community" and reflect on their struggle for survival and liberation. This is what I call reading *from* diaspora.

The third task of diaspora hermeneutics pays attention to the *prescription* of diaspora. It is an examination of the ways texts and readers promote a lifestyle and a vision of society in which diasporic people, communities, and congregations can survive and flourish in foreign lands. This is what I call reading *for* diaspora, with an option for diaspora as *vocation*. Let me develop briefly each of these reading tasks.

Reading *through* Diaspora

Diaspora hermeneutics interprets texts and readers in light of our experience and understanding of diaspora as a social situation and location. In particular, it examines the ways diasporic texts and readers represent historically or imaginatively, and reflect theologically on, three areas of diaspora social experience. The first is the processes by which people become emigrants of their homelands and expatriates in their diasporas (translocality; the postcolonial). Second are the ways diasporans turn into immigrants, foreigners, and minorities building diasporic communities (communality), negotiating their identities (ethnogenesis), and experiencing oppression and subalternity in host lands (marginality). The third area is the strategies of becoming cultural, political, and religious actors (interculturality, diaspolitics, social functions of diasporic religions) that diasporans employ while living in-between sending and receiving countries (transnationality).

Reading texts and readers "through diaspora" also involves, on the part of the diasporic readers, the option of consenting or dissenting with the representations of diaspora in texts, in other readers (diasporic and nondiasporic), and in themselves. This means that there can be competing diasporic readings of diasporic texts among diasporic readers. This variety of readings has to do, among other things, with the conditions that shape the social location, identity, and political options of the readers.

Reading *from* Diaspora

Diasporic readers evaluate and make options on their experience of becoming members of diaspora communities. Texts and readers express existential and political assessments of what life in the diaspora means and entails. They may have a negative, positive, or ambiguous assessment of the diasporic experience. Therefore, diasporic readers and texts work with some picture of diaspora as a *human condition.* There are three factors in considering the diasporic human condition: (1) a vision of the diasporic self and community, (2) the ethnic and generational identities affirmed by texts and readers, and (3) the power struggles and conflict in diaspora communities chosen by texts and readers.

Diaspora hermeneutics interrogates texts and readers on the way they construct positive, negative, or ambiguous visions of the diasporic self and community. Diasporic readers construct and react to representations about what constitutes and characterizes (positively or negatively) personal and social life in diasporic people, communities, and congregations. For example, many diasporic readers reflect on their experience of becoming "sojourners and resident aliens," "strangers and foreigners," "outsiders/insiders in home and host lands," "hybrid and mestizo people," "marginal and marginalized groups," and "border and bridge people."

Diasporic readers read texts and readers in light of their ethnic and generational identities. Diasporic readers construct imaginatively the kind of ethnic and generational identities that we think are affirmed, denied, or criticized in texts and readers. We do this by using the typologies of ethnic and generational identities to examine texts and readers. Diasporic readers read texts and readers also in light of their social location and political options. Diaspora hermeneutics explore the ways texts and readers represent those power relations, embedded in the stratification social systems (class, gender, ethnicity, race, nationality, citizenship, and generations) present in the diaspora communities, their homelands, and their host countries.[27]

In summary, diaspora hermeneutics explores and critiques the positive, negative, or ambiguous visions that readers and texts present on the human condition of diasporic people, communities, and congregations. The picture of the human condition is a political, ethical, and religious construct on what characterizes life in diaspora and what is at stake in diasporic existence. This reading strategy helps us to envision and engage with the ideological commitments of diasporic texts and readers. For diasporic interpreters this involves the task of clarifying those values and commitments that can guide actions for the survival, success, and liberation of diaspora people, communities, and congregations.

Reading *for* Diaspora

Diaspora hermeneutics explores the ways in which diasporic texts and interpreters construct an ideal vision for a diaspora community, a religious community in diaspora, and the lifestyles required to achieving them. On the one hand, I am referring to the aspiration and advocacy for a diaspora community that is protected and that flourishes toward its goals in the social environment of the receiving country. On the other hand, I am thinking about the policies, politics, and behaviors (lifestyles) that are deemed appropriate to sustain the diaspora community and its goals. "Reading for diaspora" means reading with a political, ethical, and religious option for diaspora living. This option for diaspora living is what I call diaspora as *vocation*.

It seems that all diaspora communities develop some kind of vision and strategies to secure the survival, safety, well-being, and flourishing of some form and version of diaspora life. Therefore, the use of grids to understand the multiple diasporic locations, identities, and diaspolitics could help us understand and assess the variety of diasporic political projects with their moral voices that are promoted by different sectors in diaspora communities and represented in texts and readers.[28]

In summary, a diasporic hermeneutics (reading texts and readers diasporically) is one in which the diasporic situation and location, the diasporic human condition, and a diasporic sociopolitical project (represented historically or symbolically in texts and experienced by the readers) become key interpretative concerns and entries for the exploration and interpretation of the meaning and function of the text done by diasporic people in their quest to produce meaning, reproduce their social locations and identities, and determine ways to act politically and religiously as members of diaspora communities and congregations.

Theological Diaspora Hermeneutics

Diaspora hermeneutics of biblical texts is a form of theological hermeneutics. Theological diaspora hermeneutics studies and articulates the strategies of interpreting theologically religious texts and traditions from the perspectives, experiences, and interests of sectors in diasporic communities of faith. It is concerned with the ways in which diasporic religious communities and people read their sacred texts and traditions in order to produce socioreligious meaning and mobility in response to the complex, diverse, and conflictive dynamics of being members of diaspora communities and diasporic religious groups. Theological diaspora hermeneutics interprets religious texts and traditions in light of the primary functions of diaspora religious communities and the socioreligious worldviews and commitments in these communities.

There are three complementary ways to interpret theologically texts and readers from a diasporic perspective. The first strategy is to ask for the religious value or dimension of the diasporic experience represented in texts or experienced by readers. In other words, the diasporic situation and location (in texts and readers) are interpreted in connection to the divine.

How does God relate to the origin and development of the diasporic community and people? Is the emergence and formation of the diasporic event and community represented in negative, positive, or ambiguous terms in relation to the will and action of the divinity? Is the diaspora situation one of judgment and curse, or a context of revelation, mission, and liberation? How does the divine relate or engage with the diasporic human condition and the diasporic political and congregational projects? What in the diasporic situation, condition, and project is deemed of humane and redeeming value? What are the relationships, practices, and lifestyles for diasporic living in society and congregations that are promoted or critiqued ethically, religiously, and politically? What is the religious and ethical ideal for the diasporic person, community, and congregation? In the diasporic situation, who are the voices and agents of the divine will, action, and mission, and toward what ends in relation to the diasporic situation?

The second strategy for a diasporic theological interpretation of biblical texts is to explore the diasporic value or dimension of the religious life represented in texts or experienced by readers. The divinity and the religious life are represented and interpreted through the symbolics of diaspora. In other words, the situation of diaspora is used as an analogy to describe the divine and religious life and activity. To put it differently, the divine and religious life are "diasporized."

The interpreter asks what of the diaspora experience is used as a symbol to describe God and God's relationship to the world, the human experience in the world and before God, the people of God, the ideal of the human person and community, the religious and moral life, the salvation process, the eschatological future, and so forth. In other words, how does the diaspora situation, condition, and project provide a model for understanding and responding to divine life, to live out the religious and moral life, and to enact the human vocation or project?

The third strategy of a diasporic theological interpretation is to reinterpret religious texts and traditions in light of the new insights, values, goals, and commitments that are perceived as theologically, ethically, and spiritually appropriate in light of the diasporic situation. What are the new insights of and orientations toward the divine, the human, and the religious life that the situation and challenges of a diasporic context generates? For example, diasporic religious communities may challenge ethnocentric and nationalistic religious understandings and practices. They may modify negative stereotypes of "others" and discern moral obligations toward them. They may reconsider the essentials of keeping a religious life in a sociocultural context outside the geographical and sociological boundaries of the homeland religious centers.[29]

Biblical Texts and Diaspora Hermeneutics

The reading of biblical texts from a diaspora hermeneutical perspective is possible because many biblical texts represent real or imagined experiences of migrant people and communities. A classification of these texts in light of the different dimensions in the life of immigrant communities allows us to see the importance that these texts may have for contemporary believers who are migrants and who struggle with similar issues.

There are texts in which the people of Israel, their ancestors and descendants, are represented as migrant people who experience voluntary or forced emigration and immigration in the midst of imperial/colonial dynamics (Genesis, Exodus, Deuteronomy; Joshua; exilic prophets; Lamentations; Ps. 137).[30] Stories of voluntary exodus and forced exile present people and families experiencing uproot-edness and displacement from homelands, as well as relocation and short- or long-term settlement in foreign lands. Many of these stories illustrate the main factors contributing to the migration of people: economic and political interventions of imperial countries, regional warfare and local invasions, internal political perse-cution, wars, economic crises, environmental disasters (droughts, floods, famine, plagues), family reunions, and divine calls. In these stories, Israel or its represen-tatives end up being emigrants, immigrants, exiles, refugees, conquered or con-quering people, slaves, persecuted people, and minorities or majorities.

There are other stories in which Israel and its representatives are found already in foreign lands as minority groups. They are presented as having a different social status in relation to the majority groups of the receiving country or region. Some-times Israel and Israelites are pictured as oppressed minorities settled in one place (Exodus, Jeremiah, Ezekiel, Esther, Lamentations), or as wandering and wel-comed sojourners in a region, or as resident aliens at peace or in conflict with local groups (Abraham, Jacob, Joseph in Genesis), or as members of foreign elites serving in the court of Gentile kings (Nehemiah, Esther, Daniel). Many of these stories illustrate the troubles, plights, and hardships of immigrant and minority groups in foreign lands. They also speak about the strategies of survival, negoti-ation, and resistance that foreign and minority groups develop in response to the political practices of majority groups and the hierarchical structures of power (class, race, gender, ethnicity, nationality, religious affiliation, language, etc.) in receiving countries.

Several of the biblical traditions allow us to have a sense of the debates and tensions among different sectors in the exilic and diaspora communities. There are writings that give voice to the despair and desolation of exilic people (Lamen-tations, Ps. 137), and other voices that attempt to console and give hope (Sec-ond Isaiah). There are voices that call for separation and segregation in the foreign land (Dan. 1–6), and others that seem to suggest some form of accommodation in the imperial situation (Esther, Nehemiah). There are voices that picture in neg-ative terms the encounter with the Gentile/foreigner (Joshua, Deuteronomy, Nehemiah) and other voices that offer a more positive profile of those multi-cultural experiences (Jonah, Esther, Ruth).

Apart from stories of exit and entry in a foreign land, we find stories and prophetic traditions that call the exilic Israel to hope and prepare for a new exo-dus or return migration to the native land (Second Isaiah, Jeremiah). Some of the stories narrate the return home and the work of conquering and reconstruction by returning Israelites, including their conflicts with local groups that never left or that populated the land after the exile (Ezra, Nehemiah).

Still other biblical passages present Israel as a host country and a majority group (laws toward foreigners in Deuteronomy; Joshua). There are stories and legal and prophetic traditions about Israel's internal migrants and displaced peo-ple, about Israelites returning from previous exiles or about pilgrims visiting the land, about non-Israelite natives who have turned foreigners in their own land because Israel has conquered their land, and about foreign migrants who have become resident aliens and minorities in the midst of Israel because of wars, political treaties, or the practice of slavery. Prophets and legislators sometimes encouraged the domination and social control of these minorities; at other times, they brought words of judgment against such practices.

In all of these stories that show Israel and Israelites as foreigners or in contact with foreigners as minority or majority groups, we find different ways of constructing the image of the other. For Israel, Gentile strangers can take one of three forms.[31] Strangers can be enemies of God and Israel, a threat to Israel's political and spiritual survival and well-being (Joshua, Ezra, Nehemiah, Lamentations). Sometimes Gentiles and foreigners can turn into admirers of Israel and fearers of God who turn into friends and allies of Israel (Jonah, Dan. 1–6, Esther). At other times, there are ideal pictures of foreigners becoming members of Israel as proselytes (Ruth), members of the assembly (Isa. 56:6–7; Zech. 2:10–11; Isa. 19:24–25), or part of the human diaspora that comes to Jerusalem to honor God and the city (the pilgrimage of foreigners to Jerusalem in Isa. 2, 56–66).

An interesting dimension of stereotyping the foreigners is the way that Gentile nations and empires are represented. There is a sense in which all nations are under God's rule and judgment. Nations and empires can be enemies of God (Egypt, Babylonia, Assyria, Nineveh, Edom), creatures of God (see the tables of the nations in Gen. 10), or instruments of God (Cyrus in Isa. 45). The destiny of these nations can be condemnation and destruction, a call to repentance and the doing of justice, or even a transformation into believers and servants of the one and only God. These negative and positive stereotypes of foreign persons and Gentile nations reveal different contexts in which the redefinition of self-identity and other-identity takes place according to relationships of conflict, competition, or collaboration among different sociocultural groups.

The theological interpretation of the diaspora experience finds several versions in these texts.[32] The dominant version in Hebrew Scripture presents exile and diaspora as God's judgment upon Israel's breach of covenantal relationships with God and among the community (Amos, Jeremiah). Idolatry and injustice are major accusations and reasons for the experience of being dispersed among Gentile nations. A minor version is one that understands diaspora as part of a provisional divine pedagogy to renew Israel and bring it back to a correct relationship with God, one another, and the land (Hos. 11), including the reunion of the human diaspora centered on the worship of God in Jerusalem. Still another small voice contemplates exile and diaspora as part of God's means for the blessing of the nations through the dispersion of Israel (Isa. 52:13–53:12; Jonah).

In summary, it is the diversity of these historical and imaginary representations of peoples and communities living the conditions of forced or voluntary migration, settling in host lands or returning to homelands, relating as natives and foreigners as well as majority and minority groups, and practicing and producing their faith under these circumstances that allow us to read diaspora in the texts and to read the texts diasporically.

Conclusion

As a diasporic theologian, I am trying to develop a theory for understanding and practicing diaspora hermeneutics from the experience, identities, locations, and politics of first-order diasporans. In making this proposal I have worked with several objectives in mind. The first objective has been to understand and support the efforts of Latino and non-Latino immigrant theologians, preachers, and teachers engaged in retrieving and appropriating scriptural and other religious traditions to live out their faith and politics as members of diasporic communities and congregations in the USA. The second objective has been to present a theoretical model of practicing diaspora hermeneutics that can contribute to interdisciplinary research and critical reflection on theological diaspora hermeneutics.

My last objective has been to join the efforts of Hispanic American and Asian American biblical scholars and theologians in this country who are making a significant contribution to the development of diaspora hermeneutics from the perspectives of first- and 1.5-generation immigrants.[33] Unfortunately, few Anglo-European and African American scholars in these fields are paying attention to the work of these colleagues. A case in point is the leading and important work of Daniel L. Smith-Christopher on diaspora hermeneutics. Although he recognizes the need to be engaged and informed by the resources of existing diasporic movements and people, including "the important resources of Asian, Hispanic, and African American Christian movements, as well as Pacific Islander and Native Peoples Christian movements in the United States, Canada, Australia, and New Zealand . . . but also studies of Armenian and Greek diasporic experiences," his bibliography and discussion do not incorporate these sources.[34]

My proposal of diaspora hermeneutics is a version of a theopolitical hermeneutics done for the sake of immigrant minority Christian groups in this country. It promotes a sociological, political, theological, and ethical reflection that can inspire and mobilize members of diaspora communities and congregations in their struggles for the survival, safety, recognition, freedom, and flourishing in this country. I propose a hermeneutical process that allows these groups to name and connect their experiences with a larger sociopolitical picture of the formation and dynamics of diaspora communities (reading *through* diaspora). I advance a strategy of naming and articulating options for a critical vision and existential evaluation of the religious-political meaning of living in diaspora (reading *from* diaspora). Finally, I call for the articulation and engagement of visions of society and lifestyles in diaspora that can generate multiple political and religious goals in diasporic communities and congregations (reading *for* diaspora).

I do not claim that this is the only option for diaspora hermeneutics or that it can bring hermeneutical, political, and religious consensus to different

A Schematic Picture of Diaspora Hermeneutics

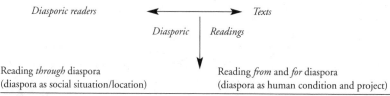

Diasporic readers ←—————→ Texts

Diasporic | Readings

Reading *through* diaspora (diaspora as social situation/location)	Reading *from* and *for* diaspora (diaspora as human condition and project)
Six dimensions of diaspora communities Translocality Communality Transnationality Interculturality Marginality Diaspolitics	*Diasporic self and community* Becoming sojourners and resident aliens, strangers and foreigners, outsiders/insiders in home and host lands, hybrid and mestizo people, marginal and marginalized groups, border and bridge people. *Ethnic and generational identities* First generation (exilic, sojourner, resident alien, diasporan)
Power relations * Three social fields: diaspora community, host land, homeland * Social stratification systems: class, gender, race, ethnicity, generations, nationality, etc. * Group dynamics: immigrants and natives in host land; expatriates and national in homeland; residents and newcomers, and different generations in diaspora communities	*Diaspolitic strategies* * Diaspora community * Homeland * Host land: assimilationist, integrationist, communalist, corporatist, autonomist, irredentist, separatist
Social functions of diasporic religions * Meeting the religious needs and fostering religious identity in continuity with religious traditions and organizations of the country of origin; * Forging ethnic communities by preserving, reproducing, or even challenging imported patterns of cultural distinctiveness, including the practice of hierarchical systems * Adapting the religious-ethnic identity to the new sociocultural environment; * Providing a network of informal and formal social service and advocacy; * Marketing the religion to coethnics, second and future generations, and outsiders; * Engaging in transnational practices through religious and nonreligious networks that operate across national borders; * Generating compliance or defiance to the structures and strategies of dominant groups to incorporate immigrant and minority groups in the political, economic, social, cultural, gender, and racial-ethnic stratification systems	*Diaspora theological hermeneutics* * Explore the religious value or dimension of the diaspora experience (theologize the diasporic situation, condition, project) * Explore the diasporic value or dimension of the divine and religious life (diasporize the divine, the human, and the religious) * Reinterpret religious texts and traditions in light of the new insights, values, goals, and commitments that are perceived as theologically, ethically, and spiritually appropriate in light of the diasporic situation

Christian diaspora communities who are retrieving and reappropriating the scriptural traditions to live out their faith and politics as diasporic people, communities, and congregations. My hope is that this intellectual exercise stimulates all those who are challenged to think and live their faith "diasporically," as well as those who want to study the religious hermeneutics of diasporans.

Notes

1. Fernando F. Segovia, introduction to *Interpreting beyond Borders* (ed. Fernando F. Segovia; Sheffield: Sheffield Academic Press, 2000), 33.
2. R. S. Sugirtharajah, *Postcolonial Criticism and Biblical Interpretation* (Oxford: Oxford University Press, 2002), 185.
3. Puerto Rico has been an unincorporated territory of the USA since 1898, and since 1952 has held the status of a commonwealth, which for a majority of Puerto Ricans of all political persuasions means a colony. Puerto Ricans were made US citizens, without their democratic consent, by an act of Congress in 1917 (the Foraker Law).
4. I am a member of the Puerto Rican diaspora, one of the many Latin American and Caribbean diaspora groups in the USA. I was born, raised, and educated in Puerto Rico, a US colony. My traveling and living between the two countries involved several trips to the United States for vacationing and professional purposes before spending seven years in Boston doing graduate theological studies (1979–1986). I returned to the Island to work at the Evangelical Seminary of Puerto Rico for nine years (1986–1995). Since 1995, I have been a faculty member at McCormick Theological Seminary. I arrived in Chicago during the years of the Republican "revolution" in Congress and the big debate on immigration that resulted in the new immigration laws of 1996. My identification with the struggles of immigrant communities and my new connections with Latino theologians and their work were the two most important factors that contributed to a new way of doing hermeneutics. The realization of my new social location as a Hispanic or a Latino in this country, and my quest to help churches and seminarians give a pastoral and theological response of advocacy toward immigrants, pushed me to look into the social sciences as resources to understand the theoretical, political, and ethical issues and options related to the new public policy on immigration.
5. See Fernando F. Segovia and Mary Ann Tolbert, ed., *Reading from This Place*, vol. 1, *Social Location and Biblical Interpretation in the United States* (Minneapolis: Fortress, 1995); Fernando F. Segovia and Mary Ann Tolbert, ed., *Reading from This Place*, vol. 2, *Social Location and Biblical Interpretation in Global Perspective* (Minneapolis: Fortress, 1995); Ada María Isasi-Díaz and Fernando F. Segovia, ed., *Hispanic/Latino Theology: Challenge and Promise* (Minneapolis: Fortress, 1996); Fernando F. Segovia, *Decolonizing Biblical Studies: A View from the Margins* (Maryknoll, NY: Orbis, 2000); Eleazar S. Fernández and Fernando F. Segovia, ed., *A Dream Unfinished: Theological Reflections on America from the Margins* (Maryknoll, NY: Orbis, 2001).
6. I see my proposal as complementing Segovia's model of diaspora hermeneutics in four ways. First, I engage with disciplines in the social sciences, particularly the contributions coming from immigration studies, diaspora studies, transnational studies, and the sociology of diasporic religions. Second, I enlarge his understanding of the varieties of locations and identities of diasporic readers by combining a typology of diasporic identities that I have developed, with a typology

of diaspora politics developed by Gabriel Sheffer. Third, I restate and supplement Segovia's profile of the "diasporic condition," which he centers on the notions of otherness, hybridity, marginality, and the postcolonial. I add and rework these categories as translocality, communality, transnationality, interculturality, marginality, and diaspolitics. Finally, I propose a definition of diaspora hermeneutics that combines three reading strategies: reading *through* diaspora, reading *from* diaspora, and reading *for* diaspora.

7. First-generation immigrants are those young adults or adults born and raised in their homelands who travel and establish residence in a host land; 1.5-generation immigrants are foreign-born children who are raised in a host country.

8. Reflecting on the different ways Latinos have entered the United States (birth, acquisition, immigration) and the different ways Hispanics experience the country, Segovia says, "Such different paths ultimately account, I believe, for different experiences with and within the country itself: (1) for those born in the country as children of immigrants, minority status vis-à-vis the dominant culture is likely to prevail as the predominant reality; (2) for the descendants of those acquired as political subjects by the country, the status of colonization may displace minority status as the fundamental optic; (3) finally, for those who entered the country as immigrants, the status of exile is likely to prove the primordial reality." Segovia, "In the World but Not of It: Exile as Theology of the Diaspora," in Isasi-Díaz and Segovia, *Hispanic/Latino Theology*, 201–2.

9. The language of diaspora and exile has become relevant to people other than immigrants who feel different, alienated, marginalized, displaced, and dispossessed by majority groups in their own countries and/or communities. The language of exile and diaspora turns into a metaphoric language of differentiation, self-affirmation, critique, and resistance used by members of minority groups, or members of majority groups that have "moved away" from centers of powers. In this sense, they claim to be political, ideological, or cultural "exiles, strangers, resident aliens, or marginal" people.

10. In a forthcoming essay, I will answer another question: How do we interpret "diasporically" biblical or other texts that do not present directly pictures of diaspora?

11. In sociological terms, *congregation* refers to a "grouping of peoples who gather together for religious purposes and who create an ongoing structure in which to worship, share a religious tradition, interact as a group, and attempt to raise their children with specific religious beliefs, customs, rituals, and values." Helen Rose Ebaugh and Janet Saltzman Chafetz, *Religion and the New Immigrants: Continuities and Adaptations in Immigrant Congregations* (Walnut Creek, CA: AltaMira, 2000), 21.

12. See Charles Hirschman, Philip Kasinitz, and Josh DeWind, ed., *The Handbook of International Migration: The American Experience* (New York: Russell Sage Foundation, 1999); Stephen Catles and Mark J. Miller, *The Age of Migration: International Population Movements in the Modern World* (2nd ed.; New York: Guilford Press, 1998); Alejandro Portes and Rubén G. Rumbaut, *Immigrant America: A Portrait* (rev. ed.; Berkeley: University of California Press, 1996); Caroline B. Brettell and James F. Hollifield, ed., *Migration Theory: Talking across Disciplines* (New York: Routledge, 2000); Darrell Y. Hamamoto and Rodolfo D. Torres, ed., *New American Destinies: A Reader in Contemporary Asian and Latino Immigration* (New York: Routledge, 1997); Alejandro Portés, ed., *The Economic Sociology of Immigration: Essays on Networks, Ethnicity, and Entrepreneurship* (New York: Russell Sage Foundation, 1995).

13. See Steven Vertovec and Robin Cohen, ed., *Migration, Diasporas, and Transnationalism* (Cheltenham, UK: Edward Elgar, 1999); Robin Cohen, *Global*

Diasporas: An Introduction (Seattle: University of Washington Press, 1997); Nicholas Van Hear, *New Diasporas: The Mass Exodus, Dispersal, and Regrouping of Migrant Communities* (Seattle: University of Washington Press, 1998); "Diaspora and Immigration," special issue editor, V. Y. Midimbe, *South Atlantic Quarterly* 98, nos. 1–2 (1999); Smadar Lavie and Ted Swedenburg, *Displacement, Diaspora, and Geographies of Identity* (Durham, NC: Duke University Press, 1996); Jana Evans Braziel and Anita Mannur, ed., *Theorizing Diaspora: A Reader* (Malden, MA: Blackwell, 2003).

14. From my perspective, diaspora communities become marginal (an act of self-definition and affirmation) and marginalized (an act of other-definition by majority groups) because of their practices of translocality, communality, transnationality, and interculturality.

15. Gabriel Sheffer, *Diaspora Politics: At Home Abroad* (Cambridge: Cambridge University Press, 2003), 162–73.

16. Ibid., 164.

17. Ibid., 169.

18. Ibid., 170.

19. See Paul Spickard and W. Jeffrey Burroughs, ed., *We Are a People: Narrative and Multiplicity in Constructing Ethnic Identity* (Philadelphia: Temple University Press, 2000); Barry Edmonston and Jeffrey S. Passel, ed., *Immigration and Ethnicity: The Integration of America's Newest Arrivals* (Washington, DC: Urban Institute Press, 1994); Sallie Westwood and Annie Phizacklea, *Trans-nationalism and the Politics of Belonging* (London: Routledge, 2000); Howard Wettstein, ed., *Diasporas and Exiles: Varieties of Jewish Identity* (Berkeley: University of California Press, 2002).

20. I am adapting a proposal on the temporal basis of ethnic identity (cultural exiles, the transnational community, and ethnic Americans) by Bryan R. Roberts, "Socially Expected Durations and the Economic Adjustment of Immigrants," in *The Economic Sociology of Immigration: Essays on Networks, Ethnicity, and Entrepreneurship* (ed. Alejandro Portés; New York: Russell Sage Foundation, 1995), 42–86; Maja Povrzanovic Frykman, *Beyond Integration: Challenges of Belonging in Diaspora and Exile* (Lund: Nordic Academic Press, 2001).

21. My construction of the differentiation between these identities suggests a continuum that pays attention to four factors: (1) the psychological interpretation of becoming emigrants and immigrants, (2) the perception of the receiving social context as hospitable or hostile, (3) the sense of affinity or distance from the culture of majority groups in the receiving country, and (4) the desire and expectation for return.

22. The resident alien and diasporic identities are distinguished from the exilic and sojourner identities by two key factors: the decision to establish long-term residency in the host country, and an increased level of sociocultural adaptation to the country of destination. The differences between the resident alien and diasporic identities are a matter of degree in three aspects: the projection of long-term residency, the sense of ethnocultural and political "home," and the degree of acculturation.

23. I think that there are other forms of identities present in second-generation groups, but this has not been my focus. Nevertheless, it is important to recognize a wider and complex variety of identities present and competing in the larger immigrant communities and families in terms of different generations.

24. The more one moves to the exilic end, the more one finds (1) a sense of cultural home and political membership centered on the homeland; (2) an ethnocultural identity oriented to the country of origin; (3) a stronger differentiation and distantiation from the culture of the country of destination; (4) lower degrees of

acculturation; and (5) higher expectations for a provisional stay and prompt return. The more you move to the diasporic end of the spectrum, the more you find a qualified sense in each of the above items as a result of processes of socio-economic, cultural and political adaptation, acculturation, and hybridity practiced by diasporans with a prolonged stay in the host lands.

25. See Helen Rose Ebaugh and Janet Saltzman Chafetz, ed., *Religion across Borders: Transnational Immigrant Networks* (Walnut Creek, CA: AltaMira, 2002); R. Stephen Warner and Judith G. Wittner, ed., *Gatherings in Diaspora: Religious Communities and the New Immigration* (Philadelphia: Temple University Press, 1998); Robert A. Orsi, ed., *Gods of the City: Religion and the American Urban Landscape* (Bloomington: Indiana University Press, 1999); Susanne Hoeber Rudolph and James Piscatori, ed., *Transnational Religion and Fading States* (Boulder, CO: Westview, 1997); Thomas A. Tweed, *Our Lady of the Exile: Diasporic Religion at a Cuban Catholic Shrine in Miami* (New York: Oxford University Press, 1997); Ana María Díaz-Stevens and Anthony M. Stevens-Arroyo, *Recognizing the Latino Resurgence in U.S. Religion: The Emmaus Paradigm* (Boulder, CO: Westview, 1998); Harold Coward, John R. Hinnells, and Raymond Brady Williams, ed., *The South Asian Religious Diaspora in Britain, Canada, and the United States* (Albany, NY: SUNY Press, 2000); Ho-Youn Kwon, Kwang Chung Kim, and S. Stephen Warner, ed., *Korean Americans and Their Religions: Pilgrims and Missionaries from a Different Shore* (University Park: Pennsylvania State University Press, 2001); Fengang Yang, *Chinese Christians in America: Conversion, Assimilation, and Adhesive Identities* (University Park: Pennsylvania State University Press, 1999).

26. I am adopting and expanding two hermeneutical dynamics that Fernando Segovia sees present in "Interpreting beyond Borders: Postcolonial Studies and Diasporic Studies in Biblical Criticism," in the collection of essays *Interpreting beyond Borders*, 11–34.

27. Segovia and others have pointed to the importance of the dynamics of the imperial and the colonial to examine the representation of power relations in texts and readers living in the empire. This perspective should be further specified by examining critically the relations, mutual perceptions, and exchanges that texts and readers present about (1) natives and foreigners, (2) native majority and minority groups and immigrants groups, (3) established diaspora groups and the new coethnic arrivals, (4) different generational groups in the diaspora community, and (5) the diasporic community and powerful groups in the sending society.

28. From my perspective, the three main strategies of diaspora hermeneutics (reading through, from, and for diaspora) are not sequential steps but simultaneous processes of approaching and interpreting texts and readers diasporically. The importance of differentiating them is to become aware of the complex process of interpretation involved in diaspora hermeneutics and to understand how they contribute to multiple diasporic readings. Finally, a careful examination of diasporic readers and their readings may reveal more strategies than those I have mentioned.

29. See a schematic summary of my diaspora hermeneutics proposal following this essay.

30. See Ralph W. Klein, *Israel in Exile: A Theological Interpretation* (Philadelphia: Fortress, 1979); Mark G. Brett, ed., *Ethnicity and the Bible* (Leiden: Brill, 1996); James M. Scott, ed., *Exile: Old Testament, Jewish, and Christian Conceptions* (Leiden: Brill, 1997); Daniel L. Smith-Christopher, *A Biblical Theology of Exile* (Minneapolis: Fortress, 2002); Rainer Albertz, *Israel in Exile: The History and Literature of the Sixth Century BCE* (Atlanta: Society of Biblical Literature, 2003).

31. See Daniel L. Smith-Christopher, "Between Ezra and Isaiah: Exclusion, Transformation, and Inclusion of the 'Foreigner' in Post-Exilic Biblical Theology," in Brett, *Ethnicity and the Bible*, 117–42.

32. See Robert P. Carroll, "Deportation and Diasporic Discourses in the Prophetic Literature in Exile," in *Old Testament, Jewish, and Christian Conceptions* (ed. J. M. Scott; Leiden: Brill, 1997), 63–85.

33. The bibliography on both Latino and Asian American theologies is growing and expanding. See, e.g., Justo L. González, *Santa Biblia: The Bible through Hispanic Eyes* (Nashville: Abingdon, 1996); Arturo J. Bañuelas, ed., *Mestizo Christianity: Theology from the Latino Perspective* (Maryknoll, NY: Orbis, 1995); José David Rodríguez and Loida I. Martell-Otero, ed., *Teología en Conjunto: A Collaborative Hispanic Protestant Theology* (Louisville, KY: Westminster John Knox, 1997); Orlando O. Espín and Miguel H. Díaz, ed., *From the Heart of Our People: Latino/a Explorations in Catholic Systematic Theology* (Maryknoll, NY: Orbis, 1999); Jung Young Lee, *Marginality: The Key to Multicultural Theology* (Minneapolis: Fortress, 1995); Andrew Sun Park, *Racial Conflict and Healing: An Asian-American Theological Perspective* (Maryknoll, NY: Orbis, 1996); Peter C. Phan and Jung Young Lee, ed., *Journeys at the Margin: Toward an Autobiographical Theology in American-Asian Perspective* (Collegeville, MN: Liturgical Press, 1999); Peter C. Phan, *Christianity with an Asian Face: Asian American Theology in the Making* (Maryknoll, NY: Orbis, 2003); and the volume, "The Bible in Asian America," in *Semeia* 90–91 (2002).

34. Smith-Christopher, *Biblical Theology of Exile*, 197.

Chapter 14

Tamar's Cry

Rereading an Ancient Text in the Midst of an HIV/AIDS Pandemic

DENISE M. ACKERMANN

We were born at the wrong end of the century. We are the AIDS generation. AIDS hit us where it hurts most. AIDS came to us and said, "Now you can't eat sadza and mabhonzo and covo. Now you can't eat!" And we said, "But how can we live without eating?" AIDS said, "You think this is drop or syphilis? All right. Glut yourselves and see what happens. . . ." We are the condom generation. . . . For some it is no use. For some it is too late. We are dying like flies. But we live on, clinging to the frayed edges of our lives with our pathetic claws. We live on, hiding our despair behind tired smiles.
Shimmer Chinodya, *Can We Talk and Other Stories*

A "Bleak Immensity": HIV/AIDS in South Africa

When I was pregnant my partner left me. Perhaps he was afraid that I was HIV because he was. I found out just before my baby was born. I was given nevirapine. I have lost two jobs. First I was a domestic worker and then I worked in a laundry. The laundry boss forced all the staff to be tested. I knew it was against my constitutional rights, but what could I do? So I was dismissed unfairly. Last week I was walking home after looking for a job. Three youths attacked me. They pulled off my clothes. They wanted to rape me. The one said, "A man's got to have a woman when it is raining." I fought with them. They left me because a car came. They did not kill me because I said that I did not see their faces. But today I am so, so happy. I have just heard that my baby is negative. My child will have a life. God is good. (Thembisa, a 26-year-old Xhosa woman)

191

He married me when I was only 18. He knew he was positive. I did not know until my baby was tested. Then I found out that I was also positive. I knew it was him. He married me because I was a virgin. He believed that if he slept with a virgin he would be cured. I walked out. Now I counsel women who are HIV-positive. There is life after infection. (Boniswa, a 35-year-old AIDS counselor)

These stories are but two among the mountain of tales that link the two themes of this essay: violence against women and HIV/AIDS.[1] In order to sketch the context in which they are told, I shall briefly introduce some facts about the HIV/AIDS pandemic in South Africa. Thereafter, I will turn to the biblical text and look at a story of rape and violence that took place in David's household. Against this background, the second half of this essay includes a series of theological reflections that arise out of both the text and the context from which I speak. This essay aims merely to introduce certain theological themes that can then be pursued further by the churches in South Africa as they struggle with their role in combatting the AIDS pandemic.

Speaking about HIV/AIDS in my context is fraught with apparent anomalies. It should be quite straightforward. Clinically speaking, HIV/AIDS is a sexually transmitted disease. The fact that it can also be spread by the transfusion of infected blood or blood products is incidental. As our pandemic escalates, these latter means of transmission play an ever decreasing role. The AIDS virus is a weak virus that cannot survive exposure to the environment.[2] HIV/AIDS can only continue if the causal pattern of sexual behavior is present. In the normal course of events, people who do not exhibit such patterns of sexual behavior run no risk of contracting AIDS. Unlike pandemics of past times that spread by means of droplet infection, AIDS isn't easy "to catch."[3] It seems quite simple. Yet the AIDS pandemic in South Africa is a complex mixture of issues. Gender inequality, attitudes toward human sexuality, the scarring and fragmentation of large sections of society, our history of migrant labor and uprooting of communities exacerbated today by increased poverty and unemployment and denial of the cause of AIDS by leading politicians are all part of the South African AIDS story.

The statistics are a nightmare.[4] By the end of the year 2000 there were approximately 36.1 million people living with HIV/AIDS, of whom 25.3 million were in sub-Saharan Africa. According to Alan Whiteside and Clem Sunter, "In the past decade 12 million people in sub-Saharan Africa have died of AIDS—one-quarter being children."[5] In South Africa there are approximately 1,500 new infections a day. UNAIDS, the joint UN Programme on HIV/AIDS, reported in June 2000 that 4.7 million (that is one in nine) South Africans are living with HIV/AIDS.[6] In the previous year, this agency had reported that 19.94 percent of fifteen-year-olds in South Africa were infected with HIV/AIDS.[7] According to the South African Medical Research Council (October 2001), 40 percent of deaths occurring in the year 2000 of people between the ages of 15 and 40 were due to AIDS-related diseases. If the pandemic continues unchecked, 10 million South Africans will have died from AIDS-related diseases by 2010. In Gauteng and KwaZulu/Natal, one in three mothers visiting prenatal clinics is infected. Approximately 5,000 infected babies are born every month. "There are no longer *any* South Africans who do not know someone or of someone who has died of AIDS or is living with HIV," say Whiteside and Sunter.[8] Over the next ten years 35 to 46 percent of medical expenditures in South Africa will be directed toward coping with AIDS-related diseases. Our fragile economy will buckle under the ravages of AIDS in the work force; productivity and growth rates will decline.[9] According to the International Labour Organization (ILO), increased absenteeism due to HIV/AIDS is exacting an enormous toll in the workplace.[10] The ILO estimates that 15 percent of our civil service is HIV-positive. The South African Teachers Union has conducted its own research. According to its statistics, ten teachers die per month. Soon we will have close to half a million AIDS orphans to care for, while the United Nations estimates that a possible 40 million children worldwide will be orphans by 2010, largely due to AIDS.[11] We are, in the words of UN Secretary General Kofi Annan, facing "a tragedy on a biblical scale."[12]

Speaking at an AIDS conference in Maputo, Mozambique, in 1990, African National Congress stalwart Chris Hani (who was later assassinated) sounded this warning: "We cannot afford to allow the AIDS epidemic to ruin the realisation of our dreams. Existing statistics indicate that we are still at the beginning of the AIDS epidemic in our country. Unattended, however, this will result in untold damage and suffering by the end of the century."[13] The year 2001 marks the twentieth anniversary of the arrival of HIV/AIDS in terms of our awareness of this disease, the first truly global epidemic in world history. In the face of this calamitous reality, it is beyond understanding that certain South African politicians can still prevaricate about the causes of AIDS and the efficacy of treatments, that they conspire to keep silent about its ravages and place political agendas and power games above the lives of citizens, the majority of whom voted them into power.[14] This state of affairs prompted Dr. Mamphela Ramphele, former vice chancellor of the University of Cape Town, to say that "no coherent management strategy [has] yet [been] developed by the Government." This failure, she stated, "results not from lack of expertise in South Africa, but in its disregard by those in Government, with tragic consequences." She concluded that the South African government's position on AIDS was "nothing short of irresponsibility, for which history will judge it severely."[15] Dr. Malegapuru Makgoba, president of the Medical Research Council of South Africa, said recently, "History may judge us, the present Africans, to have collaborated in the greatest genocide of our time by the type of choices—political or scientific—we make in relation to this HIV/AIDS epidemic."[16] The escalating health crisis in South Africa is increasing pressure on the government to officially declare HIV/AIDS a national emergency.

Not only South African politicians are parsimonious about their involvement with AIDS. Despite the fact that over 36 million people in the world are now HIV-positive or have full-blown AIDS, President Bush's first major decision as president of the USA was to deny aid to family planning organizations abroad that inform women about medical options, including abortion. As I understand it, the Bush ruling says that clinics abroad will lose US funds if they even so much as mention abortion as an alternative to their patients. The results of this are nothing short of shocking. Added to this is the shameful action of President Clinton's administration with regard to AIDS. Vice President Al Gore pressured the South African government to keep it from going ahead with a plan to impose compulsory licensing on drugs made by the big international drug companies, so that others could make and sell them far more cheaply. The drug issue in regard to AIDS is a crucial test of the morality of the US government and its understanding of what is happening in the developing world.[17] As Tim Trengove Jones states:

> The scandal of AIDS, whether viewed from the perspective of rich and poor, threatens to bring into disrepute the purportedly highest values of the international "community." The more ethics and economics clash in this debate, the more a high-toned rhetoric of human rights clashes with an escalating and preventable death toll, the more necessary it will be for the world leaders to trumpet forth an idiom of caring. The language of crisis and its concomitant vocabulary of care, point not only to the conundrum of mounting deaths but also to a demonstrable and embarrassing crisis of values.[18]

My contention in this essay is that at heart HIV/AIDS is a gendered pandemic exacerbated by poverty. As such, it requires a theological response that is prepared to wrestle with the implications of gender inequity in our traditions and our practices as well as the reasons for continuous grinding poverty in sub-Saharan Africa. Furthermore, the question of HIV/AIDS raises profound ethical questions about human sexuality and relationships between women and men. I simply cannot do justice to poverty as a theological theme in this paper other than to connect it to the story of HIV/AIDS; neither can I deal with the question of human sexuality. This essay is only a preliminary effort to raise theological issues for further consideration. After rereading the Tamar text from 2 Sam. 13:1–22, I shall attempt to set out what I mean by a "gendered pandemic" by reflecting on the position of women (and children) in relation to HIV/AIDS in the South African context. Finally, I will return to Tamar's story to look for possible clues on how the body of Christ can find its way through the present ravages of sickness and death.[19] Attending funerals every weekend is a numbing task. It is more than numbing when the church as the body of Christ itself feels amputated as its members fill coffins. There are no dividing lines between the body and some other reality "out there." We too are infected. The church today has AIDS.

Rereading an Ancient Text: The Story of Tamar

This literary reading of the Tamar story is done self-consciously from a woman's perspective.[20] Women have distinctive questions about and insights into the biblical texts derived from our life experiences. We know that the Bible, as the sourcebook of our faith, is a powerful means for defining women's place in society and that it has been invoked to justify women's subordination to men. So our readings are suspicious, critical, and questioning as we seek meaning for life. We also, in Teresa Okure's words, "read from this place." "Reading from this place" is about the relationship between the biblical text and the social location of the interpreter. Okure continues:

> By *social location* I understand the sum total of those human experiences that shape the lives of the persons connected with the Bible at three levels: (1) the level of peoples in and of the Bible itself . . . ; (2) the level of the biblical authors and their respective audiences at various epochs of history . . . ; and (3) the level of readers/interpreters of the Bible throughout the course of history up to the present day. . . . By *interpreter* I understand simply anybody who reads/hears the text with a view to deriving from it a meaning for life.[21]

My reading of the Tamar text is from my place, a place in which the bleak immensity of violence against the bodies of women and children, now haunted by the specter of HIV/AIDS, rages on. My place is also one that knows that the Bible is the book of the church and that believes that the biblical texts, despite their cultural, social, and gendered baggage, affirm God's intention that we may have life and have it abundantly (John 10:10). Furthermore, my reading from this place is tempered by an acute awareness of the gendered nature of the HIV/AIDS crisis in which women and children are too often the victims. At the same time it is also a reading that seeks hope and affirmation for life.[22]

The story in 2 Sam. 13:1–22 is well-known yet seldom preached.[23] King David's son Amnon falls in love with his beautiful half-sister Tamar. He is tormented and consults his friend Jonadab, a "very crafty man." They hatch a plan. Amnon pretends that he is sick, and at his request David sends Tamar to him to make cakes "in his sight." He refuses to eat the cakes, sends the servants away, and asks Tamar to bring the cakes "into the chamber, so that I may eat from your hand." She does so, and he grabs her and says, "Come, lie with me, my sister." She resists: "No, my brother, do not force me; for such a thing is not done in Israel; do not do anything so vile! As for me, where could I carry my shame? And as for you, you would be as one of the scoundrels in Israel." But Amnon will not listen. He is stronger than Tamar, and he rapes her. Once the deed is done, Amnon is "seized with a very great loathing for her" and says, "Get out!" Tamar protests at her treatment. Again, Amnon is deaf to her entreaties, and he calls a servant and instructs him to "put this woman out of my presence, and bolt the door after her." After this is done, Tamar puts ashes on her head, goes away, and remains "a desolate woman, in her brother Absalom's house." Later we learn that Absalom kills Amnon as revenge for Tamar's rape.

Such are the bare bones of this rapacious tale. Its truths are multiple, conflicting, and resistant to being read as a simple story of a rape. It is a text that echoes through the ages and that resonates with women's experiences today in a number of ways. Tamar is a victim of rape, betrayal, and abandonment. She is the obedient daughter who pays a price in a patriarchal clan. She does as she is told; she obeys her father and serves her "sick" brother. When she realizes what is about to happen to her, she cries out: "No, my brother, do not force me, *for such a thing is not done in Israel.*" The immorality and injustice of the violation is more than just hers. It is a shame on the name of Israel. Her words are honest and poignant. While they acknowledge female servitude, they speak of a moral vision that is tragically in contrast with that of Amnon.

Tamar is not only a victim of rape. She is betrayed by her family, raped, and then despised. She is no longer "my sister," but "this woman." Amnon ends up hating her.[24] His love for his sister is a disordered love driven by morbid desire. Once the rape is committed, he is confronted by his own morbidity mirrored to him in the tragic figure of his victim. This he cannot bear, and she is "put out" of his presence. She is also a victim of her father's abdication of his responsibility as king and as father. There is no record of him responding to this outrage with an appropriate punishment. In fact, he will not punish Amnon "because he loved him, for he was his firstborn." David does not even react to Tamar's plight personally. The house of David, tainted by David's adultery with Bathsheba, is now fouled by incestuous violence. She is also a victim of her brother Absalom's plans for revenge when she is co-opted by him into concealing them: "Be quiet for now, my sister; he is your brother; do not take this to heart." These words may be understood as consoling. They may also conceal his plans for revenge. He and not Tamar will take the law into his own hands. "For us it is clear that the process of concealment is being reactivated. This is to ensure that the victim is made silent. The word used to describe Tamar's fate means: abandoned, alone, despised."[25]

Finally, she is cast out. We last hear of her as remaining in Absalom's house "a desolate woman." Condemned to a quiet life of despair and desolation, her social and spiritual needs are not acknowledged or addressed, and she disappears into the mists of history. In 2 Sam. 14:27 reference is made to Absalom's daughter Tamar: "She was a beautiful woman." Can there be an element of restitution here for Tamar in the next generation of women in the house of David? In summary, Tamar lives in a world where men manipulate and coerce by using their power and in which her life is ruined by events over which she has no control. Amnon uses his male power and privilege to destroy. In societies where the silence about sexual violence is not broken, abuse of power is not held accountable. David abrogates the proper use of power and opts for expediency rather than justice. Absalom's wish for revenge is problematic, for it expresses his sense of being offended more than it shows concern for the victim. Revenge is easier to indulge than sharing the pain of the victim. I agree with James Poling that the "latent message of this story is that sexual violence against women is not about the humanity of women but about power between men."[26] Finally, there is no restitution or justice for Tamar.

The brutal rape in this text speaks stridently into "my place." Rape, incest, and violence are endemic in South Africa.[27] Human Rights Watch/Africa's *Report on Violence against Women in South Africa* states, "What is certain . . . is that

South African women, living in one of the most violent countries in the world, are disproportionately likely to be victims of that violence."[28] Commenting on the fact that South African women constitute 30 percent of members of Parliament, an achievement which places us in the top ten of the world's democracies, Professor Amina Mama of the Africa Gender Institute at the University of Cape Town continues:

> Yet South Africa is simultaneously topping another chart, as one of the world's most deadly environments for women. Statistical evidence tells us that post-apartheid, South African women are more likely to be murdered, raped or mutilated than women anywhere else in the democratic world, including the rest of Africa. Their assailants are not foreign invading armies demonstrating conquest, or even members of "other" racial groups in the still divided post-apartheid locales of the new nation. They are South African men, most often the very men with whom South African women live in intimate relationships.[29]

Unlike domestic violence, which cuts across all barriers,[30] recorded victims of rape are mostly concentrated among poor and disadvantaged women in South Africa.[31] While acknowledging that all women are potential rape victims, poor women in this country are more vulnerable to rape than are those from the privileged classes. This is not surprising, as poor women do not have private transportation, need to walk long distances, and live in areas plagued by crime, gangsterism, overcrowding, and poverty and, in order to work, are often required to leave and return home in the dark. Accurate statistics on rape are notoriously difficult to come by, and for the last year we have had a police-imposed prohibition on the disclosure of all crime statistics. In 1998, 49,280 rapes were reported to the South African police. These figures exclude cases of sexual assault (4,851) and incest (179) only because our definition of rape is very limited. Since January 2000, 31,780 child rape and attempted rape cases have been reported to the South African police. According to Rape Crisis Cape Town, approximately one in twenty rapes is reported; thus, approximately 985,600 rapes occurred in 1998.[32] Recently this has been exacerbated by the widespread belief that if a man has sexual relations with a virgin he will be cured of HIV/AIDS.[33] The consequence of this obscenity is that girl children, even babies, are being raped as a "cure" for HIV/AIDS. Our landscape is strewn with the wounded and dying bodies of victims.[34]

Victims of rape and indecent assault are deserted by a criminal justice system that is not able to bring offenders to justice.[35] This leads to people taking the law into their own hands. Revenge killings are occurring with increasing frequency. We have our Tamars, our Amnons, our Davids, and our Absaloms.[36] So far the lines drawn from the Tamar text to the South African context have highlighted abuse and rape. How does the Tamar story relate to the present HIV/AIDS pandemic? In order to answer this question I need to backtrack and explain what I mean by a "gendered pandemic."

HIV/AIDS—A Gendered Pandemic

African theologian Teresa Okure startled her hearers at a theological symposium on AIDS held in Pretoria in 1998 by saying that there are two viruses more dangerous than the HIV virus because they enable this virus to spread so rapidly.[37] The first virus is the one that assigns women an inferior status to men in society. According to Okure, this virus fuels the sex industry in which young women, themselves the victims of abuse, become infected with HIV and then pass it on to others, even to their babies. This is the virus that causes men to abuse women. This is the virus that is responsible for the shocking fact that in many countries in Africa the condition that carries the highest risk of HIV infection is that of being a married woman. The second virus that enables the HIV virus to spread at a devastating rate is found mostly in the developed world. It is the virus of global economic injustice that causes dreadful poverty in many parts of the developing world. Capitalist market economies are thrust on societies that are not geared for them as well as structural adjustment programs that are designed to meet the requirements of the developed world rather than those whose need is the greatest. Global economic systems disrupt traditional societies and displace economic and educational infrastructures. Moreover, the market demands of such systems make access to prevention and treatment of disease difficult and expensive. It is ironic that international organizations like UNAIDS and the United Nations call on countries to restructure their spending in order to ensure that their budgets are reallocated toward HIV prevention when these very countries are most often hamstrung by crippling foreign debt. Peter Piot, executive director of UNAIDS, has pointed out that in the year 2000, African countries were paying US $15 billion in debt repayments and that this was four times more than they spent on health or education.[38] Before moving on from this brief resumé of Okure's views, I suggest that the first virus related to the HIV/AIDS pandemic is not only about women's questionable status in society but more specifically about the disordered nature of relationships between women and men as expressed sexually and emotionally. This notion is also found in my reading of the Tamar text.

It is no coincidence that 90 percent of people infected with HIV live in developing countries. Here, according to Lisa Sowle Cahill, 800 million people lack access to clean water and are wanting for basic health care and perinatal care, primary education, nutrition, and sanitation, all of which grievously affect their physical well-being and make them vulnerable to disease. Not only do people living in poverty suffer general loss of health, but they are forced to adopt survival strategies that expose them to health risks.[39] Families break up as men seek work in cities, where they meet women, themselves under economic duress, who are willing to trade sexual access for a roof over their heads and some financial support. Inevitably less money reaches families back in the rural areas, and poverty spirals.[40]

The HIV virus causes AIDS.[41] But it does not act alone. In southern Africa HIV/AIDS is in reality a pandemic that has everything to do with gender relations and conditions of poverty. South Africa is a society in which cultural traditions of male dominance, bolstered by a particular understanding of the place of men in the Christian tradition, have resulted in continued inequity for women.[42] Poverty, both in the rural areas and in the informal settlements surrounding our cities, is an additional grinding reality. Understanding this unholy alliance should be at the heart of all HIV/AIDS programs whether located in the churches or in state structures. Gender inequality and the snaillike pace at which poverty is being tackled are the main problems blocking effective HIV/AIDS prevention. By this I do not mean that HIV/AIDS does not have devastating consequences for *all* South Africans, regardless of age, race, class, or economic status. Of course it does. But for South African women and children the AIDS pandemic is particularly perilous.[43] While it is cutting a deadly swath across the educated classes in the 20–40 age group, its greatest impact is on the most vulnerable members of society: the poor, the marginalized, and the displaced. This makes HIV/AIDS a crisis for women, particularly poor women in rural areas and those struggling to survive in shacks on the outskirts of cities.[44] And when women are affected, children suffer. Quoting from a 1997 UNAIDS report, Vicci Tallis points out that "almost four-fifths of all infected women live in Africa; in sub-Saharan Africa, there is a ratio of six women to five men infected; in the 15–24 year age group the risk of HIV infection for young women is even more disproportionate, with young women out-numbering young men by a ratio of 2:1."[45]

Probing beyond the statistics, it appears that women's vulnerability to HIV/AIDS occurs on a variety of levels: biological, social, individual, maternal, and caregiving. For instance, an HIV-positive pregnant woman runs the risk of transmitting the virus to her child, either during pregnancy, during birth, or after birth through breast feeding.[46] Rural women who have little or no education and who live in traditional patriarchal relationships have scant access to information on HIV/AIDS and generally lack the skills and the power needed "to negotiate safer sex." Tallis continues: "According to UNAIDS (1997) studies in Africa and elsewhere married women have been infected by their husbands (as their only sexual partner). Simply being married is a major risk for women who have little control over abstinence or condom use in the home, or their husband's sexual activities outside the home."[47] Strategies to deal with HIV/AIDS have failed these women because they insist on preventive behavior that they, the women, have little power to implement. There is a growing body of well-documented research in the social sciences that shows that women in patriarchal societies are "unequipped for sexual negotiation."[48] Research on teenage girls found that many experienced their first sexual encounter as coercive.[49] In the province of KwaZulu/Natal, 72 percent of teenage girls attending clinics related that they had refused to have sexual relations with their partners but were usually unsuccessful at doing so and that attempts at refusal could result in physical abuse, termination of the relationship, or financial hardship.[50]

Women who are HIV-positive are at the receiving end of prejudice, social ostracism, and violence. Countless women in South Africa who are HIV-positive have, like Tamar, been the victims of sexual violence, perpetrated within a cultural order in which power is abused and women are used for male purposes. The results? Once their status has been verified, they are often ostracized.[51] Tamar knew what it was like to be soiled goods, a status conferred on her by the power of abuse in a patriarchal order.

Tamar's cry "for such a thing is not done in Israel" is ignored. In a patriarchal system women's cries of distress are insufficiently heard, and they often disappear in a veil of silence. Breaking the silence about one's status can be life threatening. Gugu Dlamini became South Africa's first AIDS martyr when, in December 1998, she was stoned to death for speaking out about her HIV status. HIV/AIDS is nourished by silence in South Africa. The dark mystery that lies at the heart of the pandemic in this country is the stubborn multilayered silence, or what is called "the denial" by professionals. Suzanne Leclerc-Madlala, a medical anthropologist, comments that this silence "has much to do with heterosexual power, sexual life-ways, the structure and meanings of which are contoured by what is often termed 'culture.'" Wrestling with the stubbornness of the silences around HIV/AIDS in our part of the world, Leclerc-Madlala states that "well-documented social science studies . . . point to high levels of premarital activity, extramarital relations and sexual violence, making African societies, taken as a whole, more at risk for both STDs and HIV/AIDS than those in other parts of the world. In many communities women can expect a beating, not only if they suggest condom usage, but also if they refuse sex." Until such time as our leaders, like those in Uganda, speak out clearly and unambiguously about the causes and nature of HIV/AIDS, we will "continue to re-enact the high-risk sexual culture and the silence that enshrouds it."[52] As Piot insists, "No amount of dollars can make a difference if there is not concerted leadership, at all levels from the head of state to the district level, involving government in partnership with non-governmental organisations, communities and the private sector."[53]

What emerges from present research into HIV/AIDS in sub-Saharan Africa is the fact that the role of men needs to be addressed, particularly attitudes and behavior that are sexually irresponsible and that result in a certain death sentence not only for themselves but also for millions of women and children. Given the powerful role of men in society, HIV/AIDS interventions and strategies targeting men will have a substantial impact on reducing the vulnerability of women to HIV. The theoretical and practical implications of the growing awareness of men's roles in the HIV/AIDS pandemic are now being tackled by social scientists on our continent.[54] Heavily male institutions such as the military, sports clubs, and trade unions are the focus of HIV prevention.[55] The need to deal with inequities within relationships and society remains a central concern.[56] I am not negating the importance of other strategies for dealing with HIV/AIDS, such as advocating closed sexual relationships, the use of preventive measures, the need for appropriate treatment such as postexposure prophylactics, AZT, or nevirapine for pregnant mothers.[57] I am simply saying that gender relations, exacerbated by poverty, are powerful contributing factors to the present pandemic in South Africa.

Rereading the story of Tamar I feel affirmed by its truth. Women's vulnerability to abuse is unflinchingly portrayed. It speaks truth into "my place." While poverty is not Tamar's lot, this text names the evil: our human proclivity for abuse of power. It appears to leave us with little hope. But does it really? Tamar's cry, "for such a thing is not done in Israel," is a cry of resistance. The very fact that this woman's voice is heard in this text in this manner is unusual enough to leave some ground for hope, slim as it may be. The quirky power of Scripture to uncover new ways of seeing, to point to less obvious paths and to evoke hope when despair seems the only legitimate reaction, can allow clues for resistance and hope to slip through this reading that could assist the churches as they struggle to find a way forward in this present crisis.[58]

The Tamar Text: Clues for Resistance and Hope

"Saying It as It Is"

Tamar's story "says it as it is." Why is this important? There is no prevarication, no avoidance of the horror, no cover-up. Miroslav Volf speaks about "the geography of sin" and "the ideology of sin."[59] In the case of Tamar, "the geography of sin" is the scene of the crime in which her violated body is at the center. "The ideology of sin" is the context backed by eons of patriarchal traditions and practices that result in women's status being secondary to that of the male in familial relations. Saying it as it is is the place to begin. What would it take for the churches to accept responsibility publicly for our role in the promotion and maintenance of gender inequality? And when will we make the link between this woeful tradition and the present deadly impact of HIV/AIDS on the lives of women and men? Positively put, the churches can begin to deal with the present erosion of sexual morality, with its devastating consequences for women and children, by esteeming women—our entire being, our bodies, our status, and our humanity—in every respect, as well as by speaking out unambiguously about the reasons for the present scourge of HIV/AIDS.

Once the body of Christ is able to make the connection between power, gender relations, and HIV/AIDS within its own infected body, the question then is this: What will it take for the body of Christ to be a body that can bring hope to those living with HIV/AIDS? Given the existing conflicting models for being church, I suggest that a common starting point is found in our creeds. What does it mean to confess to being "one holy, catholic, and apostolic" church in the midst of this HIV/AIDS crisis?[60]

These statements are made in faith and are integral components of the confession of the triune God. As the church acquires its existence through the activity of Christ, the marks of the church are, in the first instance, marks of Christ's activity. Unity of the church lies in Christ's unifying activity. Holiness is not initially ours but is the holiness of Christ, who acts on sinners. Catholicity is really about the limitless lordship of Christ. Apostolicity refers to Christ's mission in the Spirit. Seen in this way, these confessions of faith are statements of hope—indicators of the new creation of all in Christ.[61] They are also statements of action. If we are truly *one*, we are the church with HIV/AIDS. People living with HIV/AIDS are found in every sector of society and every church denomination. We are all related; what affects one member of the body of Christ affects us all (1 Cor. 12:26). We are all living with HIV/AIDS. There is no "us" and "them." We dare not forget that inclusion, not exclusion, is the way of grace. If we are *holy*, we are not living some superhuman mode of existence, as Marjorie Suchocki reminds us: "Holiness does not require a transcendence of our human condition, but a full utilization of our condition toward the concrete reality of love."[62] Holiness is not withdrawal from the smell of crisis but engagement, often risky, in situations where God is present. If we are *catholic*, we are in solidarity because we are connected, in communion, with those who are suffering and who experience fear of rejection, poverty, and death. If we are *apostolic*, we stand in continuity with the church in its infancy, and we strive to live as Ignatius of Antioch put it, "in the manner of the apostles."[63] This means that we are true to the heart of our confession, that we are zealous for the word and that we continuously examine the ideals of the early church and measure ourselves against them. This is nothing new. It is no more than a call to put the words we mouth in the creeds into practice. Clearly, we all fall short in this regard. The marks of the church do, however, offer solid guidelines for measuring our actions as members of this one universal body, a body infected with viruses that is struggling to live faithfully.

The Power of Narrative

Tamar's story raises the issue of the power of narrative. Human beings cannot survive without a narrative identity.[64] Telling stories is intrinsic to claiming one's identity and in this process finding impulses for hope. For those living with HIV/AIDS there is a need to claim and to name their identities in order to move away from the victim status so often thrust upon them. Narrative has a further function.[65] Apart from claiming identity and naming the evil, narrative has a sense-making function. The very act of telling the story is an act of making sense of an often incomprehensible situation, of a suffering and chaotic world in which people wrestle with understanding and in so doing seek relief.

The stories of people living with HIV/AIDS are not only stories of suffering. They are also stories of triumph, of resistance, and of hope. Stories such as these need to be heard in communities of faith. Churches can offer a supportive and empathetic environment for storytelling in the search for meaning. "The self-narrative is an individual's account of the relationship among self-relevant events across time, a way of connecting coherently the events of one's own life," writes Joan Laird. Stories, she continues, are "to be thought of as narratives within the narrative."[66] The stories of people living with HIV/AIDS are individual tales within the metanarrative of the pandemic. Hearing and engaging with these stories in communities of faith has the potential to draw members into relationship. We all have stories to tell. As our stories intersect, they change. We become part of one another's stories. In this process, we are all changed. Hearing and telling stories begins a process of openness, vulnerability, and mutual engagement that challenges stigmas, ostracization, and the loneliness of suffering, and hopefully leads to acts of engagement, affirmation, and care. Most importantly, narrative has the power to break the silences surrounding this crisis and to give it a human face.

The real metanarrative is *the* story of our faith: the story of the God of Israel acting to create and redeem that culminates in the ministry, suffering, death, and resurrection of Jesus Christ. Storytelling becomes a two-way conversation—hearing stories of suffering and triumph, and retelling *the* story of suffering and triumph in our communities of faith. The intersection of our life stories with the Jesus story is our ultimate hope.

Embodiment

The HIV virus enters, lurks, then makes forays into the immune system until ultimately it destroys the body. This pandemic is all about bodies. Unfortunately, writes William LaFleur, "in spite of doctrines of incarnation, resurrection, and *imago dei*, and theories about the ingestion of the very body of Christ in the mass, both the Catholic and Protestant Churches, perhaps especially during some of the modern centuries, have conceived their principal domain as that of the soul and its salvation."[67] Thankfully, the Tamar story is a tale about embodiment. This text challenges the recurring Christian refrain that the body is secondary to the soul and that the material is less praiseworthy than the spiritual. Our social reality is an embodied reality. In Elaine Graham's words, "The effects and dynamics of power, truth, reason, good and evil never exist as transcendent ideals; they remain to be embodied, enacted, performed in human communities of bodily practice."[68] Our bodies are more than skin, bone, and flesh. Our bodies encompass the totality of our human experience: our thoughts, our emotions, our needs and memories, our ability to imagine and to dream, our experiences of pain, pleasure, power, and difference, as well as our beliefs and our hopes. Ethicist Christine Gudorf reminds us that the body is synonymous with the self: "The mind is not over and against the body but rather is part of it, as are the emotions."[69] Our bodies are, in fact, the intricate tracery of all that is ourselves. Again, in Graham's words, "embodiment is more than an 'issue' exciting our compassion; rather, it points us to the performative, incarnational nature of all theology. Bodily *praxis* is the agent and the vehicle of divine reality and the faith practices of the Body of Christ are 'sacraments' of suffering and redemption."[70] The Tamar text opens up the issue of the body and challenges any thoughts of separating soul and body, mind and emotions.

For women and children who are infected, the body is at the center of political, social, and religious struggles. This is hardly surprising. The female body has, for instance, been the subject of ridicule, adulation, envy, discrimination, abuse, and stigma. The question of stigma is particularly relevant to persons suffering from HIV/AIDS. Ignorance, prejudice, stereotypes, and issues of power and dominance all conspire to stigmatize sufferers and in so doing to label them and to distort their true identities. You simply become "an HIV-positive," a statistic whose identity is now subsumed in your status. This denies the active, meaningful, and contributing lives led by increasing numbers of HIV-positive people. Erving Goffman's influential theory of stigma points to the link between stigmas and assumed identities. He asserts that stigmas are specially constructed relationships:

> Historically, stigmas were imposed on individuals in the form of physical marking or branding to disgrace them. In modern societies, however, stigmas arise through social processes of interaction whereby individuals are marked or segregated because of an attribute they possess or because of something discrediting known about them. Hence stigmatized identities emerge through interpersonal interactions rather than as a psychological reaction to events. . . . The mere existence of stigma ensures that social interactions between stigmatized and nonstigmatized persons are usually uncomfortable, tense, and frustrating.[71]

Goffman's work on "stigmatized identities" refers to the disabled. Yet it strikes profound chords in our context. Women who are known to be HIV-positive are stigmatized by a large section of South African society. Tamar's cry is a poignant reminder of what happens when stigmas prevail. Fortunately, within the body of people living with HIV/AIDS there is an increasing band of people who are slowly gaining power by defining their experiences and claiming their reality, speaking out and breaking the silence around the disease. There is also a new brand of social activism emerging in South Africa, as bodies march in the streets demanding affordable treatment for HIV/AIDS.[72]

When, on the one hand, the body is seen merely as a vehicle for the soul, or, on the other, as some kind of a trap, it has been maltreated, vilified, and abused. This is an important clue for the churches to seize in the struggle against HIV/AIDS. Bodies are at the center of this crisis—sick, poor, and too often women and children's bodies. The gospel demands embodied acts of care, comfort, support, and acceptance.

Ethical Codes

Tamar's cry "for such a thing is not done in Israel" raises the issue of the ethical codes of a people. She cries out not only for the protection of her own body but for the honor of her people. Her people are God's people. In reality, her cry is a cry to God. It is a cry for the integrity of life. It is a cry of resistance against the disordered and morbid nature of Amnon's love and a cry for love expressed in relations of trust and respect.

In South Africa there is much talk, and very necessary talk, about abstinence, prevention, and medication in the face of the HIV/AIDS crisis. The Roman Catholics say abstinence is the only answer. The Anglicans say yes, but if you must, use condoms. There is very little being said, however, about the moral and ethical issues raised by the HIV/AIDS pandemic. So far the churches have not grasped this nettle. The recognition that the body of Christ is a community of sexual human beings is slow in coming, and centuries of ignoring any matter related to human sexuality is merely feeding the silence around HIV/AIDS.[73] It

simply is not good enough merely to preach fidelity and abstinence in sexual relations. This message cannot be heard, understood, or followed as long as it is com-
municated without a properly constructed debate on what constitutes a moral
community. Moral choices and moral accountability within a community in
which women are respected as equal partners in the church itself are essential to
this debate.

What makes a moral community? Christian ethics are communal ethics. How
people live with one another and are faithful to God are two sides of the same
coin. In Amnon's world the people of Israel received the law, according to Rowan
Williams, "when God had already established relations with them, when they
were already beginning to be a community bound by faithfulness to God and to
each other." Williams continues:

> When the Old Testament prophets announce God's judgment on the peo-
> ple, they don't primarily complain about the breaking of specific rules
> (though they can do this in some contexts) or about failure to live up to a
> moral ideal; they denounce those actions that signify a breaking of the
> covenant with God and so the breaking of the bonds of faithfulness that pre-
> serve Israel as a people to whom God has given a vocation.[74]

In the New Testament, Paul deals with ethical dilemmas (for example, Rom. 14
and 15, 1 Cor. 10) by arguing that any decisions taken should be guided by the
priority of the other person's advantage, by avoidance of judgmentalism, and by
acceptance of one another and thus by the ultimate imperative of building the
body of Christ more securely. For Christians, ethical actions flow from involvement in community with God and with one another. Actions that promote the
good of another are actions designed for the good of the body of Christ.

How can the shaping of a moral community begin? In his book *The Moral
Bond of Community*, Bernard Brady has a chapter entitled "You Don't Have Anything If You Don't Have Stories." He writes, "Narratives form and inform our
values, our dispositions and how we 'see the world.'"[75] It is indeed possible to
argue that narrative is *the* medium of moral communication. What is certain is
that narrative is at the heart of our faith, a narrative which "sets up the conditions for the possibility of the moral life."[76] Instead of a negative ethic of human
sexuality that consists only of injunctions on what not to do, people's stories can
be countered with other stories—stories from our sourcebook. Once the stories
of the Bible and from our traditions interact with our own stories, then moral
consciousness, the ability to distinguish the "is" from the "ought" and the choices
this involves, can be nurtured. Acquiring moral agency does not separate "being"
from "doing," or character from decision making and action. As Bruce Birch and
Larry Rasmussen note, to be a member of the body of Christ means "the formation and transformation of personal moral identity in keeping with the faith identity of the community."[77]

To put it differently, a moral community is one whose goal is the common
good of all. Such a community upholds the integrity of life, values the dignity of

the human person, and includes those who are on the margins or excluded, while not avoiding the reality of structural sin. The moral claim, says William Schweiker, is to "respect and enhance the integrity of life *before God*."[78] The main task of a moral community is to nurture the moral capacities of its members— by storytelling, by involvement in the work of justice and charity, and by upholding the integrity of all life, affirmed by our liturgical practices. In this way the community becomes one of moral deliberation and praxis. Birch and Rasmussen conclude, "In both Jewish and Christian traditions, faith's truth is finally a 'performative' one."[79] It becomes real when it is embodied. Moral truth and a way of life go hand in hand.

Brazilian bishop Dom Helder Camara once meditated in the middle hours of the night about the attitudes of the rich toward the poor, and then wrote a poem. This poem speaks to those of us in the church who are not HIV-positive and who may be tempted to feel virtuous about our status, perhaps even indifferent to those who are infected:

> I pray incessantly
> for the conversion
> of the prodigal son's brother.
> Ever in my ear
> rings the dread warning
> "this one [the prodigal] has awoken
> from his life of sin."
> When will the other [the brother]
> awaken
> from his virtue?"[80]

The Language of Lament

After Amnon evicts Tamar, she puts ashes on her head, rents her robe, and goes away crying loudly. Alone, without comfort, discarded and abused, her plight is that of countless women and children through the ages. There is no language in this text to deal with the horror of Tamar's experience, other than her cry. Fortunately, there are resources in Scripture that fill this lacuna. The ancient language of lament offers a vehicle for expressing the raw emotions arising from situations such as Tamar's.[81] The language of lament also offers the body of Christ the opportunity to say, "We are suffering; we stand in solidarity with all who suffer; we lament while we believe that there is hope for all in the saving grace of Jesus Christ."

What is lament? Lament is a form of mourning. It is also more. It is somehow more purposeful and more instinctive than mourning. Lamenting is both an individual and a communal act that signals that relationships have gone awry. While lamenting is about past events, it also has present and future dimensions. It acknowledges the brokenness of the present because of injustice and our role in contributing to the troubles of the world. It instinctively creates a link between healing and mourning that makes new just relationships possible in the future. Lament is not utilitarian. It is as primal as the child's need to cry. Lament is more than railing against suffering, breast beating, or a confession of guilt. It is a coil of suffering and hope, awareness and memory, anger and relief, desires for vengeance, forgiveness, and healing.[82] It is our way of bearing the unbearable, both individually and communally. It is a wailing of the human soul, a barrage of tears, reproaches, petitions, praise, and hopes that beat against the heart of God. It is, in essence, supremely human.

Once the wail is articulated, the lament usually takes on a structured form. This does not mean that lament should be tamed or domesticated but rather that it happens in spaces that are contained by liturgical boundaries and rhythms. Nevertheless, lamenting remains risky speech. It is risky because it calls into question structures of power, it calls for justice, it pushes the boundaries of our relationships with one another and with God beyond the limits of acceptability. It is a refusal to settle for the way things are. It is a reminder to God that the human situation is not as it should be and that God as the partner in the covenant must act. Lament is never an end in itself. It is undergirded by the hope that God not only can but that God *will* hear the cries of the suffering and the penitent and *will* act with mercy and compassion.

As HIV/AIDS decimates families and communities, the body of Christ can find hope and comfort in the psalms, whose undimmed quality comes to us through the ages, expressing the rawness of suffering as well as trust and hope in God. In Walter Brueggemann's words, "Israel unflinchingly saw and affirmed that life as it comes, along with joy, is beset by hurt, betrayal, loneliness, disease, threat, anxiety, bewilderment, anger, hatred and anguish."[83] Israel also saw that lament and praise go hand in hand. On the one hand, the psalmists almost assault God with facts about the human condition. On the other hand, they reveal trust and confidence that God will deliver them.

When the language of lament becomes the language of the body of Christ in circumstances of suffering it has a number of grave implications, first of all for the political and social witness of the churches and the impact of their message. The credibility in society of the churches as institutions that claim to be inclusive, caring communities is in doubt if they are not seen to lament the injustice of the patent lack of support from our government for those suffering from HIV/AIDS. Lamenting can be politically subversive and therefore dangerous, as it is never about the preservation of the status quo.

Second, the language of lament can enrich our liturgies and our pastoral care. I have seen lament at work in St. George's Cathedral in Cape Town when people faced one another across the racial divide, told their stories, wept, and joined in prayers of petition. Then I understood why so many prayers of praise are impoverished. Too often praise is not praise that emerges from grappling with radical doubt about God's presence in the world and our disquiet about suffering. I also saw how painful memories must be brought into the open. They need to be told, and, when words fail, the psalms offer a valuable resource for lament, as they honor people's pain and offer hope. Hope is nurtured in community. When the community of faith joins in lamenting, the suffering person feels that her or his pain is validated. The locus of pain is shifted from the inner world of private suffering to the outer reality of the community of faith in a movement that is potentially cathartic.

Finally, the practice of lament can contribute to a more intimate and authentic relationship with God. People living with HIV/AIDS grapple with guilt, fear, and anger. Death as judgment for sin weighs heavily on some. The ability to cry out to God, to lament sin and seek forgiveness as David did (Ps. 51), offers another way. Fear of the suffering associated with death from AIDS-related diseases is only human; anger at being a victim of infection raises legitimate questions about God, about justice, and about God's presence and power in a suffering world. Is God's justice and care for us reliable, and, if so, where is it? There is much cause for lament, yet its loss stifles our questions about evil in the world. Instead, we settle for a God who is covered with a sugar-coated veneer of religious optimism and whose omnipotence will "make everything right in the end." Religious optimism is deeply different from a life of faith that is unafraid to examine suffering but is nonetheless grounded in hope. Religious optimism prefers to sanitize God by removing God from the ugliness of evil and suffering. This is a God whom we dare not approach with our genuine grief and with whom we are in a relationship of eternal infantilism. Prayers of lament that are direct, truthful about suffering, and that name the unnameable to God are powerful in their potential to heal our doubts, address our lack of trust, and restore our faith in God's power to act on our cries. The church with AIDS must raise its voice in lament.

Life and Death

Tamar is lost in the mists of history, and we do not know how she lived out her life. Her rape undoubtedly affected her quality of life and her ability to live abundantly. Discovering that one is infected with HIV, coping with subsequent opportunistic infections and finally with full-blown AIDS challenge one's quality of life. How to live productively and hopefully with the knowledge of premature death and then how to face imminent death raise questions about the relationship between life and death that demand attention in the body of Christ. What has the good news to say to someone who is infected with HIV or who is dying of AIDS?

I suggest that the place to begin is to affirm that God is a lover of life, so much so, that life continues into eternity. Certainty about this comes from the promise of the resurrection of the body. Hope is the key to questions about life and death. Not the "pie in the sky when you die" kind of hope, which is nothing more than the thin skin of religious optimism, but creative, imaginative, expectant, and risky hope, maintained only with struggle. Hope is demanding, because we have to live our lives in such a way that that which we hope for can come about. This kind of hope takes our confessed belief in "the life everlasting" as not only something for one day when I die but as a confession of how I will live my life this day, in this moment. It is the kind of hope that enabled Dietrich Bonhoeffer, when he took leave of a fellow prisoner in Flossenbürg concentration camp and went to his execution, to say, "This is the end—for me the beginning of life."[84]

Life, death, and resurrection all belong together; they make up the whole of life. Resurrection cannot be reduced to life after death alone. When John (1 John 3:14) writes, "We know that we have passed from death to life because we love one another," he stresses that love is passionate about life, that we must say a hearty "Yes" to life. What the resurrection of the body means is the subject of theological speculation; resurrection talk, however, remains body talk according to our creeds. Resurrection does not mean a deferred life—something we put off until after we die. In Moltmann's words, "I shall live *wholly* here, and die *wholly*, and rise *wholly* there."[85] Eternal life is all of me, all of everyone, all of creation, all healed, reconciled, and completed. Nothing will be lost. Christian faith is shaped by the experience of the death of Christ and by his resurrection. The process of the resurrection of the dead begins in Christ and continues in the Spirit, "the giver of life," and will be completed in the raising of all the dead.[86] So, I would say to a person dying of AIDS, "Death is not your end. *Every life remains before God forever.*" For Moltmann, to be raised to eternal life means that nothing has been lost for God—"not the pains of this life, and not its moments of happiness." Thus, death both separates and unites. "Eternal life is the final healing of this life into the completed wholeness for which it is destined."[87]

Unfortunately, there are Christians who believe that AIDS is God's punishment for sin. In her book *AIDS and Its Metaphors*, Susan Sontag says that "plagues are invariably regarded as judgments on society."[88] We are very quick to link any sexually transmitted disease with sin as if there are no innocent victims. Insensitive zealousness has resulted in persons dying of AIDS being told, "Your sin has caused your death." I am cautious, even suspicious of this language of fear. Despite those terrifying medieval pictures of judgment that were designed to encourage women and men to seek comfort and salvation in the arms of the church, people have not stopped sinning. The mere mention of HIV/AIDS raises fear. It seeps into places where we did not know it before: fear of sexuality, fear of bodily fluids, fear of the Communion cup—as Sontag comments, "fear of contaminated blood, whether Christ's or your neighbor's."[89] (Nietzsche commented acerbically on what he called the "holy lie"—the invention of a God who punishes and rewards by holding out the afterlife as some sort of "great punishment machine.")[90] Death can be caused directly by sin. We kill one another. We are destroying our environment. But death is not God's ultimate judgment on us. Admittedly, Christian thinkers such as Paul, the church fathers, and Augustine saw death as punishment for "the wages of sin." James writes that "when that desire has conceived, it gives birth to sin, and that sin, when it is fully grown, gives birth to death" (1:15). Undeniably, death can be caused by sinful acts.

There are other traditions in Christianity that do not see death as a judgment on sin. Schleiermacher and the liberal Protestant theology of the nineteenth century disputed the causal connection between sin and physical death.[91] Moltmann argues that death may be called the "wages of sin" but that this can only be said of human beings. Angels are dubbed immortal, but according to 2 Pet. 2:4, they sinned! Animals, birds, fish, and trees don't sin, yet they die. Through human beings death has been brought into nonhuman creation. Death has been with us from the beginning. God's first commandment to human beings was "be fruitful and multiply." We were mortal right from the beginning. From a pastoral point of view, theological speculation about the relationship between sin and death is not particularly helpful for the person dying of AIDS.

The body is implicated by the process of sin. The very context in which we live is affected by sin. Innocence suffers. Everything that is born must die. It is part of our condition. Our responsibility is to live and to die in loving solidarity with that sighing and groaning community of creatures described by Paul, all waiting for "the redemption of our bodies" (Rom. 8:23).[92] We all need redemption. "The death of all the living is neither due to sin nor is it natural," writes Moltmann. "It is a fact that evokes grief and longing for the future world and eternal life."[93] We all await what Letty Russell calls "the mending of creation."[94]

At the center of our efforts to understand the link between life and death is Christ. For Paul, community with Christ, who is the subject of our hope, extends to the living and the dead: "For to this end Christ died and lived again, so that he might be Lord of both the dead and the living" (Rom. 14:9). Moltmann reads this verse as follows: "I understand this in the following sense: In dying, Christ became the brother of the dying. In death, he became the brother of the dead. In his resurrection—as the One risen—he embraces the dead and the living, and takes them with him on his way to the consummation of God's kingdom."[95] As we struggle to understand what it means to live hopefully, we are reminded that life remains unfinished. We have tried to live according to the plan for our lives, but we have failed. We are wounded, incomplete, not yet the persons that God intends us to be. We mourn the death of those we love. There is no quick fix for those who suffer. Life in the midst of suffering and death is a constant struggle; it risks moments of despair and loss of trust, and it seeks hope even in the darkest places.

Eucharist

So far my rereading of the Tamar text has raised issues of honest awareness, narrative, embodiment, moral community, lament, and issues of life and death. At heart, Tamar's story portrays what can happen when human relationships become corrupted. It is a story of failure and loss of hope, as both Tamar and Amnon are violated, albeit in different ways. Yet when it is read within the wider context of the canon, it is a story of resistance to abuse and evil power and an affirmation of the moral code of a people who knew the better way.

By grace, failure does not have the last word in the Christian life. Our hope is in Jesus Christ, the embodiment of our faith, whose life, death, and resurrection we celebrate in the Eucharist.[96] Michael Welker reminds us that the Eucharist was instituted "in the night that Jesus Christ was betrayed and handed over to the powers of this world."[97] Its origins do not lie in success or triumph but in the human betrayal of the Son, and it is precisely here that we dare to hope. I want to conclude my search for clues with a few thoughts on how the Eucharist links up with the themes that I have already raised and how it offers hope in our present context.

At the outset of this essay I said that the body of Christ has AIDS. I see a link between the violated body of Tamar, the abused bodies of women and children, the bodies of people living with HIV/AIDS, and the crucified and resurrected body of Jesus Christ, whom we remember and celebrate in the bread and the wine at the Eucharist. Deep inside the body of Christ, the AIDS virus lurks, and as we remember Christ's sacrifice we see in his very wounds the woundedness of his sisters and brothers who are infected and dying. Our hope is in Christ, who takes the church as his bride, makes it his body, and through this nuptial act sets before us the possibility of relationships in love that are the antitheses of the disordered and morbid expressions of love found in Tamar's story.

The Eucharist is the bodily practice of grace. Nancy Eisland writes, "Receiving the Eucharist is a body practice of the church. The Eucharist as a central and constitutive practice of the church is a ritual of membership. . . . The Eucharist is a matter of bodily meditation of justice and an incorporation of hope."[98] Because God chose to live with us in the flesh, sacramentality takes physical reality very seriously.[99] We are bodily partakers of the physical elements of bread and wine, Christ's presence in our lives and in our world. The very bodiliness of the celebration of the Eucharist affirms the centrality of the body in the practice of the faith. "The Supper," writes Welker, "centers on a complex, sensuous process in which the risen and exalted Christ becomes present. The Supper gives Christians a form in which they can perceive the risen and exalted Christ with all their senses."[100]

The celebration of the Eucharist makes the reign of God present "to us" in the form of Christ's body broken "for us" and Christ's blood shed "for us." Christ invites us to the feast, and he is "both the giver of the feast and the gift itself."[101] In other words, the gift of the reign of God is quite simply present in the person of Christ himself—Christ crucified and risen. Thus, the Communion meal mediates communion with the crucified One in the presence of the risen One. It becomes a foretaste of the messianic banquet of all humankind. It is the meal at which all are welcome. In Christ's body, the Eucharist is *the* sacrament of equity. Only self-exclusion can keep one away. At the Communion table we are offered the consummate step in forging an ethic of right relationship, across all our differences: "We who are many are one body, for we all partake of one bread." This visible, unifying, bodily practice of relationship with all its potential for healing is ours. For the Eucharist to have meaning in our lives, we need to feel its powerful pull to the radical activity of loving relationships with those who are different. As Duncan Forrester writes, "The Eucharist involves a commitment (*sacramentum*) to sharing with the needy neighbor, for Jesus said, 'The Bread that I shall give is my own flesh; given for the life of the world' (John 6:51)."[102]

A covenanted eucharistic community is a community in relationship with one another and with God. Paul describes us as the body of Christ, a body which though it has many members, is one body: "If one member suffers, all suffer together with it; if one member is honored, all rejoice together with it" (1 Cor. 12:26). It is a body in which the weakest are to be treated with respect, for "God has so arranged the body, giving the greater honor to the inferior member, that there may be no dissension within the body, but the members may have the same care for one another" (1 Cor. 12:24–25). The picture here is one of solidarity in suffering, of mutual support, and of a moral community in relationship with one another and with God.

Finally, much has been made of the text in 1 Cor. 11:27–29, 31–32 about eating the bread and drinking the wine in an unworthy manner, about examining ourselves, and about the threat of judgment. Welker comments that then "the Supper is no longer a feast of reconciliation but rather an anxiety-producing means of moral gatekeeping. In a sad irony, the feast of unconditional acceptance of human beings by God and among each other was misused for intrahuman moral control!"[103] There is a tension here. Welker points out that in the celebration of the Eucharist, God accepts us unconditionally, while at the same time Paul's concern is that Christians celebrate the meal in accordance with the meal's identity. Rightly so. How we partake of the meal is deeply significant for how we live as a moral community. "The Eucharist may be understood as nourishment for moral growth and formation," writes Forrester.[104] A community with a moral code and a moral identity partaking in a meal of grace, memory, and new life brings resistance to evil and hope for now and tomorrow for the church with HIV/AIDS.

In conclusion, while conceding at the outset that the Tamar text did not give much apparent cause for hope, I have tried to find clues for resistance and hope that could be useful for church praxis in our present crisis. We live in what Edward Schillebeeckx terms a world that is an "enigmatic mixture of good and evil, of meaning and meaninglessness."[105] In the midst of this bewildering mixture of experiences, there is the human capacity for indignation and moral outrage. Tamar's cry, "for such a thing is not done in Israel," allows us to find hope where there is little cause for it, enables us to say "yes" when all else shouts "no," and allows chinks of light to help us find footholds in a context that in John Chrysostom's words is "grazed thin by death."[106] Her cry jars our reality, the reality of those who, in Shimmer Chinoyda's word, were "born at the wrong end of the century." We know what should *not* be done in Israel. Tim Trengove Jones writes, "'We know what to do' is a formulation that takes us to the very heart of the scandal that is AIDS; it situates us on the frontier between hope and despair, between action and inertia, between those with the means to 'do something' and those who have little to 'do' but suffer."[107] HIV/AIDS is our *kairos*. It is a time when the ordinary rhythm of life is suspended. Will it be a time of doom, or will we find a new unveiling of God's presence and love for us here and now?[108]

Notes

1. The phrase "bleak immensity" is borrowed from Wole Soyinka, *Art, Dialogue, and Outrage: Essays on Literature and Culture* (New York: Pantheon, 1993), 16.

2. For modes of infection, see Alan Whiteside and Clem Sunter, *AIDS: The Challenge for South Africa* (Cape Town: Human & Rousseau, 2000), 10.

3. See Willem Saayman and Jacques Kriel, "Towards a Christian Response to AIDS," *Missionalia* 19, no. 2 (1991): 154–67.

4. Figures quoted here are a combination of estimates published by the United Nations health agencies and the South African National Department of Health. See also Elizabeth Pisani, "AIDS in the 21st Century: Some Critical Considerations," *Reproductive Health Matters* 8, no. 15 (2000): 63–76, for a global assessment of the AIDS situation.

5. Whiteside and Sunter, *AIDS*, 44.

6. See *Sunday Times Business Times*, July 2, 2000. See also Whiteside and Sunter, *AIDS*, 98ff.

7. Statistics on HIV/AIDS are continuously questioned and revised. A government report on HIV/AIDS released in March 2001 reports that the infection rate among women younger than 20 decreased from 21 percent in 1998 to 16.5 percent in 1999 to 16.1 percent in 2000. The HIV infection rate in KwaZulu/Natal—still the province with the highest prevalence—increased from 1999's 32.5 percent to 36.2 percent in 2000.

8. Whiteside and Sunter, *AIDS*, 134.

9. The World Economic Forum's Africa Competition Report, released in July 2000, states that 40.77 percent of South African firms rank HIV/AIDS as having a moderate to major impact on their health care costs and 30.07 percent say their training costs have increased considerably. *Sunday Times Business Times*, July 2, 2000.

10. *Cape Times*, October 11, 1999.

11. "Millennium Report of the Secretary-General of the United Nations," http://www.un.org/millennium/sg/report.

12. Accessed at www.un.org/news/press/docs/2000.

13. Quoted in Hein Marias, *To the Edge: AIDS Review 2000* (Pretoria: University of Pretoria, Centre for the Study of AIDS, 2000), 4.

14. Politicians who beat a path to the home of dying Nokosi Johnson, a courageous little boy who spoke out about living with AIDS and who pleaded for treatment to be available to sufferers, while they refuse to state publicly that HIV causes AIDS or to lobby for effective treatment for AIDS sufferers, bespeak moral turpitude. The recent report (at a cost of R2.4 million) issued by President Thabo Mbeki's AIDS advisory panel has done little to resolve any of the key issues that led to the formation of the panel. It has merely given a further platform to dissident scientists to air their controversial view that HIV does not cause AIDS. See also Tim Trengove Jones, *Who Cares? AIDS Review 2001* (Pretoria: University of Pretoria, 2001), 24–39, for a discussion of the seemingly inexplicable attitude of President Mbeki on the AIDS crisis.

15. Quoted in Justice Edwin Cameron, "Involvement of People Living with HIV/AIDS—How to Make It More Meaningful," a speech given at the Second National Conference for People Living with HIV-AIDS, March 8–10, 2000, Durban.

16. Quoted in Sipho Seepe, "A Sacrifice on the Altar of Expediency," *Daily Mail and Guardian*, September 16–21, 2001.

17. In the year 2000, thirty-nine international pharmaceutical manufacturers took the South African government to court to prevent legislation that would enable the manufacture of cheaper generic drugs in South Africa to curb the HIV/AIDS pandemic. On April 20, 2001, a settlement was reached and the case did not proceed. Since then certain pharmaceutical companies have offered the South

African government drugs for AIDS at reduced prices. So far the state has refused such offers.

18. Trengove Jones, *Who Cares?* 7. It is indeed ironic to note that after three deaths and twelve confirmed cases of anthrax in the United States, Bayer, the manufacturer of Cipro, the antibiotic of choice for treating anthrax, was pressed into dropping its prices by the US government in light of a veiled threat to resort to generic medicines.

19. Throughout this essay "body of Christ" is used as the metaphor for the church. This is intentional, because the organic nature of this metaphor is important for the argument that "if one member suffers, all suffer together with it; if one member is honored, all rejoice together with it" (1 Cor. 12:26). Thus, the church with AIDS is the church universal.

20. My reading draws, *inter alia*, on the work of the Dutch biblical scholar Fokkelien van Dijk-Hemmes. See Mieke Bal, Fokkelien van Dijk-Hemmes and Grietje van Gineken, ed., *En Sara in Haar Tent Lachte: Patriarchaat en Verzet in Bijbelverhalen* (Utrecht: HES Uitgevers, 1984). See also Phyllis Trible, "The Royal Rape of Wisdom," in *Texts of Terror: Literary-Feminist Readings of Biblical Narratives* (Philadelphia: Fortress, 1984).

21. Teresa Okure, "Reading from This Place: Some Problems and Prospects," in *Reading from This Place*, vol. 2, *Social Location and Biblical Interpretation in Global Perspective* (ed. F. F. Segovia and M. A. Tolbert; Minneapolis: Fortress, 1995), 52.

22. Long before I was aware of the technicalities of different kinds of reading, I was in fact familiar with a nascent form of interpretation used by women when studying the Bible in groups. For well over thirty years I have belonged to women's Bible study groups. We read the biblical stories through women's eyes, seeking meaning for our lives, understanding for our faith, and affirmation for our experiences. Often the texts are difficult, even off-putting. After studies in hermeneutics my approach to such contentious texts in Scripture took the route of a *sachkritiek*, and I simply rejected them. This I no longer find satisfactory. My present approach is to try and deal with the whole of Scripture with its fundamental contradictions, to mull over them, often with irritation and anger, to ascertain how I can live with such texts fruitfully.

23. In 1999 I conducted research for a workshop on homiletics and found that of the eighty-four people interviewed (which included clergy and lay people), only one had heard a sermon on this text.

24. According to Trible ("The Royal Rape of Wisdom," 47), the repetition in this passage emphasizes the hatred focused on Tamar: "*Then-hated-her* Amnon *a-hatred* great indeed (*me'od*). Truly (*kî*) greater *the-hatred* which *he-hated-her* than-the-desire which he-desired-her."

25. Bal, van Dijk-Hemmes. and van Gineken, *En Sara*, 57.

26. James N. Poling, *The Abuse of Power: A Theological Problem* (Nashville: Abingdon, 1991), 158.

27. See Jane Bennett, "Gender-Based Violence in South Africa," *African Gender Institute Newsletter* 6 (2000), 3.

28. Human Rights Watch/Africa, *Report on Violence against Women in South Africa* (New York: Human Rights Watch, 1995), 44.

29. Amina Mama, "Transformation Thwarted: Gender-Based Violence in Africa's New Democracies," *African Gender Institute Newsletter* 6 (2000), 1.

30. See Mmatshilo Motsei, "Detection of Woman Battering in Health Care Settings: The Case of Alexandra Health Clinic," *Women's Health Project* paper no. 30 (January 1993): 5, which states that contrary to conventional wisdom, research has shown that "the perpetrators of violence against women include men who

hold respectable jobs and positions in society. . . . These include lawyers, doctors, psychologists, psychiatrists, priests and business executives." Furthermore, People Opposing Women Abuse (POWA) found in a study of inquest records that every six days at least one woman is killed by her partner and that more than half of all women murdered are killed by a partner or a male friend (*Star*, November 21, 1995).

31. Human Rights Watch/Africa, *Report on Violence*, 52.

32. According to the South African police, only one in thirty-five rapes is reported. Figures given here are taken from Rape Crisis Cape Town's Web site, http://www.rapecrisis.org.sa\stats.htm.

33. See Human Rights Watch Report, *Scared at School: Sexual Violence against Girls in South African Schools* (New York: Human Rights Watch, 2001), for a sober yet shattering account of conditions for female adolescents in South African schools. See page 25 for the account of a prosecutor who describes the virgin rape myth as a major problem.

34. See Betsi Pendry, "The Links between Gender Violence and HIV/AIDS," *Agenda* 39 (1998): 30–33. See also Whiteside and Sunter, *AIDS*, 58.

35. Human Rights Watch/Africa, *Report on Violence*, deals at length with the largely inadequate state response to violence against women.

36. See Anne Mager, "Sexuality, Fertility, and Male Power," *Agenda* 28 (1996): 12–24; and Promise Mthembu, "A Positive View," *Agenda* 39 (1998): 26–30. At its core, the problem is not simply that rape occurs or that women and children experience violence and fear in the arena of sexuality. Ours is a society that is redolent with patriarchal attitudes and practices. The problem is not just that a man raped his half-sister, though this is serious enough. The problem is not just that rape, incest, and violence against women are all too common. Years of counseling and collecting anecdotal evidence have shown me that, in my context, the problem is that many perpetrators do not think they have committed rape and do not recognize the difference between ordinary heterosexual activity and sexual violence. The social construction of heterosexual activity is largely based on patterns of dominance and submission in which men are expected to be dominant and women are expected to be submissive.

37. See Kevin Kelly, "Conclusion: A Moral Theologian Faces the New Millennium in a Time of AIDS," in *Catholic Ethicists on HIV/AIDS Prevention* (ed. James F. Keenan; New York: Continuum, 2000), 325.

38. Trengove Jones, *Who Cares?* 15. Harvard economist Richard Parker commented in 1996 that "we have begun to understand the perverse consequences caused by specific models of economic development (most often imposed from above) that have in fact functioned to produce and reproduce structures of economic dependence and processes of social disintegration" (Richard G. Parker, "Empowerment, Community Mobilization, and Social Change in the Face of HIV/AIDS," paper presented at the 11th International Conference on AIDS, Vancouver, July 1996).

39. Lisa Sowle Cahill, "AIDS, Justice, and the Common Good," in Keenan, *Catholic Ethicists on HIV/AIDS Prevention*, 282–83.

40. In order to assist in this crisis, $57 million was donated by the Bill and Melinda Gates Foundation to the United Nations Population Fund; Ted Turner of AOL Time Warner has promised to donate $100 million over ten years to assist UN-led programs in combatting HIV/AIDS. Economist Jeffrey Sachs has proposed a global trust fund supervised by the World Health Organization and UNAIDS to answer the need for resources in the poorer countries. Sachs estimates that between $7 billion and $8 billion is needed. He says "The US is a $10 trillion economy, so $1 billion is about one cent out of every $100 in our economy—which to

save 5 million lives a year and a continent that is dying, is an incredibly modest effort" (*Business Day*, March 7, 2001).

41. This statement is necessary in the face of the damaging denial of the South African state president and members of his cabinet. For the four key elements used to bolster belief that HIV does not cause AIDS, see Whiteside and Sunter, *AIDS*, 3. Today the majority of the world's leading virologists believe that the HIV hypothesis is correct.

42. This is illustrated by the fact that there are mainline denominational churches in South Africa in which Communion is served in the following order: first the men, then male adolescents, then women, and lastly female adolescents—as a confirmation of the headship of men (see 1 Cor. 11:3).

43. For statistics, see Quarraisha A. Karim, "Women and AIDS: The Imperative for a Gendered Prognosis and Prevention Policy," *Agenda* 39 (1998): 15–25. For a discussion of mother-to-child transmission, see Whiteside and Sunter, *AIDS*, 12.

44. See Hilda Adams and Anita Marshall, "Off Target Messages—Poverty, Risk, and Sexual Rights," *Agenda* 39 (1998): 87–93.

45. Vicci Tallis, "AIDS Is a Crisis for Women," *Agenda* 39 (1998): 9.

46. See Gill Seidel, "Making an Informed Choice: Discourses and Practices Surrounding Breastfeeding and AIDS," *Agenda* 39 (1998): 65–81.

47. Tallis, "AIDS Is a Crisis," 9–10.

48. See, *inter alia*, A. Kline, E. Kline, and E. Oken, "Minority Women and Sexual Choice in the Age of AIDS," *Social Science and Medicine* 34, no. 4 (1992): 447–57; D. Lear, "Sexual Communication in the Age of AIDS: The Construction of Risk and Trust among Young Adults," *Social Science and Medicine* 41, no. 9 (1995): 1311–23; L. Miles, "Women, AIDS, Power, and Heterosexual Negotiation," *Agenda* 15 (1992): 14–48; I. Orubuloye, J. Caldwell, and P. Cardwell, "African Women's Control Over Their Sexuality in an Era of AIDS," *Social Science and Medicine* 37, no. 7 (1993): 859–72.

49. For a report on a recent Gauteng study in which nearly 50 percent of male youth said they believed a girl who said "no" to sex meant "yes" and 24 percent thought a girl who had been raped had "asked for it," see Human Rights Watch Report, *Scared at School*, 27. Nearly a third of both men and women surveyed said that forcing sex on someone you know is not sexual violence.

50. See Rachel Jewkes et al., "Relationship Dynamics and Teenage Pregnancy in South Africa," *Social Science and Medicine* 52 (2001): 733–44. See also Christine Varga and Lindiwe Makubalo, "Sexual Non-Negotiation," *Agenda* 28 (1996): 33.

51. Sick and without resources, these women often die. Stories such as that of Nosipho Xhape, who died in a strange shack where she tried to find shelter, are not uncommon. This woman left her two children in the Eastern Cape to find work in the city. She could only survive by linking up with a man who would look after her. When it became apparent that she had full-blown AIDS, he turned her out one night. She found shelter in a toilet until a neighbor gave her a blanket and water and she moved to a broken-down shack. Fifteen hours later she was dead (*Cape Times*, February 12, 2000).

52. Suzanne Leclerc-Madlala, "The Silences That Nourish AIDS in Africa," *Mail and Guardian*, August 11–17, 2000.

53. Quoted in Trengove Jones, *Who Cares?* 31.

54. See C. Baylies and J. Bujra, *AIDS, Sexuality, and Gender in Africa: The Struggle Continues* (London: Routledge, 2000); J. Bujra, "Risk and Trust: Unsafe Sex, Gender and AIDS in Tanzania," in *Risk Revisited* (ed. P. Caplan; London: Pluto, 2000); K. Carovano, "HIV and the Challenges Facing Men," in *Issues Paper* 15 (New York: UNDP HIV Development Programme); K. Nkosi, "Men, the Mil-

itary, and HIV/AIDS in Malawi," in *AIDS and Men* (ed. M. Foreman; London: Panos Publications/Zed Press, 1999).

55. See Janet Bujra, "Targeting Men for a Change: AIDS Discourse and Activism in Africa," *Agenda* 44 (2000): 6–23.
56. Karim, "Women and AIDS," 23.
57. See Whiteside and Sunter, *AIDS*, 147–48.
58. The remainder of this essay employs a hermeneutic of resistance and hope as the Tamar text is woven through the theological themes that follow.
59. Miroslav Volf, "Original Crime, Primal Care," in *God and the Victim: Theological Reflections on Evil, Victimization, Justice, and Forgiveness* (ed. L. Lampman; Grand Rapids: Eerdmans, 1999), 28–29.
60. This language is from the Nicene-Constantinopolitan Creed, while the Apostles' Creed speaks of "one holy, catholic church."
61. Jürgen Moltmann, *The Church in the Power of the Spirit: A Contribution to the Messianic Ecclesiology* (Minneapolis: Fortress, 1993), 338–39.
62. Marjorie Suchocki, "Holiness and a Renewed Church," in *The Church with AIDS: Renewal in the Midst of Crisis* (ed. L. M. Russell; Louisville, KY: Westminster/John Knox, 1990), 115.
63. Quoted in Robert Schreiter, "Marks of the Church in Times of Transformation," in Russell, *Church with AIDS*, 131.
64. Robert Schreiter, *Reconciliation: Mission and Ministry in a Changing Social Order* (Maryknoll, NY: Orbis, 1999), 34.
65. I am grateful to Bernard Lategan for pointing out that the narrative has the further hermeneutical function of sense making, an understanding he attributes to the work of Jörn Rüsen's concept of *Sinnbildung*.
66. Joan Laird, "Women and Stories: Re-Storying Women's Self-Constructions," in *Women and Families: A Framework for Family Therapy* (ed. M. McGoldrick, C. M. Anderson, and F. Walsh; New York: Norton, 1991), 430, 133.
67. William R. LaFleur, "Body," in *Critical Terms for Religious Studies* (ed. M. C. Taylor; Chicago: University of Chicago Press, 1998), 41.
68. Elaine Graham, "Words Made Flesh: Embodiment and Practical Theology," paper presented at the International Academy for Practical Theology's Biennial Conference, Seoul, Korea, 1997.
69. Quoted in Anne B. Gilson, "Embodiment," in *Dictionary of Feminist Theologies* (ed. L. M. Russell and J. S. Clarkson; Louisville, KY: Westminster John Knox, 1996), 82.
70. Graham, "Words Made Flesh."
71. Quoted in Nancy Eisland, *The Disabled God: Toward a Liberatory Theology of Disability* (Nashville: Abingdon, 1994), 59–60.
72. Here I have in mind the Treatment Action Campaign headed by the intrepid Zackie Achmat, who is HIV-positive and who refuses to take antiretroviral drugs until they are available to all who need them in South Africa.
73. Peter Brown has documented the variety of ways in which Christians in late antiquity found sexuality a problem. See his *The Body and Society: Men, Women, and Sexual Renunciation in Early Christianity* (New York: Columbia University Press, 1988).
74. Rowan Williams, "On Making Moral Decisions," unpublished address to Lambeth Plenary Session, Canterbury, July 22, 1998.
75. Bernard V. Brady, *The Moral Bond of Community: Justice and Discourse in Christian Morality* (Washington, DC: Georgetown University Press, 1998), 1.
76. Ibid., 22.
77. Bruce B. Birch and Larry L. Rasmussen, *Bible and Ethics in the Christian Life* (Minneapolis: Augsburg, 1989), 45.

78. William Schweiker, *Power Value and Conviction: Theological Ethics in the Post-modern Age* (Cleveland: Pilgrim, 1998), 153. See also Cahill, "AIDS, Justice, and the Common Good," 286.

79. Birch and Rasmussen, *Bible and Ethics*, 137.

80. This poem, and the story of its composition, are from Birch and Rasmussen, *Bible and Ethics*, 47.

81. See the following articles by me: "Lamenting Tragedy from the Other Side" in *Sameness and Difference: Problems and Potentials in South African Civil Society* (ed. James R. Cochrane and Bastienne Klein; Washington, DC: Council for Research in Values and Philosophy, 2000), 213–41; "Tales of Terror and Torment: Thoughts on Boundaries and Truth-Telling," *Scriptura* 63 (1997): 425–34; "On Hearing and Lamenting: Faith and Truth-Telling," in *To Remember and to Heal: Theological and Psychological Reflections on Truth and Reconciliation* (ed. H. R. Botman and R. M. Petersen; Cape Town: Human & Rousseau, 1996), 47–56; "'Take Up a Taunt Song': Women, Lament, and Healing in South Africa," in *Reconstruction: The WCC Assembly Harare 1998 and the Churches in Southern Africa* (ed. Leny Lagerwerf; Zoetermeer: Meinema, 1998), 133–50.

82. Walter Brueggemann describes lament as "a dramatic, rhetorical, liturgical act of speech which is irreversible" ("The Shape for Old Testament Theology, II: Embrace of Pain," *CBQ* 47, no. 3 [1985]: 400). It articulates the inarticulate. Tears become ideas.

83. Walter Brueggemann, "From Hurt to Joy, from Death to Life," *Int* 28, no. 1 (1974): 4.

84. Quoted in Jürgen Moltmann, *The Coming of God: Christian Eschatology* (trans. M. Kohl; Minneapolis: Fortress, 1966), xi.

85. Ibid., 67.

86. Ibid., 69.

87. Ibid., 71.

88. Susan Sontag, *AIDS and Its Metaphors* (New York: Farrar, Straus & Giroux, 1989), 54.

89. Ibid., 73.

90. Friedrich W. Nietzsche, *The Will to Power* (trans. W. Kaufmann and R. J. Hollingdale; New York: Random House, 1967), 90.

91. For an explanation of these views, see Moltmann, *Coming of God*, 87–89, who discusses Karl Barth's adaption of Schleiermacher's views: "Schleiermacher, and with him modern Protestant theology, distinguished strictly between person and nature; and he restricted himself to the religious and moral experiences of the human person. . . . With these presuppositions it is quite logical that Schleiermacher would have declared death *per se* to be neither evil nor a divine punishment but the natural end and temporal limit of the finite existence of men and women. It is only a God-consciousness deranged by sin that will experience this natural death subjectively as an evil, and fear it as a punishment. Death is not caused by sin, but it is through sin that it acquires spiritual power over human beings. . . . Liberal Protestant tradition developed Schleiermacher's position further. The underlying exegetical assumption was that the biblical traditions are talking about death both literally and in a transferred sense. In the transferred sense, 'death of the soul' means a breach of fellowship with God, while 'eternal death' is its loss. These experiences in the God-consciousness must be uncoupled from physical death. The consequences of sin are spiritual disintegration, lack of inner peace, moral corruption, and fear of eternal damnation. To derive physical death from this source is nonsensical. Physical death cannot be put down to religious and moral causes. . . . Liberal Protestant teaching concludes that the death of the soul and eternal death follow upon sin but it removes the death of

the body from this cohesion, because it distinguishes strictly between person and nature" (87–88).

92. Moltmann writes, "The modern separation between person and nature (as in Schleiermacher) or between covenant and creation (as in Barth) does neither justice to human nature nor to the community of creation. It is an expression of the anthropocentrism of the modern world, an anthropocentrism destructive of nature. . . . The patristic church's doctrine of physical redemption was more comprehensive in its cosmic dimensions" (*Coming of God*, 92).

93. Ibid.

94. This term is used by Letty Russell in many of her works to denote the eschatological implications of the reign of God.

95. Moltmann, *Coming of God*, 105.

96. Moltmann, *Church in the Power*, 244, discusses the different ways of naming the celebration and chooses to call it the "Lord's Supper," the term used by the ecumenical movement. See also Michael Welker, *What Happens in Holy Communion?* (trans. J. F. Hoffmeyer; Grand Rapids: Eerdmans, 2000), 56–59), who argues that the supper is more than a "thanksgiving." I shall use the term "Eucharist" for no other reason than that it is in keeping with my tradition.

97. Welker, *What Happens in Holy Communion?* 43.

98. Eisland, *Disabled God*, 112.

99. Susan A. Ross, "God's Embodiment and Women," in *Freeing Theology: The Essentials of Theology in Feminist Perspective* (ed. C. M. La Cugna; San Francisco: Harper & Row, 1993), 186.

100. Welker, *What Happens in Holy Communion?* 18.

101. Moltmann, *Church in the Power*, 250.

102. Duncan B. Forrester, *Truthful Action: Explorations in Practical Theology* (Edinburgh: T. & T. Clark, 2000), 96.

103. Welker, *What Happens in Holy Communion?* 70.

104. Forrester, *Truthful Action*, 95.

105. Edward Schillebeeckx, *Church: The Human Story of God* (New York: Crossroad, 1993), 4.

106. John Chrysostom, *De Virginitate* 14.1, quoted in Brown, *Body and Society*, 6.

107. Trengove Jones, *Who Cares?* 7.

108. A version of this paper appeared in Musa W. Dube and Musimbi R. A. Kanyoro, ed., *Grant Me Justice! HIV/AIDS and Gender Readings of the Bible* (Pietermaritzburg, South Africa: Cluster, 2004).

Chapter 15

Resisting Rejection by the "Elect" in Genesis 25–27

BOB EKBLAD

People who are truly on the margins do not expect to receive benefits legitimately.[1] Accustomed to being rejected by the powerful, they learn to survive by hook or by crook. If Scripture is to be relevant to today's "damned," it must be freed from the dominant theological paradigm that assumes that blessing in this world is a reward for good behavior and exclusion a punishment for bad. I encounter people at many levels of marginalization in my roles as chaplain of Skagit County Jail and director of Tierra Nueva and the People's Seminary, an ecumenical ministry to migrant farm workers and a center for Scripture study with people on the margins.

I first met Andrés in the jail when he was 22. He participated in my weekly Spanish Bible studies there over periods of three to four months while he did time on at least three occasions. Each time, he was deported by the Border Patrol to Mexico, but he always returned illegally. Andrés is short and muscular, with dark skin and hair that have earned him the nickname "el Negro" (the black one).

Andrés was orphaned at an early age and learned to fend for himself on the streets of Mexico City. He has scars on his face and elsewhere on his body that bear witness to a life marked by struggle. He crossed the border illegally in his late teens to work in the fields in California. Eventually he made his way to Washington

State and found work on a construction crew. His eyes reveal both a life of suffering and a readiness for unlimited levels of illegal adventure. He looks expectant and prepared to face any kind of fun or trouble and can invent brilliant lies, which he tells unflinchingly to police detectives, judges, and also to public defenders who are ready to represent him—and whom he does not trust. At the same time, he weeps the moment he talks about the ones he loves. He adores his partner María and their four young children, though he is constantly separated from them due to his perpetual troubles with the law.

María was also in her early twenties when I first met her. She has a dark, beautiful face and long black hair. In spite of her difficult life she is unusually quick to smile, revealing slightly crooked, protruding teeth that do not detract from her beauty but give her a slightly mischievous look. She had two young children when she met Andrés. Together they had a child, and María was pregnant with their second when I first visited her. She lived on the second floor of a rickety cockroach-infested house beside the railroad tracks with her children, struggling to make it with no income since Andrés was in jail.

María herself is one of nine children born to a street worker in Tijuana, who carried her across the border when she was several months old. María has lived her entire life moving from farm labor camps to flophouses and the lowest-level apartments, eventually earning money in questionable ways that have led some to gossip. Andrés's adoration makes him ready to pick a fight with anyone who questions her past or shows the slightest disrespect. Since she has spent all but three months of her life in the United States, she speaks English better than Spanish and considers herself more American than Mexican. Yet since her mother never applied for her permanent residence, she is in the United States illegally and has already been deported once. Her problems are compounded by the fact that she has no Mexican papers. Her mother has no memory of having a birth certificate for her, cannot remember in which poor barrio in Tijuana María was born, and is unsure whether she ever officially registered her. Consequently, María has no identification of any kind. When she and Andrés asked me to perform their wedding, I told them that I could not legally marry them because she lacked the necessary ID to obtain a marriage license.

I worked long and hard with María to pull together documents that might work to prove her identity so she could measure up to the demands of the law. The only proof we could dig up was her mug shot and personal information on file in the jail from an arrest the year before. María was unwilling to request a copy of this herself for fear that the sheriff's office would notify the Border Patrol that she was back. Her false immigration papers and social security card would have to do until someone could figure out a way to help her become an official person.

Andrés and María are somewhat typical of people on the margins with whom I read Scripture. They, like so many others from places all over the world, are accustomed to rejection by the powerful. Their spiritual outlook is subsequently impacted, as they do not naturally expect God to call them or give them any special attention. They have accurately observed that their race, social class, nationality, and other factors destine them for what they consider irremediable, eternal exclusion.

In my Bible studies and one-on-one conversations, I engage people like Andrés and María in theological reflection by helping them see themselves in the stories of struggle and liberation in the Scriptures. I seek to formulate questions that draw people out about issues that directly affect them. Most often I begin with a question about people's lives, then introduce a biblical story and ask questions that help uncover the deeper truths of the text. Other times I begin with the text, as in the following description of a Bible study on the birth of Jacob and Esau and their subsequent power struggle.

Jail guards usher me through two thick steel doors along tan cinder block corridors in the jail's multipurpose room. Tattered, coverless books lie strewn about on the table. I collect the ones I recognize as Bibles and arrange plastic blue chairs in a circle as guards usher red-uniformed inmates from their cells and pods into the room. After an opening prayer calling on God's Holy Spirit to show us the deeper meaning of the story, I invite a volunteer to read Gen. 25:19–23, which introduces the larger narrative:

> These are the descendants of Isaac, Abraham's son: Abraham was the father of Isaac, and Isaac was forty years old when he married Rebekah, daughter of Bethuel the Aramean of Paddan-aram, sister of Laban the Aramean. Isaac prayed to the LORD for his wife, because she was barren; and the LORD granted his prayer, and his wife Rebekah conceived. The children struggled together within her; and she said, "If it is to be this way, why do I live?" So she went to inquire of the LORD.

"Who are the characters in this story so far?" I ask.

"Abraham," someone says.

"No, man, it's Isaac, Abraham's son," another guy corrects. "Then there are the twins, the Lord, and finally Rebekah."

"Who has power in this story and who doesn't?" I continue.

"The Lord has the power," someone responds, assuming this to be the right answer. "The Lord answers prayers, and Rebekah gets pregnant." A few heads nod. Everyone looks to me for my reaction.

I agree with them that Isaac and later Rebekah both pray to the Lord and the that Lord answers their prayers. Since God is in the story, we assume that God has all the power. I suggest, though, that we look closely at the story again to see what it is about. "Who has power among the other characters?" I ask.

"These are the descendants of Isaac," someone reads. "Isaac has power."

"Okay, that's true. He alone is certainly getting the credit for descendants. Why doesn't the story begin, 'These are the descendants of Isaac and Rebekah?'" I ask, trying hard to free up the men to question the power relations in the narrative rather than assuming they are God-ordained.

Since four of the eight men are migrant farm workers, I suggest that this may be like someone presenting some beautiful strawberries or blueberries as harvested by Sakuma Brothers (the biggest grower and employer of Mexican farm workers in our area). "How would this make you feel?" I ask.

"Bad, man, like shit. We're the ones who sweat out there in the fields doing all the work, not the bosses."

We observe together that between Isaac and Rebekah, Isaac clearly has the power. Isaac *takes* Rebekah, praying to the Lord for *his* wife because she was barren. We observe together that Isaac's name is mentioned five times, while Rebekah is only mentioned twice in the passage. Rebekah is a weak, even powerless figure, defined in terms of her relationship with men (Isaac takes her; she is referred to as "his wife," Bethuel's daughter, and Laban's sister) and in terms of her inability to conceive. The Lord's answering Isaac's prayer shows that God stands behind him.[2] When Rebekah finally conceives as a result of Isaac's prayer, she is once again acted upon, experiencing her future "descendants of Isaac" struggling in her womb to such an extent that she does not want to continue living.

"Who are the Rebekahs in our society?" I ask.

"*Nosotros* (we are)," says José, an undocumented man, who claims he is innocent of the kidnapping and assault charges against him.

"The Mexican people here in the USA—immigrants," says another.

"Who are the people who have power over you in your life?" I ask the men.

"The judge," someone immediately replies.

"And the prosecutor," says another.

The guards, the *migra* (the INS), and drugs are all subsequently mentioned.

We look together at Rebekah's problem. An internal struggle between two children in her womb is making her life difficult. She asks God about the nature of this struggle. José Luis reads Gen. 25:23 to see how the Lord responds: "And the LORD said to her, 'Two nations are in your womb, and two peoples born of you shall be divided; the one shall be stronger than the other, the elder shall serve the younger.'"

We talk about how the Lord tells only Rebekah, the one who is powerless in the story, a special word that only she and we the readers know. The stronger, older son who normally would have the power will serve the weaker, younger son who normally would be powerless.

"God told Rebekah some information about Isaac's descendants that only she knows," I say. "Let's read on to see how that surprising word actually gets realized in real life."

The man who has been reading continues with Gen. 25:24–34:

> When her time to give birth was at hand, there were twins in her womb. The first came out red, all his body like a hairy mantle; so they named him Esau. Afterward his brother came out, with his hand gripping Esau's heel; so he was named Jacob. Isaac was sixty years old when she bore them.

> When the boys grew up, Esau was a skillful hunter, a man of the field, while Jacob was a quiet man, living in tents. Isaac loved Esau, because he was fond of game; but Rebekah loved Jacob.
>
> Once when Jacob was cooking a stew, Esau came in from the field, and he was famished. Esau said to Jacob, "Let me eat some of that red stuff, for I am famished!" (Therefore he was called Ē'dom.) Jacob said, "First sell me your birthright." Esau said, "I am about to die; of what use is a birthright to me?" Jacob said, "Swear to me first." So he swore to him, and sold his birthright to Jacob. Then Jacob gave Esau bread and lentil stew and he ate and drank, and rose and went his way. Thus Esau despised his birthright.

"So what do we know about these brothers? What does the story tell us first about Esau?" I ask the men, once the reading is done.

"He was the firstborn," someone said.

I talk briefly about how in the Mesopotamian cultures of that period, the first-born son had all the rights. Esau being the firstborn had the birthright.

Someone mentions that Esau was red and covered with hair, a man of the country, a very macho man who hunted animals for his father. "Esau was his father's favorite," says another. "His father liked to eat meat."

We observe by contrast that Jacob is the second born. He grasps Isaac's heel. He is a smooth man who lives in tents. Most importantly, he is the preferred of his mother, the one who has no power. Compared with his brother Esau, Jacob has no rights. He is not favored by his father, who has all the power.

"Since Isaac has the power that Jacob needs, he is like God to Jacob," I suggest. "If Isaac reflected who God really is, what would God be like?" I ask.

"Unfair—a God who loves the stronger and ignores the weaker," says José Luis.

"Powerful, old, and wealthy," says another. "A God who shows favorites, who blesses only some."

"Isaac likes only the strong, the skilled. He discriminates, preferring Esau because of his race, his skin color," says another.

We talk at length how if Isaac reveals God, this is a God who is distant and hard, even impossible to please. Isaac reveals a God who has his favorites and who loves because of what is brought him (i.e., meat). This image of God as sustainer of the status quo is all too familiar to the underclass in North America and in Mexico and Central America.

"What does Jacob lack that Esau has that would bring him his father Isaac's favor?" I ask.

The men repeat the list of Esau's distinguishing attributes: red color, hair, skill at hunting. In addition to these things, Jacob lacks being the firstborn and, most importantly, his father's love.

"What do you lack to have the power to do what you most want?" I ask the men, hoping they now will talk about their own lives.

"In Mexico it would help to be the son of a politician or rich person," says Armando, a Mexican man in his mid-twenties.

"Lots of money so I would not have to work," says another man.

I ask the men what nationality would be ideal? What race or skin color?

"It would be better to be an American, a US citizen," says José Luis.

"If we were white, we would definitely have more opportunities," says Armando.

"Not necessarily," insists Dominic. "I'm white and I don't have any power. To be white and to have money is to have power."

"No, there are still more benefits to being white," counters Armando. "White people get paid more than we Mexicans. Mexican children are made to work when they are very young. We are used to hard labor and are hired to do jobs that white people would never do. And we are paid less."

Dominic sees his point and nods in agreement.

The closest example in our jail Bible study of a modern equivalent of an Esau (one who has favor, power, etc.) would be me: a white, male, American.[3]

"Who are you in this story?" I ask, inviting the men to look back at the text. While they are slightly embarrassed to be associated with the tent dwelling, cooking, momma's boy Jacob, they readily state that they most closely resemble Jacob in the story.

"So was there any way for Jacob to win favor? Would there be any way for you to be white Americans?" I ask.

"No, Jacob is trapped. The only thing he can do is take advantage of his brother. He stole his birthright by taking advantage of Esau's hunger," one of the men notes. "There is nothing we can do either. We are brown skinned. We are Mexican. Unless the laws change, we will always be illegal. We are screwed," he mentions.

"But you have to do something," I say. "What do you do to get what you want?" I ask.

"Rob, break into homes, sell drugs," says Dominic matter-of-factly.

"Not me, man," responds José, insulted. "I have always worked hard. It is the only way."

"Yeah, but you steal jobs from Americans," says Dominic, getting a rise from the Mexicans. He smiles and says he's just kidding.

"What other kinds of things do you do?" I ask.

"We cross over the border without papers," says Felipe. "We walk over the hills, paying coyotes, risking our lives so we can come here to work."

"We use false papers that say we are legal," says José Luis.

"I do that too, man," says Dominic.

"Really?" I ask, wondering if there is some rivalry going on about being the baddest dude.

"Yeah, I have to work under a false name. Otherwise my wages would all be garnished to pay child support, fines, and shit," continues Dominic.

"Some of us sell drugs, steal car stereos, and do other illegal things to make more money," says another man.

Everyone laughs at this blunt assessment of each of their lives. They, like Andrés, María, and countless other undocumented and underclass people, find themselves in legally impossible situations. I think back to Andrés and María.

Andrés has been arrested, jailed, deported, and returned at least three times in the seven years that I have known him. Each time in jail he progressed further in both his self-understanding and his faith and love for God. He participated actively in the Bible studies and talked honestly about his temptations and failings. He enthusiastically welcomed any good news he could get from the Bible in ways that excited others, inspiring them to read more closely for good news. Each time he returned illegally to María, their relationship became more committed. Each time, he returned to warrants for failures to appear in one court or another, which I helped him quash with the required fifty dollars. This beautiful, young couple and their children were "damned" to an underground life, driving without driver's licenses, working with false papers—always on the lookout for law enforcement agents of every variety who could temporarily end their happiness at any time. Many of the twelve men around me there in the heart of the jail have similar stories, which emerge in response to questions and discussion in the jail Bible study.

"Do you ever feel guilty before God when you have to do these things?" I ask the men at this moment of honesty and vulnerability. "Tell me honestly, do you sometimes think that God might punish you, that God might someday make you pay for all this?" I ask.

We talk about the Mexican mothers' oft-repeated threats: "Behave yourself, my son, otherwise the good God will punish you."[4]

"Do any of you see God as punishing you now through this experience in jail?" I ask.

At least half the men nod and say, "Sí."

"Yes, whatever our mother says has to be fulfilled," says José.

Most of the men and women with whom I work view God as siding with the righteous, moral types and punishing the "bad guys." When they open their Bibles they assume that any characters that God in any way favors must be chosen because of their goodness. Jacob, though he is the youngest, they assume is good and deserving—even a moral hero. Esau, in contrast, must have been rejected because he is assumed to be evil.

Moralism and heroism are characteristics of the dominant theology in which contemporary underdogs are immersed. Yet this theology is ancient, as can be seen in the following quotes from early Jewish sources:

> And . . . Rebekah bore to Isaac two sons, Jacob and Esau, and Jacob was a smooth and upright man, and Esau was fierce, a man of the field, and hairy; and Jacob dwelt in tents. And the youths grew, and Jacob *learned to write*; but Esau did not learn, for he was a man of the field, and a hunter, and he learned war, and all his deeds were fierce. And Abraham loved Jacob, but Isaac loved Esau. (*Jubilees* 19:13–15)

> And the two boys grew up, and Esau was a skilled hunter, a man who went out to the fields, and Jacob was a perfect man who frequented the school-house. (*Targum Onqelos* Gen. 25:27)[5]

> . . . the righteous Jacob, who observed the entire Torah, as it is said, "And Jacob was a perfect man, dwelling in tents." (*Sifre Deuteronomy* 336)

> When she passed by houses of idol-worship, Esau would squirm about, try-ing to get out, as it says, "The wicked turn astray [*zōrû*] from the womb" (Ps. 58:4); when she would pass synagogues or study-houses, Jacob would squirm to get out, as it says, "Before I formed you in the womb, I knew you" (Jer 1:5). (*Genesis Rabba* 63:6)

Assumptions of Jacob's worthiness in these commentaries and within today's dominant reading community rob this story of its relevant meaning for those most in need of its message.[6] A careful read of the text with the dominant theol-ogy in mind can help take the text back from its usurpers and return it to its right-ful contemporary beneficiaries. There are clear connections between people on the margins and Jacob, who exhibits the ethics of survival.

I invite the men to look more closely at how Jacob and then Rebekah and Jacob deal with their powerlessness. I invite a volunteer to reread Gen. 25:29–34.

> Once when Jacob was cooking a stew, Esau came in from the field, and he was famished. Esau said to Jacob, "Let me eat some of that red stuff, for I am famished!" (Therefore he was called Edom.) Jacob said, "First sell me your birthright." Esau said, "I am about to die; of what use is a birthright to me?" Jacob said, "Swear to me first." So he swore to him, and sold his birthright to Jacob. Then Jacob gave Esau bread and lentil stew, and he ate and drank, and rose and went his way. Thus Esau despised his birthright.

The men are quick to label Jacob an opportunist who takes advantage of Esau's desperation for food to get the birthright. I remind them that Jacob's name means heel grabber, deceiver, or even trickster.[7] But he still lacked the most important thing that would guarantee success for him and his descendants: his father's blessing.

"Where is God in this story?" I ask the men. We observe that God is absent or at least silent. God does not stop Jacob from his scheme.

I remind the men that the Lord had given Rebekah the secret, that the stronger, older one would serve the weaker, younger one. Yet in the story this looks like an impossibility.

"Let's see how Rebekah and Jacob deal with these obstacles." I invite the men to turn to Gen. 27 and ask someone to read the entire chapter.

As Armando reads the story the other men follow closely. They appear sur-prised by Rebekah's bold scheme to deceive her husband.

As we read we overhear with Rebekah Isaac's special arrangement with his favored son, Esau, that he hunt for wild game, make him a meal, and come for the blessing before Isaac dies (27:1–4). The men are intrigued that Rebekah is listening in and that she acts with such bold cunning, ordering and coaching Jacob to change his identity by imitating Esau before their blind father to deceptively steal the blessing (27:5–9). The inmates are amazed that Rebekah helps Jacob so much (27:9), even to the extent of taking any curse upon herself should Jacob be discovered (27:13). The details of Jacob's counterfeit identity—the skins of the kids on his hands and neck (27:16), the savory food that his father loved (27:17)—make the story more intriguing and believable to these men, many of whom have given fake names to the police and have been involved in identity theft and forgery. Jacob's boldfaced lies about his identity (27:19) and even about God helping him get the game quickly (27:20) shock the men. They are expecting failure and grow increasingly sure that powerful Isaac, though blind, will discover the trickery.

The men I am reading with have all been caught for their crimes in varying degrees. Their very presence in jail is a constant reminder. Yet many have succeeded in getting away with crimes numerous times. They can see that Jacob's crime was no easy feat. Isaac's command that he come near so he can feel whether or not he is really Esau reminds Armando of a time when the police pulled him over and ran a background check on a false name he gave at the spur of the moment hoping to escape arrest due to a warrant he knew he had. The trick worked that time, as Jacob's ruse succeeded.[8] I think to myself of Andrés's most recent adventures.

Andrés's most recent return involved crossing alone through the desert of Arizona, since he and María had no way to pull together the $1,400 needed to pay a coyote. He tells the story of praying without ceasing as he crossed the border and of how the Border Patrol drove right past him without stopping as he entered a border town on foot.

"It was like God made me invisible or something," said Andrés. "It was a miracle, Roberto! God helped me."

Would Andrés's next close encounter with the law be similarly successful? Would Jacob's next moment with his blind but intelligent father lead to detection? Suspense grows among the men as Jacob's success is achieved step by agonizing step. These are men who know firsthand Jacob's stress, as Isaac notices the voice of his lying son is Jacob's and not Esau's (27:22), as he asks Jacob one more time, "Are you really my son Esau?" (27:24), and as he utters his final request: "Come near and kiss me, my son" (27:26).

"Is this *mika* (permanent residency card) really good?" I ask, pretending to be an employer or a Border Patrol agent. Everyone laughs.

To sum up our findings so far, I ask the men how the powerless, discriminated-against people in the story, Jacob and Rebekah, get the power and favor they lack. "How do you get favor if you are damned by the one with power? What means did Jacob and Rebekah use that allowed them to succeed?"

Together we make up a list with ease, as criminal minds are quick to see the survival wisdom of the Bible's underclass. Trickery, lies, using false identities, counterfeiting, and fraud are all mentioned as part of Jacob and Rebekah's arsenal. I remind the men that Jacob's name actually means trickster or deceiver. They smile uneasily, looking surprised to encounter a character they can so easily identify with and such a real-life story in the Bible. I remind the men that Rebekah was driven to help her son Jacob by a word from God in a dream that the stronger and older would serve the younger. We still do not know how God feels about Jacob and Rebekah's criminal behavior, though they have clearly succeeded in the world of power-struggling humans.

"How do you think God looks at these kinds of actions?" I ask. "How do you think God will respond to Jacob and Rebekah?"

"Probably God was not in agreement," says Armando.

"God will probably punish them later," says José Luis.

After briefly telling the story of Esau's angry discovery of Jacob's crime, his plot to kill his brother, and Jacob's escape to a foreign country, I invite someone to read the story of the Lord's first encounter with fugitive Jacob after this incident. One of the men reads the story of Jacob's dream at Bethel in Gen. 28:11–16:

> He came to a certain place and stayed there for the night, because the sun had set. Taking one of the stones of the place, he put it under his head and lay down in that place. And he dreamed that there was a ladder set up on the earth, the top of it reaching to heaven; and the angels of God were ascending and descending on it. And the LORD stood beside him and said, "I am the LORD, the God of Abraham your father and the God of Isaac; the land on which you lie I will give to you and to your offspring; and your offspring shall be like the dust of the earth, and you shall spread abroad to the west and to the east and to the north and to the south; and all the families of the earth shall be blessed in you and in your offspring. Know that I am with you and will keep you wherever you go, and will bring you back to this land; for I will not leave you until I have done what I have promised you."

I ask the men again how God responds to Jacob's crime.

"God doesn't say anything. It's like it didn't matter," says one of the men.

"God blessed Jacob, promising that he would be with him," says another man in amazement.

"God is different than we expect here," I comment. "If we were to look at Jacob's life, what does Jacob do that makes him worthy of God's presence with him and promise of blessing?" I ask. "Was Jacob a religious person? Was he a person who prayed, went to church, read his Bible?"

The men look down at their Bibles. Hesitantly they begin to comment.

"He wasn't a religious man. He didn't do anything good," says Armando. "He took advantage of his brother, stealing his birthright. He had just lied to his father and stolen his brother's blessing."

"He wasn't seeking God when God came to him. He was escaping his brother," says José Luis. "He committed a crime and fled."

"He was sleeping when God visited him," says another man, stirring everyone to laughter.

"So is this story telling us that it is okay with God if we commit crimes?" I ask.

"Maybe God is not worried about every crime. Some crimes are okay," someone says. "Maybe this story is telling us that even when we commit crimes, God can still come to us and bless us."

"I don't know, man. This don't feel like a total blessing to me," says Dominic. "Jacob has to flee. He has the birthright and the blessing, and God is with him and shit, but he's on the run, he's separated from his mom and dad, his brother and his country. This looks like a hard road."

I think back to Andrés and María. I did not doubt Andrés's perception that God had helped him. He was full of faith wrought from the furnace of his recent suffering, which always burned away all the distractions and left him glowing. I had visited him and María in the months after this incident. I watched him struggle with the temptation to do unnecessary illegal actions, which he carefully sought to distinguish from the necessary illegalities. Being caught driving without a license for his fifth or sixth time would most certainly land him in jail and into the hands of the Border Patrol. Yet when his ride did not show up for work he would take the calculated risk rather than lose his hard-to-come-by construction job. Working with counterfeit immigration papers and social security number was no different than Jacob's covering his arms and neck with goatskins and lying to his blind father.

One afternoon when I showed up unexpectedly to Andrés's marijuana-smoke-filled apartment, I began to worry that he might be slipping into an old pattern that included justifying more and more unnecessary and risky behaviors. Andrés was eventually arrested on suspicion of knowingly using and selling counterfeit twenty-dollar bills and for possession of stolen property—crimes for which he may well have been guilty. After the prosecutor was unsuccessful in convicting him, the jail turned him over to the INS for deportation. Since he was undocumented and had numerous prior deportations, the INS decided to prosecute Andrés for illegal reentry and sentenced him to two years in federal prison. Andrés called me collect from prison on numerous occasions. He was going through a dark period of worry and doubt. He asked me how María was doing, since she had long since had her phone service disconnected due to her inability to pay her phone bill. Meanwhile, María surprised him by preparing to move back to Mexico to start a new life with hopefully fewer troubles. When Andrés was recently deported, María left the country she considers home to join him in Mexico, where they now live with their four children. God is with Andrés and María, whether in the land of their dreams or in exile, as God is with my inmate brothers in Skagit County Jail.

I look around at other immigrant men like Andrés in a big circle, Bibles open upon their red, jail-issue panted laps, plastic thongs planted on the brown cement floor of the jail's multipurpose room. I encourage the men to take the story of God's appearance to and blessing of fugitive Jacob as a clear announcement of God's love for and willingness to bless the underdogs—the ones who have no legal rights to benefits and who often feel paralyzed by the restrictions and enforcement imposed on them by the principalities and powers. I suggest that we look together at Jacob's reaction to God's appearance to him. We read together Gen. 28:16–18, 20–22:

> Then Jacob woke from his sleep and said, "Surely the LORD is in this place—and I did not know it!" And he was afraid, and said, "How awesome is this place! This is none other than the house of God, and this is the gate of heaven."
>
> So Jacob rose early in the morning, and he took the stone that he had put under his head and set it up for a pillar and poured oil on the top of it. . . . Then Jacob made a vow, saying, "If God will be with me, and will keep me in this way that I go, and will give me bread to eat and clothing to wear, so that I come again to my father's house in peace, then the LORD shall be my God, and this stone, which I have set up for a pillar, shall be God's house; and of all that you give me I will surely give one tenth to you."

We end the study by talking about how Jacob recognizes after his dream that God was there with him even though he did not know it—a reminder to all of us that God's presence is perhaps hard to discern and unexpected. The men notice the unbelief of Jacob too, and that his vow is full of conditions: "*If* God will be with me and protect me, and feed me and bring me back home in peace, *then* the Lord will be my God." The men are delighted. They feel like there is room for them and their unbelief. I encourage them to not believe too quickly but to look for signs of God's presence with them and to not be afraid to ask God to demonstrate God's presence and care for them.

"So who is God according to this story? What is God like?" I ask, wrapping things up before our closing prayers.

"God is with us and cares for us even when we are doing bad things, like committing crimes," someone says.

"God comes to people and blesses them, even when we are not looking for him. God came to Jacob when he was running away."

We talk about how God works through other people, like Rebekah. Rebekah had a special word from the Lord that the younger, undeserving son was the chosen one. Her response to this word represents her becoming a separate subject, an actress in her own and another's liberation. God's word to her freed her to break allegiance with the dominant theology/culture and to help her son, taking risks by serving as an accomplice in Jacob's crime.

The men appear to be encouraged as we gather in a circle and hold hands. We pray the Lord's Prayer as brothers. I feel some peace and can see that the men are more hopeful. Armando approaches me with a smile and says he is really excited and needs to talk right away. I press the buzzer for the guards and ask them to bring Armando up to the front of the jail, where I wait for him in a small visiting cell. After the guard locks us into the privacy of our cell, Armando excitedly tells me his plan.

"This study was incredible. I feel free to do something now and want to know what you think," he began. "The *narco* detectives [drug task force police] visited me this week and want to make a deal with me. You see, I was very active dealing drugs here, and I know lots of people who sell drugs—big dealers, who they would like to catch. They told me that if I work with them on the street to point out and help them arrest seven to nine people, they will drop charges and let me return to Mexico. Otherwise, they want to give me thirty-six to forty-eight months in prison. I can't go to prison, Roberto. I have a wife and three kids back in Mexico. They need me. I want to go back to be with them. After this study I feel like I am free to cooperate with the *narcos*. What do you think?"

I sit there stunned, feeling my friend's predicament but at the same time resisting his interpretation. I have little sympathy for the destruction wrought by drug abuse, but I see no wisdom in the federal government's strategies of incarcerating offenders in its unsuccessful war on drugs. Drug task forces often make use of desperate people who are facing delivery of controlled substance charges and almost certain conviction. They release them on condition they cooperate in undercover sting operations, buying and selling drugs while others videotape or listen in through their planted microphones. "Turn in three and go free" is a dangerous deal that some cannot refuse. I ask Armando some careful questions about the risks involved in telling on other drug dealers. He responds in a way that surprises me all the more, pushing the ethical implications of our Bible study to new levels of complexity.

"No, Roberto, don't get me wrong," continues Armando. "I couldn't tell on my brothers. I'm not a *rata* and never would actually do what they want. What I want to talk with you about is this. I need your help. You see, the name I am using here is not my real name. I am wondering whether you think it would work if my family sent you my real Mexican ID, with my real name. With this do you think I could buy a plane ticket and fly to Mexico?" he asks.

"Yes, I do not see any problem with this. If you have any kind of identification with your photo that says you are a Mexican citizen, you can get a plane ticket and fly," I respond, still not clear about what Armando wants from me.

"Okay, good. What I want is your help. I do not have an address in Skagit County. Could my family send you my papers? Would you then be willing to do me the favor of buying me a plane ticket to Mexico for the day that I get out? I need to know whether on the day that the drug task force lets me out to work for them you would be willing to pick me up and drive me to the airport so I can get away from here. Maybe you cannot, but I have to ask you anyway," he says in a calm but urgent voice.

What should I do? The story of Rebekah and Jacob plays back in my brain. Armando has interpreted this story well, seeing implications that go far beyond my vision for this story's relevancy. Armando sees himself as Jacob and me as Rebekah. Indeed, I had received the word from God over and over that God sides with the weak, advocates for the least, and gives his life for the sheep. Was I willing to serve as a Rebekah for Armando?

I think about the cost of Rebekah's advocacy for herself. She had told her son, "Let your curse be on me, my son" (27:13).[9] Rebekah's success meant enmity between the two brothers and permanent separation from her beloved son. I point this out to Armando and tell him that I need to think about the risk and potential cost for myself and my family of this sort of aiding and abetting an escape. I tell him that if we were caught I would face time in prison and separation from my wife and children. I tell him that I oppose my government's treatment of drug dealers with long prison sentences and wish I could help him rejoin his wife and children, but that I am not ready to take the risk that helping him would involve. I warn him that if he were caught he could face as much as six additional years for escape. I offer to look more into the consequences and the probabilities of him being apprehended, so that he can have a clear idea about the risks. I pray with him and leave, amazed and deeply unsettled by yet another night in the jail.

I think back to the man who visited me at our first farm in Honduras, where my wife and I worked with peasants for six years beginning in the early 1980s. He had asked me for money to take a bus to the capital and to buy a shirt so he would look more presentable for a job. I had freely given him these things, only to be hit up for a pair of pants and finally my own shoes. I am deeply aware of the limits of my love both in Honduras and here in El Norte. I am both inspired and unsettled by my encounters with people like Armando and with the Scriptures, which together push my faith and understanding to places I would rather not go. I recently came upon one of the sayings of the Desert Fathers that speaks to one of my ongoing questions, which I now quote in full:

> Going to town one day to sell some small articles, Abba Agathon met a cripple on the roadside, paralyzed in his legs, who asked him where he was going. Abba Agathon replied, "To town, to sell some things." The other said, "Do me the favor of carrying me there." So he carried him to the town. The cripple said to him, "Put me down where you sell your wares." He did so. When he had sold an article, the cripple asked, "What did you sell it for?" and he told him the price. The other said, "Buy me a cake," and he bought it. When Abba Agathon had sold a second article, the sick man asked, "How much did you sell it for?" and he told him the price of it. Then the other said, "Buy me this," and he bought it. When Agathon, having sold all his wares, wanted to go, he said to him, "Are you going back?" and he replied, "Yes." Then said he, "Do me the favor of carrying me back to the place where you found me." Once more picking him up, he carried him back to that place. Then the cripple said, "Agathon, you are filled with divine blessings, in heaven and on earth." Raising his eyes, Agathon saw no man; it was an angel of the Lord, come to try him.[10]

I feel continually tested through my encounters with people on the margins. I, like Rebekah, have heard the word: The older will serve the younger, the last shall be first, by grace you have been saved. I am continually seeing that God has chosen what is foolish in the world to shame the wise; God has chosen what is weak in the world to shame the strong; God has chosen what is low and despised in the world, things that are not, to reduce to nothing things that are, so that no one might boast in the presence of God (1 Cor. 15:27–29). Am I willing to follow Rebekah's bold path of resistance, breaking allegiance with the dominant religion and mainstream culture in my solidarity with the underdog? In Armando's case the drug task force never ended up making a deal with him. He was convicted of dealing drugs and sentenced to thirty-six months in prison. Still I have no sense of having passed the many tests that come my way. Rather, I am humbled by my limitations and pushed to pray and discern more clearly God's voice and presence to me as I am met and challenged by people on the margins. Isaac's unwitting and unwilling part in Jacob's blessing, in spite of his role as representative of the dominant theology and mainstream, comes strangely as a word of grace to me. Maybe his violent trembling, when he discovers he has been tricked, represents a sort of conversion (Gen. 27:33). Finally, this story assures me that God's will can be done on behalf of others, both when I am a willing accomplice like Rebekah and when I am a blind and unwilling actor in people's liberation like Isaac. My faith and my lack of faith both can serve God's purposes. This is good news for the damned and good news for me.

Notes

1. An earlier version of this essay appeared in Bob Ekblad, *Reading the Bible with the Damned* (Louisville, KY: Westminster John Knox, 2005).
2. Isaac and Rebekah's first encounter supports Isaac's dominance. Isaac brings her into the tent, takes her, knows her, loves her, and is comforted (Gen. 24:27). This contrasts with the betrothal narrative, where Abraham's servant treats her with more respect. In Gen. 26 Isaac continues to treat Rebekah as an object, putting her at risk among the men of Gerar (26:6–17).
3. I told the men how in trying to get a job teaching theology, however, it would help me if I were black or Hispanic and female—things I could never be.
4. "Pórtate bien, mi hijo, sino Diosito te va a castigar."
5. See also *Targum Neophyti* Gen. 25:27. Rashi writes that Jacob "is a plain man" and comments, "He is not expert in all these (worthless pursuits), as his heart (mind) so is his mouth. One who is not sharp minded in deceiving is called *tām* (plain)." Rabbi Abraham Ben Isaiah and Rabbi Benjamin Sharfman, *The Pentateuch and Rashi's Commentary: A Linear Translation into English* (Brooklyn: S. S. & R. Publishing Co., 1976), 244.
6. The Jewish interpreters are in part correct in translating *tām* as "perfect." The Hebrew may very well include this meaning (cf. Job 8:20; 9:20, 21; Ps. 64:4 [Heb. 5]), appearing in poetic parallelism with "upright" (Job 1:1, 8; 2:3; Ps. 37:37) or in contrast to "the wicked" (Job 9:22). In the context of Gen. 25, where Esau is described as a "skillful hunter, a man of the field," this meaning is less compelling. For this reason Jacob is contrasted to Esau in the RSV and NRSV as "a quiet man, dwelling in tents." "Simple man" (Robert Alter, *Genesis: Translation and Commentary* [New York: Norton, 1996], 128) and "mild man" (Nahum M. Sarna, *Genesis* [JPS Torah Commentary; Philadelphia: Jewish Publication Society, 1989], 180) are also possibilities. Isaac is then described as loving Esau because he ate of his game, supporting the translation "skillful hunter." In contrast, no reason (i.e., that he is perfect/blameless) is given for Rebekah's love of Jacob (Gen. 25:28).
7. Adrien Janis Bledstein argues that Isaac's name can be translated "trickster" and Jacob's "heel" in "Binder, Trickster, Heel, and Hairy-Man," in *A Feminist Companion to Genesis* (ed. A. Brenner; Sheffield: Sheffield Academic Press, 1999),

283. However, the narrator presents an etymology suggesting Jacob means "heel," "supplanter" (Walter Brueggemann, *Genesis* [Interpretation; Atlanta: John Knox, 1982), 217, or even "trickster," though the original meaning of Jacob's name is likely "God protects" (Sarna, *Genesis*, 180) or "God follows after" (Alter, *Genesis*, 128).

8. Bledstein's assertion that trickster Isaac knew Jacob's true identity all along and sought to test his "resolve and stamina" before passing on "the mantle to the next-generation trickster" ("Binder, Trickster, Heel, and Hairy-Man," 288–89) has little support from the text. Rather, it reflects yet another attempt typical of Rabbinic exegesis to deny or in some way justify the weakness of the father(s). This reading disempowers true tricksters, attributing the success of their plots to the patronage of the powerful.

9. The LXX's semantic equivalent for the MT's *qᵉlālâ* (curse) is *katára*, which links Rebekah's action in this text to Gal. 3:13–14, where Jesus is described as taking on the curse (*katára*) of the law in order that the excluded nations might be brought in. "Christ redeemed us from the curse [*katára*] of the law by becoming a curse [*katára*] for us—for it is written, 'Cursed is everyone who hangs on a tree'—in order that in Christ Jesus the blessing of Abraham might come to the Gentiles, so that we might receive the promise of the Spirit through faith."

10. *The Sayings of the Desert Fathers: The Alphabetical Collection* (trans. Benedicta Ward; Kalamazoo, MI: Cistercian Publications, 1975), 25.

Chapter 16

Toward a Culture of Peace and Nonviolence in Postwar Guatemala

J. RAFAEL ESCOBAR R.

> Surely his salvation is at hand for those who fear him,
>   that his glory may dwell in our land.
> Steadfast love and faithfulness will meet;
>   righteousness and peace will kiss each other.
> Faithfulness will spring up from the ground,
>   and righteousness will look down from the sky.
>   (Ps. 85:9–11)

This psalm of David captures the great hope of all of humanity and the longing of a people to live in another dimension—a dimension where peace is a reality of a life saturated with the presence of God, manifested in justice, harmony, reconciliation, and togetherness.

The valid human aspiration to live in a peace that is manifested in healthy fraternal relations and in power structures that are at the service of justice and truth seems like an impossible and unobtainable dream, as we observe the sad reality that surrounds us. This utopia is the great challenge that is proposed by biblical and theological education. How, from biblical formation itself and being at the service of the people of God, can we promote God's dream? How do we revitalize the keys that will help us to break our culture of violence—a culture that has become imbedded in our daily experience and our sentiments as people who dream, sing, laugh, and desire to find ourselves in true peace?

Our Context

Guatemala is a multicultural country, as the indigenous world is present in practically the entire nation. The indigenous presence is found in the physical features of the people, in the form of land cultivation, in our worldview, in small businesses, and in our artisan work. The country's ethnic and linguistic maps register the existence of twenty-two ethnic groups in the national territory. The largest groups in number are the Quichés, the Mames, the Cackchiqueles, and the Kekchíes. The total number of different Mayan languages is fifty-two, and the Mayans represent between 50 and 60 percent of the total population. The rest of the nonindigenous population is *mestizo* or *ladino* and use Spanish as their common language. We also have the Xinca and Garífuna ethnic groups. These numbers do not begin to express the complex, conflictive, and fluid sociocultural relations in a country such as Guatemala.

Sixty-five percent of the population is Roman Catholic, 25 percent is Protestant, and the rest is made up of other religious groups. Over the years the percentage of evangelical Christians has not grown, as many have argued. However, today in our country we can say that we have a greater proportion of evangelical Christians than in many other Latin American countries. Due to this, we also are responsible to lift up the weak and deliver the message to those who walk in darkness. There remains a lot to do.[1] This complex Guatemalan reality has allowed the population to be vulnerable and fragile, a victim of the ideological polarizations that have promoted a life of violence and oppression.

Characteristics of the Culture of Violence

The culture of violence in Guatemala is a product of human experience, where historically the right to live in dignity and with one's own identity has not been respected. For some, the marked contrast between rich and poor, and between satisfaction and dissatisfaction, allowed violence to become the only solution to historic injustice.

The outcome of the war between our brothers that lasted almost forty years remains an open wound in the life and history of our people. The many years of armed violence cost the lives of more than 150,000 people, leaving more than 30,000 widows, close to 100,000 orphans, and more than 1 million displaced persons or refugees. The armed conflict has given way to the experience of great poverty and terrible social debt. The document *Guatemala Nunca Más* (*Guatemala Never Again*) refers to this context:

> The social conflict in Guatemala historically has been based on political exclusion, ethnic discrimination and social injustice, which are rooted in the configuration of the political state of Guatemala. Since 1954 until the present the story of Guatemala has been characterized by continuous experiences of violence that have been concentrated in different eras, historical cycles, and in distinct areas and population groups.
> During the decade of the 1960s, in addition to the encounters between the guerrillas and the army, state-sponsored violence was directed against the peasant population in the east of the country. In the decade of the 1970s, the political violence became very strong in the city and was directed against lead-

ers of social movements and sectors opposed to the military governments. In the early 1980s, political counterinsurgency turned into state terrorism, which went with politics of mass destruction, especially in the indigenous communities and organized peasant groups. For its part, the guerrillas used violence as a way to eliminate people who collaborated with the army, or on other occasions as a form of eliminating the opposition within the civil population. Beginning in the mid-1980s, the state-sponsored political repression adopted a more selective character, but continued developing against individuals, social and community opposition groups, which suffered persecution, assassinations, [and] forced disappearances with the accusation that they were collaborating with the guerrillas.[2]

In this same vein, Monseñor Próspero Penados del Barrio, the recently retired archbishop of Guatemala, has said:

> One asks oneself: How was it possible to arrive at this depth of degradation? How was it possible to achieve this degree of disregard for the human person, the handiwork of a loving creator? . . .
>
> What were the roots of this conflict? We must consider the living conditions of the vast majority, deprived of their basic needs (access to food, healthcare, education, housing, a decent salary, the right to organize, respect of political thought, etc.) so that they were not able to develop in conditions befitting human beings. We must reflect on the prevailing anarchy in our country at that time and the enduring wound inflicted by an armed intervention that allowed a glimpse of humankind's hidden capacity for destruction.[3]

One of the biggest factors in forming this culture of death and destruction is the profound social gap that separates Guatemalan society into distinctively marked classes. It did not appear just of its own accord.

An Ethnic Reading of Classism

The history of Guatemala blends blood and power in a mix of invasion, conquest, and colonization. One of the first projects of the conquest and colonization was the negation of the indigenous as a class. In other words, the invaders made the indigenous people invisible, as a subject of the past, and relegated them to an object of conquest and domination. Fray Francisco Jiménez tells us, "During the colonial era the indigenous appear to disappear or be diminished, not being absent from the social square, but badly drawn and denied their human worth."[4] The Indians, while in the numerical majority, were pushed into a situation of social exclusion.

The children of the Europeans born in Guatemala without any racial mix were called *criollos*. They explained the natural advantages of their social position by invoking an inherent superiority that was shared with the Spanish. They also embraced the idea of having pure blood. It was a superiority that came with their persons.[5]

Historian Severo Martínez Peláez, in his attempt to interpret Guatemalan colonial reality, explains:

> Francisco Antonio Fuentes y Guzmán was a direct descendant of the first conquerors and first Spanish immigrants in Guatemala. . . . In the genealogy of our man appear the Alvarados, the Becerras, the Chávez, the Castillos, the Polancos, and the Cuevas. But, since the swords of the conquistadors had not been bathed in blood in vain, but rather with the purpose of putting the indigenous societies under the dominion of their new masters, from there the genealogy tree is filled with public offices and positions of authority . . . and with no lack of ecclesiastical positions along with these civil authorities: an uncle of Antonio had been the provincial of the opulent religious order of Santo Domingo.[6]

This kind of experience did not end here. The result of relations between Europeans and the indigenous was that a new social group surfaced called the *mestizos*—a people with a profound lack of identity that is the product of the systematic and inhuman violation of thousands of indigenous women, producing what Severo Martínez Peláez calls a *feudal mixture*. As had been the case with the abuses of feudalism in Central Europe, these landholding men would help themselves sexually to indigenous women.[7] Very soon after, the mestizos became known as *ladinos*, those who were not Indians, or Spaniards, or criollos—a group of people without specific characteristics. The judicial order of the dominant Spanish system quickly categorized them, ordering that the mestizos could not consider themselves able to form a social class.[8] In modern times these violent and complex relationships between cultural groups became even more explosive with the introduction of classism. Janet May explains this social phenomenon as

> a human social division between rich and poor, with a little bit of blending between the two. This means that there is a small minority that dominates the society in relation to political, economic, judicial, educative and military power. The majority of humankind lives in poverty or in conditions barely above survival level. Some social groups live precariously adjusted to the situation or even to the point of being well adjusted, but their resources do not come even close to what the elite possess. This reality gives reason to consider classism as a conscious force of the privileged class to maintain and increase their power at the expense of the rest of the social sectors.[9]

This is what Guatemala is like: a world of contrasts, which reflect the reality of our society. This fractured culture is the first fruit of an experience of violence that has not respected women, children, or elders. We have lost human sensitivity and a respect for life. The gap between the contradictions grows more every day. Every day peace and justice move farther beyond our reach. People continue to lose faith in institutions, including the Christian churches, since we are not the best example of unity or of solidarity. Because of this, it is important to analyze some of the confessional and religious factors that group us together and give us our identity.

Contradictions and Confessional Characteristics

A historic tension exists in our country between Catholicism and Protestantism. From 1831 to 1838 Guatemala experienced a new political movement under the leadership of Mariano Gálvez, a powerful Liberal governor. Admiring the modernity of northern Atlantic Protestant nations, he modeled his leadership after them by establishing the basis for a republican style of government and the development of capitalism. Gálvez implemented a series of anticlerical laws designed to reduce the most colonial of all the institutions: the Roman Catholic Church. He left the Church with minimum functions, expropriated many of its properties, and expelled some of the religious orders. In May 1832, the most lethal attack against the Catholic Church came when Gálvez endorsed an amendment to the federal constitution that called for "freedom of conscience and freedom of religion," which repealed the 1824 article of the constitution that had said, "The religion of the united provinces is Catholic, Apostolic, and Roman with the exclusion of all others." Under the new arrangement, the first Bible distributors arrived from England, representing the first Protestant presence in Guatemala.[10] Many years later, the Catholic Church managed to recuperate its lost power under the auspices of President Rafael Carrera, who established a prolonged Conservative government. During his term, the Church was able to reestablish the Catholic religious orders that Gálvez had expelled and reinstall the archbishop, who had been in exile during Gálvez's regime. The death of Carrera in 1865 marked the end of the Conservative governments. In 1871 the Liberal Revolution began, led by General Justo Rufino Barrios. Barrios had the idea of introducing Protestantism as part of the Liberal project. The spread of Liberal thought occurred in this new Guatemalan context as it had in other parts of the world. On March 15, 1873, Justo Rufino Barrios proclaimed decree number 93, which permitted freedom of thought and religion in the country.

This new environment paved the way for the arrival of the first Protestant churches in Guatemala. The Presbyterian Church arrived in 1882, the Central American Mission (CAM) in 1899, the Quaker Church (Friends) in 1902, the Nazarene Church in 1904, and the Primitive Methodist Mission in 1921. They divided the country into areas of influence in order to alleviate the conflicts that were arising. In 1937 the first interdenominational organization was founded: the Synod of Evangelical Churches of Guatemala.[11]

The arrival of Protestantism was surrounded by an official halo, not only because of the agreement of freedom of worship but also because at that time the government of Guatemala took action to bring the first of these churches (Presbyterian) to the country and to provide every opportunity for its establishment and consolidation. Accordingly, Álvaro Velásquez says, "the arrival of Protestantism in Guatemala came within the framework of the political tactic to consolidate the ideal of North American liberal democracy, which the first missionaries reflected well in their lifestyle and beliefs."[12]

With the Protestant presence an era began that, although it brought new opportunities for the country, also generated a religious tension that has contributed to the establishment of a culture of violence. The multiplication of religious perspectives disconnected from the social, political, and spiritual realities of our people makes it clear that the culture of violence has its real prolongation in the symbolic field. Julio de Santa Ana comments about this kind of culture:

> An incontestable fact about the life of Guatemala is the very important role that the different religious expressions in the socio-political processes have protagonized. In circumstances where the role of the civil society has become more controlled, its traditional institutions have had less space to develop their activities. The symbolic field appears to be the area where the popular sectors can still express their desires and hopes. This is how the various millennial movements appear and take shape in other movements much more embodied in history. The religious expressions have taken part in this situation, and with the shout "Christ is coming" there are those who support the possibility of an Armageddon, interpreted according to world politics at the moment. Diverse components of the electronic church have amply contributed as well. Others, proclaiming that Christ is King, have supported various dictators and, at the same time, use liturgies that symbolically express a radical social protest. From the centers of ecclesiastical power are organized neo-conservative defenses and evangelization programs, which make viable ideologies that legitimize the existing domination.[13]

In Guatemala, we should recognize that our contribution has been tainted by personal interests and the search for power, riches, and prestige.

A Brief Panoramic Version of Our History

What role has the reading of the Bible played in this context? How do we read it in a context of conflict? How can the word of God influence the formation of new attitudes and new forms of seeing and living life? A high percentage of textual readings, their interpretations, and applications have supported sectarian doctrines and dogmas and consolidated rigid categories, but very few have been used as tools of change for life.

In the 1970s, a group of evangelical seminary students and professors in Costa Rica joined together to rethink their theology and pastoral practice in light of their particular place and time. They tackled tough questions, like what it means to be faithful to the gospel of Jesus Christ in Latin America today. They were especially influenced by the far-reaching pastoral, theological, and liturgical reforms that were sweeping through Latin America's churches. Under the leadership of Dr. Orlando Costas, these pioneers created CELEP, *Centro Evangélico Latinoamericano de Estudios Pastorales* (the Latin American Evangelical Center for Pastoral Studies). In more than two decades of pioneering work, CELEP has designed and implemented flexible research and training programs especially intended to respond to the needs of church leaders, women and men, who are actually "in the trenches" doing pastoral work but who have little access to continuing theological, pastoral, and technical training.

In September 1985 those Central Americans who had participated in this initiative set up a semi-autonomous regional office named CEDEPCA, *Centro Evangélico de Estudios Pastorales en Centro América* (the Evangelical Center for Pastoral Studies in Central America). Similar regional initiatives had been set up in Mexico, Brazil, and Peru. By 1998, CELEP, the umbrella organization, had devolved into these various regional offices. Today CEDEPCA continues this innovative tradition through cutting-edge training programs in the areas of (1) biblical, theological, and pastoral reflection, (2) a women's pastoral program, with special attention to the problem of violence against women, (3) the Women's Pastoral North-South and South-South Immersion Seminars, and (4) publications and communications training.[14]

The Biblical, Theological, and Pastoral Reflection program has developed a reflexive, inclusive, and participatory methodology that allows reflection based on faith and in life. Because of this, we promote biblical reflection from a triple perspective that we call "Given in Life," "Learned from the Bible," and "Responded to in Life."

Given in Life

This first moment has as its focus the problems of daily life. At this point we do not look for solutions or for Bible teachings, but we analyze the reality that surrounds us. To achieve this, we use techniques that allow the participants to place themselves in their own context and to begin a common search.

Learned from the Bible

At this stage we open the biblical text, following these steps.

Observation of the Text

Every evangelical Guatemalan owns one or more Bibles.[15] However, usually we make very little effort to read the Bible seriously. We look at the text literally, which quickly kills the spirit of the text and gives way to establishing and sustaining rigid fundamentalist categories. At the same time, our readings are mixed with the sensationalist eschatologies that invite people to speculate, to depend on emotions that awaken fears and frustrations. A brief example can illustrate this tendency: With much excitement, a church in the western part of the country initiated a radio program called "The Voice of God and Not of Men." For a long time the program was known by this name, and a pastor in a rural area asked the producers where they had gotten the name. Immediately they said that it was biblical, taken from Acts 12:22, the account of the death of Herod. In that passage Herod is mad at the inhabitants of Tyre and Sidon and calls them together. In response to his address the people yell, "The voice of God and not of men." The interesting thing is that these Guatemalan brothers and sisters believed that because the words were in the Bible, they were the words of God. When we helped them to discover the context of the expression, they felt embarrassed and immediately changed the name of the program.

When people first take hold of a text, they think that to read it differently from how it was taught to them would be to turn against their school, doctrine, and experience. Because of this, when we come to the biblical text, we read slowly and carefully and in various versions, observing the people, situations, geography, key words, proposed ideas, and literary genre. This work is extremely important, as this is the time when many questions are posed, new discoveries made, doubts and agreements expressed, and—above all—a new world of discovery is opened up for them.

Research

Here we can research the discoveries made in the last step. Sadly, we do not have many bibliographical resources at hand. There are very few libraries and research materials, and the lack of a culture of reading makes this a difficult step. However, students are encouraged to continue their search. A double temptation exists during this step: to skip it entirely and jump immediately to interpretation (which is the most common inclination), or to look firsthand at biblical commentaries of doubtful academic worth to which most all have access. The commentary saves time and effort and can offer expert thought, but many times it is not based on our reality.

Interpretation

This is the act of taking a position on what the text is proposing to us. It is the moment of making a theological argument that responds from faith and the word to the reality in which we live. It is an encounter between the interpreter and the spirit of the text to discover its virtues, secrets, and mysteries. It is fascinating to accompany groups of people when they discover all the possibilities of interpretation. In the beginning they come up with very simple interpretations and are very fearful, but little by little they dare to do theology from a living perspective and from a faithful practice.

This was the case of a group of sixteen Quiché peasants—Presbyterians in Cantel, Quetzaltenango—who at the end of their course "How to Study the Bible" presented a sociodrama, "The Lost and the Found." In a brief interpretation of Luke 15, where Jesus narrates the parable of the Lost Sheep, they discovered that we have always used this parable to illustrate the love of Jesus for the lost, but we have never questioned the context of the lost persons. The parable points out the bad attitudes of the religious people of the time, who believed that they were good and holy and who scorned and marginalized those who were apparently bad. The group of students concluded their presentation by saying that we should be careful not to have the same attitudes of the religious people during the time of Jesus. We should demonstrate Jesus' passion for everyone and not discriminate against anyone who is not like us.

Communication

Communication is the act of being a bearer of good news and of supporting each other in our struggles with these new tools to confront life and to make God's presence known.

Respond in Life

In this final part, our participants think of situations they must face on the basis of their commitment to and their following of the word of God. As an example, I would like to share an experience of a group of brothers and sisters of the Pentecostal Church Tabernacle of Faith in Huehuetenango. For several years we had been offering them a process of biblical formation, using this method. The group of students varied from fifty to sixty per week.

> Encounter nos. 16, 17, 18
>
> Theme: "Walking in the Desert"
>
> Subtheme: The needs of the people in the desert
>
> Biblical texts: Exodus 15:22–27; 16:1–36; 17:8–12
>
> Prayer of intercession and illumination

First Step: We Begin with Life

What are the needs of our people today? With this question we began a reflection on the reality of our families, neighbors, towns, and cities. Many responses arose, but three were the most frequent: water, security, and work. We heard many different accounts and experiences of life. We noted the spoken needs on a flip chart so that we were able to see everything that had been said. We first celebrate and live our faith, and then we reflect theologically.

Second Step: We Learn from the Bible

After rereading the texts, we returned to the questions that were generated by the reflection, and we dialogued. What were the needs of the people in the desert? How were they satisfied? What did God do? What did the people do?

Working in small groups, the students discovered three great necessities of the people in the desert: water, bread, and security. In bipartisan fashion, God acted together with the people to solve the needs in different ways. For example, in Exod. 15:22 the people are desperate because they cannot drink the bitter water. God tells them to throw a piece of wood into the water, and the water becomes drinkable. We saw that a concrete need was satisfied. In the same way we reviewed the other two needs.

Third Step: We Return to Life

What is our reality today? Do we have these same needs in our communities and in our churches? How can we resolve them? How does God participate?

One of the student groups brought the following case to class. For three months an indigenous community had not had water. The only source of water that they had was closed off by the owner at its spring. How could we help them? At this time, during the worst days of the armed violence that destroyed the western part of the country, life for everyone was very difficult, and the easiest thing to do was not to get involved in others' problems. Nevertheless, nothing held them back, and they began a prayer campaign asking God to show them what to do. After realizing that they could not distance themselves from this problem, they decided to do two things.

First, they visited the community to spread hope and celebrated an open-air worship service, asking God to intervene. It was an interdenominational experience, and many people joined in. Second, they decided to write a letter to the owner of the water source, and everyone signed the letter. It turned out that the owner was a doctor and a member of the Baptist church. He received the people and the letter and was asked to consider the damage that his attitude and action were inflicting upon the community, which had lived in this place for many years and had never caused problems. Sadly, the attitude of the doctor did not reflect the love of Christ. He accused them of being subversives and reported them to the army.

Even this threat did not detain their struggle, and they initiated a prayer chain and invited many churches in the area to join them. Another doctor, a friend and study partner of the other individual for many years, knew of the situation and of the action of the church. He offered to mediate and to speak with his friend, and a few simple words served to soften that owner's heart. A few days later they made an appointment with the community board and arrived at an agreement. The people paid to construct a small canal, which branched off to their community and satisfied their very important need for water. The rural community invited the church members to a celebration in honor of God, because life had triumphed and God had been present. It is by experiences such as this that God has incorporated in our paths a space for reflection and meeting.

Conclusion

Why do we study the Bible? For people in a country like Guatemala studying the Bible is not a simple social activity but a nucleus for generating values. It is a transforming meeting space. In the same sense, the reading of biblical texts is not a mere academic exercise; it is a discovery of how and where God is present in our history and human reality. The challenge for the Christian churches in Guatemala is to continue to provide spaces for reflection, understanding, cooperation, and, above all, brotherhood. The challenge is to put the values and principles of the reign of God at the service of life, with the hope of changing the culture so that we can truly live as brothers and sisters in peace and harmony.

Notes

1. See Gary Lengheeh, *Estado de la Iglesia en Guatemala: Reporte preliminar del Servicio Evangelizador para América Latina* (Guatemala City: SEPAL, 2001).
2. *Guatemala: Nunca Más. Impactos de la violencia* (Guatemala City: Arzobispado de Guatemala, Oficina de Derechos Humanos, 1998), 1:xxxiii (author's translation).
3. Quoted in *Guatemala*, ix–x (author's translation).

4. Fray Francisco Jiménez, *Historia de la provincia de San Vicente de Chiapas Guatemala: Sociedad de Geografía e historia* (Guatemala City: n.p., 1930), 1:6 (author's translation).

5. Severo Martínez Peláez, *La patria del criollo: Ensayo de interpretación de la realidad colonial guatemalteca* (San José, Costa Rica: Editorial Universitaria, 1979), 23–25 (author's translation).

6. Ibid., 20–21.

7. Ibid., 267–72.

8. Ibid., 269.

9. Janet May, "Género, Raza y Clase: Un replanteo conceptual," unpublished paper presented at the Universidad Bíblica Latinoamericana in San José, Costa Rica, in 1999) (author's translation).

10. Virginia Garrard-Burnett, *Protestantism in Guatemala: Living in the New Jerusalem* (Austin: University of Texas Press, 1998), 3–4.

11. Luis Samandu, "Breve Reseña Histórica del Protestantismo en Guatemala," *Cuadernos de Investigación USAC* 2 (1987), 9–11.

12. Alvaro Velásquez, "Iglesias cristianas y proyecto de nación en Guatemala," *Diálogo* 1 (1988): 18–19 (author's translation).

13. Julio de Santa Ana, *Fundamentos para la paz* (San José, Costa Rica: Editorial Nueva Sociedad, 1999), 3 (author's translation).

14. www.cedepca.org. The previous two paragraphs summarize the history of CEDEPCA as presented on the group's Web site at http://www.cedepca.org.

15. Francisco Mena, *Cómo Estudiar la Biblia I y II* (Curso de Educación Pastoral; San José, Costa Rica: SEBILA, 1991).

Index of Ancient Sources

Index of Names